PRINCIPLES OF PROGRAM DESIGN

PROBLEM SOLVING WITH JAVASCRIPT

PRINCIPLES
OF PROGRAM DESIGN

PROBLEM SOLVING WITH JAVASCRIPT

PAUL ADDISON

COURSE TECHNOLOGY
CENGAGE Learning™

Australia • Brazil • Japan • Korea • Mexico • Singapore • Spain • United Kingdom • United States

COURSE TECHNOLOGY
CENGAGE Learning™

Principles of Program Design: Problem Solving with JavaScript, International Edition
Paul Addison

Executive Editor: Marie Lee

Acquisitions Editor: Brandi Shailer

Senior Product Manager: Alyssa Pratt

Development Editor: Lisa M. Lord

Editorial Assistant: Stephanie Lorenz

Content Project Manager: Matthew Hutchinson

Art Director: Faith Brosnan

Associate Marketing Manager: Shanna Shelton

Quality Assurance: Serge Palladino

Copyeditor: Camille Kiolbasa

Proofreader: Brandy Lilly

Indexer: Sharon Hilgenberg

Compositor: Integra

Library of Congress Control Number: 2010938073

For permission to use material from this text or product, submit all requests online at **cengage.com/permissions**
Further permissions questions can be emailed to
permissionrequest@cengage.com

International Edition:

ISBN-13: 978-1-111-82556-0

ISBN-10: 1-111-82556-4

Cengage Learning International Offices

Asia
www.cengageasia.com
tel: (65) 6410 1200

Australia/New Zealand
www.cengage.com.au
tel: (61) 3 9685 4111

Brazil
www.cengage.com.br
tel: (55) 11 3665 9900

India
www.cengage.co.in
tel: (91) 11 4364 1111

Latin America
www.cengage.com.mx
tel: (52) 55 1500 6000

UK/Europe/Middle East/Africa
www.cengage.co.uk
tel: (44) 0 1264 332 424

Represented in Canada by Nelson Education, Ltd.
www. nelson.com
tel: (416) 752 9100 / (800) 668 0671

Cengage Learning is a leading provider of customized learning solutions with office locations around the globe, including Singapore, the United Kingdom, Australia, Mexico, Brazil and Japan. Locate your local office at **www.cengage.com/global**

For product information: **www.cengage.com/international**
Visit your local office: **www.cengage.com/global**
Visit our corporate website: **www.cengage.com**

AVAILABILITY OF RESOURCES MAY DIFFER BY REGION. Check with your local Cengage Learning representative for details.

Printed in the United States of America
1 2 3 4 5 6 7 17 16 15 14 13 12 11

Brief Contents

Contents

vi

x

Preface

Principles of Program Design: Problem Solving with JavaScript gives beginning programmers the fundamental concepts of good program design, illustrated and reinforced by hands-on examples of using JavaScript. Why JavaScript? Many beginning programming books have no actual programming examples students can use to test programming principles, or they use a programming language with an interface so complex that students have difficulty separating programming principles from operating instructions for a particular software application. JavaScript requires no special editor, doesn't need to be compiled, and runs in any browser without needing additional software or an Internet connection. In short, there's practically no overhead, so every programming statement is related to solving the problem at hand.

This book isn't about learning JavaScript; it's about learning programming concepts, techniques, and practices, using JavaScript as a set of tools for examining and testing each idea. Programming is introduced as a craft, with the right tool applied to each task. Nor is this book about learning HTML. Only the tags needed to enclose JavaScript sections are used, with two exceptions: Chapter 3 introduces graphical user interfaces (GUIs) along with object-oriented programming (OOP), so the HTML tags for creating forms are included, and Appendix A describes several HTML tags for making browser pages more visually appealing.

One more thing this book is not: It's not about creating Web pages or designing Web sites. JavaScript is contained in HTML files rendered by Web browsers, but the JavaScript examples simply illustrate the programming concepts in the book. No Internet connection is needed; the browser runs solely on the client machine.

This book assumes students have little or no programming experience. The writing is nontechnical and on the light side. The examples are business or school oriented, and good programming practices (such as adding comments to code) are emphasized from the beginning. No math beyond high school algebra is required.

Pseudocode is introduced as a method for developing algorithms to solve problems. In other words, students are encouraged to think in terms of the logical steps needed to solve a problem. After the logic is developed, the pseudocode is converted to JavaScript. With this approach, students can apply the programming concepts they learn in this book to any programming language. Flowcharts are also introduced as another method of algorithm development. Other helpful logic development tools include decision tables and binary trees for multiple conditions and hierarchy charts for module development and documentation. These tools are especially useful for visual learners.

This book includes several features to help students apply and practice what they're learning. The Programmer's Workshop is a project that has students apply the chapter's concepts to a new situation, using a problem-solving approach and the IPO (input-processing-output) method. In addition, students build on a case study at the end of chapters in which they develop a program to simulate the card game War. New features are added to the program as students learn practical applications for the concepts discussed in each chapter as well as program development, documentation, testing, and maintenance. As mentioned, OOP concepts and GUIs are introduced early, and instructors can choose to include an OOP and GUI track by assigning the Object Lesson, which has students develop programs incorporating these concepts.

JavaScript doesn't allow opening, creating, or editing data files, so the topic of file manipulation isn't covered in this book. User input and programmer assignments of variables and array values are used to supply data to programs. All other common programming concepts are included in this book.

Organization and Coverage

Principles of Program Design is about learning to "think like a programmer" and apply problem-solving skills and programming tools to a situation. Chapter 1 introduces programming as a craft and gives students an overview of computer components and fundamental programming concepts, such as data types, variables, and constants. Chapter 2 summarizes the types of programming languages and the history of the Internet and JavaScript. It also introduces pseudocode and the JavaScript language and shows students how to convert pseudocode into simple JavaScript programs.

Chapter 3 introduces object-oriented programming, and from this chapter on, an object-oriented application is in every chapter.

This Object Lesson feature can be skipped without any detriment to learning, but including it gives students a practical understanding of OOP concepts. The difference between JavaScript (a "prototyping" language) and regular object-oriented languages is explained but doesn't diminish students' understanding of object-oriented programming.

Chapters 4, 5, and 6 explain the three standard control structures used in programs: sequence, selection, and repetition. Many examples are given to show variations in these structures, and good programming style is encouraged consistently. Complex conditions aren't covered until Chapter 7, by which time students have a grasp of using simple conditions in selection and repetition structures.

In the next four chapters, students use the logic tools they've learned in previous chapters and begin looking at overall program design. Chapter 8 covers functions and modular programming, arguments and parameters, return values, and design considerations about when to modularize. Chapter 9 combines menus and data validation, two separate but compatible concepts, and emphasizes ease of use, data integrity, and robust programs. Chapter 10 examines arrays, a data structure that's useful in simplifying large or complex data collections. Chapter 11 brings together concepts covered throughout the book by exploring design considerations in practical applications and answering the question "What tool should be used in which situation?"

Chapters 12 and 13 cover topics that are often considered nonessential for beginning programmers: sorting data and recursion. Although a programmer can get a job these days without knowing these skills, these chapters more than any others stretch students' ability to think both logically and imaginatively and help students gain a better understanding of several programming concepts, including data storage, function calling, loops, and data structures. Students who complete these chapters will be well on their way to thinking like a programmer.

Appendix A is an HTML tutorial. Although it's not essential for learning programming, it gives students a basis for further study of HTML and Web site development, and students can use this information to make the output of their JavaScript programs more visually appealing.

Features

Principles of Program Design includes the following features:

EARLY INTRODUCTION OF OOP AND GUIS Many introductory programming books put object-oriented programming off until very near the end. This book covers OOP and GUIs with hands-on examples in Chapter 3. An optional project, called the Object Lesson, is included in this chapter and each subsequent chapter so that students can apply the traditional programming concepts discussed in the chapter to OOP and GUI applications.

DIRECT APPLICATION OF CONCEPTS Problem solutions are developed in pseudocode and converted to JavaScript in each chapter so that students get to see programming concepts put into action. In addition, debugging strategies and techniques are explained so that students can find and fix their own mistakes. Flowcharts are introduced as an algorithm development method along with other logic development tools, such as decision tables, binary trees, and hierarchy charts.

GOOD PROGRAMMING PRACTICES Students are encouraged to develop good techniques and habits and follow prescribed conventions and styles, including program documentation, comments in code, and consistent indentation and naming procedures.

PROGRAMMER'S WORKSHOP A project in each chapter, called the Programmer's Workshop, has students put the chapter's concepts to work on a full-scale program, giving them an opportunity to get hands-on experience with program development, testing, and documentation.

Principles of Program Design also includes the following chapter components:

OBJECTIVES Each chapter begins with a list of objectives as an overview of the topics discussed in the chapter and as a useful study aid.

NOTES, WANT MORE INFO?, PROGRAMMING TIPS, AND CAUTIONS Notes provide additional information about programming concepts. The Want More Info? features give links that guide students to Web sites where they can explore topics in more depth or find useful resources. Programming Tips give advice on approaching problems from a programmer's point of view. Cautions warn students about situations that are easy to get into and likely to cause big problems.

FIGURES AND TABLES Chapters contain diagrams to clarify programming concepts and screenshots to show program output. In addition, many tables are included to give students an at-a-glance summary of useful information.

DETECTIVE WORK Many chapters have this feature, in which students are challenged to apply a concept to a new situation, complete a task started in a previous exercise, or convert pseudocode to JavaScript. This feature helps ensure that students are learning to apply concepts, not just following instructions.

SUMMARIES At the end of each chapter is a summary list that recaps the programming concepts and techniques covered in the chapter so that students have a way to check their understanding of the chapter's main points.

KEY TERMS Each chapter includes definitions of new terms, alphabetized for ease of reference. This feature is another useful way to review the chapter's major concepts.

HOW-TO EXERCISES Program examples are given in a step-by-step "how-to" format to help students understand what each section of code does. Many of these examples include screenshots at the end to show students the result of running the program.

REVIEW QUESTIONS Each chapter contains multiple-choice and true/false review questions, along with discussion questions for a review of key concepts in the chapter.

HANDS-ON ACTIVITIES Each chapter includes programming problems involving concepts explained in the chapter. Students are encouraged to work through the problems and have instructors check their work against the solution files.

PROGRAM CODE The downloadable student data files provide the code for each full program presented in the chapter. (For more information, see "To the User.") With these files, students can run the programs, view the results for themselves, and experiment by entering different values. Students can also use these files to modify programs without having to retype all the code.

QUALITY Every program example, hands-on activity, and case study was tested by the author in four major browsers (Internet Explorer, Mozilla Firefox, Google Chrome, and Safari) and again by Cengage Quality Assurance testers.

Teaching Tools

The following supplemental materials are available when this book is used in a classroom setting. All the teaching tools for this book are available to instructors on a single CD and for download at *login.cengage.com*:

ELECTRONIC INSTRUCTOR'S MANUAL The Instructor's Manual that accompanies this book includes additional instructional material to assist in class preparation, including suggestions for lecture topics, and solutions to review questions, end-of-chapter hands-on activities, and case studies.

EXAMVIEW® This book is accompanied by ExamView, a powerful testing software package that allows instructors to create and administer printed, computer (LAN-based), and Internet exams. ExamView includes hundreds of questions that correspond to the topics covered in this book, enabling students to generate detailed study guides that include page references for further review. The computer-based and Internet testing components allow students to take exams at their computers and save instructors time by grading each exam automatically.

POWERPOINT PRESENTATIONS Microsoft PowerPoint slides are available for each chapter. These slides are included as a teaching aid for classroom presentation; teachers can make them available on the network for chapter review or print them for classroom distribution. Instructors can add their own slides for additional topics they introduce in the class.

DATA FILES Code for JavaScript and pseudocode programs developed in chapters as "how-to" exercises are available in student data files so that students can compare their work with these files. For more information on data files, see "To the User."

SOLUTION FILES Solutions to all review questions, hands-on activities, and case studies are available on the Instructor Resources CD-ROM and at *login.cengage.com.* The solutions are password protected.

DISTANCE LEARNING Cengage Learning is proud to present online test banks in WebCT and Blackboard to provide the most complete and dynamic learning experience possible. Instructors are encouraged to make the most of the course, both online and offline. For more information on how to access the online test bank, contact your local Course Technology sales representative.

Acknowledgments

I would like to thank all the people who helped move this book from a dream to a reality, especially Lisa Lord, my development editor, who guided me every step of the way, including the times when several chapters were in different stages of development and production simultaneously. Thanks also to Alyssa Pratt, Senior Product Manager, Amy Jollymore and Brandi Shailer, Acquisitions Editors, and Serge Palladino, the MQA tester who made sure all JavaScript programs ran correctly. There are also many people at Course Technology and Cengage who encouraged me and introduced me to people who were able to take this idea off the ground.

Thanks also to the many reviewers who provided helpful comments and encouragement during this book's development, including Ali Fazelpour, Palm Beach Community College; Keyuan Jiang, Purdue University Calumet; Michael Kaltwang, Northeastern Technical College; and Jim McKeown, Dakota State University.

I would also like to thank my wife Jan, who supported me throughout the project and endured many evenings of watching me sitting on the sofa staring at a laptop computer. This book is dedicated to Jan and to our wonderful kids, Mark and Rachel.

Paul Addison

Read This Before You Begin

To the User

You can use a computer in your school lab or your own computer to do the exercises in this book. To check your work on hands-on activities, you can get solution files from your instructor. For the programs developed in chapters, you can check the student data files available for download at *www.CengageBrain.com*. At the home page for this Web site, search for this book's ISBN by using the search box at the top. This search takes you to the product page, where you can find the resources you're looking for. Click the Access Now link under the book cover image to find data files and other study tools for students. The data files for this book are organized by chapter, and you can save them to your hard drive or a flash drive. To prevent overwriting these files, you should set up different folders to store your own program files containing pseudocode or JavaScript.

Pseudocode files have the file extension .txt and are named according to the program title. For example, if the program title is Weekly Interest Calculator, the pseudocode filename is weeklyInterestCalculator.txt. In the program documentation lines in chapters, you see the program title—Weekly Interest Calculator, for instance—listed.

JavaScript programs are scripts included in HTML files, so they have the file extension .html to enable you to open them in browsers. Like pseudocode files, they're named according to the program title, such as rainfallAverages.html for the program called Rainfall Averages. To differentiate them from pseudocode files in chapters, the program documentation lists them by filename rather than program title.

To help you learn consistent filenaming procedures, filenames start with a lowercase letter for the first word and capitalize each subsequent word, as in modeFinder.html. The only exception is class files you create for some object-oriented programs; these files start with an uppercase letter, as in AccountClass.txt.

Also, you can open .txt data files by simply double-clicking filenames to open them in Notepad. To open .html files for viewing or modifying the code, make sure you right-click the filename, point to Open With, and click Notepad. Otherwise, the .html file opens in a browser and shows you the program output, not the actual code.

Using Your Own Computer

To use your own computer to do the exercises and activities, you need the following:

- **Software**. A text editor such as Notepad, which comes with any Windows operating system. You also need any of the major browsers (Internet Explorer, Mozilla Firefox, Google Chrome, or Safari), with JavaScript enabled. The screenshots in this book were taken in Mozilla Firefox.

- **Hardware**. Microsoft specifies these minimum requirements: 1.6 GHz CPU, 1024 MB of RAM, 3 GB of available hard disk space, 5400 rpm hard disk drive, DirectX 9–capable video card that runs at a 1280 × 1024 or higher display resolution, and a DVD-ROM drive.

- **Operating system**. Windows 7, Vista, or XP.

To the Instructor

Solution files are included on the Instructor Resources CD. You can also get these files electronically through the Cengage Learning Web site at *login.cengage.com.* Follow the instructions in the Help file to copy the user files to your server or stand-alone computer. You can view the Help file with a text editor, such as WordPad or Notepad. After the files are copied, you can make copies for users yourself or tell them where to find the files so that they can make their own copies.

License to Use Data Files

You are granted a license to copy the files accompanying this book to any computer or computer network used by people who have purchased this book.

CHAPTER 1

The Craft of Programming

In this chapter, you learn to:

◎ Explain computer programming and what it includes

◎ Describe how data and instructions are stored in the computer

◎ Explain the difference between hardware and software, with examples of each

◎ Summarize the basic operating functions of the central processing unit, memory, and storage drives

◎ Describe an algorithm and name some tools for developing one

◎ Describe methods for testing programs

◎ Name the two main data types a programmer uses and give an example of each

◎ Define the binary and decimal numbering systems and convert a number from one system to another

◎ Explain the difference between the two main character-coding systems, ASCII and Unicode

◎ Define variables and named constants and explain how to declare them and assign values to them

◎ Define and contrast input and output

◎ Explain the need for and use of program comments

◎ Describe the input-processing-output method

◎ Use pseudocode to begin solving a problem by developing an algorithm

"You come in here with a skull full of mush,
and if you survive, you leave thinking like a lawyer."
—PROFESSOR CHARLES KINGSFIELD, *THE PAPER CHASE*

Your skulls aren't necessarily full of mush, and you won't have to worry about surviving as you read this book. However, if you substitute the word "programmer" for "lawyer" in this quote, you'll understand this book's goal, which is for you to leave *thinking like a programmer.*

Becoming a programmer is more than learning a computer language. It's learning a set of skills to use when you want to solve a problem with the computer's help. It's understanding the problem you're trying to solve and selecting suitable, efficient tools to solve it. It's formulating a logical solution of steps, known as an algorithm, to solve the problem. It's recognizing which programming structures to use in different situations. (The good news is that you need only three structures.) It involves lots of hands-on practice so that you can see immediately whether your idea actually does help solve the problem. In this book, you'll develop projects by using solid building blocks, testing and improving them along the way.

Learning this set of skills—understanding the problem, recognizing what tools to use, and practicing—is, in effect, learning a craft. With this book, you're guided through all kinds of programming exercises and projects so that you learn how to use the right tool for the right job. The exercises and projects vary from the simplest statements to complex working programs. You'll develop programming skills in the same way an apprentice learns a trade, and you'll learn to approach a business problem as programmers do.

You use the JavaScript scripting language in this book. Why JavaScript? It doesn't require software installation or a special editor. Furthermore, when you want to test a few lines of code, you simply save your file and open it in any Web browser; you don't even need to be connected to the Internet. With JavaScript, you can think more about programming and less about the programming environment.

What Is Computer Programming?

Computer **programming** is the process of formulating instructions to operate a digital computer, an electronic device that can receive, process, store, and send data. Both instructions and data in a digital computer are represented as binary digits.

Binary digits (that is, 0s and 1s), referred to as **bits**, are the building blocks of a digital computer. The most basic instructions to the computer's processor are stored as sequences of bits and make up the computer's **machine language**. You might be familiar with the names of some programming languages, such as C#, Java, or Visual Basic, or scripting languages, such as JavaScript or Python. Although these languages are understandable to people, they must be translated into the computer's machine language so that the computer can run (execute) the instructions.

Data, the raw information processed by computers, is also stored in digital form. However, different types of data are stored differently for reasons of compatibility and processing efficiency. There are three general categories of data types: numeric data (values that can be used in mathematical calculations), text data (letters, punctuation marks, and digits that can be displayed or printed), and raw binary data (including special formats, such as image, video, and sound files).

Instructions for the computer include single commands, which are grouped into units called modules that perform specific tasks. Modules are grouped into programs. Computer applications can be made up of several program files, and operating systems can consist of thousands of programs. Instructions at any of these levels are categorized as **software**, a digital representation of instructions on the computer.

A computer and its related equipment are collectively called **hardware** (see Figure 1-1). The computer system unit (the box enclosing the equipment) includes the motherboard, which is the electronic circuit board that connects the system's main components. The processor and the system memory are connected to the motherboard, and numerous slots allow connecting other kinds of circuit boards, such as video cards and network cards, to the motherboard.

The terms "data" and "information" are often used interchangeably, but most programmers make a distinction, referring to unprocessed and unorganized facts, names, and numbers as "data," and the useful results of the computer's processing and organizing as "information."

When you package and send merchandise items, you need information, such as the items' sizes and shapes, to determine the kinds of packaging and shipping methods to use. When you write instructions to process data, you need to ask similar questions: What are the data types? What are reasonable or valid values for the data? How will the data be gathered?

Various cables and wires connect the motherboard to other system devices, such as disk drives and built-in webcams. A variety of connections called "ports" allow connecting external devices, such as USB flash drives, network cables, a keyboard, and a mouse, to the computer. All these units, devices, cards, ports, and cables are classified as hardware. Figure 1-1 shows some examples of computer hardware.

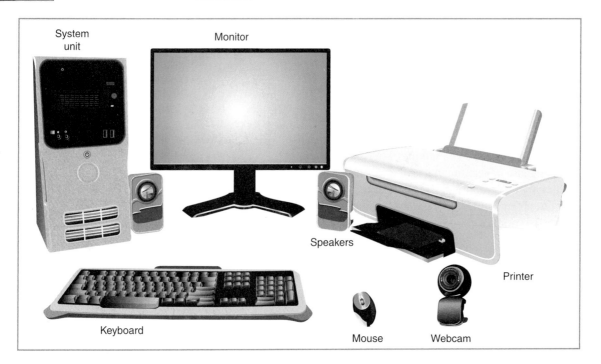

Figure 1-1 Examples of computer hardware

The processor (or microprocessor) and system memory make up the core of a computer's activity. The processor is an integrated circuit contained on a chip usually made of silicon. It contains the **central processing unit (CPU)**, which performs the computer's processing activity. The CPU is made up of two functional parts: the control unit and the arithmetic logic unit (ALU).

The control unit can be thought of as a traffic manager, which handles the instructions sent to it by application programs, the operating system, and system devices. For each instruction, a cycle of activities must be performed. The activities, or steps, in the information processing cycle, are as follows:

- Fetch (get the next instruction from system memory)

- Decode (get any data required by the instruction and find the address of the next instruction)

- Execute (perform required actions, which might involve sending data and instructions to the ALU)

- Store (write results to main memory or send them to an output device)

The ALU is like an intelligent calculator. The arithmetic portion does all kinds of mathematical calculations, including basic arithmetic, trigonometry, and statistics. The logic portion compares two values and returns one of three results:

- The values are equal.

- The first value is greater than the second.

- The second value is greater than the first.

Memory is the other main component of computer processing. The most common type of memory is **random access memory (RAM)**, also called "main memory." It's the temporary storage place for instructions and data while the computer is running. You can think of it as a whiteboard, where you write notes and erase portions and rewrite notes many times. The reason you must save your files to a hard drive, flash drive, or other long-term storage medium is that RAM is erased when the computer is powered down, and the RAM for a particular application is erased when that program ends. For this reason, RAM is considered volatile memory. The term "random access" refers to data not being fetched in a predetermined order; rather, data is located by using spinning disks and moving heads. As a result, the average time to fetch a piece of data from memory is roughly the same for any piece of data, no matter what its location in memory is. In contrast, sequential access memory is accessed in order.

RAM is like a CD or DVD, in that you can go directly to the track or segment you want with no delay. Sequential access memory is like a cassette tape or VHS tape, which requires starting at the current location and fast-forwarding or rewinding to get to the track or segment you're looking for.

Another type of memory is **read-only memory (ROM)**. "Read-only" means the data can be read, or accessed, but not changed. This small area of memory contains instructions for the system to perform a self-test as it powers up and to load the operating system from hard drive storage into main memory. ROM is persistent, meaning it's *not* erased when the computer is powered off.

Long-term storage is handled with disk drives and storage media. The most common storage devices are electromagnetic hard drives, electronic USB flash drives and memory cards, and optical CDs and DVDs. Figure 1-2 shows some examples of storage devices.

USB flash drive

DVD

Removable hard drive

Figure 1-2   Examples of storage devices

Programming Skills: Using the Right Tool for the Right Job

In some programs, you keep repeating a set of steps as long as there are items to process. Repetition is one of the three programming structures, and it's a valuable tool in the programmer's toolbox. You learn more about programming structures in Chapter 4.

Like any craft, programming involves learning a set of skills and a set of tools. One of the most important skills is learning how to analyze the problem to be solved and selecting the right tool. Each structure, concept, method, and process you learn is another tool you can add to your toolbox.

Good programming skills also include basic mathematics and a familiarity with common statistics, including calculating the average, minimum, and maximum.

Algorithms: The Logic of Problem Solving

Computers are used to solve problems. They're machines, but they have the following capabilities that make them preferable to humans for certain applications:

- They can operate extremely fast, performing billions of operations per second.

- They can operate for extremely long periods of time without getting tired or making mistakes.

- They can perform the same tasks repeatedly, also without getting tired or making mistakes.

Computers are often accused of making mistakes, but in most cases, the mistake is caused by human error in programming or data input. Occasionally, the mistake is caused by equipment or power failure. In this book, you're concerned with first preventing and then correcting errors in programming and data input. You can leave it to engineers and technicians to prevent and correct equipment or power failures.

Because you're using a machine to solve a problem, you must first understand the problem to be solved. In the business world, there are unlimited sources of problems, and for many, the computer is a useful tool. For example, business problems in order processing might include the following:

- How do you take an order from a customer?

- How do you calculate the total price for an order?

- How do you determine from where the order should be shipped?

- How do you check the customer's credit status and process payment?

In the second question, for example—calculating an order's total price—there are many steps in solving this problem. Some steps might need to be done only once, some might need to be done more than once, and some might not need to be done at all. The steps formulated to solve a problem, stated clearly and correctly, make up what's called an **algorithm**.

The steps in calculating an order's total price depend on many factors, including the type of business, whether sales tax is charged, and what shipping method is preferred. Some assumptions are made for this example, but remember that when you're solving a real business problem, you need to understand the conditions and policies for *your* particular situation.

In this algorithm, several products of varying descriptions and prices have been ordered. There's a 6% sales tax on the purchase, and the customer can choose between ground shipping for a flat charge of $10 or air shipping for a flat charge of $20. The algorithm might look something like this:

```
Set the total purchase price to 0
While there are still items to be processed:
   Get the quantity and price of the current item
   Multiply the quantity by the price
      to get the total for the current item
   Add the current item total to the total purchase price
```

```
Multiply the total purchase price by the 6% sales tax rate
    to get the sales tax amount
Ask the customer to choose ground or air shipping:
    If ground shipping, set the shipping charge to $10
    If air shipping, set the shipping charge to $20
Add the total purchase price, the sales tax amount, and the
    shipping charge to get the order total
```

There might well be more than one way to solve the same problem, just as there's more than one route from Chicago to Atlanta. Some routes are faster, some are less expensive, and some are more scenic. The best algorithm depends on the priorities for the situation, but in general, a programming algorithm should have these characteristics:

- It's logically correct (provides a satisfactory solution to the problem).

- It's efficient (uses suitable programming tools without wasting time or resources).

- It's easy to understand (can be explained in ordinary language).

When programmers develop algorithms, they use **pseudocode**, a structured, English-like language used to represent steps in an algorithm. Pseudocode was developed as a consistent and easily understood method of describing logic. It's not an actual programming language but can be converted to almost any current language easily. It has a few **syntax rules** for order, spacing, indentation, and punctuation and has some **keywords**, which are terms reserved for special purposes. There are many variations of pseudocode, but the differences are minor. You learn about the type of pseudocode used in this book in "Programming Basics" later in this chapter.

Testing Your Programs

Businesses can succeed on a single good idea, and they can fail on a single faulty product. Manufacturers will recall millions of products, even if just a few have proved defective, to assure the public that they care about quality. However, manufacturers go to great lengths to avoid reaching the point of recalling a product. Before a product ever reaches the market, it's tested for quality and safety numerous times.

Software companies are in the business of selling computer applications, so-called because the software is "applied" to a particular task, such as Microsoft Word for word processing, Adobe Photoshop for photo editing, and Sibelius for music printing. Like any product, software applications must be tested thoroughly at all stages of development.

Similarly, programs written for a company by a person or team inside the company also need to be tested thoroughly. Suppose you wrote a payroll program that inadvertently added an extra zero to the dollar amount for every employee's check, so someone who was supposed to receive $400 got $4000 instead, for example. If the checks were actually distributed before the mistake was discovered, employees might be delighted at first, but the company would certainly recall or stop payment on the checks (just before you're fired!).

Software testing can be done on several different levels: in small sections of program code (sometimes called snippets), in task-oriented modules, in interaction between modules, as complete programs, and in interaction between programs. Programs are often designed from the top down (breaking a large task into smaller tasks), but they're built and tested from *both* the top down and the bottom up, making sure every line of code performs its job correctly and works correctly with every other line of code in the program.

 There are three main categories of errors: syntax errors (violations of language rules), logic errors (incorrect instructions, such as adding instead of multiplying), and runtime errors (errors not known until the program runs, such as a missing data file).

One method of testing a program is to create **data sets** to see how the program behaves at data boundaries. For example, if you want to award bonus points to every customer who orders $100 or more of merchandise, your data set should include values such as 99.99, 100.00, and 100.01, values around the "boundary" of $100. You should also include data such as 0.00 and -1.00. How your program handles invalid or illogical data is important, and this topic is covered in Chapter 9. It's crucial that your program doesn't crash or freeze while it's being used, but it's just as crucial that it doesn't process invalid data.

Programming Basics

In addition to developing a logical set of steps to solve a problem—an algorithm—you need to know how programming languages enable you to implement your algorithm by using the computer.

Data Types and Numbering Systems

As mentioned, the three main categories of data are numeric, text, and raw binary. Programmers are usually concerned only with the first two: numeric and text. Text data consists of letters, digits, punctuation, and other characters you can type on a standard keyboard. Numeric data consists of values that can be used in mathematical calculations. Because these kinds of data are stored

 Other programming mistakes can have even more serious consequences. Mistakes in bank software can result in money being lost or assigned to wrong accounts. Programs are also written to control stoplights, railroad-crossing signals, and air traffic controller monitors, for example, and mistakes in these applications can be disastrous.

9

 The "Y2K scare" was a computer-related phenomenon just before 1999 ended and 2000 began. The problem was that many business programs written in the 1960s and 1970s, when storage and memory were expensive and processing was slow, stored data for the year as two digits, not four, assuming the first two digits would be "19." This problem created monumental concerns that programs would instantly shut down at the turn of the century. As a result of the Y2K scare, a lot of program code was checked and corrected or rewritten. Fortunately, none of the disastrous predictions (which included worldwide power grid outages) came true.

differently, programmers need to indicate in their programs which type they're using.

The familiar **decimal numbering system** uses the value 10 as its base, and the **binary numbering system** uses the value 2. Otherwise, the systems are remarkably similar. Values in either system use a notational system in which a number's value is equal to the sum of the values in its positions. The position on the far right represents the "ones" column in all numbering systems. The value of this position is the digit's value multiplied by 1. The digit 0 in any position makes the value in that position 0 because it equals 0 times whatever the positional value is.

The value of the next position to the left is equal to the numbering system's base (2 in binary and 10 in decimal). In the decimal system, a 1 in this position has the value 10, and in the binary system, it has the value 2. Table 1-1 shows the positional values in the decimal numbering system.

Exponent	7	6	5	4	3	2	1	0
Positional value (10 × exponent)	10,000,000	1,000,000	100,000	10,000	1000	100	10	1

Table 1-1   Positional values for an eight-digit decimal number

As you can see, the value in each position is equal to the base times the exponent, and it's the same for the binary system. Table 1-2 shows the positional values in the binary numbering system.

Exponent	7	6	5	4	3	2	1	0
Positional value (2 × exponent)	128	64	32	16	8	4	2	1

Table 1-2   Positional values for an eight-digit binary number

Converting Binary Numbers to Decimal

You can convert a binary number to its decimal equivalent by using a simple process of multiplication and addition. You multiply each digit by its positional value to get the decimal value for that position, and then add the products for the final decimal number. The procedure in Table 1-3 works for any binary number of eight or fewer digits.

Exponent		7	6	5	4	3	2	1	0
Multiplier (2 ^ exponent)		128	64	32	16	8	4	2	1
Multiplicand (binary digits)									
Product (multiplier × multiplicand)									
Final decimal number									

Table 1-3   Binary-to-decimal conversion table

Here's how to use the binary-to-decimal conversion table:

1. If the binary number has fewer than eight digits, write zeros to the left of the number until there are eight digits.

2. Write your eight-digit binary number in the multiplicand row from left to right, one digit per space.

3. For each column, multiply the multiplier by the multiplicand, and write the product in the product row.

4. Add the numbers in the product row, and write the total in the last row for the final decimal number.

The example in Table 1-4 shows the table filled out for converting the binary number 00001111 to its decimal equivalent, 15.

Exponent		7	6	5	4	3	2	1	0
Multiplier (2 ^ exponent)		128	64	32	16	8	4	2	1
Multiplicand (binary digits)		0	0	0	0	1	1	1	1
Product (multiplier × multiplicand)		0	0	0	0	8	4	2	1
Final decimal number					15				

Table 1-4   Converting binary 00001111 to its decimal equivalent

The example in Table 1-5 shows the table filled out for converting the binary number 10101010 to its decimal equivalent, 170.

Exponent	7	6	5	4	3	2	1	0
Multiplier (2 ^ exponent)	128	64	32	16	8	4	2	1
Multiplicand (binary digits)	1	0	1	0	1	0	1	0
Product (multiplier × multiplicand)	128	0	32	0	8	0	2	0
Final decimal number				170				

Table 1-5   Converting binary 10101010 to its decimal equivalent

Detective Work

Use Table 1-6 (or print binaryToDecimalTable.doc in the student data files) to convert the binary number 11111111 to decimal.

Exponent	7	6	5	4	3	2	1	0
Multiplier (2 ^ exponent)	128	64	32	16	8	4	2	1
Multiplicand (binary digits)								
Product (multiplier × multiplicand)								
Final decimal number								

Table 1-6   Binary-to-decimal conversion table

If you're having trouble with the conversions in this section or the next, review conversionTables.doc in your student data files.

Converting Decimal Numbers to Binary

Converting a decimal number to its binary equivalent involves whole number division, using the quotient and the remainder. In programming, when dividing whole numbers, the division operator (/) is used to find the quotient, and the modulus operator (%) is used to find the remainder. The decimal number is divided by the binary positional value in each column, calculating from left to right. The quotient becomes the binary digit for that position, and the remaining decimal value is moved to the next position, until the entire decimal value has been "distributed" across the binary positions. The procedure in Table 1-7 works for any decimal number of 255 or less.

Exponent	7	6	5	4	3	2	1	0
Divisor (2 ^ exponent)	128	64	32	16	8	4	2	1
Dividend (remaining decimal value)								
Quotient (dividend / divisor)								
Remainder (dividend % divisor)								
Final binary number								

Table 1-7 Decimal-to-binary conversion table

Here's how to use the decimal-to-binary conversion table:

1. Write the decimal number in the dividend row in the Exponent 7 column.

2. Starting with the Exponent 7 column and proceeding to the Exponent 0 column:

   a. Using whole number division, divide the dividend by the divisor.

   b. Write the quotient in the quotient row for that column.

   c. Write the remainder in the remainder row for that column.

   d. Copy the remainder to the dividend row for the next column to the right (except for the last column).

3. When you're finished, write the eight binary digits in the row for the final binary number.

The example in Table 1-8 shows the table filled out for converting the decimal number 155 to its binary equivalent, 10011011.

Exponent	7	6	5	4	3	2	1	0
Divisor (2 ^ exponent)	128	64	32	16	8	4	2	1
Dividend (remaining decimal value)	155	27	27	27	11	3	3	1
Quotient (dividend / divisor)	1	0	0	1	1	0	1	1
Remainder (dividend % divisor)	27	27	27	11	3	3	1	0
Final binary number				10011011				

Table 1-8 Converting decimal 155 to its binary equivalent

14

The example in Table 1-9 shows the table filled out for converting the decimal number 62 to its binary equivalent, 00111110.

Exponent	7	6	5	4	3	2	1	0
Divisor (2 ^ exponent)	128	64	32	16	8	4	2	1
Dividend (remaining decimal value)	62	62	62	30	14	6	2	0
Quotient (dividend / divisor)	0	0	1	1	1	1	1	0
Remainder (dividend % divisor)	62	62	30	14	6	2	0	0
Final binary number				00111110				

Table 1-9 Converting decimal 62 to its binary equivalent

Detective Work

Use Table 1-10 (or print decimalToBinaryTable.doc in the student data files) to convert the decimal number 116 to binary.

Exponent	7	6	5	4	3	2	1	0
Divisor (2 ^ exponent)	128	64	32	16	8	4	2	1
Dividend (remaining decimal value)								
Quotient (dividend / divisor)								
Remainder (dividend % divisor)								
Final binary number								

Table 1-10 Decimal-to-binary conversion table

Standard ASCII code, which includes all characters commonly used in the English language, uses only 7 bits and includes 128 characters. Extended ASCII code makes use of the 8th bit to expand the number of characters to 256.

Character-Coding Systems

Bits are grouped in standardized coding schemes to represent characters. The **American Standard Code for Information Interchange (ASCII)** character-coding system uses 8 bits, consisting of a unique arrangement of eight 0s and 1s for each character. In ASCII (pronounced AS-kee), an uppercase A, for instance, is represented by the digits 01000001, equivalent to the decimal value 65.

Although 256 characters is enough for English and other languages based on the English alphabet, it doesn't come close to the number of characters needed in alphabets such as Chinese, Japanese, Arabic, Farsi, and Hebrew. The **Unicode** character set was developed in the late 1980s to address these alphabets. Unicode is a 16-bit system, capable of 65,536 characters. For purposes of compatibility, the characters represented by the first 8 bits in the Unicode system are identical to those in the 8-bit ASCII system.

You can view the ASCII table on the Web at *www. asciicodes. us*. This table lists codes in the binary, decimal, and hexadecimal numbering systems as well as characters or their abbreviations. (For example, BS stands for the backspace character.)

15

Variables and Named Constants

As mentioned, the computer deals with binary digits. For example, every memory location has a binary address. Programmers must use memory all the time. When you need to keep track of something in a program, you designate a memory location for it. However, keeping track of memory locations by their binary addresses is a cumbersome, time-consuming task. For this reason, programming languages include **variables**, which are simply programmer-designated names for memory locations. Memory locations are used to store **values**, the numeric or text data you want to keep track of. These values can be changed at any time during the program—hence the name "variable."

A programmer uses variables in two main ways: declaring them and assigning values to them. **Declaring** a variable simply informs the computer that you want to associate a particular name with a particular data type. (The operating system keeps track of what binary address is associated with the name.) In most programming languages, the data type must be declared along with the variable name so that the operating system can store the data correctly, as text or a numeric value. In this book, you develop algorithms by using only two data types: `Numeric` and `String`.

- Numeric variables can store any type of number, with or without decimal places.

- String variables can store any text data, including single characters, a collection of characters in a particular order, and an "empty string" (represented by two quotation marks with nothing between them).

Programmers assign values to variables in several ways. One of the most common is with the **assignment statement**, in which the variable name is followed by an equals sign and the value to be assigned. Most languages allow declaring the variable and assigning it an initial value in the same step.

For example, you might need to calculate the gross pay for an employee named Monica Vanderkolk, who worked 40 hours at a pay rate of $15.00 an hour. To solve this problem, you need to keep track of these pieces of data:

- Hours worked (40)

- Pay rate per hour (15.00)

- Gross pay (to be calculated)

- The employee's last and first name

You need to designate variables for each item. The first three pieces of data represent number values, and the last two are text, so you declare three variables as Numeric and two as String. Use hoursWorked for the first variable, payRate for the second one, and grossPay for the third. For the employee's name, use two variables, lastName and firstName. You're choosing these names for two main reasons:

- The names must comply with the programming language's rules.

- The names should be easy to read and understand.

Most current programming languages allow using **camel casing** for names, and this convention is followed in this book for naming variables. With this convention, names are made up of words and digits, and all letters are lowercase except the first letter of each new word, starting with the second word, as in lastName. (The term "camel casing" comes from the shape of an imaginary curve over the top of the name, resembling a camel's humps.) Camel casing doesn't use underscores or hyphens between words in a name, although these characters are permitted in most languages. The rules for variable names and other identifiers vary, but most agree on the following:

- Identifiers can include letters, digits, underscores, and hyphens.

- Identifiers can't begin with a digit.

- Identifiers can't contain spaces.

Variables should also be easy to read and understand. Early programming languages severely restricted the length of variable names (for example, some allowed a maximum of six letters or digits), but modern languages allow an almost unlimited length. Algebra uses letters, such as x and y, to represent unknown quantities and explain what they're used for in the problem statement, but programmers choose variable names that convey their meaning.

For example, if you're choosing a name for the total adjusted gross income tax for the year 2011, the name tAdGrIncTx11 is too short for its meaning to be recognized and remembered easily, but totalAdjustedGrossIncomeTaxForTheYear2011 is probably longer than what you need. A reasonable length between these extremes would be totAdjGrossTax2011. The word "income" might not be necessary as part of the name, unless you're dealing with other kinds of taxes besides income tax. "Tot" and "adj" are common abbreviations for "total" and "adjusted." The full four-digit date was chosen, not so much because of leftover Y2K scare, but because the digits "11" are easy to confuse with the lowercase letters "ll." The point is to make the variable's purpose clear to you and to others who might need to look at your work: a manager, a colleague, or the person who replaces you when you take another job.

Remember that you aren't the only one who has to read your program code. Those who have to figure out what your programs are doing will praise you for using easy-to-understand variable names or curse your name for writing hard-to-understand code.

The first keyword you use is the instruction to declare a variable: Declare. The next two keywords are for the two data types, Numeric and String. In this payroll example, you have five variables to declare, so your pseudocode should have the following statements:

```
Declare Numeric hoursWorked
Declare Numeric payRate
Declare Numeric grossPay
Declare String lastName
Declare String firstName
```

In this payroll program, you need to assign values to four of the variables and calculate the value of the fifth one (grossPay). To do this, you use assignment statements. After a variable has been declared, it can be used in an assignment statement. The value to be assigned to the variable, placed to the right of the equals sign, must be similar in data type to the type of variable receiving it. (You learn more about assignment statements in the next section.) The following statements assign values to the first four variables and calculate the value of the fifth.

```
lastName = "Vanderkolk"
firstName = "Monica"
hoursWorked = 40
payRate = 15.00
grossPay = hoursWorked * payRate
```

The following statements cause errors because the data types don't match; note the explanations of what causes the errors:

lastName = 10 (A numeric constant can't be assigned to a string variable.)
firstName = hoursWorked (The value of a numeric variable can't be assigned to a string variable.)
payRate = "15.00" (A string constant can't be assigned to a numeric variable.)
grossPay = firstName (The value of a string variable can't be assigned to a numeric variable.)

Named constants are also identifiers, names that represent values. The difference is that a named constant's value, as its name implies, *can't* be changed while a program is running. Named constants are often used for rates, such as tax rates, that need to be used throughout a program. You use named constants for the same reason you use variables—to identify and use values in your programs.

The naming rules for constants are similar to the rules for naming variables, except that uppercase letters and underscores are used instead of camel casing to make constant names stand out in the code and make it clear they're not variables and, therefore, can't be changed. The value of a constant is set at the time the constant is declared, near the beginning of the program. In this book, the words `Declare Constant` are used, followed by the constant's name, an equals sign, and the constant's value.

Constant values are **literals**. As in English, "literal" means that something is exactly what it says it is. In other words, the value 2 is always 2; it can't be changed to anything else. Numeric literals include numbers, such as 0, 1, 120, and -33. Numbers without decimal places are called whole numbers or, more commonly, integers. Numeric literals that include a decimal point and decimal places, such as 0.0, 3.14159, 98.6, and -22.35, are categorized as real numbers or floating-point numbers. (The term "floating-point" refers to the high precision that's possible for very large and very small numbers in the same number of bits, by "floating" the decimal point to the left or right as needed.) String literals have quotation marks around them. Notice in the following statements that numeric literals don't have quotation marks around them, but string literals do. A special kind of string literal is represented by quotation marks with nothing between them; it's known as an "empty string."

Here are some declarations of program constants:

```
Declare Constant INT_RATE_SAVINGS = 0.025
Declare Constant INT_RATE_CHECKING = 0.015
Declare Constant MINS_PER_HOUR = 60
Declare Constant COMPANY_NAME = "Zodiac Designs, Inc."
```

If you have a state sales tax rate of .07 and a county sales tax of .01, the use of constants can clarify your calculation statement. For example, the following line is easy to understand only if you already know what the .07 and .01 values represent:

```
totSalesTax = (totSales * .07) + (totSales * .01)
```

The following statement, although slightly longer, makes it clear how the calculation is being performed:

```
totSalesTax = (totSales * STATE_TAX_RATE) +↵
  (totSales * COUNTY_TAX_RATE)
```

Remember that by definition, the value of a named constant can't change after it's declared, so it must be given a value *at the time* it's declared. Also, because constant values are literals, specifying the data type isn't necessary. If the value is enclosed in quotation marks, it's text, and if it isn't, it's numeric.

The use of named constants also has a major benefit when you have to change a constant value. Suppose the state sales tax rate changes from .07 to .08. If you're using a named constant, you have to change its value in only one place in the program. However, if you're using the "hard-coded" value .07, you have to find every instance in which the state sales tax rate is used and change the value .07 to .08 each time. You can't apply a global "find and replace" to change every instance of .07 to .08 because the value .07 might appear in different contexts. For example, what if another rate in the program is also .07?

Assignment Statements

You've already seen the basic components of the assignment statement:

- The name of the variable that's to receive the value. It's the only item on the left of the equals sign and specifies where the result of the statement will be stored.

- An equals sign, which is used as the assignment operator.

- The value to be assigned, which can range from simple to complex.

Assignment statements differ from algebraic equations, although both use the equals sign. In algebra, an equation is a statement that the values on both sides of the equals sign are already equal. In programming, an assignment statement says to take the value on the right side of the equals sign and store it in the memory location for the variable on the left side.

Here are some assignment statements with numeric variables being assigned literal values. Assume that all these variables have been declared as `Numeric` types:

```
gradeLevel = 6
patientAge = 62
areaRoom2231 = 232.5
semesterGPA = 3.89
```

Here are some assignment statements with string variables being assigned literal values. All these variables have been declared as `String` types:

```
lastName = "Nelson"
firstName = "George"
streetAddress = "123 Dutch Elm Street"
city = "Kouts"
state = "IN"
zip = "46347"
```

Remember that the computer takes the value on the *right* side of the equals sign and places it in the memory location for the variable named on the *left* side.

Variables can also be assigned the value of another variable, as long as they both have the same data type. Here's an example, with both variables already declared as `Numeric`:

```
itemCost01 = 9.99
itemCost02 = itemCost01
```

After these statements are executed, both variables have the value 9.99. If the value on the right of the equals sign is a variable name instead of a literal, the computer goes to the memory location for that variable name, fetches the value, and copies this value into the memory location for the variable name on the left of the equals sign. Here's an example for strings:

```
homeCity = "Miami"
homeState = "Florida"
currentCity = "Tampa Bay"
currentState = homeState
```

After these statements are executed, both `homeState` and `currentState` contain the value "Florida".

For string assignments, the value on the right must be a string literal or the name of a string variable. For numeric assignments, the value on the right must be a numeric literal or the name of a numeric variable. If not, an error results.

The value on the right of the equals sign in an assignment statement can also be more complicated than a single value. Numeric assignments can include arithmetic calculations, and string assignments can be used to build a long string from shorter string segments. Both tasks can include literals and variables.

Numeric Operations

Numeric calculations use arithmetic operators, which are similar to the familiar symbols used for common arithmetic. Besides addition, subtraction, multiplication, and division, most programming languages have an operator for the modulus operation, which returns the remainder after one integer is divided by another. The following are the common operators used in this book, and the values these operators work on are called operands:

- \+ for addition
- \- for subtraction
- * for multiplication
- / for division
- % for modulus

Here are some examples of assignment statements, some using numeric calculations (all variables are numeric):

Example 1: An employer decides that bonuses for the year 2011 will be double what they were in 2010.

```
bonus2010 = 125
bonus2011 = bonus2010 * 2
```

Example 2: A man wants to keep track of how much weight he has lost since he started exercising and dieting.

```
startingWeight = 185
currentWeight = 174
weightLostToDate = startingWeight - currentWeight
```

Example 3: A woman wants to know how far she can drive in a specific amount of time if she drives constantly at the speed limit.

```
speedLimit = 70
hoursDriven = 5
totalMilesDriven = speedLimit * hoursDriven
```

Example 4: A restaurant manager wants to know the average number of customers served in an 8-hour period.

```
hoursWorked = 8
totCustomersServed = 140
avgCustomersServedPerHour = totCustomersServed /↵
  hoursWorked
```

The use of the modulus (mod) operator (%) isn't as common as the basic arithmetic operations, but it comes in handy when you want to divide a quantity of items equally and find out how many items will be left over. For example, a first-grade student brings a box of small granola bars to class for snack time. The box has 48 granola bars in it, but there are 22 students in the class. If they're divided up equally, how many are left over?

```
totalBars = 48
numStudents = 22
barsLeftOver = totalBars % numStudents
```

Have you figured out that the value of `barsLeftOver` is 4? The number 22 goes into 48 evenly two times, with a remainder of 4. The mod operator calculates the remainder value.

What happens when the arithmetic is more complicated than two numbers, or you have multiple variables joined by different operators? When multiple operations are to be performed in a single assignment statement, it's important to know the order in which operations should be performed. Before you get into mathematical trouble, read the tip on the right.

Now that you've been cautioned, you can look at an example without parentheses and spot the potential danger. A customer purchases one item at $5.00, two items at $40.00, and three items at $20.00. You're

You have already seen how the modulus operation is used to convert a decimal number to binary.

Operations enclosed in parentheses are performed before other operations, and operations in an inner set of parentheses are performed before operations in outer, or enclosing, sets.

Dollar signs and commas used with numbers don't affect their numeric value. They're used only when the number is displayed and are considered **formatting** elements only.

going to calculate the total cost. Notice that dollar signs aren't used in the calculation, only numeric values.

```
totalCost = 5 + 2 * 40 + 3 * 20
```

Three operations are performed in this assignment statement. Which order will the computer take? If it goes from left to right, it adds 5 + 2 (giving 7), multiplies this number by 40 (giving 280), adds 3 (giving 283), and multiplies this number by 20 (giving 5660). This result could be a problem.

You know that the total for the first item is 5, the total for the second item is 2 * 40 (giving 80), and the total for the third item is 3 * 20 (giving 60). The totals for the second and third items should be calculated before adding them to the first item price (5) to get the final total (145). Are you sure the computer will do these operations in the correct order?

The best solution is to put parentheses around the operations that need to be done first: the two multiplication operations. The statement expressed this way guarantees correct results in any programming language:

```
totalCost = 5 + (2 * 40) + (3 * 20)
```

Each programming language has a defined order of operations, in which some types of operations take precedence over others. There are even similarities in the order of precedence for the exponential operation and the basic arithmetic operations (addition, subtraction, multiplication, and division). Without parentheses, in most languages, operations are carried out in this order:

- Exponential operations are performed before any basic arithmetic operation.

- Multiplication and division are performed left to right in a "pass" through the calculation.

- Addition and subtraction are performed left to right in the next "pass" through the calculation.

So would this example have been calculated correctly without parentheses? Before you figure that out, look at the two examples of assignment statements. Which one is easier to read? It turns out that the computer would have computed the correct answer in this case, but you have to look at the first one more closely to make that determination. Remember that making your code easy to understand is the mark of a good programmer.

Now that you know the order of operations, take a look at some examples of numeric calculations that involve multiple operations:

Example 1: Cash revenue for five days is recorded to find the average daily revenue for the work week.

```
revMon = 174
revTue = 181
revWed = 166
revThu = 237
revFri = 277
avgDailyRev = (revMon + revTue + revWed + revThu + revFri) ↵
  / 5
```

Example 2: A customer wants to know her balance after one year, with an initial deposit of $1000 at 3.5% annual interest.

```
initDeposit = 1000
annualIntRate = 0.035
balYearEnd1 = initDeposit + (initDeposit * annualIntRate)
```

String Operations

If a string is a group of characters, it makes sense that you can make longer strings out of shorter ones by putting them together. This process is called **concatenation**, and it uses the same operator used for arithmetic addition: +. Numerous operations can be performed on strings, such as finding what character is at a certain position or converting the string to all uppercase letters, but the most basic operation is concatenating strings. Like numeric calculations, string concatenation can involve operands that are literals or other string variables.

For example, a library wants to send a postcard to a patron and use the patron database to print the address on the postcard. The first and last names are stored separately, as are the street address, city, state, and zip code. All these variables are declared as String types. (Zip codes don't have any mathematical value and should be stored as a five-character string.)

Assign the known variables first:

```
firstName = "Debi"
lastName = "Tippett"
streetAddr = "19125 Peach Orchard Road"
city = "Kalamazoo"
state = "MI"
zip = "49002"
```

You can build the three address lines by using concatenation:

- The first line should contain the first name and last name, separated by a space.

- The second line is the same as the street address.

- The third line contains the city, a comma, a space, the state abbreviation, a space, and the zip code.

Below the assignment statements, you're ready to build the three address lines. A literal space is placed between the first and last name and between the state and zip code for readability. Between the city and state, a comma and a space are inserted:

```
addrLine1 = firstName + " " + lastName
addrLine2 = streetAddr
addrLine3 = city + ", " + state + " " + zip
```

Remember that with numeric variables, the plus sign is for arithmetic addition. With string variables, it's used to connect smaller strings, or segments, to build a larger string.

Input and Output

So far, you have given values to all your variables by using assignment statements. This method is excellent when you know what all the values are, but in the business world, programmers almost never know the actual data values for variables in any program. Employees' names and addresses, wage rates, product codes, and sales amounts are usually gathered during **runtime**—that is, when the program is running (executing).

Input to a program is gathered in two main ways: A data input operator or a user enters values while interacting with the program, or the values are input, or read, from a file or database. The pseudocode keyword for getting input from a user is `Input`, followed by the variable that's receiving the value. The value the user enters is stored in the variable. For example, the following statement causes the program to pause and wait for the user to type something and press Enter (or click OK in a program with a graphical user interface):

```
Input age
```

Whatever number the user types is stored in the variable named `age`.

Information can also be sent from the computer and is called **output**. The most common types of output are to the user's screen (called "soft copy") or to a printer (called "hard copy"). The pseudocode keyword to display text on the user's screen is `Display` followed by the string (or concatenated string) to be displayed. Each `Display` statement causes a single line of output to be displayed onscreen.

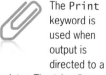

The `Print` keyword is used when output is directed to a printer. The `Display` keyword is used when output is directed to the user's screen.

A `Display` statement is often used at the beginning of a program to welcome the user or display the name of the program. This statement does both:

```
Display "Welcome to the Ticket Reservation System!"
```

For the user to know what values are to be entered at the right time, the instruction, or **prompt**, must be displayed onscreen. When a user is expected to enter data, a `Display` statement is paired with an `Input` statement, as in the following example. The space before the closing quotation mark is used to separate the last displayed character of the prompt (the colon) from the user's entry.

```
Display "Enter the customer ID number: "
Input custID
```

With this ability to send information to and receive information from users, you have added a new dimension to your programming experience: Your programs are now interactive, meaning users can enter relevant data at the time the program is running.

Program Comments

Programming involves learning new languages. Whether the language is pseudocode, JavaScript, Python, C++, Java, Visual Basic, or any other, nonprogrammers don't understand the languages programmers use, which can be a handicap in situations such as the following:

- When a manager needs to look at your program to understand what it's supposed to do

- When your colleague has to make a change to your program in your absence

- When you move on to another job and a new programmer takes your place

Do these situations sound familiar? Similar ones were stated earlier in this chapter as reasons for using easy-to-understand variable names. It's not just variable names that should be understood easily by others. Your entire program, and every one of your programs, should be written so that a nonprogrammer can understand what the program accomplishes and other programmers can understand how the program accomplishes it.

The way to achieve this goal is by using **comments**. Every program should have consistent basic documentation that includes the program's name and purpose, who wrote it, and the date it was written or modified. In addition, each section of each program should include brief but useful comments on what each variable is used for and what each section of code is doing.

The operative words here are "consistent" and "brief." Your company might have a specific style for commenting programs, or you might have to establish your own. In any case, a nonprogrammer should be

You shouldn't expect others to admire you for your clever or complicated programming code. Any admiration you earn should come from writing programs that run correctly and efficiently and are easily understood so that they can be maintained. If your programs are to be useful to your company, they must be able to be modified and updated to adapt to changing times and business needs.

able to look at your program code and see what it's doing. You don't, however, have to explain every line of code and every calculation. The level of detail is a judgment call on your part. Simple calculations with basic arithmetic don't need to be described in detail, for example, but a complicated calculation might require an explanation. In general, a description of *what* a section of your program accomplishes is more important than *how*.

Comments in a program are simply descriptions in plain language. They aren't executed by the computer, so they don't need to conform to the programming language's syntax rules. Programming languages differ in how to include comments, but several languages, including JavaScript, C++, and Java, use two slashes (//) at the beginning of each comment line. Use this practice for pseudocode in this chapter and for JavaScript in later chapters.

In this book, every program starts with four items of documentation: the program name, a brief description of the program's purpose, the author's name, and the date the program was written or last modified. Here's an example:

```
// Program name: Label Maker
// Purpose: Create mailing labels from a list of names
// and addresses
// Author: Paul Addison
// Date last modified: 01-Sep-2011
```

In most languages, comments can start after a programming instruction, on the same line. Everything after the two slashes is treated as a comment. This convention makes variable descriptions and other short comments easy to read without having to take up a lot of space.

Be consistent in naming variables. Don't use `mar2012` in one place and `apr12` in another. Making names of similar variables the same length is a good idea, too. Your code will line up better and be easier to read.

As mentioned, using meaningful variable names goes a long way in helping someone understand your code. Still, a short definition at the time each variable is declared can prevent confusion and misinterpretation later. For example, does the variable name `monEnd` mean "month end" or "Monday end"? Does `address` mean just the street address or the full address, including the street address, city, state, and zip code? Simple explanations can make your intentions clear and give programmers who have to modify your code necessary information.

Here are some examples of variable declarations with definitions as comments.

```
Declare Numeric qtr1avg        // quarter 1 average sales
Declare Numeric qtr2avg        // quarter 2 average sales
Declare Numeric qtr3avg        // quarter 3 average sales
Declare Numeric qtr4avg        // quarter 4 average sales
Declare Numeric totSales = 0   // total sales for year
```

```
Declare String fname          // first name of employee
Declare String lname          // last name of employee

Declare Numeric numCansDonated // # cans a customer donates
Declare Numeric totCansDonated // total # of cans donated
```

Many languages allow you to declare multiple variables on the same line if they're the same data type, as in these examples:

```
Declare String player1, player2    // names of game players
Declare Numeric score1, score2     // scores for players
```

In the program's code, each section should have a brief comment describing what that code does. How big is a section? That's up to you, but a few examples should help:

Example 1:

```
// Get principal and rate from user
// Calculate and display interest
Display "Enter the principal amount: "
Input principal
Display "Enter the annual interest rate (example:↵
  3% is .03): "
Input intRate
intAmt = principal * intRate
Display "The interest earned in the first year is:↵
  " + intAmt
```

Example 2:

```
// Ask user for two numbers
Display "Enter the first number: "
Input num1
Display "Enter the second number: "
Input num2

// Calculate and display sum and product
sum = num1 + num2
prod = num1 * num2
Display "The sum of the two numbers is: " + sum
Display "The product of the two numbers is: " + prod
```

Using blank lines and spaces in your program code keeps the page from looking too crowded and can make the code much easier to read. These empty areas are referred to as "white space."

Complete pseudocode programs in this book begin and end with the keywords Start and Stop. Everything between these two keywords is indented for readability.

The Input-Processing-Output Method

How do you keep track of all the variables and programming steps needed in an algorithm? When analyzing a problem and developing an algorithm for a solution, listing the algorithm's components in the categories of input, processing, and output is helpful. This process is called **input-processing-output (IPO)**. The IPO method is useful when deciding what variables are necessary. Interestingly, however, the most logical order to deal with these components is output, then input, and then processing because you know ahead of time what the program's outputs should be; they're the reason for writing the program. Next, the inputs are listed: What information is available to use in creating the required output? Finally, using logical, mathematical, and programming skills, you determine the processing steps.

 ## Detective Work

A clerk wants to print a payroll statement for one employee, entering the employee's name, hours worked, wage rate, and total deductions. The program calculates gross pay and net (take-home) pay. (Remember that the dollar sign isn't included in a numeric variable; it's used only for formatting.)

Start with the IPO method:

- What outputs are requested? Gross pay and net pay

- What inputs are available? Employee's name, hours worked, wage rate, and total deductions

- What processing is required? Get input, multiply hours by wage to get gross pay, and subtract total deductions to get net pay

Use that information to determine the variables you need:

- Gross pay and net pay (numeric): grossPay, netPay

- Hours worked, wage rate, and total deductions (numeric): hoursWorked, wageRate, totDeductions

- Employee's last and first name (string): lastName, firstName

Pseudocode Program 1-1

```
// Program name: Payroll Statement
// Purpose: Create payroll statement from pay data
// Author: Paul Addison
// Date last modified: 01-Sep-2011

Start
    Display "Welcome to the Payroll Statement Program!"

    // Declare variables
    Declare String lastName        // employee's last name
    Declare String firstName       // employee's first name
    Declare Numeric hoursWorked    // hours worked
    Declare Numeric wageRate       // pay rate per hour
    Declare Numeric totDeductions  // total deductions
    Declare Numeric grossPay       // gross pay
    Declare Numeric netPay         // net pay
```

```
    // Get input from user
    Display "Enter the employee's last name: "
    Input lastName
    Display "Enter the employee's first name: "
    Input firstName
    Display "Enter the number of hours worked: "
    Input hoursWorked
    Display "Enter the wage rate for this employee: "
    Input wageRate
    Display "Enter the total deductions for this employee: "
    Input totDeductions

    // Calculate gross and net pay
    grossPay = hoursWorked * wageRate
    netPay = grossPay - totDeductions

    // Display payroll information
    Display "Payroll statement for " + firstName↵
     + SP + lastName
    Display "Hours worked: " + hoursWorked
    Display "Wage rate: $" + wageRate
    Display "Gross pay: $" + grossPay
    Display "Total deductions: $" + totDeductions
    Display "Net pay: $" + netPay

    // Close program
    Display "Thank you for using this program!"

Stop
```

Now see what this pseudocode would look like if you ran it on a computer. The text the program displays is in regular code font and what the user types is in bold code.

Pseudocode Program 1-1 Simulation

```
Welcome to the Payroll Statement Program!
Enter the employee's last name: Siebenthal
Enter the employee's first name: Melanie
Enter the number of hours worked: 30
Enter the wage rate for this employee: 15.50
Enter the total deductions for this employee: 25.00
Payroll statement for Melanie Siebenthal
Hours worked: 30
Wage rate: $15.50
Gross pay: $465.00
Total deductions: $25.00
Net pay: $440.00
Thank you for using this program!
```

When you need a blank line of output, simply issue this statement:

```
Display
```

Sometimes your line of pseudocode, even if it's meant to display one line of output, is too long to fit on one line in your program. You can split a line of code, as long as you don't split a literal string, a variable, or a constant name over two lines. You should indent the second line for easier reading. Here's an example of breaking a pseudocode line into two lines:

```
Display "The final score was: Central High School " +
    score1 + ", South Side High " + score2
```

 ## Programmer's Workshop

In the Programmer's Workshop, you study a business problem and develop an algorithm for a solution as a programmer would approach it. For this problem, you use pseudocode as the programming tool. In future chapters, you use other tools, including flowcharts and JavaScript. These problems help you put together what you've learned throughout the chapter, paying special attention to good programming style.

Problem: Sunshine Books is a bookstore that's open every morning from 8:00 a.m. to 12:00 p.m. The manager wants information about the number of customers in the store at different times. A clerk, whose station is near the door, counts customers by making a mark on a piece of paper each time a customer enters. The paper is divided into four segments, one for each hour, and the clerk notes the time before making each mark. When the store closes at noon, the clerk wants to enter the numbers in a program, which then displays the total number of customers for the day and the average number of customers per hour.

Your job, as the programmer, is to develop an algorithm by using pseudocode. If the manager likes your pseudocode proposal, you might be invited back to write the program in an actual computer language.

Discussion: Use the IPO method to get started:

- What outputs are requested? Total customers and average customers per hour

- What inputs are available? Number of customers for each hour

- What processing is required? Get input, add numbers for total, and divide by number of hours for average

The next step is deciding what variables and constants you need. You need a variable for each item you want to keep track of (that is, each input and output) and sometimes a temporary variable for calculations. You should use a constant when you know ahead of time how many of something you have. Choose your variables and constants, giving them the following names and data types:

- Total customers (numeric): `totCust`

- Average customers per hour (numeric): `avgCust`

- Count of customers each hour (numeric): `count1, count2, count3, count4`

- Number of hours (numeric constant): `NUM_HOURS`

    1. Open a new file in Notepad and save it as **customerStats.txt**.

    2. Start by entering your four documentation items, substituting your name for the author name and today's date for the date last modified:

    ```
    // Program name: Customer Statistics
    // Purpose: Compute total and average number
    //    of customers over 4 hours
    // Author: Paul Addison
    // Date last modified: 01-Sep-2011
    ```

    3. Next, declare your variables and constants. Labeling the section with a comment is helpful. Notice that some comments are placed on a separate line from the declaration for better readability. The entire program after the documentation lines is placed between the keywords `Start` and `Stop`.

    ```
    Start
        // Variables and constants
        Declare Numeric totCust     // total customers
        Declare Numeric avgCust     // average customers
            per hour
        Declare Numeric count1, count2, count3, count4
                            // count of customers each hour
        Declare Constant NUM_HOURS = 4 // number of hours
    ```

    4. Now you're ready to get the input, do the calculations, and display the output. Don't forget to display a program heading and thank the user at the beginning and end of the program!

    ```
    // Program heading
    Display "Sunshine Books Customer Statistics Program"

    // Get number of customers for each hour
    Display "Enter the # of customers for the first hour: "
    Input count1
    Display "Enter the # of customers for the second hour: "
    Input count2
    Display "Enter the # of customers for the third hour: "
    Input count3
    Display "Enter the # of customers for the fourth hour: "
    Input count4
    ```

```
// Compute total and average, and display results
totCust = count1 + count2 + count3 + count4
avgCust = totCust / NUM_HOURS
Display "Total number of customers: " + totCust
Display "Average customers per hour: " + avgCust
// Thank the user and end the program
Display "Thank you for using this program. Good-bye!"
Stop
```

The following shows what your pseudocode program looks like if you run it on a computer:

Pseudocode Simulation

```
Sunshine Books Customer Statistics Program
Enter the # of customers for the first hour: 22
Enter the # of customers for the second hour: 37
Enter the # of customers for the third hour: 47
Enter the # of customers for the fourth hour: 38
Total number of customers: 144
Average customers per hour: 36
Thank you for using this program. Good-bye!
```

Chapter Summary

- Computer programming is the process of formulating instructions to operate a digital computer.

- Binary digits (0s and 1s) are the building blocks of a digital computer and are referred to as bits. The computer stores instructions and data as bits.

- Data is unprocessed pieces of information and is classified into three data types: text, numeric, and raw binary.

- A computer and its related equipment are called hardware.

- Software includes all kinds of instructions to the computer, including commands, modules, and programs.

- Understanding the problem to be solved is the essential first step in formulating a successful solution.

- The logical steps formulated to solve a problem are called an algorithm.

- Pseudocode is a structured, English-like language used to express logic and develop algorithms.

- Software testing can be done on several levels, such as in small code sections, in modules, and as complete programs. Although programs are often designed from the top down, they're tested from both the top down and the bottom up.

- One method of software testing is creating data sets to see how the program behaves at data boundaries.

- All numbering systems have a base (the number of digits used), and use positional notation to determine the value of each position. The binary system (base 2), decimal system (base 10) and hexadecimal system (base 16) are the most common. Numbers in one system can be converted to another.

- Text data includes characters such as letters, digits, and punctuation marks, which are represented by binary character codes. The ASCII system uses 8 bits for each character, and the Unicode system uses 16 bits.

- Variables are names for memory locations. Programmers declare variables by giving them a name and specifying their data types. Names given to variables must conform to the programming language's syntax rules. The value of data stored in a variable can change when the program runs.

- Constants, values that don't change, are given names by programmers to make it easier to understand their use and to make code modifications easier.

- Programmers often don't know ahead of time what data a program needs; it must be entered (input) at the time the program is running, usually by a user interacting with the program or by getting the input from a file or database.

- Data sent out from the computer is called output and is usually displayed onscreen (soft copy) or printed on paper (hard copy).

- Comments are used to document a program's name, purpose, author, and creation date; define variables and named constants; and explain what specific sections of program code do. They're also useful to other programmers who have to maintain or modify the program.

- Programmers use the IPO method to specify the inputs, processing, and outputs required for an algorithm before writing the actual steps needed to solve the problem.

Key Terms

algorithm—The logical steps formulated to solve a problem.

American Standard Code for Information Interchange (ASCII)—A character-coding system that uses 8 bits to represent each character; Standard ASCII uses only 7 bits and includes 128 characters, and Extended ASCII makes use of the 8th bit to expand the number of characters to 256.

assignment statement—A programming statement that assigns values to variables; typically, the variable name is followed by an equals sign and the value to be assigned.

binary numbering system—A numbering system that uses two digits, 0 and 1.

bits—Derived from the term "binary digits," they're the 0s and 1s a computer's processor uses to store instructions.

camel casing—A convention for naming variables and other identifiers in which all letters are lowercase except the first letter of each new word, starting with the second word, as in lastName.

central processing unit (CPU)—The computer component that processes instructions and performs calculations on data; made up of the control unit and the arithmetic logic unit (ALU).

comments—Documentation added to a program that includes the program's name and purpose, who wrote it, and the date it was written or modified; also used to define variables and constants and describe the purpose of each code section to make program maintenance and modification easier.

concatenation—Joining shorter strings with the + operator to create longer strings.

data—The raw information, stored in digital form, that's processed by computers.

data sets—Collections of data designed to test how a program behaves at data boundaries.

decimal numbering system—A numbering system that uses 10 digits, 0 through 9.

declaring—The process of designating a memory location for program use by associating a variable name with a data type.

formatting—Characters or symbols used to enhance the display of text or numeric data to improve its readability; they don't affect the value of text or numeric variables.

hardware—The physical components of a computer system.

input—Data a program gathers by having users enter values while interacting with the program or by reading values from a file or database.

input-processing-output (IPO)—A method for determining the inputs, processes, and outputs an algorithm needs to solve a programming problem.

keywords—Terms in pseudocode or a programming language that are reserved for special purposes.

literals—Values that have only one meaning and can't be changed; for this reason, specifying the data type isn't necessary. *See also* named constants.

machine language—The sequence of bits that make up a computer's internal set of instructions. Programming languages must be translated into machine languages so that computers can execute program instructions.

named constants—Identifiers representing literal values that *can't* be changed while a program is running; used for easy reference and modification in program code.

output—Information that's sent from the computer to the user's screen (called "soft copy") or to a printer (called "hard copy").

programming—The process of formulating instructions to operate a digital computer.

prompt—An instruction displayed onscreen that directs a user to enter data.

pseudocode—A structured, English-like language used to represent steps in an algorithm; developed as a consistent and easily understood method of describing logic. Although it's not a programming language, it can be converted to one easily.

random access memory (RAM)—Also called "main memory," it's the temporary storage place for instructions and data while the computer is running. RAM is considered volatile because its contents are lost when the computer is powered down.

read-only memory (ROM)—An area of nonvolatile memory containing instructions for the system to perform a self-test as it powers up and load the operating system; "read-only" means the data can be accessed but not changed.

runtime—The period during which a computer is running (executing) a program.

software—A digital representation of instructions on the computer, including commands, modules, and programs.

syntax rules—The rules in pseudocode or a programming language for spacing, punctuation, indentation, and order of language elements.

Unicode—A character-coding system that uses 16 bits to represent each character and is capable of 65,536 characters; developed to address a variety of alphabets.

values—Numeric or text data stored in variables. *See also* variables.

variables—Programmer-designated names for memory locations.

Review Questions

True/False

1. Binary digits (0s and 1s), the building blocks of a digital computer, are referred to as bytes. True or False?

2. Software includes all computer hardware and communication devices. True or False?

3. The processor does the main work of the computer and contains the CPU. True or False?

4. The essential first step in formulating a successful solution is compiling program code. True or False?

5. Software testing is always done from the top down. True or False?

6. All numbering systems have a base, which is the number of digits used in the system. True or False?

7. An assignment statement is used to store a value in a variable's memory location. True or False?

8. The use of comments can override the order of precedence and make calculations easier to understand. True or False?

9. Syntax rules include specifications about spacing, indentation, punctuation, and order of items. True or False?

Multiple Choice

1. Computer programming is the process of formulating _____ to operate a digital computer.

   a. variables

   b. instructions

   c. memory

   d. hardware

2. A computer uses which of the following to operate on instructions?

   a. assembly language

   b. high-level language

   c. scripting language

   d. machine language

3. Data is classified into which general data types?

   a. text, numeric, and binary

   b. first-generation, second-generation, and third-generation

   c. integers, real numbers, and irrational numbers

   d. easy, medium, and difficult

4. The CPU contains the _____ , which handles instructions, and the _____ , which performs calculations and comparisons.

   a. RAM, ROM

   b. control unit, arithmetic logic unit

   c. input, output

   d. hardware, software

5. System memory includes main memory or _____ , which is volatile, and _____ , which is persistent.

   a. flash drive, hard drive

   b. instructions, data

   c. programming, operating systems

   d. RAM, ROM

6. Which of the following is handled by disk drives, including hard drives, USB flash drives, CDs, and DVDs?

   a. data communication

   b. long-term storage

   c. arithmetic calculation

   d. logical comparison

7. The logical steps for solving a problem are called which of the following?

   a. application

   b. high-level language

   c. algorithm

   d. data boundary

8. Text data includes characters such as _____, which are represented by binary character codes.

   a. integers and real numbers

   b. calculations and instructions

   c. logical comparisons

   d. letters, digits, and punctuation marks

9. Variables are names for which of the following?

   a. constant values

   b. arithmetic calculations

   c. memory locations

   d. programs

10. Programmers declare a variable by giving it a name and specifying its _____ .

   a. data type

   b. value

   c. endpoint

   d. opposite

11. Which of the following is a value that doesn't change and is given a name to indicate its use and make modifications easier?

    a. equation

    b. command

    c. program

    d. constant

12. Which of the following is a structured, English-like language used to express logic and develop algorithms?

    a. solution language

    b. C++

    c. pseudocode

    d. decision table

13. Programming languages have an order of _____ that determines the sequence in which arithmetic operations are performed.

    a. precedence

    b. syntax

    c. variables

    d. punctuation

14. Text characters are grouped into strings and can be joined with other strings by using which process?

    a. multiplying

    b. commenting

    c. concatenating

    d. copying

15. A programmer doesn't usually know ahead of time what data a program needs, so it must be entered, or _____, at the time the program is running.

    a. input

    b. written

    c. sorted

    d. output

Hands-On Activities

Hands-On Activity 1-1

Employees at Morning Buzz Coffee Shop have been told they'll get a bonus if they bring in enough pounds of recyclable newspapers. They want a program to calculate the amount they need to bring in each day to make this total, based on the total number of pounds to be collected and the number of days they'll be bringing in newspapers. The program should ask for these amounts and calculate how many pounds they need to bring in each day to make the total in that number of days. They plan to run the program several times until they can find a number of pounds per day that seems reasonable.

Using pseudocode, develop an algorithm to solve this problem. Include standard documentation and comments, and save your algorithm in a file named recyclingCalculator.txt in Notepad.

Hands-On Activity 1-2

Brianna Watt, a consultant doing business as Watt Gives, wants a program to create an invoice for consulting services. Normally, she works on a project for five days before sending an invoice. She writes down the number of hours worked on each day and needs a program that asks for these amounts, totals them, and multiplies the amount by her standard rate of $30 per hour. The invoice should include Brianna's business name, the client's business name, the total number of hours worked, the rate, and the total amount billed. The information will be displayed onscreen.

Using pseudocode, develop an algorithm to solve this problem. Include standard documentation and comments, and save your algorithm in a file named consultingInvoice.txt in Notepad.

Hands-On Activity 1-3

Zach Stern, a floor tiler doing business as Zach Stern's Tile, needs to know the area of any rectangular floor he's tiling. He wants a program that asks for the room's length and width and the cost per square foot of tile. The program should calculate and display the room's area in square feet and the cost of the tile needed to cover the room.

Using pseudocode, develop an algorithm to solve this problem. Include standard documentation and comments, and save your algorithm in a file named floorTileCalculator.txt in Notepad.

Hands-On Activity 1-4

Justin Kace is promoting the metric system and wants people to be able to convert miles to kilometers and kilometers to miles. You are to develop a program that asks the user for a number of miles and converts miles to kilometers (multiplying miles by 1.609), and then asks for a number of kilometers and coverts kilometers to miles (multiplying kilometers by 0.6214).

Using pseudocode, develop an algorithm to solve this problem. Include standard documentation and comments, and save your algorithm in a file named metricConverter.txt in Notepad.

It's War!

Throughout this book, you'll be building an application in JavaScript. At the end of each chapter, you add a little to the project, based on programming principles and skills you have learned in the chapter. This chapter lays out the project's scope and specifics, so you don't have any tasks to do in this first chapter.

The project is developing a simulation of the card game War. In the real card game, a deck of 52 cards is shuffled and dealt to two players, who keep their cards in a face-down stack. To play a hand, each player turns over the top card, and the player whose card value is higher takes both cards, keeping them in a "take" pile. If there's a tie, the cards are left out, and the players turn over the next card on their stacks. This process continues until one player turns over a higher card than the other player's, and the player with the higher card takes all the cards played in the tie hand. When each player's stack is depleted, the take pile becomes the stack. Play continues until one player wins all 52 cards.

The game for this project is slightly different. The user enters the value of each player's card, and it has to be a valid card value (2 through ace). Instead of keeping track of each card, the game keeps track of point values for each player. At the beginning of each game, the program asks how many points are needed to declare one player the winner, and the game continues until one of the players reaches or exceeds this score.

The names of the two players are entered first, followed by the number of points needed to win. For each hand, the program asks for the card value of the first player (called Player 1). Card values include the numbers 2 through 10 plus the letters J, Q, K, and A for jack, queen, king, and ace, worth 11, 12, 13, and 14 points. If an invalid card value is entered, the program displays an error message and prompts the user repeatedly until a valid card value is entered. When a valid card value is entered, the program asks for the card value of the second player (Player 2).

The two cards played are then compared. If one player has a higher card value than the other, the combined point value of the cards is added to this player's score. If the cards have an identical value, the point values are placed in a "hold" area, and the next two card values are entered. As long as there's a tie, the new card points are added to the hold area. When one player finally has a higher card than the other, this player gets the two new cards plus all points in the hold area. Play continues until the game score is reached.

You'll add documentation and comments and test this program thoroughly at every stage. As you learn new programming techniques, you can revise or rewrite sections of code, keeping in mind the characteristics of a good program algorithm listed earlier in this chapter:

- Logically correct (provides a satisfactory solution to the problem)

- Efficient (uses suitable programming tools without wasting time or resources)

- Easy to understand (can be explained in ordinary language)

Although the game will be simulated with a computer program, an excellent way of testing the program is for two players to play the game with a real deck of cards to help verify that you have built the program correctly. Get ready—it's War!

CHAPTER 2

The JavaScript Language

In this chapter, you learn to:

◎ Describe generations of programming languages and explain the difference between compiled and interpreted languages

◎ Summarize the history of the Internet and JavaScript

◎ Explain the relationship between JavaScript and HTML

◎ Convert pseudocode into JavaScript code

◎ Write JavaScript statements for getting user input

Speak properly, and in as few words as you can, but always plainly; for the end of speech is not ostentation, but to be understood.

—WILLIAM PENN (1644–1718)

This book isn't about JavaScript. It's about programming and learning how to solve business problems by thinking like a programmer and using a programmer's skills and tools. In this book, JavaScript is the tool of choice for helping you understand programming concepts. If you're interested in learning more details about JavaScript, plenty of excellent books are available to help you do that.

Likewise, it's not about learning Web design, although that's the most common application of JavaScript. JavaScript code is placed in an HTML file, where it's interpreted by a Web browser, such as Internet Explorer, Mozilla Firefox, or Safari. Appendix A has information on HTML, which can improve the visual appeal of the Web pages where your JavaScript programs are displayed.

JavaScript is used in this book because it allows you to focus on programming concepts without getting bogged down by software installation or the quirks of a program's interface. JavaScript has these advantages over the leading programming languages, including Java, C++, C#, or Visual Basic:

- No installation is required, and it runs in a Web browser, with no Internet connection needed.

- You don't need to learn any special editor or development environment software; you can use any text editor.

- No compiling is necessary. Only three simple HTML tags are needed to enclose JavaScript code and enable it to run.

In short, there's almost no "overhead" for JavaScript programs. If you want to display one line of output onscreen, you need only one line of JavaScript code. If you want to test a condition, you can write a single statement in JavaScript, save the file, and run it in your Web browser with no other statements needed. JavaScript enables you to write clear code, in very few words and plainly, which helps ensure that your programs will be understood. William Penn would be pleased.

Types of Programming Languages

Chapter 1 discussed different categories of computer languages. Referring to their evolution over time, these categories are often called "generations" of computer languages. **First-generation languages (1GLs)** consisted of machine languages, written in binary code and executed by the computer's processor. Even today, all languages must be translated in some way into a computer's machine language, but at first, the instructions were written in binary code.

However, computer scientists understood early how time consuming and tedious this job is. For this reason, abbreviations called mnemonics (pronounced nee-MAH-nicks) were developed for each instruction contained in the processor's instruction set, and variable names were used for memory locations. These **second-generation languages (2GLs)** were called **assembly languages**, and the programs to translate them into machine language were called assemblers. Assembly languages still had as many instructions as machine language did, but they were much easier for people to understand.

This example of assembly language code can be explained as follows:

```
GET         NUMA,1
GET         NUMB,2
ADDINTO     1,2
STORE       2,NUMC
```

- The first instruction gets, or fetches, the value from the memory location NUMA and puts it into register 1. (A register is a short-term memory location in the processor.)

- The second instruction gets the value from NUMB and puts it into register 2.

- The third instruction adds the values of registers 1 and 2 and keeps the result in register 2 (adding 1 "into" 2).

- The fourth instruction takes the value from register 2 and stores it in the memory location NUMC.

Assembly languages were a quantum leap over machine languages in terms of understandability, but programmers still had to break down each logical step into as many steps as the processor required to perform the operation. What was still lacking was a language for expressing problems more like a person would express them. For example, using the pseudocode you learned in Chapter 1, you can express the four assembly language steps shown previously in one assignment statement, like this:

```
numC = numA + numB
```

You don't need to know which registers the processor uses to hold numbers while the addition is taking place. What's important is instructing the processor to add the values numA and numB and store the result in numC. This one pseudocode statement expresses the problem more like the way a person does than the assembly language statements do.

The third generation of programming languages came to be known as "high-level" languages because statements could be expressed more closely to the way people think than the way the computer "thinks."

These languages are also called "procedural" languages because they focus on the steps to solve the problem. Many **third-generation languages (3GLs)** still exist, and programs written in these languages are still running flawlessly on computers today. Some of these languages are as follows:

- FORTRAN (FORmula TRANslator), 1955
- LISP (LISt Processor), 1958
- ALGOL (ALGOrithmic Language), 1958
- COBOL (Common Business-Oriented Language), 1960
- BASIC (Beginner's All-purpose Symbolic Instruction Code), 1964
- Pascal (named after the mathematician), 1970
- C (developed at Bell Labs for use with the UNIX operating system), 1972

The BASIC language has undergone a few transformations. It was originally known as "line-number BASIC" because every line of code had to be designated by a number, but in the 1980s, a version known as QuickBASIC or QBasic that didn't need line numbers was developed. Later, a version with a graphical user interface, called Visual Basic (VB), was developed. Visual Basic was one of the first languages to have an **integrated development environment (IDE)**, in which the editor, compiler, and executer are combined in the same application. In addition, the C language was enhanced to become C++ in the 1980s to incorporate object-oriented programming (OOP), in which the focus is less on a program's procedures and more on the objects (or things) on which these procedures operate. In 2000, C# (pronounced C-sharp), a Web-oriented version, was introduced.

 If you were going to hear a visiting professor's speech in a foreign language, you might be given two choices: to have a previously translated copy of the speech to read or to have someone translate it into your headphones as the professor is speaking. The first method is similar to compiling, in which the entire program has been translated ahead of time, and the second is similar to interpreting, with the translation taking place in real time as the program is running.

As mentioned, programs have to be translated from the language in which they're written (the **source code**) into the binary machine language the computer understands. Two methods are used for this translation: **compiling** and **interpreting**. Complete programs that are translated into complete machine-executable programs are said to be compiled, and programs translated and executed line by line from the source code are said to be interpreted.

Compiled programs have two distinct advantages: They're free of syntax errors (because they can't be compiled with them), and they run faster than interpreted programs (because they're already in machine-executable form). When interpreted programs run on the computer, they seem identical to compiled programs to users. However, if a program contains a syntax error (that is, an instruction the computer can't understand), it usually just halts or crashes. Still, interpreted languages, such as BASIC, have one thing in their favor: They can be modified and tested immediately. There's no need to wait for a program to be compiled; this capability made BASIC a popular programming language for students of high school age or younger. JavaScript is also considered an interpreted language because it's interpreted by a Web browser.

At one time, 3GLs were clearly in one category or another (compiled or interpreted). Most languages were compiled, creating a machine-executable file (often with the extension .exe) that the operating system could run directly. Line-number BASIC was the only popular interpreted language. However, compiled languages had a major problem: A different compiler was needed for each operating system (platform), and the source code often had to be modified because operating systems required special commands or different syntax rules to prepare the program for compiling. In other words, a programmer had to write different versions of the program for each platform on which the program would run.

Today, a kind of hybrid process for the leading programming languages is used that requires programmers to write only one version of the source program. The program can be compiled into an intermediate version of the language, which is then interpreted or compiled on the target (or "client") computer by a translator written specifically for that operating system. Java, for example, calls the intermediate compiled version "bytecode," which is compiled into machine code by a just-in-time compiler. This process means programmers don't have to write different versions of programs and can keep the source code from public view if it's proprietary, not open source.

There's some disagreement about what defines a fourth-generation language (4GL). The most common definition is that a 4GL is "application specific"—that is, tied to an application such as a database or a report writer. 4GLs are also associated with visual interfaces and natural languages in some definitions.

A **scripting language** is one that doesn't run as a separate (stand-alone) program. Scripts are segments of program code that another program runs. So in addition to being an interpreted language, JavaScript is considered a scripting language because it doesn't run as a stand-alone program. It's embedded in an HTML file and interpreted by a Web browser, such as Mozilla Firefox, Internet Explorer, Google Chrome, or Safari.

History of the Internet and JavaScript

No single person, company, or agency created the Internet. What's known as the Internet today is the culmination of a series of developments during the 1960s to the 1990s. These developments were like pieces of a puzzle, and nobody knew what the puzzle would look like

47

until the pieces came together. Actually, the history of computing can be traced back to the ancient abacus. However, the concept of the Internet and the technology to support it finds its roots in research papers published in the 1960s.

J.C.R. Licklider of MIT published several influential papers in the 1960s and jokingly nicknamed his research team the "Intergalactic Computer Network." In 1962, he joined the Advanced Research Project Agency (ARPA) of the U.S. Department of Defense, which created ARPANET, a network connecting the largest computer systems at research institutions and universities. In 1964, Paul Baran of RAND Corporation published the series "On Distributed Communications," which describes a decentralized network of computers and digital packet switching as a means of communication between these systems. His work was incorporated into ARPANET. Although the initial motivation for developing ARPANET was national defense, participating institutions began to explore peaceful uses for it. In the mid-1980s, the National Science Foundation established NSFNET, which included four new supercomputer networks as well as ARPANET. In the early 1990s, searching tools with the names Archie, Gopher, Veronica, and Jughead established the use of **hyperlinks**, which made it possible to click a text link and retrieve a document from another location in the vast Internet resources known as "cyberspace."

In the 1970s, minicomputers and multiuser operating systems became more common in the workplace, and in the 1980s, businesses began using available technology to establish local area networks (LANs) that connected workstations in a business. Also during that decade, the use of personal computers (PCs) grew exponentially, mainly because of the introduction of the Apple II computer in 1977 and the IBM PC in 1981. Not only did the average consumer learn how to use a computer, but applications that called for intercomputer connections, such as e-mail and multiplayer gaming, pushed the development of network communication. A popular application for the Apple Macintosh called Hypercard used links that enabled users to switch from one "card" (or page) to another.

In 1989, Tim Berners-Lee developed **Hypertext Markup Language (HTML)**, which became the language of the modern Internet, and **Hypertext Transfer Protocol (HTTP)**, which specified how communication should take place. The last piece of the puzzle to fall into place was the development of the **graphical browser**, which could display pictures and play sounds from documents in addition to displaying text and providing hyperlinks. Mosaic was released in 1993, Netscape Navigator in 1994, and Microsoft Internet Explorer in 1995.

HTML is a markup language, meaning it describes the layout of a Web page onscreen. As the Internet became hugely popular in the mid-1990s, the fascination with pretty pages yielded to a need for more interaction between computer users and Web sites. HTML simply didn't have the tools for this interactivity. Credit for the development of JavaScript, first known as Mocha and then LiveScript, goes to Brandon Eich of Mozilla Corporation. JavaScript provided what HTML couldn't: programmable dialogues between program and user, the use of variables, and assignment statements and programming structures, such as selection and repetition. JavaScript was first used in Netscape Navigator in 1995.

The collection of HTML pages stored, transmitted, and displayed on the Internet became known as the **World Wide Web** or, more commonly, the Web. A computer that stores and sends out Web pages on the Internet is called a **Web server**, and a collection of related Web pages on a server is called a **Web site**. The Web browser on the user's computer that receives Web pages is called the **client**. Although many people consider the Web and the Internet to be identical, the Web is just one application that runs on the Internet. E-mail and File Transfer Protocol (FTP) are two other applications that use the Internet as their principal medium. In general terms, you can think of applications such as the Web and e-mail as software and the Internet as hardware.

HTML Tags for JavaScript

As you've learned, JavaScript programs aren't compiled, and they don't run separately as standalone programs. Instead, they're included in HTML documents and marked off as separate sections, and the HTML documents are saved as text files with the extension .htm or .html. Although this book doesn't cover HTML in detail, understanding the relationship between JavaScript and HTML is essential to understanding JavaScript's environment, its capabilities, and its limitations.

Appendix A has more detailed information about HTML.

HTML uses a system of **tags** to identify sections of a Web page. A tag consists of a pair of angle brackets (< >), with an identifier (the tag's name) inside the brackets. For example, the <b> tag stands for "bold" and instructs the browser to format the text following it in bold type. All text after the <b> tag is bolded until the closing tag, </b>, is encountered. Take a look at this example:

```
<b>Calling all entrepreneurs!</b>
```

On the browser page, the sentence is displayed like this:

Calling all entrepreneurs!

Each tag has a matching closing tag consisting of a pair of angle brackets, a forward slash (/), and the identifier of the section being closed. Sections marked off by tags don't overlap each other; therefore, a section can be contained inside another section, but it's still a complete, distinct section. For example, the following HTML code is acceptable (with the `<i>` and `</i>` tags to format the text in italics):

```
<i>Type the following words:
<b>2011 Annual Report
</b></i>
```

However, the following isn't acceptable because the sections overlap:

```
<i>Type the following words:
<b>2011 Annual Report
</i></b>
```

Only three HTML tags are needed to set up a section for writing JavaScript:

```
<html>
<body>
<script type="text/javascript">
```

The preceding tags, placed at the beginning of an HTML document, are matched at the end by their closing tags in reverse order:

```
</script>
</body>
</html>
```

The `<html> </html>` tag pair is the root tag, marking off the section that encloses all others. It identifies the entire document as being written in HTML. The second tag pair, `<body> </body>`, marks off the main part of the HTML document. The third tag pair, `<script> </script>`, identifies the section where you place JavaScript code. Notice that the opening tag has more than just an identifier. It includes information about the kind of script being used. When an identifier needs further specifications, the tag includes a pair of data items: an attribute and a value, commonly known as an **attribute-value pair**. In the `<script type="text/javascript">` tag, for example, the attribute-value pair indicates the following:

- The attribute `type` indicates that the type of script needs to be identified.

Other HTML tags are introduced in later chapters as they're needed.

- The value `text/javascript` is actually two pieces of data, telling the Web browser that the script is in text format (rather than binary) and the script type is JavaScript.

All the JavaScript code you need for now can be placed between the opening and closing `<script>` tags.

XHTML and HTML 5

Shortly after the Web became popular in the early 1990s, competing Web browser vendors started developing their own versions of HTML, some of which weren't compatible with each other. So in 1994, Tim Berners-Lee formed the World Wide Web Consortium (W3C) to promote standards and cooperation among Internet participants. The establishment of the W3C helped standardize HTML, but there were still a number of problems. For example, there was no way to test an HTML document's syntax, such as checking that every opening tag had a matching closing tag. A Web browser encountering incorrect HTML code simply rendered what it could onscreen and ignored what it couldn't render. HTML's limitations were becoming apparent.

You can find out more about the W3C, including the history of HTML and XHTML, at *www.w3.org*.

In the late 1990s, a new markup language, **Extended HTML (XHTML)**, was created. It included features such as user-defined tags for describing data, a capability not available in HTML. For example, to describe a collection of books, you could create XHTML tags such as `<book>`, `<title>`, `<author>`, `<ISBN>`, and `<publisher>`. A principle of XHTML is that it contains the content of data and leaves the formatting specifics to external documents, such as Cascading Style Sheets (CSS).

Additionally, XHTML includes the capability of **validating** code, meaning it can be checked for correctness. XHTML seemed to be the right way to clean up the millions of existing Web pages with sloppy HTML code. After the release of HTML version 4.01, development shifted to XHTML version 1.0 and subsequent versions. It was expected that Web developers would need to convert Web pages from HTML to XHTML eventually. However, Web developers resisted, or simply ignored, the expected transition to XHTML. Work then began on a new version of HTML, and in July 2009, the W3C announced that it would discontinue development of XHTML version 2 and focus its efforts on a new version of HTML. HTML 5 will include new tags and capabilities, including syntax checking.

From Pseudocode to JavaScript

One reason for selecting JavaScript to use in this book is its low "overhead," which are extraneous commands that don't relate to the logic of the algorithm being used. Except for the HTML tags to create a JavaScript section and lines for documentation and comments, all lines in JavaScript programs relate to solving the problem at hand.

Chapter 3 explores JavaScript's many object-based capabilities. You start a new series of activities in that chapter, called the Object Lesson, which includes an exercise using object-based programming.

52

JavaScript is considered an object-based language, meaning it uses objects, most commonly objects of a Web browser. It has many object-oriented programming (OOP) features, such as creating objects from the generic `Object` class and calling methods from predefined classes (the `Math` class, for example). However, it doesn't allow actual programmer-defined classes, so it's not a true object-oriented language.

Comparing Pseudocode and JavaScript Statements

In this book, an empty set of parentheses is used when discussing any JavaScript statement that requires enclosing **arguments** (data needed by the command) in parentheses. So using the format `document.write()`, for example, is a visual reminder to include the parentheses in your JavaScript code.

In object-based programming, a statement is often made up of two parts: the name of the object initiating an action (such as `document`) and the action itself (`write`, for example). The syntax is as follows:

object.action()

In this format, the object is named first, followed by a period, the name of the action, and parentheses, sometimes containing arguments.

Take a look at an example of converting pseudocode to JavaScript. Here's a pseudocode statement from Chapter 1:

```
Display "Welcome to the Payroll Statement Program!"
```

The equivalent JavaScript statement is as follows:

```
document.write("Welcome to the Payroll Statement Program!");
```

Now examine the differences between these two statements:

- In pseudocode, the keyword `Display` is followed by the text expression.

- In JavaScript, the `document.write` is followed by the text expression in parentheses, and a semicolon is placed at the end of the statement.

Although most Web browsers can interpret JavaScript code that doesn't have a semicolon at the end of each line, you use it in this book for the following reasons:

- A semicolon is required at the end of each statement in most major programming languages.

- Multiple statements can be written on one line, but only if they're separated by semicolons.

- A semicolon marks the end of a statement clearly, leaving no doubt as to whether it continues to the next line.

This book uses a hands-on approach, so it's time for you to get your hands on the keyboard and the mouse and create your first JavaScript program to compare it with pseudocode. Before you start, here are a few things to know:

- Notepad and Windows 7 are used for all examples. Any text editor will work, as long as you make sure to save files in a text format with the file extension .html (not .txt or any other extension). Notepad saves in a text format automatically.

- After the instructions for typing your HTML and JavaScript code, this chapter shows screenshots of the program in Mozilla Firefox 5.0 for comparison purposes.

- Programs have been tested in the major Web browsers (Firefox, Internet Explorer 8, Safari 4.0.4, and Google Chrome) and should be displayed correctly in all four, but you might see slight differences in alignment, fonts, size, and other formatting features if you use a Web browser other than Firefox.

- You're encouraged to keep your HTML and JavaScript files in the same folder on the same drive, preferably a USB flash drive or a new subfolder of the Documents folder on your hard drive (called My Documents in earlier Windows versions).

You learned about the importance of comments in Chapter 1, and they're just as important in JavaScript as they are in pseudocode. In fact, they're often more important because you run JavaScript programs on a computer, and comments can help you and others develop JavaScript statements that run correctly. Comments in JavaScript start with two slashes (//), as in pseudocode.

PROGRAM 2-1 JavaScript Program welcome.html

1. Open a new Notepad document by clicking **Start**, pointing to **All Programs**, **Accessories**, and clicking **Notepad**.

2. Type the three HTML tags required to create a JavaScript section in an HTML file. Be sure to type these tags exactly as shown here, and press **Enter** after each line:

```
<html>
<body>
<script type="text/javascript">
```

(continues)

(continued)

3. To save the file, click **File**, **Save** from the menu. In the Save As dialog box, navigate to and select the drive and folder where you're keeping files for this book, and then type **welcome.html** in the File name text box. (You can leave "Text Documents (`.txt)" in the Save as type text box, even though you're changing the file extension.) Click **Save**.

4. Press **Enter** to insert a blank line, and then type the four documentation lines (substituting your name for the author's name and today's date for the "Date last modified" line), pressing **Enter** after each line.

```
// Program name: welcome.html
// Purpose: Use a display statement in a
// JavaScript program
// Author: Paul Addison
// Date last modified: 01-Sep-2011
```

5. Press **Enter** again to insert a blank line, and type the following comment and JavaScript display statement, pressing **Enter** after each line:

```
// Welcome the user
document.write("Welcome to my first JavaScript ↵
  program!");
```

6. Press **Enter** again to insert a blank line, and then type the three closing tags (in reverse order from the opening tags), pressing **Enter** after each line:

```
</script>
</body>
</html>
```

You can compare your file with the welcome.html file in the student data files for this chapter. Be sure to use Notepad to open any HTML file when you want to see the code. If you double-click the file icon, the file opens in a browser.

7. Save the file again, and leave Notepad open so that you can go back and fix any errors, if necessary.

8. Start Firefox by clicking **Start**, pointing to **All Programs**, **Mozilla Firefox**, and clicking **Mozilla Firefox**. Open your HTML file by clicking **File**, **Open File** from the Firefox menu, navigating to and clicking the **welcome.html** file you saved in Notepad, and clicking **Open**.

Figure 2-1 shows what your Notepad file should look like, and Figure 2-2 shows what the page should look like in Firefox.

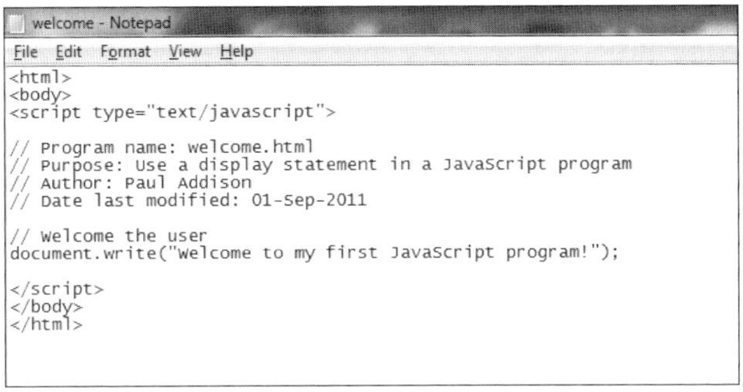

Figure 2-1   The welcome.html program in Notepad

Figure 2-2   The welcome.html program in a Web browser

If no output appears, go back to Notepad, and make sure all the lines are typed correctly. Common typing mistakes in HTML and JavaScript programs include the following:

- Tag identifiers misspelled or not closed correctly

- Single slashes instead of double slashes for comment lines

- A missing quotation mark in the <script> tag

- A missing parenthesis or quotation mark in the document.write() line

When you have made any necessary corrections in Notepad, save the file again, and then refresh the page in your Web browser. In Firefox, you click the Reload icon (shown in Figure 2-2). If you do have the correct output in your Web browser, congratulations! You have written and run a program successfully.

Now it's time to look at the other pseudocode statements you learned in Chapter 1 and discover the JavaScript equivalents, shown in Table 2-1. Notice that pseudocode and JavaScript statements are the same when assigning values to a variable, writing arithmetic expressions, and concatenating strings.

Task	Pseudocode	JavaScript
Display text	Display followed by the text expression: `Display "Welcome!"`	`document.write` followed by the text expression in parentheses and a semicolon: `document.write("Welcome!");`
Declare a variable	Declare followed by the data type and variable name: `Declare Numeric numHours`	var followed by the variable name: `var numHours;`
Assign a value to a variable	The variable name, an equals sign, and the value to be assigned: `wageRate = 15.00`	The variable name, an equals sign, and the value to be assigned: `wageRate = 15.00`

Arithmetic expressions	Operands associated by operators, clarified if necessary by parentheses:
	`profit = revenue - expenses`
	`avg = (val1 + val2) / 2.0`
		Operands associated by operators, clarified if necessary by parentheses:
		`profit = revenue - expenses`
		`avg = (val1 + val2) / 2.0`

String concatenation	Operands associated by the concatenation operator (+): `deptCode = "DEPT" + deptNum`	Operands associated by the concatenation operator (+): `deptCode = "DEPT" + deptNum`

Table 2-1   Pseudocode and JavaScript equivalents

A few notes are in order here:

- JavaScript, unlike most full programming languages, doesn't require declaring a data type. The data type is inferred by the value assigned to it or the method by which it's assigned.

- JavaScript has no separate declaration for constants, so constants are declared as variables. However, you use the same naming conventions—camel casing for variables and uppercase letters combined with underscores for constants—to clarify how they're being used.

- Using parentheses in a string concatenation makes no difference in the resulting string because of the associative property of addition. Therefore, the value resulting from (a + b) + c is equal to the result of a + (b + c), with a, b, and c as the names of string variables.

- In pseudocode, each `Display` statement is presumed to start output on a new line, but JavaScript output doesn't go to the next line until the line is full or a line break tag (explained in the next section) has been used.

JavaScript Input

The JavaScript function for receiving input is `prompt()`. JavaScript gets user input by means of a prompt box, a pop-up window containing an instruction for entering a value, a text box where the user types the value, and two buttons: OK and Cancel. You can also supply a default value that's displayed in the text box. The syntax of the assignment statement that calls the `prompt()` function follows. Assume the variable has already been declared.

```
variableName = prompt("prompt text","optional default value");
```

To store the user-entered value in a variable, an assignment statement is used that specifies the following:

- The name of the variable to receive the input is declared.

- If the user types something in the text box and clicks OK, the text is assigned to the variable.

- If a default value has been provided and the user clicks OK without typing anything, the default text is assigned to the variable.

- If no default value has been provided and the user clicks OK without typing anything, an empty string is assigned to the variable.

- If the user clicks Cancel, nothing is assigned to the variable.

The assignment statement actually calls the `prompt()` **function** (a code module that returns a value), which displays the prompt box and accepts the user-entered value.

 If you don't supply a default value, Internet Explorer inserts the word "undefined" in the text box. To override this display, you can include an empty string as the default. Firefox, Chrome, and Safari don't display anything in the text box if you haven't specified a default value.

The empty string as an optional default value is a good example of using a named constant. It's represented by two quotation marks with nothing between them and appears in the `prompt()` statement after the comma and before the closing parenthesis. That's a lot of punctuation and can look confusing, as you can see:

```
// prompt for employee's last name
var lastName = prompt("Enter the employee's last name:","");
```

By declaring an empty string as a constant named `ES` (a logical name for an empty string), you eliminate two punctuation characters and

Named constants should be used when they serve to improve readability and understanding.

58

have a visual reminder of what's represented. This `prompt()` statement is easier to read:

```
// prompt for employee's last name
// use ES constant for optional default
var ES = "";
var lastName = prompt("Enter the employee's last name:",ES);
```

The preceding code displays a prompt box in a Web browser (see Figure 2-3).

Figure 2-3 A prompt box displayed in Firefox

Another named constant can be used when you need to insert a line break in your output. In pseudocode, each `Display` statement causes output to appear on a new line, but in JavaScript, a `document.write()` statement must end with a line break tag, `<br />`, for the output to appear on the next line of the browser page. Even if you have two separate `document.write()` statements, the text is displayed as a single line if you don't include the line break tag. Here are two JavaScript statements, each displaying some output text:

```
document.write("This is line 1.");
document.write("This is line 2.");
```

When this code is entered in an HTML file and run in a browser, the output looks like this:

```
This is line 1.This is line 2.
```

If you declare the line break tag as a named constant (`BR`), you can concatenate it with the text in your `document.write()` statement, ensuring that the text is displayed on the next line of the browser page, as shown in these JavaScript statements:

The line break tag in HTML is an example of an "empty tag," meaning it encloses no text, so there's no need for both an opening and a closing tag. The slash before the ending bracket (`/>`) denotes an empty tag.

```
var BR = "<br />";
document.write("This is line 1." + BR);
document.write("This is line 2." + BR);
```

The output looks like this in the browser:

```
This is line 1.
This is line 2.
```

Note that anything entered in a text box is stored as text data. This rule sounds logical enough, but it has a serious consequence: A number entered in a text box is stored as a string of digits, not as a numeric variable, and an expression using the + operator between two variables assigned with the prompt() statement concatenates the variables as strings instead of performing arithmetic addition on them. For example, this JavaScript code might seem to prompt for and add two numbers, and then display the result. Assume the variables and the empty string constant have already been declared:

```
num1 = prompt("Enter the first number:",ES);
num2 = prompt("Enter the second number:",ES);
sum = num1 + num2;
document.write("The sum of the two numbers is: " + sum);
```

However, if the user enters 37 and 44 in the two prompt boxes, the following line is displayed:

```
The sum of the two numbers is 3744
```

What you need is a way to convert text data the user enters into a numeric format that can be used in an arithmetic statement. JavaScript provides two functions for this purpose: parseInt() for converting text to integers (whole numbers) and parseFloat() for converting text to real numbers (numbers with decimal places). Like the prompt() function, parseInt() and parseFloat() are usually used in an assignment statement. Here's the syntax of both statements:

```
variableName = parseInt(text literal or text variable);
variableName = parseFloat(text literal or text variable);
```

In this case, there's no need to create a new variable for numbers the user enters. You can simply reassign the variables to their new numeric values. The following code produces the correct results:

```
num1 = prompt("Enter the first number:",ES);
num1 = parseInt(num1);
num2 = prompt("Enter the second number:",ES);
num2 = parseInt(num2);
sum = num1 + num2;
document.write("The sum of the two numbers is: " + sum);
```

Why not prove this for yourself? Start Notepad and write your second JavaScript program.

60

PROGRAM 2-2 JavaScript Program textToNumbers.html

1. Open a Notepad document by clicking **Start**, pointing to **All Programs**, **Accessories**, and clicking **Notepad**. Save the file as **textToNumbers.html**.

2. Type the three HTML tags required to create a JavaScript section in an HTML file, and then type the four lines of program documentation, as shown. Press **Enter** at the end to add a blank line for readability. Make sure you add a blank line at the end of the code section in each step.

```
<html>
<body>
<script type="text/javascript">

// Program name: textToNumbers.html
// Purpose: Convert text input to numbers and add them
// Author: Paul Addison
// Date last modified: 01-Sep-2011
```

3. Declare variables and constants for the line break tag and the empty string, and add short comments after each declaration:

```
// Declare variables and constants
var num1, num2;      // numbers entered by user
var sum;             // sum of two numbers
var BR = "<br />";   // HTML line break tag
var ES = "";         // empty string
```

4. Display a message to welcome the user:

```
// Welcome the user
document.write("Welcome!" + BR);
document.write("This program converts text to numbers,");
document.write(" adds them, and displays the sum." + BR);
```

5. Prompt the user for two numbers and convert them to integers. Use the empty string constant for the default prompt value, as shown:

```
// Prompt for two numbers, convert to integers
num1 = prompt("Enter the first number:",ES);
num1 = parseInt(num1);
num2 = prompt("Enter the second number:",ES);
num2 = parseInt(num2);
```

(continues)

(continued)

6. Add the numbers and display the sum. Notice that you're concatenating three elements in your output statement: the text to display, the value of the sum, and the line break tag:

```
// Add the numbers, display the sum
sum = num1 + num2;
document.write("The sum of the numbers is: " + sum + BR);
```

7. Thank the user and end the file with the three closing HTML tags:

```
// Thank user and end program
document.write("Thank you!" + BR);

</script>
</body>
</html>
```

8. Save the file again, and leave Notepad open in case you need to correct any code.

9. Start Firefox by clicking **Start**, pointing to **All Programs**, **Mozilla Firefox**, and clicking **Mozilla Firefox**. Open your HTML file by clicking **File**, **Open File** from the Firefox menu, navigating to and clicking the **textToNumbers.html** file you just saved in Notepad, and clicking **Open**.

10. When prompted for the first number, enter **37** and click **OK** (or press **Enter**). For the second number, enter **44** and click **OK** (or press **Enter**).

You can compare your file with the textToNumbers.html file in the student data files. (Be sure to open it in Notepad.) Figure 2-4 shows what your program should look like in Firefox.

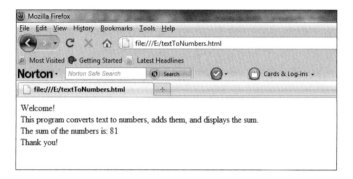

Figure 2-4   The textToNumbers.html program in a Web browser

Converting Complete Pseudocode Programs to JavaScript

Pseudocode was developed to describe logic. When it's converted into a programming language, you need to take into account any differences between pseudocode and that language. At this point, you should be able to convert any algorithm you've seen from pseudocode to JavaScript. Here are the basic guidelines for this conversion:

- JavaScript statements (excluding comments) end with a semicolon.

- In JavaScript, variables are declared with var and use camel casing, but the data type isn't specified.

- Constants are declared as variables, using uppercase letters and underscores for the constant name.

- Display/Input pairs for prompting and input in pseudocode are replaced by the JavaScript prompt() function, followed by a parseInt() or parseFloat() function if the variable is to be used as a numeric variable.

- Display statements in pseudocode become document.write() statements in JavaScript, with the text to be displayed inside the parentheses.

- Constants for string literals, such as an empty string and a line break tag, can make output easier to read.

Next, take the pseudocode you developed in Chapter 1's Programmer's Workshop and turn it into a JavaScript program.

PROGRAM 2-3 JavaScript Program customerStats.html

If you didn't save the pseudocode you developed in
Chapter 1, it's repeated here for easy reference. It's also in
the student data files for this chapter.

```
// Program name: Customer Statistics
// Purpose: Compute total and average number
// of customers over 4 hours
// Author: Paul Addison
// Date last modified: 01-Sep-2011

Start
    // Variables and constants
    Declare Numeric totCust    // total customers
    Declare Numeric avgCust    // average customers/hour
    Declare Numeric count1, count2, count3, count4
                    // count of customers each hour
    Declare Constant NUM_HOURS = 4  // number of hours

    // Program heading
    Display "Sunshine Books Customer Statistics Program"

    // Get number of customers for each hour
    Display "Enter the # of customers for the first hour: "
    Input count1
    Display "Enter the # of customers for the second ↵
     hour: "
    Input count2
    Display "Enter the # of customers for the third hour: "
    Input count3
    Display "Enter the # of customers for the fourth ↵
     hour: "
    Input count4

    // Compute total and average, and display results
    totCust = count1 + count2 + count3 + count4
    avgCust = totCust / NUM_HOURS
    Display "Total number of customers: " + totCust
    Display "Average customers per hour: " + avgCust

    // Thank the user and end the program
    Display "Thank you for using this program. Good-bye!"
Stop
```

(continues)

(continued)

1. Using the guidelines you've learned for converting pseudocode to JavaScript, create an HTML file in Notepad with the following JavaScript code for the Customer Statistics program. Save the file as **customerStats.html**.

```
<html>
<body>
<script type="text/javascript">

// Program name: customerStats.html
// Purpose: Compute total and average customers over
// 4 hours
// Author: Paul Addison
// Date last modified: 01-Sep-2011

// Variables and constants
var totCust;            // total customers
var avgCust;            // average customers per hour
var count1, count2, count3, count4;
                        // count of customers each hour
var NUM_HOURS = 4.0;    // number of hours
var BR = "<br />";      // HTML line break tag
var ES = "";            // empty string

// Program heading
document.write("Sunshine Books Statistics Program" + BR);

// Get number of customers for each hour
count1 = prompt("Enter # of customers for Hour 1:",ES);
count1 = parseInt(count1);
count2 = prompt("Enter # of customers for Hour 2:",ES);
count2 = parseInt(count2);
count3 = prompt("Enter # of customers for Hour 3:",ES);
count3 = parseInt(count3);
count4 = prompt("Enter # of customers for Hour 4:",ES);
count4 = parseInt(count4);

// Compute total and average, and display results
totCust = count1 + count2 + count3 + count4
avgCust = totCust / NUM_HOURS
document.write("Total # of customers: " + totCust + BR);
document.write("Average customers/hour: " + avgCust + BR);

// Thank the user and end the program
document.write("Thank you for using this program!" + BR);

</script>
</body>
</html>
```

(continues)

(continued)

2. Start Firefox, and open the **customerStats.html** file. Enter the numbers **5**, **6**, **7**, and **8** in the prompt boxes, pressing **Enter** after typing each number. Your output should be similar to Figure 2-5.

65

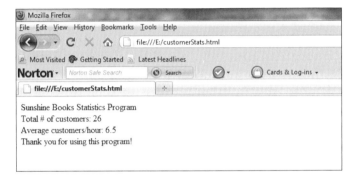

Figure 2-5 The customerStats.html file in a Web browser

Now that you've learned how to create an algorithm with pseudocode and convert the pseudocode to JavaScript, you're ready to tackle a business problem. Remember, programming is about problem solving. After you have a good algorithm, converting the logic into a programming language is straightforward.

 You don't have to wait until your entire program is developed in pseudocode to begin building it. Start building your program early, and make sure it works correctly from the start. Develop your changes carefully in pseudocode, and put them into your program one section at a time, testing all the way. Debugging (correcting errors in your program) is much easier when you introduce only one change at a time.

 Make frequent backups of your programs as you develop them. Always make a backup of a working program before making changes so that if your change doesn't work, you can easily go back to a version that does work correctly.

 Programmer's Workshop

In this chapter's workshop, you build a program in pseudocode, test it, and then make a change to a section of code, simulating a more realistic work environment in which program requirements change constantly. By doing this, you also learn to test your programs frequently and develop the habit of making backups of your program before making new changes so that you can always go back to a working program.

In this workshop, you have been asked to create an interactive program that computes and displays paycheck information for employees. The program should prompt users to enter an employee's first and last name, the number of hours worked, and the hourly wage rate. After the program computes gross pay, it deducts three types of income tax withholding—federal (at a rate of 15.0%), state (at 3.4%), and county (at 1.1%)—as well as the amount of the employee's medical insurance deduction. Finally, the program totals the deductions and computes net pay (what's left over after deductions). It should display all this information, including the employee's name, onscreen. Design the algorithm with pseudocode, and then create a JavaScript program from the pseudocode.

For this JavaScript program, you use a new constant named PA for the HTML paragraph tag (`<p />`), which is equivalent to two line breaks.

Discussion: Start with the IPO method:

- What outputs are requested? Gross pay; federal, state, and county income tax withholding; total deductions; and net pay

- What inputs are available? First and last name; hours worked and hourly wage; federal, state, and county tax rates; and medical insurance deduction

- What processing is required? Multiply hours by wage to get gross pay, multiply gross pay by federal tax rate to get federal income tax withholding, multiply gross pay by state tax rate to get state income tax withholding, multiply gross pay by county tax rate to get county income tax withholding, add all income tax withholding amounts and medical insurance deduction to get total deductions, and subtract total deductions from gross pay to get net pay

The next step is deciding what variables and constants you need and determining their data types, based on the IPO method:

- Gross pay (numeric): `grossPay`

- Federal, state, and county tax withholding (numeric): `fedTaxWith`, `stateTaxWith`, `countyTaxWith`

- Total deductions (numeric): `totDeductions`

- Net pay (numeric): `netPay`

- First and last name (text): `firstName`, `lastName`

- Hours worked and hourly wage (numeric): `hoursWorked`, `wageRate`

- Medical insurance deduction (numeric): `medInsDed`
- Federal, state, and county tax rates (numeric constants): `FED_RATE`, `STATE_RATE`, `COUNTY_RATE`

In the following steps, remember to press Enter to add a blank line after the code section in each step. You should get into this habit to improve the readability of your programs.

1. Open a new document in Notepad, and save the file as **payrollCalc.txt**. Start with the four documentation lines:

```
// Program name: payrollCalc.txt
// Purpose: Get payroll information, calculate
// deductions, display all information
// Author: Paul Addison
// Date last modified: 01-Sep-2011
```

2. Next, declare variables and constants, grouping them for better understanding and lining up the comments for readability: Remember that your program is contained between the keywords `Start` and `Stop`.

```
Start
    // Declare variables
    Declare String firstName      // employee's first name
    Declare String lastName       // employee's last name
    Declare String fullName       // employee's full name
    Declare Numeric grossPay      // gross pay
    Declare Numeric netPay        // net pay
    Declare Numeric hoursWorked   // hours worked
    Declare Numeric wageRate      // wage rate
    Declare Numeric fedTaxWith    // federal withholding
    Declare Numeric stateTaxWith  // state withholding
    Declare Numeric countyTaxWith // county withholding
    Declare Numeric medInsDed     // medical ins
deduction
    Declare Numeric totDeductions // total deductions

    // Declare constants (withholding rates)
    Declare Constant FED_RATE = .15      // federal rate
    Declare Constant STATE_RATE = .034   // state rate
    Declare Constant COUNTY_RATE = .011  // county rate
```

3. Display a program heading, get the input, do the calculations, display the output, and thank the user. Remember to add blank lines between sections to improve readability.

```
    // Program heading
    Display "Employee Payroll Calculator"
    Display
```

```
// Get employee's name, hours worked, and wage rate
Display "Enter the employee's last name: "
Input lastName
Display "Enter the employee's first name: "
Input firstName
Display "Enter the number of hours worked: "
Input hoursWorked
Display "Enter the employee's hourly wage rate: "
Input wageRate

// Calculate gross pay
grossPay = hoursWorked * wageRate

// Calculate federal, state, and county withholding
fedTaxWith = grossPay * FED_RATE
stateTaxWith = grossPay * STATE_RATE
countyTaxWith = grossPay * COUNTY_RATE

// Get medical insurance deduction
Display "Enter medical insurance deduction: "
Input medInsDed

// Calculate total deductions and net pay
totDeductions = fedTaxWith + stateTaxWith + ↵
countyTaxWith + medInsDed
netPay = grossPay - totDeductions

// Concatenate first and last name
fullName = firstName + " " + lastName

// Display all information
Display "Payroll information for: " + fullName
Display "Hours worked: " + hoursWorked
Display "Hourly wage rate: $" + wageRate
Display "Gross pay: $" + grossPay
Display
Display "Withholdings:"
Display "Federal income tax: $" + fedTaxWith
Display "State income tax: $" + stateTaxWith
Display "County income tax: $" + countyTaxWith
Display "Medical insurance: $" + medInsDed
Display "Total deductions: $" + totDeductions
Display
Display "Net pay: $" + netPay
Display

// End the program
Display "End of program. Good-bye!"
Stop
```

4. Next, convert the pseudocode to JavaScript, applying what you've learned in this chapter. When you're finished, save the file in Notepad as **payrollCalc.html**.

```
<html>
<body>
<script type="text/javascript">

// Program name: payrollCalc.html
// Purpose: Get payroll information, calculate
// deductions, display all information
// Author: Paul Addison
// Date last modified: 01-Sep-2011

// Declare variables
var firstName;       // employee's first name
var lastName;        // employee's last name
var fullName;        // employee's full name
var grossPay;        // gross pay
var netPay;          // net pay
var hoursWorked;     // hours worked
var wageRate;        // wage rate
var fedTaxWith;      // federal withholding
var stateTaxWith;    // state withholding
var countyTaxWith;   // county withholding
var medInsDed;       // medical ins deduction
var totDeductions;   // total deductions

// Declare constants (withholding rates)
var FED_RATE = 0.15;       // federal rate
var STATE_RATE = 0.034;    // state rate
var COUNTY_RATE = 0.011;   // county rate

// Declare constants (display)
var BR = "<br />";         // HTML line break
var PA = "<p />";          // HTML paragraph break
var ES = "";               // empty string

// Program heading
document.write("Employee Payroll Calculator" + PA)

// Get employee's name, hours worked, and wage rate
lastName = prompt("Enter the employee's last name:",ES);
firstName = prompt("Enter the employee's first name:",ES);
hoursWorked = prompt ↵
("Enter the number of hours worked:",ES);
hoursWorked = parseFloat(hoursWorked);
wageRate = prompt("Enter the employee's hourly wage:",ES);
wageRate = parseFloat(wageRate);
```

```
// Calculate gross pay
grossPay = hoursWorked * wageRate;

// Calculate federal, state, and county withholding
fedTaxWith = grossPay * FED_RATE;
stateTaxWith = grossPay * STATE_RATE;
countyTaxWith = grossPay * COUNTY_RATE;

// Get medical insurance deduction
medInsDed = prompt("Enter medical insurance deduction:",ES);
medInsDed = parseFloat(medInsDed);

// Calculate total deductions and net pay
totDeductions = fedTaxWith + stateTaxWith +↵
 countyTaxWith + medInsDed;
netPay = grossPay - totDeductions;

// Concatenate first and last name
fullName = firstName + " " + lastName;

// Display all information
document.write("Payroll information for: " +
fullName + BR);
document.write("Hours worked: " + hoursWorked + BR);
document.write("Hourly wage rate: $" + wageRate + BR);
document.write("Gross pay: $" + grossPay + BR);
document.write("Witholdings:" + BR);
document.write("Federal income tax: $" + fedTaxWith + BR);
document.write("State income tax: $" + stateTaxWith + BR);
document.write("County income tax: $" + countyTaxWith + BR);
document.write("Medical insurance: $" + medInsDed + BR);
document.write("Total deductions: $" + totDeductions + BR);
document.write("Net pay: $" + netPay + PA);

// End the program
document.write("End of program. Good-bye!" + BR);

</script>
</body>
</html>
```

5. Open your HTML file in a browser, and enter **Fitch** for the last name, **Meredith** for the first name, **40** for hours worked, **15.50** for the hourly wage rage, and **55** for the medical insurance deduction. Your output should look like Figure 2-6.

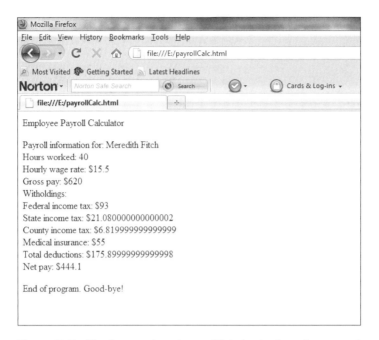

Figure 2-6 The first version of payrollCalc.html, after all prompts have been answered

What's wrong with this picture? You probably noticed that some dollar amounts have many decimal places, some have very few, and some have none at all. Multiplying tax rates by dollar amounts results in numbers with varying precision, which creates confusing-looking output. However, you can use the JavaScript method toFixed() to specify the exact number of decimal places for a number. You place this number inside the parentheses as the argument to the method. Dollar amounts are usually displayed with two decimal places, so if you attach this method to all document.write() statements for dollar amounts and include the value 2 as the argument, the dollar amounts are displayed correctly.

At this point, you should start developing the habit of backing up your working program frequently. Whenever you're about to make changes to a working program, save a backup copy first. That way, if your changes don't work or you decide you don't like them after all, you can go back to the previous version. This habit is a good way of making sure you always have a working version.

Go back to Notepad so that you can edit the payrollCalc.html file as follows:

1. Click **File**, **Save As** from the menu. Change the filename to **payrollCalc-backup.html** and click **Save**.

2. Click **File**, **Open** from the menu, click the **File type** list arrow, and then click **All Files** in the list of options. Click the **payrollCalc.html** file, and click **Open**.

3. Change the Display code section to the following, and save the file again:

```
// Display all information
document.write("Payroll information for: " ↵
  + fullName + BR);
document.write("Hours worked: " + hoursWorked + BR);
document.write("Hourly wage rate: $" + ↵
  wageRate.toFixed(2) + BR);
document.write("Gross pay: $" + grossPay.toFixed(2) + BR);
document.write("Withholdings:" + BR);
document.write("Federal income tax: $" + ↵
  fedTaxWith.toFixed(2) + BR);
document.write("State income tax: $" + ↵
  stateTaxWith.toFixed(2) + BR);
document.write("County income tax: $" + ↵
  countyTaxWith.toFixed(2) + BR);
document.write("Medical insurance: $" + ↵
  medInsDed.toFixed(2) + BR);
document.write("Total deductions: $" + ↵
  totDeductions.toFixed(2) + BR);
document.write("Net pay: $" + netPay.toFixed(2) + PA);
```

The output, using the same input you used previously, should look like Figure 2-7.

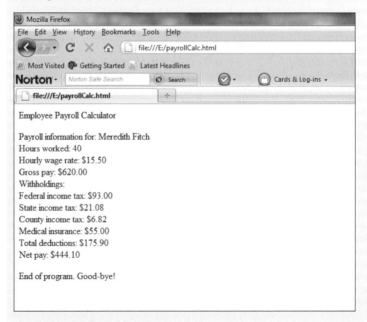

Figure 2-7 The second version of payrollCalc.html, changed to display two decimal places for dollar amounts

Chapter Summary

- Binary machine language was the first generation of programming languages.

- The second generation of programming languages, called assembly languages, used mnemonics instead of binary code for instructions and variables.

- The third generation of programming languages is known as high-level languages or procedural languages.

- A compiled program is translated as a whole into machine language, and an interpreted program is translated and executed line by line.

- A scripting language doesn't run on its own as a stand-alone program. JavaScript is both a scripting language and an interpreted language.

- The Internet started in the 1960s with the Department of Defense's ARPANET and included the development of network communication, hyperlinked documents, HTML, and graphical browsers.

- HTML is a markup language that uses tags to identify sections of a Web page or document.

- JavaScript code is included in the `<script>` section of an HTML document, which is contained in the `<body>` section.

- XHTML is a newer markup language that separates content and formatting. It was expected to replace HTML, but a new HTML version is now being developed instead of XHTML.

- Algorithms expressed correctly in pseudocode can be translated into scripting or programming languages easily.

- Most pseudocode statements have a direct correspondence to JavaScript statements.

- JavaScript gets input from a user by means of a prompt box.

- JavaScript has some differences from pseudocode, including ending statements with a semicolon, not specifying a data type, and using different keywords for input and display statements.

- Good programming habits include developing your programs one section at a time, testing your programs as you're building them, and making frequent backup copies.

Key Terms

arguments—Data that's passed to a function so that it can perform its task.

assembly languages—Machine-specific languages for computers; they use mnemonics for commands and memory locations.

attribute-value pair—Two components that define a specific instance of a tag.

client—The Web browser on a user's computer that receives Web pages from a Web server. *See also* Web server.

compiling—The process of translating a program written in a high-level language into machine language; in this process, the entire program is translated ahead of time.

Extensible HTML (XHTML)—A markup language for Web pages that allows user-defined tags to separate data content from its formatting description; includes the capability to validate code.

first-generation languages (1GLs)—The first category of programming languages, which consisted of binary instructions; also called machine languages.

function—A code module that returns a value to the module that called it.

graphical browser—An application that enables users to retrieve Web pages, including a variety of multimedia elements, such as text, pictures, video, and sound.

Hypertext Markup Language (HTML)—A markup language that describes the layout of a Web page onscreen.

Hypertext Transfer Protocol (HTTP)—The communication specification for sending Web page information on the Internet.

hyperlinks—Connections that allow retrieving a resource on the Web, usually by clicking a text or graphical reference to it.

integrated development environment (IDE)—A programming tool that includes an editor, a compiler, and an executer in the same application.

interpreting—The process of translating statements written in a high-level language, one at a time, into machine language.

scripting language—A language that doesn't run as a stand-alone program and is interpreted by other applications, such as Web browsers.

second-generation languages (2GLs)—A category of programming languages that use abbreviations for commands and variable locations.

source code—Program statements written in a high-level language; must be translated to the computer's machine language.

tags—A system used in HTML to identify a section of a document; a tag consists of a pair of angle brackets (< >), with an identifier (the tag's name) inside the brackets.

third-generation languages (3GLs)—A category of programming languages that are written with procedural statements; also called high-level languages.

validating—The process of checking HTML code for correctness.

Web server—A computer that stores Web pages on the Internet and makes them available to users on request.

Web site—A collection of related Web pages on a server.

World Wide Web—The term for all Web sites and Web pages stored and transmitted on the Internet.

Review Questions

True/False

1. A compiled program is translated into machine language one line at a time. True or False?

2. An interpreted program is translated into machine language as an entire program. True or False?

3. Version 5 of HTML is currently under development. True or False?

4. Variables in JavaScript must be declared as numeric or string types. True or False?

5. Data entered in a JavaScript prompt box is automatically considered numeric. True or False?

6. The text of each output statement in JavaScript automatically starts on a new line on the browser page. True or False?

7. JavaScript has a method for specifying the number of decimal places to display for a numeric variable. True or False?

Multiple Choice

1. Which of the following describes a scripting language? (Choose all that apply.)

    a. It's compiled.

    b. It's run inside another application.

    c. It doesn't run on its own as a stand-alone program.

    d. It has a visual interface.

2. Machine language is considered which of the following generations of programming languages?

    a. first

    b. second

    c. third

    d. fourth

3. Third-generation programming languages are also called which of the following? (Choose all that apply.)

    a. assembly

    b. procedural

    c. mnemonics

    d. high-level

4. Compiled programs have which of the following advantages? (Choose all that apply.)

    a. They're free of syntax errors.

    b. They're translated one line at a time, which makes testing easier.

    c. They run faster than interpreted programs.

    d. They can be modified and tested immediately.

5. The Defense Department's _____ computer network evolved into the Internet.

    a. Mark I

    b. ENIAC

    c. COBOL

    d. ARPANET

6. Which of these developments in the evolution of the Internet occurred last?

    a. the personal computer (PC)

    b. computer gaming

    c. a graphical browser

    d. hyperlinks

7. Which of the following is a markup language for describing a document's layout onscreen?

    a. HTTP

    b. HTML

    c. URL

    d. DNS

8. HTML uses _____ to identify the sections of a document.

    a. tags

    b. scripts

    c. protocols

    d. pseudocode

9. JavaScript's output is interpreted by a _____.

    a. Web server

    b. Web browser

    c. compiler

    d. database

10. Which of the following is a markup language that was expected to replace HTML?

    a. XML

    b. HTTP

    c. XHTML

    d. SGML

11. Which of the following does JavaScript use to declare a variable?

    a. `Declare`

    b. `document.write()`

    c. `prompt()`

    d. `var`

12. The `Display`/`Input` pair in pseudocode is replaced in JavaScript by which of the following?

    a. `prompt()`

    b. `parseInt()`

    c. `parseFloat()`

    d. `document.write()`

13. If a variable assigned in a `prompt()` statement is to be used as a number containing decimal places, you should use _____ to convert the input to a numeric type. (Choose all that apply.)

    a. `var`

    b. `parseInt()`

    c. `parseFloat()`

    d. `toFixed()`

14. Constants can be declared for _____. (Choose all that apply.)

    a. a blank space

    b. an empty string

    c. an HTML line break tag

    d. replacing JavaScript keywords

15. In a JavaScript prompt box, if no default text value has been provided and the user clicks OK without typing anything, which of the following happens?

    a. Nothing is assigned to the variable.

    b. The user is prompted again.

    c. An empty string is assigned to the variable.

    d. An error message is displayed.

Discussion Questions

1. What are some reasons for using named constants?

2. Why does a number entered in a JavaScript prompt box need to be converted to a numeric data type?

3. What is the purpose of pseudocode, if you can't run it on a computer?

Hands-On Activities

Hands-On Activity 2-1

You have been asked to design a program for calculating the percentage increase or decrease of the market value of the Connors Building from January 2010 to January 2011. The program should ask the user for the January 2010 price and the January 2011 price, compute the difference, and then calculate and display the percentage increase or decrease over the January 2010 price.

Using pseudocode, develop an algorithm to solve this problem. Include standard documentation and comments, and then convert the pseudocode to JavaScript. Save your pseudocode file in Notepad as buildingPriceInc.txt and your JavaScript program as buildingPriceInc.html.

Hands-On Activity 2-2

You have the final sales figures for the four quarters in 2010 for Bennet's Used Auto Sales, and you are to design a program that asks for the sales figures, computes the total sales for the year, and calculates and displays the average quarterly sales for the year.

Using pseudocode, develop an algorithm to solve this problem. Include standard documentation and comments, and then convert the pseudocode to JavaScript. Save your pseudocode file in Notepad as autoSalesStats.txt and your JavaScript program as autoSalesStats.html.

Hands-On Activity 2-3

You've been asked to write a program that computes percentages for specific categories in a personal budget. The program should ask the user to enter estimated monthly expenditures for the following categories: Rent Payment, Food, Utilities, and All Other. Your program should add the amounts, display the total, and compute and display the percentage for each category. Dollar amounts should be displayed with two decimal places and percentages should be displayed with one decimal place.

Using pseudocode, develop an algorithm to solve this problem. Include standard documentation and comments, and then convert the pseudocode to JavaScript. Save your pseudocode file in Notepad as budgetViewer.txt and your JavaScript program as budgetViewer.html.

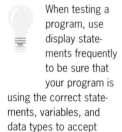

When testing a program, use display statements frequently to be sure that your program is using the correct statements, variables, and data types to accept input and perform calculations.

CASE STUDY: Algorithm Development for It's War!

Chapter 1 described the War card game you're creating throughout this book. At this point, you don't have enough programming knowledge to validate the input of card values or compare the cards played, but you can set up the documentation, welcome the user, ask for the two players' names, and ask for the number of points (the "point goal") needed to determine the winner. To make sure data is entered correctly, you can display or "echo back" what was entered. Of course, you can also thank the user for playing the game, even if it's still a test version!

In this chapter, you develop the pseudocode for part of the program's algorithm, and then convert it to JavaScript. By now, the IPO process should be familiar. You can apply it to each new section of the program as you develop it.

- What outputs are requested? None at this time

- What inputs do you have available? Players' names and point goal

- What processing is required? Getting players' names and point goal from the user

From this information, you can set up your first variables as shown:

- Names of the two players (text): player1, player2

- Point goal (numeric): pointGoal

Open a new document in Notepad, and save the file as warGame. txt. Start with the four documentation items. You might need more than one line to describe the program's purpose. You can create the description in your own words, using the following as a guideline:

```
// Program name: War Game
// Purpose:
//    Keep score for the card game War, simplified version.
//    A point goal for the game is entered.
//    The user enters card values for two players each hand.
//    The values are compared, and the player with the
//    higher value wins the combined point value.
//    In case of a tie hand, the points are held while two
//    more card values are compared, until one player wins,
//    getting the points for those cards and all held cards.
//    The first player to reach the point goal wins.
// Author: Paul Addison
// Date last modified: 01-Sep-2011
```

Next, declare the variables and constants you're using in this version. In later chapters, you add to this section as you develop the program further. At this point, you don't have to include the constants needed only for JavaScript.

```
// Declare variables
Declare String player1, player2    // names of the players
Declare Numeric pointGoal          // points needed to win
```

Now welcome the user to the game, ask for the two players' names and the point goal, and thank the user for playing:

```
// Welcome the user
Display "Welcome to the Game of War!"

// Ask for the names of the two players
Display "Enter the first player's name: "
Input player1
Display "Enter the second player's name: "
Input player2

// Ask for the point goal
Display "How many points will you play to? "
Input pointGoal

// Display the data
Display "First player: " + player1
Display "Second player: " + player2
Display "Game will be played to: " + pointGoal

// Thank the user
Display "Thank you for playing the game of War!"
```

Save your file again. Next, open a new document in Notepad, save it as warGame.html, and use what you have learned to convert the pseudocode to JavaScript. Test your program by opening it in a Web browser. If the program doesn't display the data correctly, examine your JavaScript code, find the errors, and try again until it works correctly. Debugging is an important part of being a programmer.

Objects, Events, and Graphical User Interfaces

In this chapter, you learn to:

◎ Explain how object-oriented programming differs from procedural programming

◎ Use class diagrams to name a class, its properties, and its methods

◎ Write class definitions and methods in pseudocode

◎ Explain how JavaScript uses classes differently from true object-oriented languages

◎ Define your own classes with constructor functions in JavaScript

◎ Instantiate objects from your classes in JavaScript

◎ Use methods and properties from existing JavaScript objects

◎ Distinguish between static and instance methods and properties

◎ Create a graphical user interface with HTML and JavaScript

◎ Define and create event-driven programs

In my third experiment, participants described in words the same information expressed in a single diagram by others. From the average number of words used, I calculate that—a picture is worth 84.1 words.

—ALAN BLACKWELL, UNIVERSITY OF CAMBRIDGE
(USED BY PERMISSION)

Object-oriented programming and graphical user interfaces were developed because programmers and users wanted to do more complicated things in simpler ways. Focusing on objects rather than procedures requires taking a different view of programming. This chapter discusses object-oriented programming and how it differs from traditional procedural programming. You learn about using object-oriented features in JavaScript, creating graphical user interfaces with JavaScript, and writing JavaScript code for responding to button clicks, which is known as event-driven programming. Using icons and buttons and mice (oh, my!) is a more effective means of interacting with computers because a picture is worth a thousand (or at least 84.1) words.

Object-Oriented Programming: Classes, Objects, and Methods

Until the mid-1980s, most programming languages were **procedural**, meaning each step of a program performs an action of some kind on a variable or a collection of variables. These languages, such as FORTRAN, COBOL, Basic, Pascal, and C, focused on actions to be performed. They were written by using modules and procedures to act on variables, but the modules and variables were never permanently linked to each other. However, during the 1980s, a new kind of programming language became popular: **object-oriented programming (OOP)**. Object-oriented languages focus on the objects of programming, not just the actions performed on them.

What is an object? The classic definition of a noun (a person, place, or thing) applies. An **object** is an entity, something with a distinct existence. In programming, objects have **properties**, which describe the object's characteristics, and **methods**, which define what the object can do or be made to do. Examples of programming objects include customers, employees, data folders, printers, and transactions. If you have an object representing customers, for instance, this object has properties such as first and last name, address, phone numbers, birthdate, and e-mail address to identify and describe each customer.

Object methods might include creating a customer account and updating customer information.

Object-oriented programming was developed, in part, to keep programmers from having to reinvent the wheel with each program. If a description of a bank account is well developed in one program, why not use it in another program? This idea of reusable code is an important OOP concept.

To understand object-oriented programming, you need to understand the relationship between classes and objects. A **class** is the template or description a programmer uses to create an object. It's often compared to a blueprint for a house. The blueprint isn't the house itself, but it contains the specifications needed to build a house. Each house created from the blueprint can have some variations (for example, in paint color and carpet choice), but all houses created from this blueprint are basically the same. An object created from a class is also called an **instance** of the class, and the act of creating an object is called **instantiation**.

For example, a bank account can be an object, and the class to describe it could be called Account. By convention, a class name starts with an uppercase letter and is otherwise similar to a variable name, with each new word starting with an uppercase letter, as in PartTimeEmployee or FullTimeEmployee.

An object's properties (also called attributes) are defined in the class. What properties does a bank account have? There are many, but at a minimum, they include the following:

- An account type (checking, savings, loan, and so on)
- An account number
- The name of the account owner
- A balance

Properties are represented by variables. When you instantiate an object from this Account class, a set of memory locations is reserved for the object, and the values stored in its variables describe this object. You might instantiate an object from this class definition by using these values:

- Account type: C (for checking)
- Account number: 67475648
- Name: Mike Rowave
- Balance: $200.00

You might then create a different bank account object with these values:

- Account type: S (for savings)

- Account number: 68437522

- Name: Mac Remay

- Balance: $3500.00

Each bank account object has its own memory locations for storing these variables and can be treated independently of variables stored by other objects. For example, checking account variables are separate from savings account variables.

An object's methods define what the object can do or what can be done to it. Methods are usually represented by modules or functions, which are run or "called" when needed. A method is a procedure that can be performed on an object, similar to pressing a button on a remote control. Calling an object's method is sometimes described as sending a message to the object.

What kinds of methods would a bank account have? They would likely include the following:

- Depositing money in the account

- Withdrawing money from the account

- Changing the name on the account

- Inquiring about the balance

- Displaying information about the account

Each method contains program code to perform its task. Some methods might need additional information, which is sent in the form of arguments. For example, if you deposit or withdraw money, the method needs to know the amount of the deposit or withdrawal, so the method call might include `deposit(100.00)` or `withdraw(75.50)`. For withdrawals, the method might also check the existing balance to be sure funds are available. Other methods, such as inquiring about the balance or displaying account information, might not need additional information.

Creating Objects with Constructor Methods

A special type of method is the **constructor method**, which is called when an object is instantiated. The computer creates an object in two steps: associating a class name with an object name and then calling

Think of your objects as having remote control devices. To control a TV, you press the remote control's Power On button or Volume Up button or press some numbers to choose a channel. It's similar to calling methods of the "television object" to turn the TV on, increase the volume, or select a channel.

the constructor method to prepare memory space for the object. A constructor usually has the same name as the class and is called with the keyword new in an assignment statement. The two steps to create an Account object can be written in pseudocode as follows:

```
Account myCheckingAcct
myCheckingAcct = new Account()
```

However, most programming languages allow combining these two steps. This statement declares the object to be of the Account class type and calls the constructor method in one step:

```
Account myCheckingAcct = new Account()
```

When you instantiate an object from a class, you give a name to this particular object so that your program can distinguish it from other objects you instantiate from the same class. For example, if you want to instantiate two Account objects from the Account class, you might name them myCheckingAcct and mySavingsAcct.

In some OOP languages, a default constructor method is provided, so you don't always have to write one. In this case, instance variables are created for each new object, but the programming language's default values are assigned to them. Normally, numeric variables are assigned the value 0, and text variables are assigned an empty string or the null value.

If you want to assign values different from the defaults to a new object's variables at the time it's created, the constructor method can do that. You have the choice of initializing variables with the same values for each new object (in which case, literal values can be assigned in the constructor), or they can be supplied as arguments to the constructor method, similar to calling any other method.

Sometimes looking at the method call first makes understanding the method easier. If you want to create a new Account object and specify the account type, number, last name, and first name and make an initial deposit for the opening balance, you can call the constructor method like this:

```
Account mySavingsAcct = new Account("S", 1376433, ↵
  "Dunes", "Sandi", 80.00)
```

You can determine the constructor's makeup from this method call. The Account() method needs **parameters** (variables to receive arguments) to match each argument, and it needs statements in the method body to assign arguments to the property variables. Here's the pseudocode for a constructor method for the Account class, which takes five arguments (represented by the parameters in parentheses) and assigns them to the class variables:

```
// Constructor method with five parameters
Constructor Method Account(String type, Numeric num, ↵
 String lName, String fName, Numeric bal)
    acctType = type
    acctNumber = num
    lastName = lName
    firstName = fName
    acctBal = bal
End Method
```

When programmers choose parameter names for arguments that set or modify class variables, they often use names similar to the variable names but somewhat shorter to suggest the parameter's temporary nature. For example, with variables named lastName and firstName, you might name the parameters lName and fName.

Using Class Diagrams

The two languages you're learning in this book, pseudocode and JavaScript, are text-based languages. Graphics-based languages are also available, including flowcharts (which you learn about in Chapter 4) and Unified Modeling Language (UML), a graphical language developed especially for describing classes, objects, the relationships between them, and the activities an object-based system can perform.

A **class diagram** is a UML diagram describing the makeup of a class. It has a simple format, with three sections (see Figure 3-1).

Class name
Class properties
Class methods

Figure 3-1   Structure of a class diagram

Class names should be simple and general, such as Account, Vehicle, or Animal. You can specify the properties when you create object instances from your class. Remember that the class is like a blueprint; it's not the actual object.

Choosing variable names for class properties is similar to choosing names for variables in procedural programs. Data types must be declared, and camel casing is usually used. You continue using the pseudocode data types Numeric and String, both in pseudocode for classes and in class diagrams. For example, you might choose the following data types and names for the five property variables in the Account class:

- Account type (String): acctType (such as C for checking and S for savings)

- Account number (Numeric): acctNumber

- Name (String): lastName, firstName

- Balance (Numeric): acctBal

Although many languages have a special data type for date variables, they're represented in this book with the String type for simplicity.

Methods in class diagrams include the method name and data types as well as parameter names in parentheses to match any arguments the method needs.

After determining this information, the Account class definition can be updated as shown in Figure 3-2 with the properties and a constructor method to set the values of an instantiated object.

Account
String acctType
Numeric acctNumber
String lastName
String firstName
Numeric acctBal
Account(String type, Numeric num, String lName, String fName, Numeric bal)

Figure 3-2   Structure of the Account class diagram

Writing Pseudocode for Classes and Methods

In object-oriented programming, class definition files can be stored separately from programs that use them to instantiate objects, or class definitions can be combined with a program into one file. For convenience, they're combined in this chapter. The class definition part of the file starts with the keywords Class Account and ends with the keywords End Class.

The constructor method is usually listed as the first method, after variables are declared. In pseudocode, a constructor method starts with the keywords Constructor Method and ends with the keywords End Method. As you write the following pseudocode program, add a blank line after each code section to improve readability.

 PROGRAM 3-1 Pseudocode Program AccountClass.txt

1. Open a new document in Notepad, and save the file as **AccountClass.txt**.

2. Type the following documentation lines:

```
// Program name: Account Class
// Purpose: Pseudocode for defining a class
// for Account
```

(continues)

(continued)

```
// Author: Paul Addison
// Date last modified: 01-Sep-2011
```

3. Type the name of the class, add a blank line, and then declare variables:

```
Class Account

    // Declare class variables
    String acctType       // account type
    Numeric acctNumber    // account number
    String lastName       // owner's last name
    String firstName      // owner's first name
    Numeric acctBal       // account balance
```

4. Type the pseudocode for the constructor method with its five parameters (one for each variable), and then end the class definition:

```
    // Constructor method with five parameters
    Constructor Method Account(String type, ↵
      Numeric num, String lName, String fName, ↵
      Numeric bal)
        acctType = type
        acctNumber = num
        lastName = lName
        firstName = fName
        acctBal = bal
    End Method

End Class
```

5. The next part of your pseudocode file is a module that creates an account by calling the constructor method. Begin with the keyword `Start`, and then add the following lines to display the program's name and purpose:

```
Start
    // State program purpose
    Display "Account program."
    Display "This program creates an account."
```

6. Call the constructor method, sending five arguments as values for the class variables:

```
    // Create an account object
    Account mySavingsAcct = new Account ("S", ↵
      1376433, "Dunes", "Sandi", 80.00)
```

(continues)

(continued)

7. Thank the user and end the program:

```
// Thank the user
Display "Thank you!"
Stop
```

8. Save the file again.

Defining Classes in JavaScript

If you use JavaScript in both the <head> and <body> sections of your HTML file, you need a separate <script> section for each one.

You can define your own classes and instantiate objects in JavaScript. The notion of classes in JavaScript differs from regular object-oriented languages. Instead of actual classes, JavaScript creates "prototypes" that allow you to create instances of an object containing all the properties and methods of the class definition. By using constructor functions, you can define your own classes with variables and methods in the <head> section of your HTML file and create objects from these classes in the HTML <body> section.

In JavaScript, a function is a section of code starting with the keyword function, followed by the function name and a parameter list in parentheses. As with variables, JavaScript doesn't require declaring specific data types for parameter names. The statements in the function, called the function body, are enclosed in a pair of braces: { }. The opening brace is placed at the end of the function header (the first line). All statements in the function are indented three spaces, and the closing brace lines up under the "f" in the keyword function. Here's an example of a function that returns the value of the argument times 10:

```
// This function returns the argument value times 10
function timesTen(num) {
   var result = num * 10;
   return result;
}
```

Because you can create several instances of an object from a class, JavaScript needs to know which instance is being referenced. In the constructor function, you can use the keyword this to refer to the current object.

Many programmers put the opening brace under the first letter of the function header and indent statements so that the first letter of the header and both the opening and closing braces line up. However, putting the opening brace at the end of the first line saves space and makes it easier to see the beginning and end of the function. This method is used in this book.

Now you're ready to convert your pseudocode program for the Account class to a JavaScript program.

PROGRAM 3-2 JavaScript Program AccountClass.html

Don't forget to add a blank line after each code section to improve your program's readability.

1. Function definitions are placed in the `<head>` section of an HTML file. Open a new document in Notepad and save it as **AccountClass.html**. Type the required HTML tags at the beginning, as shown:

```
<html>
<head>
<script type="text/javascript">
```

2. Add the documentation lines:

```
// Program name: AccountClass.html
// Purpose: Use a constructor function
// to create an object
// Author: Paul Addison
// Date last modified: 01-Sep-2011
```

3. You can refer to the pseudocode you developed for Program 3-1 to determine the code for the Account class constructor. Place a comment line before the function header to describe its purpose:

```
// Constructor function for the Account class
function Account(type, num, lName, fName, bal) {
```

4. The JavaScript function statements are similar to the pseudocode statements, but you use the keyword this to refer to the object, followed by a dot and the variable name. Each argument is assigned to one of the object's variables. Don't forget the semicolon at the end of each statement. After the last statement, add the closing brace at the left margin, and end the `<script>` and `<head>` sections with the closing HTML tags:

```
    this.acctType = type;
    this.acctNumber = num;
    this.lastName = lName;
    this.firstName = fName;
    this.acctBal = bal;
} // end Account function

</script>
</head>
```

(continues)

91

(continued)

5. Start the `<body>` section with the HTML tags and a constant for the line break tag:

```
<body>
<script type="text/javascript">

// Variables and constants
var BR = "<br />";    // HTML line break tag
```

6. Display a message stating the program's purpose:

```
// State program purpose
document.write("Account program." + BR);
document.write("This program creates an ↵
 account." + BR);
```

7. Next, set the values for an account (Sandi Dunes, the same example used in the pseudocode program) by calling the constructor function. You create an object with the keyword `new`. Just as you don't need to specify data types in JavaScript, you don't need to precede object names with their class names; the keyword `var` is enough. The following lines create a savings account for Sandi Dunes:

```
// Create an account object
var mySavingsAcct = new Account("S", 1376433, ↵
 "Dunes", "Sandi", 80.00);
```

8. Thank the user and add the HTML tags to end the program:

```
// Thank the user and end the program
document.write("Thank you!" + BR);

</script>
</body>
</html>
```

9. Save the file again, and then open it in a browser. Because you haven't written any functions to display the information from the class, only the program's purpose and the closing message are displayed (see Figure 3-3).

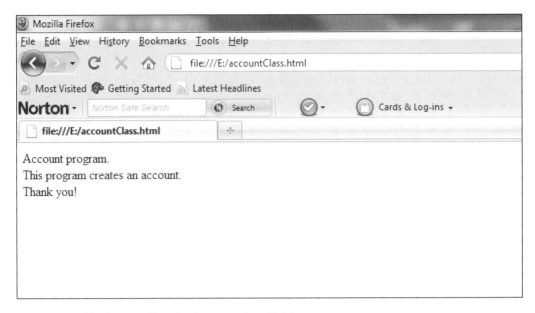

Figure 3-3   The AccountClass.html program in a Web browser

Adding Methods for the **Account** Class

Besides code reusability, another design principle of OOP is **data hiding**. When you press the Volume Up button on a TV remote, you don't need to understand all the electronics behind the operation; you just need to know what button to press. When a method is called to deposit money into an account, the programmer using the method doesn't need to know all the details (even if they're simple); he or she needs to know just enough to accomplish the task. In this case, the details are the object name, the method name, and any arguments needed, written in this format: *objectName.methodName(arguments)*. Suppose you have an Account object named myCheckingAcct and a method called deposit(), and you want to deposit $500.00 in the account. The method call looks like this:

```
myCheckingAcct.deposit(500.00)
```

The programmer using this method doesn't need to know the specific code contained in the deposit() method, only that it accomplishes the purpose of putting $500 into the account.

Variables are usually nouns because they describe things, and method names are usually verbs because they describe actions. As you choose method names, you should also determine whether the method needs to receive an argument to perform its task, and if so, create a variable name—a parameter—to receive this value. The parameter is specified by a data type and a name, just like a variable declaration. When the deposit() method is called in the previous example, the argument value of 500.00 is copied into the parameter and used in the method as a variable representing the deposit amount.

Now it's time to write pseudocode definitions for the other methods in the Account class: deposit(), withdraw(), changeName(), inquire(), and displayInfo(). The logic is fairly simple. Methods consist of two main parts:

- The method header, which includes the keyword Method, the method name, and the parameter list in parentheses

- The method body, which contains the pseudocode for the method's algorithm

For example, the purpose of the deposit() method in the Account class is to add the deposit amount to the current balance. For verification purposes, your method should display the new balance to the user. The current balance is kept in the acctBal variable. The deposit amount is the parameter amt, which receives the value of the argument sent to it when the method is called.

For better readability, the lines making up the method body are indented three spaces, and the last line is End Method. Following these guidelines, the deposit() method is written like this:

```
Method deposit(Numeric amt)
   acctBal = acctBal + amt
   Display "The new balance is: $" + acctBal
End Method
```

The withdraw() method subtracts the withdrawal amount from the balance and displays the new balance. In Chapter 5, you learn how to compare values and make decisions based on these comparisons, and then you could test whether the withdrawal amount exceeds the balance. For now, you simply allow the transaction to take place. The withdraw() method is similar to the deposit() method, but it subtracts from the balance instead of adding to it:

```
Method withdraw(Numeric amt)
   acctBal = acctBal - amt
   Display "The new balance is: $" + acctBal
End Method
```

The changeName() method requires two arguments: the account owner's last name and first name. The order in which arguments are sent *must* match the order in which the method expects to receive them as parameters (or the first and last names will be reversed). The method takes one argument and assigns this value to the object's lastName variable and takes the other argument and assigns it to the firstName variable. No computations are performed; the method simply performs two assignment statements. The Display statement confirms the transaction, as shown:

```
Method changeName(String lName, String fName)
    lastName = lName
    firstName = fName
    Display "The name has been changed to " +↵
  firstName + " " + lastName
End Method
```

If a method returns a value, the statement immediately before the
End Method statement consists of the keyword Return followed by
the variable or literal value to be returned to the calling module. The
inquire() method returns a value and no parameters are needed, so
the method body consists solely of the Return statement:

```
Method inquire()
    Return acctBal
End Method
```

Here's an example of a method that returns a literal value:

```
Method returnZeroBalance()
    Return 0.00
End Method
```

Finally, the displayInfo() method doesn't take an argument or return
a value:

```
Method displayInfo()
    Display "Account #: " + acctNumber
    Display "Account type: " + acctType
    Display "Owner name: " + lastName + ", " + firstName
    Display "Current balance: " + acctBal
End Method
```

With these new methods added, the class diagram now looks like
Figure 3-4.

Account
String acctType
Numeric acctNumber
String lastName
String firstName
Numeric acctBal
Account(String type, Numeric num, String lName, String fName, Numeric bal)
deposit(Numeric amt)
withdraw(Numeric amt)
changeName(String lName, String fName)
inquire()
displayInfo()

Figure 3-4   Expanded structure of the Account class diagram

PROGRAM 3-3 Expanded Pseudocode Program
AccountClass-2.txt

Remember to add a blank line after each code section to improve readability. To help you determine where to add new code, some lines from Program 3-1 have been repeated in these steps. These lines aren't bolded, so type only the bold code lines in the following steps.

1. Open your **AccountClass.txt** file in Notepad and save it as **AccountClass-2.txt**. After the End Method line of the constructor method definition (which is repeated in the following code) and before the End Class line, add these lines to define the five methods just discussed:

```
// Constructor method with five parameters
Constructor Method Account(String type, ↵
  Numeric num, String lName, String fName, ↵
  Numeric bal)
    acctType = type
    acctNumber = num
    lastName = lName
    firstName = fName
    acctBal = bal
End Method

// Method to deposit an amount in the account
Method deposit(Numeric amt)
    acctBal = acctBal + amt
    Display "The new balance is: $" + acctBal
End Method

// Method to withdraw an amount from the account
Method withdraw(Numeric amt)
    acctBal = acctBal - amt
    Display "The new balance is: $" + acctBal
End Method

// Method to change the first and last name
Method changeName(String lName, String fName)
    lastName = lName
    firstName = fName
    Display "The name has been changed to " + ↵
      firstName + " " + lastName
End Method

// Method to inquire about the account balance
Method Numeric inquire()
    Return acctBal
End Method
```

(continues)

(continued)

```
// Method to display all information
// about the account
Method displayInfo()
    Display "Account #: " + acctNumber
    Display "Account type: " + acctType
    Display "Owner name: " + lastName + ", ↵
      " + firstName
    Display "Current balance: " + acctBal
End Method
```

2. In the code section stating the program's purpose, insert the following bold line after the `Display` statement shown here:

```
Display "This program creates an account."
Display "It also modifies the account with ↵
  class methods."
```

3. After the statement calling the constructor method to create a new account for Sandi Dunes, add a blank line and type the code to deposit $100, withdraw $50, inquire about the balance, and display all information on the account:

```
// Create an account object
Account mySavingsAcct = new Account("S", 1376433, ↵
  "Dunes", "Sandi", 80.00);

// Deposit $100
mySavingsAcct.deposit(100.00)

// Withdraw $50
mySavingsAcct.withdraw(50.00)

// Inquire about balance
mySavingsAcct.inquire()

// Display the information to verify
mySavingsAcct.displayInfo()
```

4. Save the file again.

Next, you can convert your JavaScript program to include the new methods and modify the account information for Sandi Dunes. Remember that methods are called functions in JavaScript. Also, in JavaScript, a constructor needs to link an object to other functions so that methods are performed only on the object that calls them. Here's the JavaScript code to link an object to the `deposit()` method:

```
this.deposit = deposit;
```

Objects are linked to other methods in a similar way.

PROGRAM 3-4 Expanded JavaScript Program
AccountClass-2.html

Again, some lines from Program 3-2 have been added to help you determine where to add new code. Remember to type only the bold code lines in the following steps.

1. Open your **AccountClass.html** file in Notepad and save it as **AccountClass-2.html**. Just before the line that ends the Account constructor function, add these new lines that link the object to the new functions:

```
    this.acctBal = bal;

    // Link the current object to the class methods
    this.deposit = deposit;
    this.withdraw = withdraw;
    this.changeName = changeName;
    this.inquire = inquire;
    this.displayInfo = displayInfo;
} // end Account function
```

2. After the end of the Account constructor function and before the tags ending the `<script>` and `<head>` sections, add these lines of code to define the new functions:

```
} // end Account function

// Function to deposit in the account
function deposit(amt) {
    this.acctBal = this.acctBal + amt;
    document.write("New balance: $" +↵
      this.acctBal + BR);
}

// Function to withdraw from the account
function withdraw(amt) {
    this.acctBal = this.acctBal - amt;
    document.write("New balance: $" +↵
      this.acctBal + BR);
}

// Function to change the first and last name
function changeName(lName, fName) {
    this.lastName = lName;
    this.firstName = fName;
    document.write("The name has been changed to "↵
      + this.firstName + " " + this.lastName + BR);
}

// Function that returns the current balance
function inquire() {
```

(continues)

(continued)

```
        document.write("Balance: $" + this.acctBal + BR);
    }

    // Function that displays all account information
    function displayInfo(amt) {
        document.write("Account type: " + ↵
          this.acctType + BR);
        document.write("Account #: " + ↵
          this.acctNumber + BR);
        document.write("Last name: " + ↵
          this.lastName + BR);
        document.write("First name: " + ↵
          this.firstName + BR);
        document.write("Balance: $" + this.acctBal + BR);
    }

    </script>
    </head>
```

3. In the `<body>` section where you state the program's purpose, add the following line as shown:

```
document.write("This program creates an ↵
  account." + BR);
document.write("It also modifies the account." + BR);
```

4. After the line that calls the constructor to create the account for Sandi Dunes, add a blank line and type the following code to call the functions to deposit $100, withdraw $50, inquire about the account, and display all information on the account:

```
var mySavingsAcct = new Account("S", 1376433, ↵
  "Dunes", "Sandi", 80.00);

// Deposit $100
mySavingsAcct.deposit(100.00);

// Withdraw $50
mySavingsAcct.withdraw(50.00);

// Inquire about balance
mySavingsAcct.inquire();

// Display info for verification
mySavingsAcct.displayInfo();
```

5. Save the file again, and open it in a browser. Your output should look like Figure 3-5.

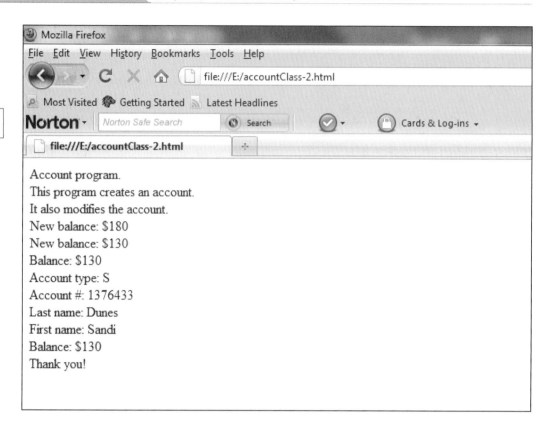

Figure 3-5   The AccountClass-2.html program in a Web browser

Many programming languages require declaring methods that return a value as the same data type as the value they're returning. They also require declaring methods that don't return a value (such as the ones you have just written) as `void` data types.

You can learn more about the Document Object Model at *www .w3schools. com/htmldom/default.asp*.

Many programming languages make their methods available to other programs but do not allow modifying the properties directly. The keywords `Public` and `Private` are used to allow and disallow access by other programs, so they're called **access modifiers**.

Using Existing JavaScript Objects

You have already used the `document` object in JavaScript, which refers to the Web page where the text in HTML documents and output from your JavaScript programs are displayed. This object is instantiated automatically when an HTML file is opened in a Web browser, and it belongs to the Document Object Model (DOM), which is a hierarchy of elements belonging to a document. For example, the `<head>` and `<body>` sections are the document's major sections. In the `<body>` section, you can have tags such as `<h1>` for heading text or `<form>` to create a form. The `write()` method is defined for the `document` object and allows you to display output on the browser page. Other objects are defined in the DOM, including `window`, `button`, and `form` objects.

A number of other objects are part of the JavaScript language, including the Array object (discussed in Chapter 10), the Date object (for retrieving and using dates), the Boolean object (for objects that can be classified as true or false), and the Math object. In this section, you learn about properties and methods available in the Math object.

Classes have been described as templates or blueprints for instantiating objects. Properties and methods belonging to each object instantiated from a class are known as **instance properties** and **instance methods**. If you create two objects from the Account class and name them cdAccount and iraAccount, for example, each has its own properties, and any methods defined in the class can be applied to the objects separately.

Another category of properties and methods, in which only one property or method exists for the entire class instead of one for each object, is called **static properties** and **static methods**. A static property has only one value for the whole class, and a static method can be called independently of a separate object. For example, you could define a static variable called numAccounts, which is incremented each time a new Account object is created from the class. A static method called getNumAccounts() could be called to retrieve the number of accounts that have been created.

An easily recognized static property of the Math object represents the constant value PI, defined geometrically as the ratio of a circle's circumference to its diameter, with the numerical value 3.14159.... Static properties are written in uppercase letters, similar to named constants (which they essentially are). You can use the value Math.PI in a calculation. If you know a circle's radius, you can compute the circumference in JavaScript by multiplying twice the radius (which equals the diameter) by the constant PI, as shown:

```
var radius;
var circumference = 2 * radius * Math.PI;
```

Using Static Properties and Methods of the Math Object

It's time to put your newfound programming skills to work and write a program that asks the user to enter a circle's radius and then computes the circle's diameter, circumference, and area. In this program, you allow the user to enter numbers with any number of decimal places but display all numbers to two decimal places by using the toFixed() method.

The toFixed() method is from the JavaScript Number object.

PROGRAM 3-5 JavaScript Program circleStats.html

Remember to add a blank line after each code section to improve your program's readability.

1. Open a new document in Notepad, and save it as **circleStats.html**.

2. Enter the HTML tags and documentation lines:

```
<html>
<body>
<script type="text/javascript">

// Program name: circleStats.html
// Purpose: Uses the PI property of the Math object
// Author: Paul Addison
// Date last modified: 01-Sep-2011
```

3. Next, declare variables for a circle's radius, area, circumference, and diameter plus literal constants for the empty string and the HTML line break and paragraph break tags:

```
// Variables and constants
var radius;          // radius of circle
var area;            // computed area of circle
var circum;          // computed circumference
                     // of a circle
var diameter;        // computed diameter of a
                     // circle
var ES = "";         // empty string for prompt
var BR = "<br />";   // HTML line break
var PA = "<p />";    // HTML paragraph break
```

4. Now welcome the user and explain the program's purpose:

```
// Welcome the user
document.write("JavaScript Math program:" + BR);
document.write("This program asks for the radius ");
document.write("of a circle, and computes the↵
  diameter, ");
document.write("circumference, and area." + PA);
```

5. Next, prompt for the circle's radius and convert the input to a number:

```
// Prompt user for a radius, convert to number
radius = prompt("Enter the radius of a circle:",ES);
radius = parseFloat(radius);
```

(continues)

(continued)

6. Do the math to calculate circle statistics:

```
// Compute and display circle statistics
diameter = 2 * radius;
circum = Math.PI * diameter;
area = Math.PI * radius * radius;
document.write("Diameter: " +↵
  diameter.toFixed(2) + BR);
document.write("Circumference: " +↵
  circum.toFixed(2) + BR);
document.write("Area: " + area.toFixed(2) + PA);
```

7. Thank the user and enter the closing HTML tags:

```
// Thank the user
document.write("Thank you for using this↵
  program!" + BR);

</script>
</body>
</html>
```

8. Save the file again, and open it in a browser.

When you run this program in Firefox, it should look like Figure 3-6 if you enter the value 40.2 in the prompt box that asks for the radius.

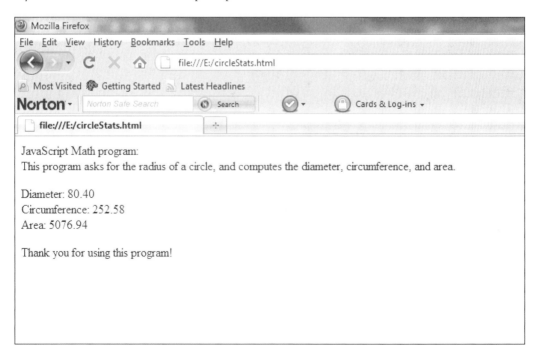

Figure 3-6   The circleStats.html program in a Web browser

Another method from the Math object is one that computes square roots: sqrt(). This method obviously requires an argument, as you use it to find and display the square root of a number, like this:

```
var someNum = 122;
var someSqRoot = Math.sqrt(someNum);
document.write("The square root is " + someSqRoot);
```

Other methods from the Math object include the following:

- abs(), which returns the absolute value of a number

- ceil(), which returns the value of the next highest whole number

- floor(), which returns the value of the next lowest whole number

- max(), which takes two arguments and returns the higher value

- min(), which takes two arguments and returns the lower value

Next, you write a JavaScript program that asks the user for a number and computes and displays the number's square root, absolute value, next highest whole number, and next lowest whole number. It then asks for a second number and computes and displays which is the larger number and which is the smaller one.

PROGRAM 3-6 JavaScript Program mathMethods.html

Remember to add a blank line after each code section to improve your program's readability.

1. Open a new document in Notepad, and save it as **mathMethods.html**.

2. Enter the HTML tags and documentation lines:

```
<html>
<body>
<script type="text/javascript">

// Program name: mathMethods.html
// Purpose: Uses several Math methods
// Author: Paul Addison
// Date last modified: 01-Sep-2011
```

3. Declare variables for the first user-entered number and its square root, absolute value, next highest whole number, and next lowest whole number; the second user-entered number; the higher and lower of the two user-entered numbers; and literal constants for the empty string and the HTML line break and paragraph tags:

(continues)

(continued)

```
// Variables and constants
var someNum1;          // 1st number entered by user
var sqRoot;            // square root of number
var absolute;          // absolute value of number
var nextHighest;       // next highest whole number
var nextLowest;        // next lowest whole number
var someNum2;          // 2nd number entered by user
var higherNum;         // higher of two numbers entered
var lowerNum;          // lower of two numbers entered
var ES = "";           // empty string for prompt
var BR = "<br />";     // HTML line break
var PA = "<p />";      // HTML paragraph break
```

4. Welcome the user and explain the program's purpose:

```
// Welcome the user
// and explain the program's purpose
document.write("Welcome to the Math methods↵
  program." + BR);
document.write("This program asks for a decimal↵
  number, ");
document.write("and calculates the square↵
  root, " + BR);
document.write("absolute value, and the next↵
  highest ");
document.write("and next lowest whole↵
  number. " + BR);
document.write("It then asks for a second↵
  number, ");
document.write("and calculates the higher↵
  and the lower ");
document.write("of the two numbers." + PA);
```

5. Prompt for the first number and convert it to a numeric decimal type:

```
// Prompt user for the first number
// Convert to numeric
someNum1 = prompt("Enter a number:",ES);
someNum1 = parseFloat(someNum1);
```

6. Call the Math methods to find the required statistics and display the results:

```
// Compute and display square root, absolute value,
//    and next highest and next lowest whole numbers
sqRoot = Math.sqrt(someNum1);
absolute = Math.abs(someNum1);
nextHighest = Math.ceil(someNum1);
```

(continues)

(continued)

```
nextLowest = Math.floor(someNum1);
document.write("Square root: " +↵
  sqRoot.toFixed(2) + BR);
document.write("Absolute value: " +↵
  absolute + BR);
document.write("Next highest whole number: " +↵
  nextHighest + BR);
document.write("Next lowest whole number: " +↵
  nextLowest + PA);
```

7. Prompt the user for the second number and convert it to a numeric decimal type:

```
// Prompt user for the second number
// Convert to numeric
someNum2 = prompt("Enter another number:",ES);
someNum2 = parseFloat(someNum2);
```

8. Call the Math functions to find the maximum and minimum of the two numbers:

```
// Compute and display the higher and lower numbers
higherNum = Math.max(someNum1, someNum2);
lowerNum = Math.min(someNum1, someNum2);
document.write("Higher of the two: " +↵
  higherNum + BR);
document.write("Lower of the two: " + lowerNum + PA);
```

9. Thank the user and enter the closing tags, and then save the file again:

```
// Thank the user and end the program
document.write("Thank you for using this↵
  program!" + BR);

</script>
</body>
</html>
```

If you open this program in a browser, and enter the numbers 56.78 and -32.1, your browser page should look like Figure 3-7.

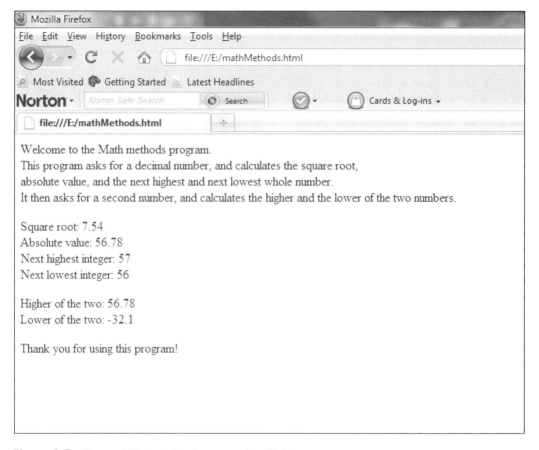

Figure 3-7 The mathMethods.html program in a Web browser

Graphical User Interfaces

From the early days of computing well into the 1970s, a programmer's interaction with a computer often consisted of using a keypunch machine to create cards containing the program code and feeding them into the computer by means of a card reader. The computer ran the program and printed the results on paper for the programmer to read. If the program was unsuccessful because it had a syntax error or a logic error, the programmer had to determine the error, correct it, repunch the faulty cards, resubmit all the cards, and wait for the next printed output.

At that time, most business users worked with computers by means of a keyboard and monitor, called a terminal. These computers were similar to today's workstations, but it had no mouse, no storage device, and no processing power. Until the development of microcomputers (PCs), computer systems were mainframe or minicomputer systems, with all computing and storage done centrally, and multiple users were connected to them by means of their terminals.

Report Program Generator (RPG) was one of the few early programming languages based on the screen position of data instead of procedural statements to determine what tasks to perform.

Users of mainframe and minicomputer systems used one of two interaction methods: a **command-line interface** or a **screen form**. With a command-line interface, users had to type commands to start programs or perform operations. Application programs using this interface asked users questions one at a time, to which the user would respond. Screen form programs were early versions of what are now called **graphical user interfaces (GUIs)**. Screen forms resembled paper forms, with specific areas where users could enter data; they used designated keys, such as the Tab key or a function key, to move from one area to another.

Douglas Engelbart is credited with inventing the mouse in 1968.

When the microcomputer was developed, users still interacted with it by using a combination of command-line interfaces and screen forms. The release of the Apple Macintosh in 1984 signaled a new era in human-computer interaction. Although much research had been done on using a mouse and other pointing devices, the Macintosh was the first commercial computer to use a GUI as the sole interaction method.

GUI components were once named according to the WIMP model (window, icon, menu, and pointing device), but this name is rarely used today.

The Macintosh introduced the concept of the desktop as a metaphor for a user's computer workspace and used a trashcan icon to indicate deleting data. Both concepts are still used in operating systems. Many educators as well as people in business and industry believed that a GUI was easier to learn and use than the command-line interface.

PC-DOS was the operating system name for IBM PCs, and MS-DOS was the name for IBM compatibles. The two operating systems were nearly identical.

Microsoft developed Disk Operating System (DOS) for IBM and IBM-compatible computers, which became known as PCs. DOS had a command-line interface. Microsoft did some research and development with a GUI system in the 1980s, but it wasn't until the release of Windows version 3.0 in 1990 that PC users began using a GUI. Windows 3.0 was a huge application that still ran under DOS. Finally, with the release of Windows 95, the GUI was in charge, and the command-line interface (now known as the "command prompt") became an application under the Accessories menu.

Creating GUI Forms

Screen forms now have more variety than they did when most users had connections to mainframe computers. They include not only text areas to type in, but also buttons, radio buttons, check boxes, and drop-down boxes. Forms are normally used in Web pages to collect information from the user and submit it to the Web server. A form is created with HTML tags, not JavaScript code, in the <body> section of the HTML file with the `<form>` tag. It has two attributes: `name` to assign a name to the form and `action` to tell the Web browser what to do if the information users enter is submitted to a Web site or an e-mail address. In this case, you're creating a form for the purpose of manipulating objects and elements, such as buttons and text boxes, so the value of the `action` attribute is an empty string. This tag creates a form with the name `OrderForm`:

```
<form name="OrderForm" action="">
```

Elements of a form—including buttons, text boxes, radio buttons, check boxes, and other graphical items used to interact with a program—are placed on a Web page with the `<input>` HTML tag. To introduce you to programming a GUI, you're going to create a form with three elements: radio buttons, text boxes, and buttons. The radio buttons are used for selecting from a group of colors, and the text boxes are used to enter first name and last name. One button is used to change the Web page's background to the selected color, and another button is used to combine the contents of the two text boxes in a third text box. The background color is set by the `bgcolor` attribute of the `<body>` HTML tag.

You don't need a `<script>` section in the body of an HTML file used to create a form. Each element is created with an `<input>` tag followed by a `type` attribute to specify the type of element. Each element is also given a name so that you can access it when you want to get or change its value, and it might have other attributes, as described in the following examples. All `<input>` tags are empty tags, so instead of a separate closing tag, the tag ends with `/>`. The following lines create a group of two radio buttons, a text box, and a button:

```
<input type="radio" name="year" value="2011" />2011<br />
<input type="radio" name="year" value="2012" />2012<br />
<input type="text" name="zip" value="Zip" size="5" /><br />
<input type="button" name="exit" value="Exit" /><br />
```

Radio buttons are a group of circular buttons, used to select one item from a group. They have the following attributes:

- The `type` value of a radio button is `"radio"`.

- The `name` attribute of all radio buttons in a group must be identical for the Web browser to ensure that only one is selected at a time. When the user selects one radio button, the others are deselected.

- The `value` attribute holds text that can be passed as an argument when action is taken as the result of clicking the radio button.

- The label for the radio button appears as text after the end of the `<input>` tag (`/>`).

You use JavaScript later to program the actions that take place when a user does something with the form, such as clicking a button.

You can see a list of color names supported by all major browsers at *www.w3schools.com/html/html_colornames.asp*.

Text boxes are used for two purposes: to give the user a place to enter text and to give the programmer a label with text that can be changed. They have these attributes:

- The `type` value of a text box is `"text"`.
- The value of the `name` attribute is different for each text box.
- If you're using the text box as a label and you don't want the user to be able to change its value, set the `readonly` attribute to `"true"`.
- A `value` attribute can be assigned to a text box and is displayed as a prompt when the form is created, similar to the second argument used when creating a prompt box.
- A `size` attribute can be specified to set the maximum number of characters that can be entered.

All values in an attribute-value pair should be placed inside quotation marks, as in `name="exitButton"`.

Buttons are the rectangular buttons used to initiate an action and have these attributes:

- The `type` value of a button is `"button"`.
- The value of the `name` attribute is different for each button.
- The `value` attribute specifies what text is displayed on the button.

Comments in HTML are noted differently than in JavaScript. The symbols `<!--` mark the beginning of a comment section, and the symbols `-->` mark the end.

You need a `<script>` section for JavaScript functions in the `<head>` section of your HTML file. In the following example, you put the documentation lines with the program description in that section.

PROGRAM 3-7: JavaScript Program formTest.html

As usual, add a blank line after each code section to improve your program's readability.

1. Start a new document in Notepad, and save the file as **formTest.html**.

2. Enter the following code to start your form:

```
<html>
<head>
<script type="text/javascript">

// Program name: formTest.html
// Purpose: Creates a form
// Author: Paul Addison
// Date last modified: 01-Sep-2011

</script>
</head>
```

(continues)

(continued)

3. For the `<body>` section, start with a comment in HTML style, and then add the `<body>` and `<form>` tags. To create a white background for your page, set the `bgcolor` attribute to `"white"`. Then assign the name `"ColorAndText"` to the form. The `action` attribute is set to an empty string because the form isn't being submitted to a Web site or an e-mail address.

    ```
    <!-- set body color to white, name the form -->
    <body bgcolor="white">
    <form name="ColorAndText" action="">
    ```

4. Next, create the three radio buttons for selecting a background color:

    ```
    <!-- three radio buttons to set the color -->
    <input type="radio" name="colors"↵
     value="Azure" /> Azure<br />
    <input type="radio" name="colors"↵
     value= "LightYellow" /> Light Yellow<br />
    <input type="radio" name="colors"↵
     value= "Cornsilk" /> Cornsilk<br />
    ```

5. Create the Change Color button:

    ```
    <!-- a button to change the color -->
    <input type="button" name="change"↵
     value="Change Color" /> <p />
    ```

6. Enter the following code to create the text boxes for first and last name:

    ```
    <!-- text boxes for first and last name -->
    <input type="text" name="firstName"↵
     value="First name" size="40"><br />
    <input type="text" name="lastName"↵
     value="Last name" size="40"><br />
    ```

7. Create the text box to display the full name and add the Display Name button:

    ```
    <!-- text box and button to display full name -->
    <input type="text" name="fullName" readonly="true"↵
     size="40"><br />
    <input type="button" name="displayName"↵
     value="Display Name" /><br />
    ```

8. Finish up with the closing tags, and save your program:

    ```
    </form>
    </body>
    </html>
    ```

When you open the file in a Web browser, it should look like Figure 3-8.

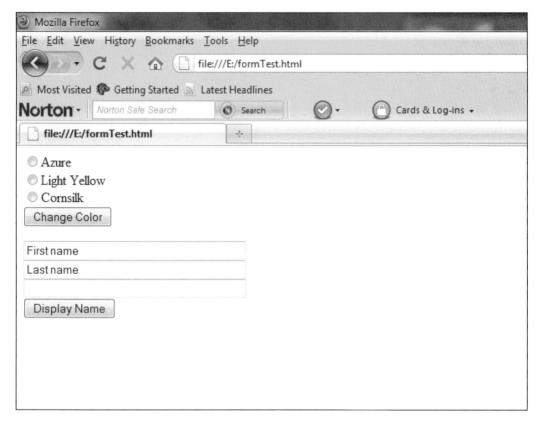

Figure 3-8   The formTest.html program in a Web browser

In this form, when you click one radio button, the others are deselected. You can type your first and last name in the first two text boxes, but you can't enter text in the third one because you set it to be a read-only text box. You can also click the Change Color or Display Name button, but for now, nothing happens when you do. So now that you have created a form, it's time to put some programming power behind it in the next section.

Event-Driven Programming

Procedural languages, including third-generation languages such as Pascal and COBOL, enabled programmers to determine the order in which questions were answered and input was received from the user. Even if users could make choices in these programs, programmers controlled when these choices were presented. Both the languages and the style of program execution were considered procedural.

Object-oriented programming languages, especially those with a GUI, encouraged the development of a different style of program execution, called **event-driven programming**. Instead of users being asked predetermined questions in a specified order, they can decide what options to choose at any time. Several choices can be displayed simultaneously on a screen form, and the user picks one, usually by clicking a button—an activity called an event. This event triggers running a section of program code called an event handler, which is usually a module, such as a JavaScript function.

Object-oriented programs continuously monitor graphical elements, such as buttons, that can trigger events. For buttons and radio buttons, JavaScript has an attribute for the <input> tag called onclick, which is matched with the name of a JavaScript function to be called when the button is clicked. The function can be called with or without arguments, depending on how it's set up. The following code creates a button and calls a function named changeYear() when the button is clicked:

```
<input type="button" name="change" value="Change Year" ↵
  onclick="changeYear()" />
```

Two events should be programmed for selecting your form's background color. Each time the user clicks a radio button, a different color is selected, and when the user clicks the Change Color button, the screen background should change to the selected color. To use event-driven programming in your form, you need to add these functions:

- A function called setColor(), which is called each time a radio button is clicked. It assigns the current radio button's value to the nextColor variable. The color value is sent as an argument to the setColor() function by using the property this.value, in which this refers to the radio button being clicked.

- A function called changeColor(), which is called each time the Change Color button is clicked and changes the page's background color. You can do this in JavaScript by setting the form's bgcolor property.

- A function called displayName(), which is used to concatenate the user's first and last names (taken from the first two text boxes), add a space between them, and display the user's full name in the read-only text box.

PROGRAM 3-8 JavaScript Program
formAndFunctionTest.html

Don't forget to add a blank line after each code section to improve your program's readability.

1. To preserve the test program for your form, open **formTest.html** in Notepad, click **File**, **Save As** from the menu, and save the file as **formAndFunctionTest.html**. The opening tags are the same, but you need to modify the program name and purpose, as indicated in bold code:

```
<html>
<head>
<script type="text/javascript">

// Program name: formAndFunctionTest.html
// Purpose: Creates a form and calls functions to
//    set and change color and display text
// Author: Paul Addison
// Date last modified: 01-Sep-2011
```

2. Next, set up your variables and constants:

```
// Variables and constants
var nextColor = "";      // new background color
var BR = "<br />";       // HTML line break
var PA = "<p />";        // HTML paragraph break
```

3. The `setColor()` function includes a parameter, `newColor`, to receive the argument from the radio button that's clicked and assigns this value to the `nextColor` variable:

```
// This function takes the color passed from the
// radio button and assigns it to nextColor.
function setColor(newColor) {
   nextColor = newColor;
}
```

4. The `changeColor()` function doesn't need an argument. It gets the color value from the `nextColor` variable and assigns it to the `bgcolor` property of the document body:

```
// This function changes the background color of the
// page to the color stored in nextColor.
function changeColor() {
   document.body.bgColor=nextColor;
}
```

(continues)

(continued)

5. The `displayName()` function doesn't need an argument, either. It gets the values of the names from the two text boxes. For readability, the names are assigned to variables before the step that concatenates and displays them:

```
// Concatenate the first and last names from the
// first two text boxes with a space in between
// and display them in the third text box.
function displayName() {
    var firstName = document.ColorAndText.↵
      firstName.value;
    var lastName = document.ColorAndText.↵
      lastName.value;
    document.ColorAndText.fullName.value =↵
      firstName + " " + lastName;
}
```

6. The closing `<script>` and `<head>` tags remain unchanged and so do the `<body>` section and the `<form>` header, as shown:

```
</script>
</head>

<!-- set body color to white, name the form -->
<body bgcolor="white">
<form name="ColorAndText" action="">
```

7. The radio buttons and the button for changing colors have to be modified to include the `onclick` attribute, paired with the corresponding function call. Insert the code indicated in bold:

```
<!-- three radio buttons to set the color -->
<input type="radio" name="colors" value="Azure"↵
  onclick="setColor(this.value)" />Azure<br />
<input type="radio" name="colors" value="LightYellow"↵
  onclick="setColor(this.value)" />Light Yellow<br />
<input type="radio" name="colors" value="Cornsilk"↵
  onclick="setColor(this.value)" />Cornsilk<br />

<!-- a button to change the color -->
<input type="button" name="changeButton"↵
  value="Change Color" onclick="changeColor()" /><p />
```

(continues)

(continued)

8. The code for the text boxes is unchanged, but the Display Name button has to be modified to call the `onclick` attribute. Insert the code indicated in bold:

```
<!-- text boxes for first and last name -->
<input type="text" name="firstName"↵
 value="First name" size="40"><br />
<input type="text" name="lastName"↵
 value="Last name" size="40"><br />

<!-- text box and button to display full name -->
<input type="text" name="fullName"↵
 readonly="true" size="40"><br />
<input type="button" name="displayButton"↵
 value="Display Name" onclick="displayName()" /><br />
```

9. The closing tags are unchanged:

```
</form>
</body>
</html>
```

10. Save your program.

11. Now comes the fun! Open the file in a Web browser, click the radio button for the background color you want, and click the **Change Color** button. Then type your first and last names in the first two text boxes, and click the **Display Name** button.

Your browser page should look like Figure 3-9 if you select the Light Yellow radio button and type "Paul" and "Addison" in the text boxes.

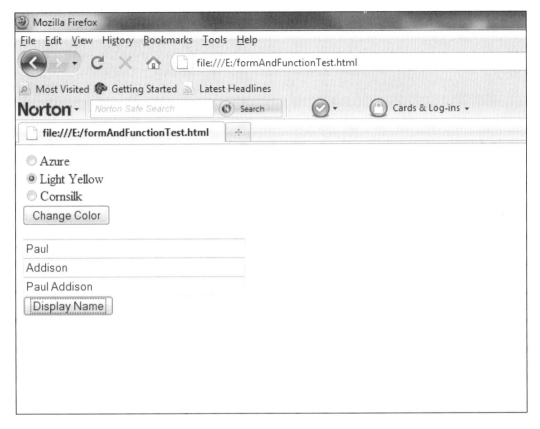

Figure 3-9   The formAndFunctionTest.html program in a Web browser

In Chapter 1, this rather dry definition of programming was given: "formulating instructions to operate a digital computer." However, programming is about a lot more. It's about power! You, as the programmer, control how users will interact with your program. Now you have choices: procedural programs, in which the order of tasks is predetermined, and event-driven programs, in which you let users take control. There are applications suitable for each choice. Use your power wisely!

Object Lesson

In this chapter, the Programmer's Workshop is replaced by the Object Lesson, a project using object-oriented programming and GUIs. Beginning with Chapter 4, both the Programmer's Workshop and Object Lesson are included in each chapter. Your instructor might ask you to follow a procedural programming track and complete the Programmer's Workshop or follow an object-oriented track and complete the Object Lesson, or maybe both.

In this project, you're designing a customer order form for Music Delivered, an online store with sheet music available for download. For simplicity, all sheet music purchases are $0.99, and only one purchase is made with each order. The form should consist of these elements:

- A heading (you learn how to create HTML headings)
- A drop-down list to select a song for sheet music purchase (a new form element)
- A set of radio buttons to select a credit card type
- Text boxes for the customer to enter first name, last name, and e-mail address
- A Display Order button
- A multiline text box for displaying the full order

HTML has heading tags from <h1> (the largest) to <h6> (the smallest). Headings are automatically bold, and the heading text is placed between the open and closing tags. For example, the following line in an HTML document displays the words "Breakfast Menu" in bold and in the largest heading size:

```
<h1>Breakfast Menu</h1>
```

A drop-down list containing options to choose is created in HTML with a <select> tag. Each option in the list has a value attribute (for the programmer) and a label (for the user), similar to a radio button. However, the text box is given a name for the whole group with the name attribute, so the options in the list don't need a name or an event trigger, such as onclick. The text box's value is the same as the option that's currently selected. Here's an example of a drop-down list that allows a user to choose a movie time:

```
<select name="movieStartTime">
   <option value="1:30pm">1:30 pm</option>
   <option value="4:00pm">4:00 pm</option>
   <option value="6:30pm">6:30 pm</option>
   <option value="9:00pm">9:00 pm</option>
</select>
```

A multiline text box, called a text area, is created in HTML with the <textarea> tag. It has a name (for the programmer to refer to), and the height and width are specified by the rows attribute (number of rows, starting with 0) and the cols attribute (the width of a line in characters). If the text area is for the programmer to place text, as in this example, you can specify a readonly attribute set to "true." The following tag creates an empty text area named "Messages" that's

6 rows high (although you use 5 as the setting because the browser starts counting at 0) and 50 characters wide:

```
<textarea name="Messages" value="" rows="5" cols="50"> ↵
  </textarea>
```

Inside a text box, a line break can be specified as "\n", called the new-line character, instead of using an HTML line break tag.

There's no processing to be done in the sense of calculating values. The output information is only what the user has selected. In this case, an IPO analysis can be bypassed, as long as you list the variables and constants you need:

- A variable for the selected song title: songTitle
- A variable for the selected credit card type: creditCardType
- A constant for the sheet music price: SONG_PRICE
- The usual literal string and HTML constants
- A new constant for a text line break (the newline character): NL

Follow these steps to write the code for your order form, remembering to add a blank line after each code section to improve readability:

1. Open a new document in Notepad and save the file as **musicOrderForm.html**.

2. Type the following HTML tags and documentation lines:

```
<html>
<head>
<script type="text/javascript">

// Program name: musicOrderForm.html
// Purpose: Creates a form and calls functions to
//   order sheet music for download.
// Author: Paul Addison
// Date last modified: 01-Sep-2011
```

3. Now declare your variables and constants and include comments, of course:

```
// Variables and constants
var songTitle;          // song selection
var creditCardType;     // selected credit card type
var SONG_PRICE = .99;   // fixed price of song
var BR = "<br />";      // HTML line break
var PA = "<p />";       // HTML paragraph break
var NL = "\n";          // JavaScript newline character
```

4. Next, add the function to set the credit card type with a radio button; this function is similar to setting the background color in the formAndFunctionTest.html program. The setType() function is called with the onclick attribute of each radio button.

```
// Take the credit card type passed from the
// radio button and assign it to
// the variable creditCardType.
function setType(ccType) {
    creditCardType = ccType;
}
```

5. Type the comments explaining what information the function should display. To make the output statements easier to understand, assign the text box values to variables before creating the output text:

```
// This function displays order information, including
// the selected song from the drop-down list,
// the name and e-mail address of the customer,
// the credit card type selected from the radio button
// group, the order total (a constant charge),
// along with a heading and a thank-you line.
function displayOrder() {
    var firstName = document.OrderForm.firstName.value;
    var lastName = document.OrderForm.lastName.value;
    var email = document.OrderForm.email.value;
    var songTitle = document.OrderForm.songChoice.value;
```

6. The command to display the output simply concatenates literal and string values, including newline characters, to create an easy-to-read summary of the order. Don't forget to add the closing tags for the <script> and <head> sections. The concatenated string is assigned to the value attribute of the text area named fullOrder, which is part of the OrderForm form (part of the document object).

```
    document.OrderForm.fullOrder.value =
        "HERE IS YOUR ORDER:" + NL + NL
        + "TITLE: " + songTitle + NL
        + "YOUR NAME: " + firstName + " " + lastName + NL
        + "YOUR EMAIL ADDRESS: " + email + NL
        + "CREDIT CARD: " + creditCardType + NL
        + "AMOUNT CHARGED TO CARD: $"
        + SONG_PRICE.toFixed(2) + NL + NL
        + "Thank you for placing your order!";
}
</script>
</head>
```

7. Now it's time to create your form. Start with the <body> tag and specify the background color, the heading size, and the form name, as shown:

```
<!-- Set background color, display heading, ↵
 name form -->
<body bgcolor="Azure">
<h2>Music Delivered Order Form</h2>
<form name="OrderForm" action="">
```

8. Above the drop-down list, add a label in bold text. The tag for bold text is <strong>, with the text between the opening and closing tags. For the drop-down list, the current options are some popular songs from the 1960s. (Of course, you can fill the list with any selections you like.) The text paired with the value attribute is what appears by default in the text area when the order is displayed, and the label in the opening <option> tag is what the user sees in the list. The default text and the label don't have to match exactly.

```
<!-- Create drop-down list for song selection -->
<strong>Select your song:</strong><br />
<select name="songChoice">
   <option value="She Loves You (Beatles)"> ↵
The Beatles: She Loves You</option>
   <option value="Ruby Tuesday (Rolling Stones)"> ↵
The Rolling Stones: Ruby Tuesday</option>
   <option value="My Generation (The Who)"> ↵
The Who: My Generation</option>
   <option value="Light My Fire (The Doors)"> ↵
The Doors: Light My Fire</option>
   <option value="Somebody to Love (Jefferson ↵
      Airplane)"> Jefferson Airplane: Somebody ↵
      to Love</option>
</select><p />
```

9. Add a bold label over the radio button group for selecting a credit card type. When each button is clicked, the setType() function is called, with the button's value sent as an argument:

```
<!-- Create radio buttons for credit card type -->
<strong>Select your credit card type:</strong><br />
<input type="radio" name="creditCard" value="MasterCard" ↵
 onclick="setType(this.value)" />MasterCard<br />
<input type="radio" name="creditCard" value="Visa" ↵
 onclick="setType(this.value)" />Visa<br />
<input type="radio" name="creditCard" value="Discover" ↵
 onclick="setType(this.value)" />Discover<br />
<input type="radio" name="creditCard" value="American ↵
 Express" onclick="setType(this.value)" />American ↵
 Express<p />
```

10. Now add a bold label and text boxes for the user's first name, last name, and e-mail address:

```
<!-- Create text boxes for user information -->
<strong>Enter your name and e-mail address:</strong><br />
<input type="text" name="firstName"↵
 value="First name" size="40"><br />
<input type="text" name="lastName"↵
 value="Last name" size="40"><br />
<input type="text" name="email"↵
 value="E-mail address" size="40"><p />
```

11. Next, add the Display Order button, which calls the displayOrder() function, and the text area where the order details are displayed:

```
<!-- Create display button and multiline text↵
 box for info -->
<input type="button" name="displayButton"↵
 value="Display Order" onclick="displayOrder()" /><p />
<textarea name="fullOrder" readonly="true"↵
 value="" rows="8" cols="50"></textarea><br />
```

12. Finally, enter these closing tags, and then save the file again:

```
</form>
</body>
</html>
```

13. Now open the **musicOrderForm.html** file in a Web browser. Figure 3-10 shows the results if you select the Jefferson Airplane song "Somebody to Love," use a Discover card, and enter "Jonah Vark" as your name and "jvark@hotstakes.com" as your e-mail address.

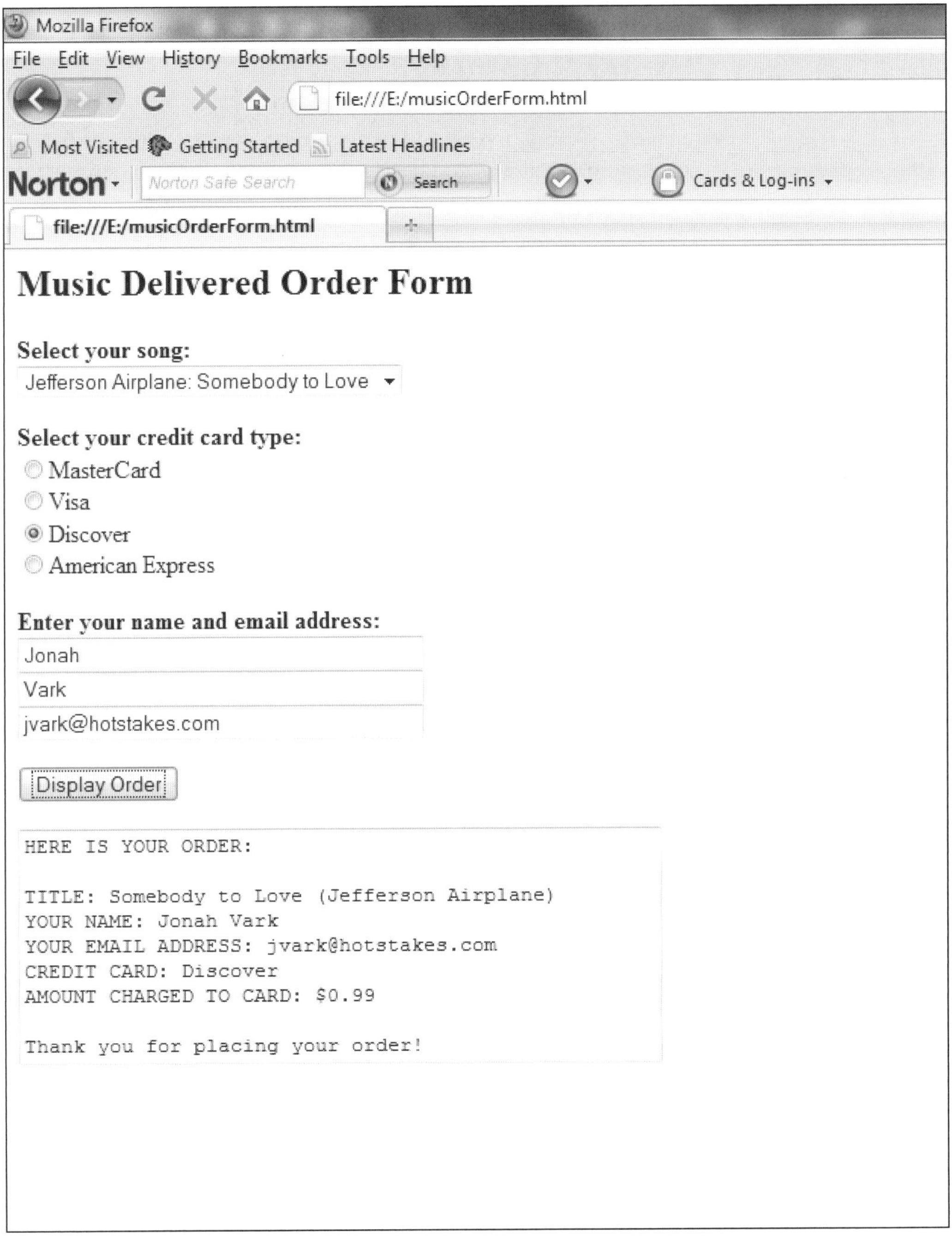
Mozilla Firefox
File Edit View History Bookmarks Tools Help
file:///E:/musicOrderForm.html
Most Visited Getting Started Latest Headlines
Norton
Norton Safe Search
Search
Cards & Log-ins
file:///E:/musicOrderForm.html
Music Delivered Order Form
Select your song:
Jefferson Airplane: Somebody to Love
Select your credit card type:
MasterCard
Visa
Discover
American Express
Enter your name and email address:
Jonah
Vark
jvark@hotstakes.com
Display Order
HERE IS YOUR ORDER:
TITLE: Somebody to Love (Jefferson Airplane)
YOUR NAME: Jonah Vark
YOUR EMAIL ADDRESS: jvark@hotstakes.com
CREDIT CARD: Discover
AMOUNT CHARGED TO CARD: $0.99
Thank you for placing your order!

Figure 3-10 The musicOrderForm.html program in a Web browser

Chapter Summary

- Object-oriented programming focuses on objects, which are created from classes, and have properties and methods. Properties describe characteristics of an object, and methods specify what an object does.

- A class is a blueprint or template containing the definition of objects to be created from it.

- Class diagrams, part of the Unified Modeling Language (UML), show class definitions in graphical form. A class diagram consists of three parts: class name, class properties, and class methods.

- Objects created from classes have their own set of properties, called instance properties, and methods that operate only on these objects are called instance methods.

- JavaScript has a number of existing objects with static properties and methods that you can use without having to instantiate a separate object.

- JavaScript uses constructor functions to define classes and allows objects to be instantiated from them.

- Graphical user interfaces (GUIs) have windows, icons, and menus that enable users to interact with a program by using a pointing device, such as a mouse.

- Graphical elements in HTML include the browser page, forms, and form elements, such as buttons, radio buttons, check boxes, and text boxes, all of which can be manipulated with JavaScript.

- Event-driven programming, which gives users choices in their interactions with a program, is highly compatible with object-oriented programming languages using GUIs.

Key Terms

access modifiers—Words used to specify how other programs can access the properties and methods in a class; usually specified with the keyword Private or Public.

class—A definition of an entity, used to create objects in object-oriented programming languages.

class diagram—A graphical representation of the name, properties, and methods of a class.

command-line interface—An interaction method in which the user is given a prompt and responds by entering a command from the keyboard.

constructor method—A method used to create instances of objects; optionally allows assigning specific values to properties.

data hiding—A concept of OOP languages that means programmers don't need to know the details of properties or methods, only the instructions for accessing or modifying them.

event-driven programming—A style of program execution in which the user is given choices in determining the order of steps.

graphical user interfaces (GUIs)—Interfaces that incorporate graphical objects, such as forms, buttons, and text boxes, as tools for users to interact with a program.

instance—A single occurrence of an object created from a class definition. The process of creating an object is called "instantiation."

instance methods—Methods associated with specific instances of objects.

instance properties—Properties associated with specific instances of objects.

method—An action that an object can perform or have performed on it, represented by a program function. Calling an object's function is referred to as sending a message to the object.

object—An entity or thing used by programs; contains properties and methods.

object-oriented programming (OOP)—A category of programming that focuses on objects along with their properties and methods.

parameters—Variables in a function that receive the value of arguments sent to the function.

procedural programming—A category of programming that focuses on actions performed on variables.

property—An attribute describing an object, represented by a class-defined variable.

screen form—An interaction method in which the user fills in data at predefined locations onscreen.

static methods—Methods that occur only once for a class, instead of for each instance of a class.

static properties—Properties that occur only once for a class, instead of for each instance of a class.

Review Questions

True/False

1. Classes are created from objects. True or False?

2. Properties are represented by functions, and methods are represented by variables. True or False?

3. Class diagrams are one of the graphical tools in the Unified Modeling Language. True or False?

4. The access modifiers Public and Private are used to specify whether programmers can use properties and methods of objects. True or False?

5. The Arithmetic class has several methods for programmers to use, including methods to calculate square roots, absolute values, and minimum and maximum values of a pair of numbers. True or False?

6. A programmer must write a specific constructor method for each class, or objects can't be created. True or False?

7. The GUI was first popularized by the IBM PC. True or False?

8. A command-line interface displays a prompt that requires the user to enter a response from the keyboard. True or False?

9. In a group of radio buttons, only one can be selected at any time. True or False?

10. In event-driven programs, the programmer determines the order of steps. True or False?

Multiple Choice

1. Classes are defined to create objects and include _____ and _____.

   a. properties, methods

   b. windows, forms

   c. events, actions

   d. radio buttons, text boxes

2. A class is often compared with which of the following?

    a. compiler

    b. function

    c. blueprint

    d. meeting agenda

3. Methods are used to do which of the following? (Choose all that apply.)

    a. assign values to variables

    b. retrieve values from variables

    c. rename variables

    d. test the validity of values to be assigned to variables

4. The UML contains graphical tools for doing which of the following?

    a. automating program code generation

    b. eliminating procedural programming rules

    c. describing classes, objects, and their relationships and activities

    d. depicting a computer's hardware components

5. If a constructor method isn't specifically written for a class, most languages do which of the following?

    a. don't allow objects to be created

    b. provide a default constructor

    c. don't allow a program to be compiled

    d. prompt the user for values for the object variables

6. GUIs usually include which of the following?

    a. command prompts

    b. text responses to questions

    c. voice recognition

    d. a pointing device

7. Objects created in HTML can be accessed and manipulated in JavaScript by referencing which of the following?

    a. Unified Modeling Language (UML)

    b. Document Object Model (DOM)

    c. Hypertext Transfer Protocol (HTTP)

    d. Domain Name System (DNS)

8. Programs that give users choices in determining the order of steps are called _____.

    a. object-oriented programs

    b. procedural programs

    c. GUI programs

    d. event-driven programs

9. An event can cause a JavaScript function to be called by using which attribute?

    a. `onclick`

    b. `name`

    c. `value`

    d. `type`

Discussion Questions

1. What are some advantages in using object-oriented programming languages?

2. Describe the relationship between classes and objects.

3. What are the main differences between a UML class diagram and a pseudocode description of a class?

4. What are static properties and static methods? What are some examples from this chapter?

5. What are instance properties and methods?

6. What is the purpose of an explicitly written constructor method? What can it do that a default constructor can't?

7. How does a command-line interface differ from a GUI?

8. How do radio buttons on a form differ from buttons?

9. Can arguments be sent to methods in event-driven programs?

Hands-On Activities

Hands-On Activity 3-1

The manager of an electronics appliance store has asked you to develop a class to help in tracking inventory for TVs. Variables include manufacturer, screen diagonal size (in inches), and retail price (in dollars and cents). Methods include a setPrice() method with a parameter for the new price and a displayInfo() method that displays the three variables' values in sentences. There's also a constructor method with three parameters for the three variables.

Using pseudocode, write a class definition. Save your pseudocode file in Notepad as TelevisionClass.txt.

Hands-On Activity 3-2

The store manager from Hands-On Activity 3-1 likes your class definition and wants you to test your logic by writing a program that creates a Television object with Sony as the manufacturer, 52 as the screen size, and $1299.00 as the price. Your program should call the displayInfo() method to display information about the television, change the price to $999.00 by using the setPrice() method, and then call the displayInfo() method again.

Using pseudocode, write a module that creates an object from the Television class definition. Open the pseudocode file TelevisionClass.txt you created in Hands-On Activity 3-1, and save it in Notepad as TelevisionClass-2.txt.

Hands-On Activity 3-3

In case the manager likes your model enough to ask you to try it in a working environment, you decide to test a scaled-down version, using the pseudocode from Hands-On Activity 3-2 to write a JavaScript program that includes a constructor method in the <head> section for the Television class (no other methods). In the <body> section, the program should create a new Television object called myTV by calling the constructor with the values you used in Hands-On Activity 3-2, and then display the values of the variables and thank the user.

Using JavaScript, write a program that creates a `Television` object. Save your JavaScript file in Notepad as TelevisionClass.html.

Hands-On Activity 3-4

The owner of a flower shop wants you to develop a form for use on the shop's Web site. The form should have a single text box for the user to enter his or her name. Under the text box should be a group of radio buttons for three different kinds of flowers: Roses, Carnations, and Daisies. Below the radio buttons should be a button labeled Request Info, with a read-only text box under it for thanking the user for requesting information. This program doesn't need any functions or `onclick` attributes for the graphical elements.

Using JavaScript, create this form. Save your JavaScript file in Notepad as flowerForm.html.

Hands-On Activity 3-5

The flower shop owner in Hands-On Activity 3-4 wants to see whether you can make the form interactive and asks you to have the form display a message in the bottom text box that includes the user's name, a comma, and the words "thank you for your inquiry about" followed by the flower name the user selected. Write a function named `displayMessage()` that accesses the user's name from the first text box and displays the message in the read-only text box. You also need to make the Request Info button call the `displayMessage()` function when it's clicked.

Using JavaScript, make this form active by including event triggers and functions. Open the flowerForm.html file and save it as flowerFormAction.html.

CASE STUDY: It's War!

The case study is based on procedural programming and resumes in Chapter 4.

The Sequence Structure

In this chapter, you learn to:

- ◎ Define structured programming and explain its advantages
- ◎ Describe the sequence structure
- ◎ Define a flowchart and describe its relationship to pseudocode
- ◎ Convert flowcharts to their equivalent pseudocode
- ◎ Explain how programming concepts are implemented in pseudocode, flowcharts, and JavaScript

Just do what must be done. It may not be happiness, but it is greatness.

—GEORGE BERNARD SHAW

Electricians, plumbers, and other professionals are required to operate under codes established by professional organizations, industry, and government agencies. Although programmers aren't legally bound by similar codes, a standard programming method known as "structured programming" is widely considered to be the best way to develop and maintain programs. Three control structures are used in programming: sequence, selection, and repetition.

This chapter deals with the first and simplest of these three structures: sequence. In contrast with the other two control structures, sequence structures run straight through, with no variation, and they run only once. This chapter gives you an overview of the three structures, focusing on sequence structures. It also introduces flowcharts as a visual method for developing programming logic and compares similar programming concepts and how they're implemented in pseudocode, flowcharts, and JavaScript. The computer has no choice in the matter of sequence; it has to do what must be done. So if George Bernard Shaw is right, your computer may not be happy, but it will be great!

What Is Structured Programming?

Structured programming is a way of designing, writing, and modifying programs that focuses on this core concept: Use only the three recognized control structures—sequence, selection, and repetition. Structured programming is widely accepted as the most efficient method of program development, resulting in faster development, reusable code, easier maintenance, and fewer errors.

An advantage of structured programming is that it works well with the concept of modular programming. Structures can be pulled out of programs and inserted into other programs without adversely affecting the flow of the surrounding code. When code isn't written by using modules, it's difficult to know what effect changing a line of code will have on surrounding statements. Structures are easy to find and change: They have one entry point and one exit point—a clear beginning and end.

The need for structured programming can be illustrated best by describing the alternative. Nonstructured programming is most often characterized by the GOTO statement, common in early line-number BASIC programs. Here's an example:

```
100 PRINT "Enter a number (or 0 to quit): "
110 INPUT N
120 IF N < 0 THEN GOTO 150
130 IF N > 0 THEN GOTO 170
140 GOTO 200
150 PRINT "Your number is negative."
160 GOTO 100
```

```
170 PRINT "Your number is positive."
180 GOTO 100
200 PRINT "Thank you!"
```

Nonstructured programming is commonly called "spaghetti code." If you draw lines on the preceding code statements to trace their order, your drawing will resemble a pile of spaghetti, going all over the place with no apparent control. The flow of control jumps forward and backward, with no clues to what will be done when a number is negative or positive. You have to go to the statement and connect it with the statement that sent you there. In contrast, a structured program has a flow that's much easier to follow and understand:

```
100 PRINT "Enter a number (or 0 to quit): "
110 INPUT N
120 WHILE N <> 0
120     IF N < 0 THEN PRINT "Your number is negative."
130     IF N > 0 THEN PRINT "Your number is positive."
140     PRINT "Enter a number (or 0 to quit): "
150     INPUT N
160 END WHILE
200 PRINT "Thank you!"
```

The Three Control Structures

Here's a brief explanation of the three control structures:

- *Sequence*—A **sequence structure** consists of one or more statements performed in order with no variation. You could say that the statements are performed with "no ifs, ands, or buts." Example: "Go to the grocery store. Buy milk and eggs. Get gas in the car on the way home."

- *Selection*—This structure evaluates a logical condition, one that's true or false, and then performs one or more statements (or ignores those statements), based on the evaluation of this condition. The selection structure, discussed in detail in Chapter 5, usually starts with the keyword If and sometimes includes Else. Example: "If it's raining outside, take an umbrella."

- *Repetition*—This structure also evaluates a logical condition and performs or ignores one or more statements based on the evaluation. The difference is that it evaluates the condition again and, based on the outcome, repeats the statements. It's discussed in detail in Chapter 6. Example: "Deposit $100 into savings every week, as long as your balance is below $1000."

In this chapter, you focus on the sequence structure, discussed in the next section.

The GOTO command is mentioned only as an example of poor programming practice, and its use should be avoided.

133

The concept of structured programming has been traced back to the "stored programming" concept developed by John von Neumann. This concept, which states that *any* program can be written by using only sequence, selection, and repetition structures, was introduced in a paper written by Corrado Bohm and Giuseppe Jacopini. Edsger Dijkstra's paper "GoTo Statement Considered Harmful" and articles by computer scientists Niklaus Wirth (the creator of Pascal) and Donald Knuth continued the discussion.

The Sequence Structure

A common example used for a sequence structure is the instruction part of a recipe. After assembling the ingredients and utensils for cooking a cup of macaroni, the instructions might read like this:

```
Pour 2 quarts of cold water in cooking pot
Add 1/2 teaspoon salt
Place pot on stove
Turn stove to a high setting
Wait for water to boil
Pour 1 cup of macaroni in pot
Reduce heat to a medium setting
Stir macaroni every 2 minutes
After 10 minutes, remove pot from stove
Turn off stove
Pour macaroni and water into colander
Rinse with cold water for 20 seconds
```

These steps are meant to be performed in order. Imagine the results you would get if you performed the steps in this order:

```
Pour 1 cup of macaroni in cooking pot
Rinse with cold water for 20 seconds
Stir macaroni every 2 minutes
After 10 minutes, remove pot from stove
Pour macaroni and water into colander
Pour 2 quarts of cold water in cooking pot
Place pot on stove
Add 1/2 teaspoon salt
Turn stove to a high setting
Wait for water to boil
Reduce heat to a medium setting
Turn off stove
```

What would happen? You'd end up with a colander of uncooked macaroni and a pot of hot water! Order matters. You would also get very different results if you ignored some steps and performed the others in this order:

```
Place pot on stove
Pour 1 cup of macaroni in cooking pot
Turn stove to a high setting
Stir macaroni every 2 minutes
After 10 minutes, remove pot from stove
Turn off stove
```

Because you didn't use any water, you have scorched a cup of macaroni, ruining it and possibly your cooking pot, too.

Programmers have an easier time getting a computer to obey the sequence structure than many parents do with their children.

Although many parents don't realize it, they're using the sequence structure when they give the following instructions to their children:

```
Wash the dishes.
Clean your room.
Do your homework.
```

A programmer can convert the following pseudocode to a programming language and run it on the computer:

```
Display "Enter your full name: "
Input fullName
Display "Enter your age in years: "
Input age
Display "Hi, " + fullName
Display "You are " + age + " years old."
```

Here's the same algorithm after converting it to JavaScript. Assume that constants for an empty string (ES) and the line break tag (BR) have been declared:

```
fullName = prompt("Enter your full name:",ES);
age = prompt("Enter your age in years:",ES);
document.write("Hi, " + fullName + BR);
document.write("You are " + age + "years old." + BR);
```

If the computer had performed the document.write() statements before the prompt statements, the variables fullName and age would have no values. Again, order matters.

Statements in a sequence structure are performed without any conditions. They can be grouped into sections and commented, but the order still proceeds from top to bottom. Although there are groups of statements in the following example, they're still performed in order:

```
// Declare variables
   Declare Numeric score1, score2, score3   // test scores
   Declare Numeric total                     // score total
   Declare Numeric average                   // average score

// Ask for test scores
   Display "Enter the first test score: "
   Input score1
   Display "Enter the second test score: "
   Input score2
   Display "Enter the third test score: "
   Input score3

// Compute and display an average of the scores
   total = score1 + score2 + score3
   average = total / 3
   Display "Average score is: " + average
```

The result of the preceding algorithm would be much different if the average had been computed before all three test scores had been entered or if the statements computing the total and the average had been switched. However, when statements are listed in sequence, they're performed in the order in which they appear, and all statements are performed.

Representing Control Structures with Flowcharts

In Chapter 3, you learned how to define a class by using a class diagram. There's another graphical tool for expressing an algorithm's logic that conveys the same information as pseudocode. Known as a **flowchart**, it can represent a single module or an entire program. Flowchart components include the following:

- **Terminal symbols** (ovals) that mark the beginning and ending of a flowchart

- **Process symbols** (rectangles) for variable declarations or assignment statements

- **Input/output symbols** (parallelograms) for display statements, prompts, and input statements

- **Module symbols** (rectangles with stripes), used to call a module or function, with the module definition in a separate flowchart section

- **Flowlines** (lines with arrowheads) for connecting other symbols

- **Annotation boxes** (open-sided boxes) for comments

Take a look at an example to see how statements that prompt users to enter their age and then input the data are expressed in pseudocode, JavaScript, and flowcharts. In pseudocode, you use the following statements:

```
Display "Please enter your age: "
Input age
```

In JavaScript, the two statements are combined in a single prompt statement:

```
age = prompt("Please enter your age:",ES);
```

For convenience, the prompt text and input command are combined in a single flowchart symbol (see Figure 4-1).

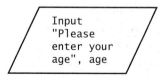

```
Input
"Please
enter your
age", age
```

Figure 4-1 Input symbol that combines the prompt text and input command

The flowcharts in this book were created with Microsoft Visio 2007. Microsoft Visio Toolbox offers a free trial version at *http://visiotoolbox.com/visio2007freetrial/*. Other flowcharting software includes SmartDraw (free trial version at *www.smartdraw.com*) and Gliffy (free trial version at *www.gliffy.com/flowchart-software/*).

The following algorithm asks for the user's age, adds 10 years to it, and displays how old the user will be in 10 years, and the flowchart in Figure 4-2 describes the same algorithm.

```
Start
    // Declare variables
    Declare Numeric age, newAge

    // Get user's age
    Display "Please enter your age: "
    Input age

    // Compute age in 10 years
    newAge = age + 10

    // Display new age
    Display "In 10 years, you will be " + newAge
Stop
```

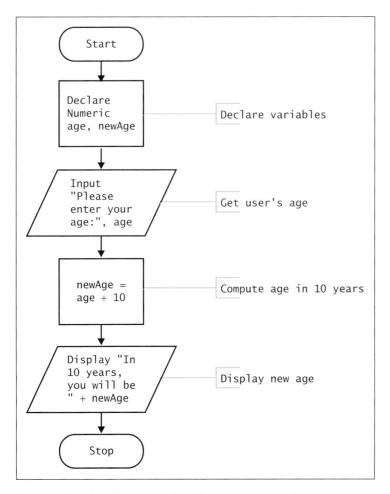

Figure 4-2   Flowchart for adding 10 years to the user's age

Note the correlations between the pseudocode and flowchart:

- The Start and Stop keywords, used to indicate the beginning and end of a pseudocode program, are represented by terminal symbols.

- A variable declaration is considered a process, so it's placed in a rectangle.

- An Input statement is considered input, so it's placed in a parallelogram along with the prompt text.

- Adding 10 years to the age variable and storing the result in the newAge variable is an assignment statement, so it's placed in a rectangle.

- The Display statement for the result is considered output, so it's also placed in a parallelogram.

- Symbols are connected by flowlines that indicate the order of processing.

- Comments are placed in annotation boxes, which are attached to the corresponding symbols by straight lines.

The flowlines simply trace the order of steps, and in the sequence structure, there's only one order: from beginning to end. Flowcharts can be drawn to move from top to bottom or from left to right, whichever fits the page better.

You can convert an algorithm from a flowchart to pseudocode. Look at the flowchart in Figure 4-3, and see whether you can understand what the program is doing.

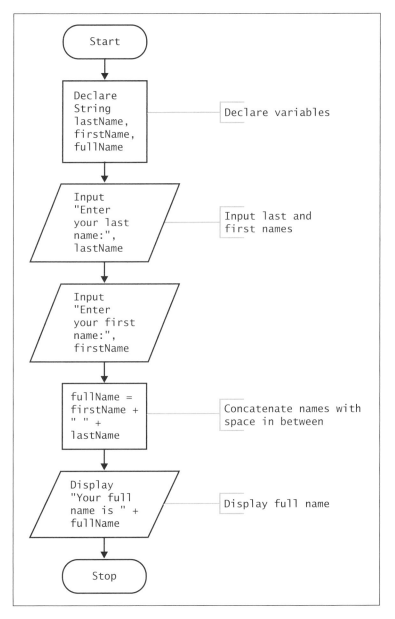

Figure 4-3   Flowchart for concatenating first and last names

Flowcharts are so similar to pseudocode that the conversion process shouldn't be difficult. However, instead of looking just at converting single steps, try to see what the entire program is accomplishing.

This program asks for the user's last and first names, concatenates them with a space in between, and displays the full name. Here's the pseudocode:

```
Start
    // Declare variables
    Declare String lastName, firstName, fullName

    // Input last and first names
    Display "Enter your last name: "
    Input lastName
    Display "Enter your first name: "
    Input firstName

    // Concatenate names with space in between
    fullName = firstName + " " + lastName

    // Display full name
    Display "Your full name is " + fullName
Stop
```

The flowchart and pseudocode have the following similarities:

- The `Declare` statement is identical in both; it appears in a rectangle in the flowchart.

- The `Input` statements in the flowchart combine the corresponding `Display` and `Input` statements in pseudocode.

- The assignment statement is identical in both; it appears in a rectangle in the flowchart.

- The annotation boxes in the flowchart correspond to comments in the pseudocode.

Try to determine what an entire program is accomplishing, not just what's done in each step.

The Sequence Structure and Modules

What about programs that call modules, such as object-oriented programs that create objects by calling constructor methods and instance methods? Are they sequential? The answer is that they can be. Modules (which include methods and functions) are sections of programming code, and as a result, they're made up of sequence, selection, and repetition structures, just as other program code is. When a function or method is called, the computer temporarily halts processing of the current module (or **calling module**), runs the function or method, and then returns to the calling module, resuming with the statement following the call.

For example, in Chapter 3, the pseudocode program AccountClass-2 contains the following code, which makes up the main module:

```
Start
   // State program purpose
   Display "Account program."
   Display "This program creates an account."
   Display "It also modifies the account."

   // Create an account object
   Account mySavingsAcct = new Account ("S", 1376433, ↵
 "Dunes", "Sandi", 80.00)

   // Deposit $100
   mySavingsAcct.deposit(100.00)

   // Withdraw $50
   mySavingsAcct.withdraw(50.00)

   // Inquire about balance
   mySavingsAcct.inquire()

   // Display the information to verify
   mySavingsAcct.displayInfo()

   // Thank the user
   Display "Thank you!"
Stop
```

Remember that the computer doesn't process comments; they're included for the programmer's use. The statements in this pseudocode program run until these statements are encountered:

```
   // Create an account object
   Account mySavingsAcct = new Account ("S", 1376433, ↵
"Dunes", "Sandi", 80.00)
```

At this point, program control shifts to the constructor method for the Account class, where the following code runs:

```
// Constructor method with five parameters
   Constructor Method Account(String type, Numeric num, ↵
 String lName, String fName, Numeric bal)
      acctType = type
      acctNumber = num
      lastName = lName
      firstName = fName
      acctBal = bal
   End Method
```

The statements in the constructor method are processed sequentially, and then program control returns to the AccountClass-2 program, resuming with the next statements:

```
// Deposit $100
mySavingsAcct.deposit(100.00)
```

When the call to the deposit() method is made, the computer finds the code for it:

```
// Method to deposit an amount into the account
Method deposit(Numeric amt)
   acctBal = acctBal + amt
   Display "The new balance is: $" + acctBal
End Method
```

After these statements are processed, programming control returns to these statements:

```
// Withdraw $50
mySavingsAcct.withdraw(50.00)
```

This process continues until the end of the main program. Every time a module is called, the computer suspends execution of the main program, runs the module, and then returns to the next statement in the main program.

Representing Modules in Flowcharts

As mentioned, modules are represented by rectangles with stripes. Modular programming helps keep your main program uncluttered and easy to understand, and you can see this advantage when using a flowchart to represent a program that calls modules. Figure 4-4 shows the AccountClass-2 pseudocode converted to a flowchart. (For easy reference, the AccountClass-2.txt file is included in the student data files for this chapter.)

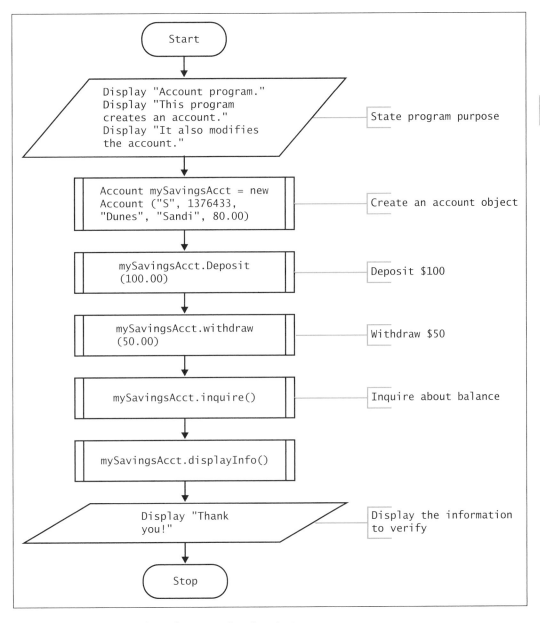

Figure 4-4 The AccountClass-2 program in a flowchart

Each rectangle with stripes in the flowchart represents a call to a module. For each module, which contains statements in a sequence structure, a separate flowchart section includes the module's code. This flowchart section is similar to a flowchart for a main module, except the terminal symbols include the module's name at the beginning and the Return keyword at the end. Figure 4-5 shows the flowchart section for the constructor method.

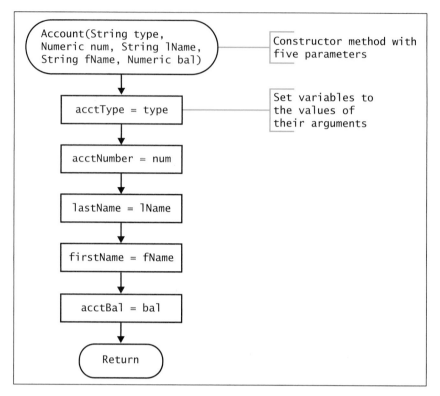

Figure 4-5 The constructor method for the AccountClass-2 program in a flowchart

Figure 4-6 shows the deposit() method as a flowchart. Each module has its own flowchart section.

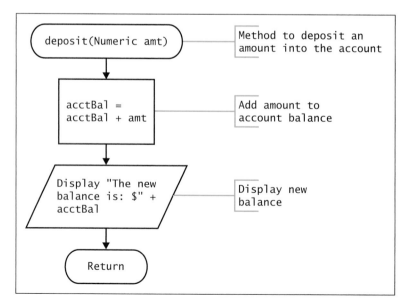

Figure 4-6 The deposit() method for the AccountClass-2 program in a flowchart

Except for the `inquire()` method, the other methods in AccountClass-2 are similar to the `deposit()` method. They take one or more arguments and set or recalculate the value of class variables based on these arguments. The `inquire()` method is different, in that it takes no arguments but returns a value to the calling program. There are no calculations in the module, but the name of the variable whose value is to be returned is included with the `Return` keyword in the ending terminal symbol. Figure 4-7 shows the flowchart section for the `inquire()` method.

Class methods that return values to the calling module are called "accessor" or "get" methods. Methods that assign values to class variables are called "mutator" or "set" methods.

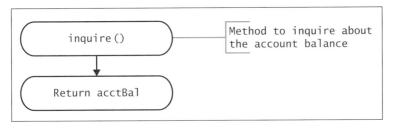

Figure 4-7   The `inquire()` method for the AccountClass-2 program in a flowchart

 **Think Tank**

Draw the flowchart sections for the remaining methods in the AccountClass-2 program, `withdraw()` and `changeName()`. Check your results against the flowcharts in the student data files for this chapter.

Comparing Pseudocode, JavaScript, and Flowcharts

People are sometimes categorized into two groups, based on whether they're more inclined to think in words or in pictures. People who think in words are often referred to as "left-brained," and those who think in pictures and images are called "right-brained." Using this categorization, left-brained people tend to favor pseudocode as a method of developing algorithms for programs, and right-brained people tend to favor flowcharts. Whichever method you prefer, remember that you can convert one to the other easily, and either one can be converted to JavaScript or another programming language easily, too.

Programming is largely about communicating. You're communicating instructions to the computer, and you're communicating with programmers who need to look at your code and perhaps modify it in the future. You have learned three different methods of communication already: pseudocode, JavaScript, and flowcharts. All three can describe the same processes and information. Table 4-1 compares these three methods.

Pseudocode	JavaScript	Flowchart symbol
Start	N/A	⬭
Stop	N/A	⬭
Display	document.write()	▱
Input	prompt()	▱
Declare	var	▭
Assignment statements	Assignment statements	▭

Table 4-1   Comparison of pseudocode, JavaScript, and flowcharts

Pseudocode and flowcharts are both tools to help you develop the logic for an algorithm. Based on your left-brain or right-brain tendencies, you might already have a preference for one tool or the other. Either one can be converted to JavaScript. As a programmer, you should learn which tool helps you clarify your logic most effectively.

Programmer's Workshop

Now is a good time to incorporate what you've learned so far by solving a business problem with flowcharts and JavaScript. In this Programmer's Workshop, you create an interactive program that computes annual interest for a savings account. The program asks the user for the beginning balance in the account and the annual interest rate, and then computes the annual interest and adds it to the account balance, displaying the interest and the new balance. Design the program with a flowchart, and then convert it to JavaScript and test it.

Discussion: Start with the IPO method. At this point in your programmer's apprenticeship, you can choose variable types and names as you use the IPO method:

- What outputs are requested, and what data type should they be? Annual interest (`interest`) and new balance (`balance`)
- What inputs do you have available, and what data type should they be? Beginning balance (same variable as new balance: `balance`) and annual interest rate (`intRate`)
- What processing is required? Compute interest by multiplying account balance by interest rate, and add interest to balance.

    1.   Start the program and declare your variables, as shown in Figure 4-8.

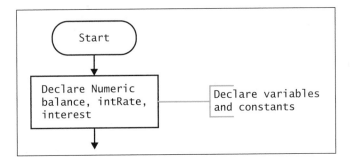

Figure 4-8   Starting the program and declaring variables

    2.   Welcome the user and ask for the beginning balance and annual interest rate (see Figure 4-9).

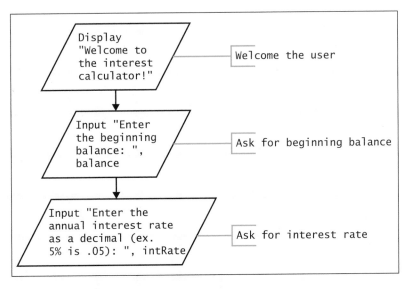

Figure 4-9   Welcome and prompt for input

3. Calculate the interest, add it to the balance, and display both amounts, as shown in Figure 4-10.

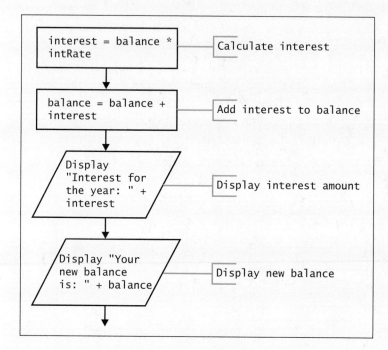

Figure 4-10 Performing calculations and displaying the results

4. Finally, thank the user and end the program (see Figure 4-11).

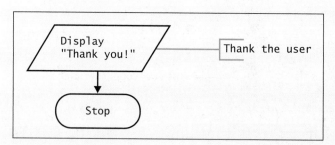

Figure 4-11 Thanking the user and ending the program

Figure 4-12 shows the flowchart for the entire program. You can also look at the Visio file interestCalculator.vsd in your student data files.

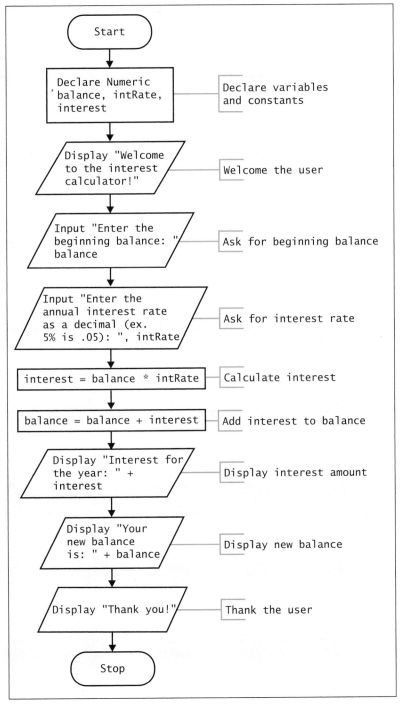

Figure 4-12 The complete flowchart for the interest calculator program

In the following steps, you convert the flowchart to JavaScript, and test the program. When entering JavaScript code, remember to add a blank line after each code section to improve your program's readability.

1. Open a new document in Notepad and save it as **interestCalculator.html**. Enter the beginning HTML tags and the usual documentation lines, and convert the first flowchart section by declaring variables and adding JavaScript constants:

```
<html>
<body>
<script type="text/javascript">

// Program name: interestCalculator.html
// Purpose: Compute annual interest
// Author: Paul Addison
// Date last modified: 01-Sep-2011

// Declare variables and constants
var balance;          // current balance
var intRate;          // annual interest rate
var interest;         // interest amount
var ES = "" ;         // literal empty string
var BR = "<br />";    // HTML line break
```

2. Convert the next flowchart section by welcoming the user and prompting for the current balance and the interest rate. Remember to convert your input to decimal values with the parseFloat() function.

```
// Welcome the user, ask for beginning balance
// and interest rate
document.write("Welcome to the interest calculator!" + BR);
balance = prompt("Enter the beginning balance:",ES);
balance = parseFloat(balance);
intRate = prompt("Enter the annual interest rate as a ↵
  decimal (ex. 5% is .05):",ES);
intRate = parseFloat(intRate);
```

3. Convert the next flowchart section by calculating and displaying the interest amount and the new balance:

```
// Calculate interest, add to balance, and display both
interest = balance * intRate;
balance = balance + interest;
document.write("Interest for the year: $" + interest + BR);
document.write("Your new balance is: $" + ↵
  balance.toFixed(2) + BR);
```

4. Convert the last flowchart section by thanking the user and entering the closing HTML tags:

```
// Thank the user and end the program
document.write("Thank you!" + BR);

</script>
</body>
</html>
```

5. Save the file, and open it in a Web browser. To test the program, enter **500.00** for the balance and **.03** as the interest rate (see Figure 4-13).

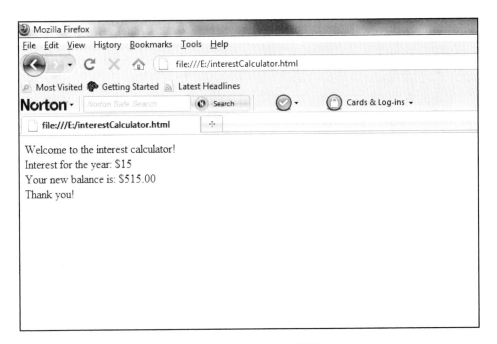

Figure 4-13 The interestCalculator.html program in a Web browser

 **Object Lesson**

In the Object Lesson for this chapter, you design the MenuItem Class program, using a class for menu items and creating and displaying several menu item objects. Specifically, a menu item consists of an item name, a category (sandwich or drink), and a price. You should

have a constructor method and a method to display all an item's properties. Your program should create the following objects:

- Pastrami sandwich, sandwich, $4.95

- Ham sandwich, sandwich, $5.25

- Milk shake, drink, $2.95

- Soft drink, drink, $1.49

1. Start with a class diagram for the MenuItem class, as shown in Figure 4-14.

MenuItem
String itemName
String category
Numeric itemPrice
MenuItem(String name, String cat, Numeric price)
displayInfo()

Figure 4-14   The class diagram for the MenuItem class

2. Next, create the pseudocode for the class. The top section (from Class MenuItem to End Class) is the class definition, and the bottom section (from Start to Stop) is the module that creates objects from the class. Your pseudocode should look like this:

```
// Program name: MenuItem Class
// Purpose: Pseudocode for defining the MenuItem class
// Author: Paul Addison
// Date last modified: 01-Sep-2011

Class MenuItem
    String itemName       // name of menu item
    String category       // item category (sandwich or ⏎
      drink)
    Numeric itemPrice  // price of item

    // Constructor method with three arguments
    Constructor Method MenuItem(String name, String cat, ⏎
      Numeric price)
        itemName = name
        category = cat
        itemPrice = price
    End Method
```

```
    // Method to display all information about the menu item
    Method displayInfo()
        Display "Item name " + itemName
        Display "Category " + category
        Display "Price of item: " + itemPrice
    End Method
End Class

Start
    // Welcome the user
    Display "Welcome to the Menu Maker!"

    // Create four menu item objects
    MenuItem pastrami = new MenuItem ↵
("Pastrami", "Sandwich", 4.95)
    MenuItem ham = new MenuItem ↵
("Ham", "Sandwich", 5.25)
    MenuItem milkShake = new MenuItem ↵
("Milk shake", "Drink", 2.95)
    MenuItem softDrink = new MenuItem ↵
("Soft drink", "Drink", 1.49)

    // Display the information for all menu items
    pastrami.displayInfo()
    ham.displayInfo()
    milkShake.displayInfo()
    softDrink.displayInfo()

    // Thank the user
    Display "Thank you!"
Stop
```

3. Now you can convert the pseudocode program to JavaScript. Open a new document in Notepad, and save it as **MenuItemClass.html**. Start by entering the HTML tags and documentation lines and declaring class variables and JavaScript constants. Remember to add a blank line after each code section.

4. When you have converted the program to JavaScript, save the file again, and open it in a Web browser. Test your program and make sure it works. The output should look like Figure 4-15. If your program doesn't run correctly, compare it with MenuItemClass-solution.html in your student data files.

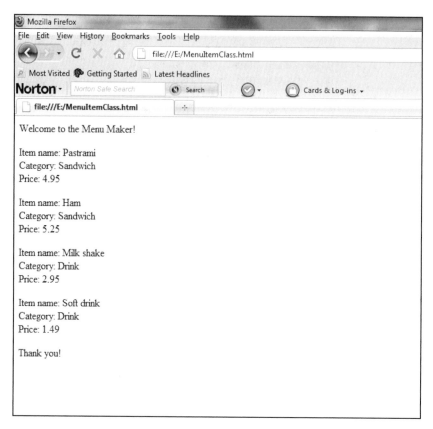

Figure 4-15 The MenuItemClass.html program in a Web browser

All the statements in this Object Lesson use the sequence structure. You have now written programs in JavaScript that use the sequence structure and JavaScript's object-oriented features.

Chapter Summary

- Structured programming is a method for building programs from three control structures: sequence, selection, and repetition. It makes programs easier to read and follow.

- Nonstructured program code is difficult to follow and is often called "spaghetti code."

- In a sequence structure, steps are performed in order with no variation.

- Flowcharts are a visual representation of an algorithm and are used to develop a program's logic.

- Flowcharting symbols correspond to pseudocode statements.

- Pseudocode algorithms can be converted to flowcharts, and vice versa.

- Both flowcharts and pseudocode can be converted to JavaScript or other programming languages.

Key Terms

annotation boxes—Open-sided boxes containing comments that are connected to flowchart symbols by straight lines.

calling module—A program module containing a call to another module.

flowchart—A diagram representing the logic of an algorithm.

flowlines—Lines with arrowheads that connect symbols in a flowchart to indicate the order of steps.

input/output symbols—Flowchart symbols (parallelograms) used for display statements, prompts, and input statements.

module symbols—Flowchart symbols (rectangles with stripes) used to indicate calling a module or function, which has its own flowchart section.

process symbols—Flowchart symbols (rectangles) used for variable declarations or assignment statements and other processing commands.

sequence structure—The programming control structure in which all steps are performed in order with no variation.

structured programming—A method for building programs from three control structures: sequence, selection, and repetition.

terminal symbols—Flowchart symbols (ovals) that represent the beginning and end of the algorithm.

Review Questions

True/False

1. The sequence structure indicates that the top-down programming method is being used. True or False?

2. The sequence structure performs all statements in the order specified. True or False?

3. In a sequence structure, some steps can be skipped. True or False?

4. Flowcharts and pseudocode represent the same logic for an algorithm. True or False?

5. A flowchart uses a terminal symbol to indicate performing a calculation. True or False?

6. Assignment statements are indicated with the rectangle symbol in flowcharts. True or False?

7. Input and output statements use different symbols in flowcharts. True or False?

8. Comments are listed in annotation boxes in flowcharts. True or False?

9. Flowlines are used to connect flowchart symbols to comments. True or False?

10. Pseudocode can be converted to JavaScript or another programming language, but flowcharts can't. True or False?

11. Decision symbols are often used to flowchart a sequence structure. True or False?

12. Unstructured programs can often be identified by their use of the GOTO statement. True or False?

Multiple Choice

1. Which of the following is a basic control structure? (Choose all that apply.)

   a. flow

   b. selection

   c. repetition

   d. sequence

2. What's the term for unstructured code that jumps to other statements frequently?

   a. loose code

   b. transition code

   c. spaghetti code

   d. faux code

3. Which flowchart symbol is used to mark the beginning and ending of an algorithm?

   a. terminal

   b. process

   c. input/output

   d. annotation box

   e. module

4. Which flowchart symbol is used for displaying a message to the user?

   a. terminal

   b. process

   c. input/output

   d. annotation box

   e. module

5. Which flowchart symbol is used for an assignment statement?

   a. terminal

   b. process

   c. input/output

   d. annotation box

   e. module

6. Which flowchart symbol is used to call a function?

   a. terminal

   b. process

   c. input/output

   d. annotation box

   e. module

7. Which flowchart symbol is used to display comments?

   a. terminal

   b. process

   c. input/output

   d. annotation box

   e. module

8. Which of the following can be converted easily into JavaScript or another programming language? (Choose all that apply.)

   a. pseudocode

   b. flowcharts

   c. IPO charts

   d. data types

   e. control structures

Discussion Questions

1. What's one advantage of using structured programming?

2. Can programs that call functions or modules use a sequence structure?

3. What's the difference between a sequence structure and event-driven programming?

4. Which method of algorithm development do you prefer: writing pseudocode or flowcharting? Why?

Hands-On Activities

Hands-On Activity 4-1

A sales manager wants to know the percentage increase in sales for 2011 compared with 2010. Using pencil and paper, draw a flowchart to design an algorithm for a program that asks for the two sales numbers, computes the difference, divides the difference by the base (2010) number, and displays the result.

Hands-On Activity 4-2

The sales manager in Hands-On Activity 4-1 thinks your program will work and wants to see it in action. Convert the flowchart to JavaScript and test the program. Convert percentages to the standard format (multiplying the decimal amount by 100) and display them with two decimal places.

Using JavaScript, write a program that implements the sales increase percentage algorithm you wrote for Hands-On Activity 1. Save your JavaScript file as salesIncrease.html.

Hands-On Activity 4-3

In Chapter 3, you used the Math.max() method with two arguments. Write a program that asks the user for three sales amounts, sends all three as arguments to Math.max(), and then displays the result. Does the Math.max() method accept three arguments?

Using JavaScript, write a program to find the maximum of three sales amounts by testing whether the Math.max() method can accept three arguments. Save your JavaScript file as maxOfThree.html.

Hands-On Activity 4-4

BuzzButtons is a novelty item company manufacturing personalized lapel buttons that buzz randomly. The buttons are marketed as a conversation starter, and the company's slogan is "It starts the buzz!" The owner is promoting his buttons by offering them at 99 cents each. He wants you to design a program asking the user for his or her name for the button, an e-mail address, and the number of buttons to order. The program should then add a 6% sales tax and a flat shipping rate of $2.00. The program displays the information the user enters as well as the button price total, sales tax amount, shipping amount, and order total. The company contacts the user by e-mail later for shipping address information.

Using pseudocode, design an algorithm that asks the user for the number of fixed-price items to order, adds sales tax and flat-rate shipping, and displays the result. Save your pseudocode file in Notepad as buzzButtons.txt.

Hands-On Activity 4-5

The owner of BuzzButtons thinks you have the solution for promoting his product and asks you to produce a working program that asks for this information. Use the algorithm from Hands-On Activity 4-4 and test it.

Using JavaScript, write the button order program. Save your JavaScript program as buzzButtons.html.

CASE STUDY: **Declaring Variables and Adding a Prompt for It's War!**

In Chapter 2, you designed the pseudocode and JavaScript to start the War card game. Now it's time to decide what other variables are needed to play this game and set them up. You can also provide the prompt for the first card played by each player.

In Notepad, open the warGame.txt file, and save it as warGame-ch4.txt.

So far, you have these variables declared:

```
Declare String player1, player2    // names of the players
Declare Numeric pointGoal           // points needed to win
```

Reread the rules for the game in Chapter 1, and think of what items you need to keep track of as you develop the algorithm to keep score and track the progress for the game:

- The cards are input by name (2 to 10, J, Q, K, or A).

- You convert the card name to its correct point value.

- Each player's score starts at 0.

- The current score is displayed after each hand.

- In case of a tie, the combined point count for the two cards is put into a hold area (initially 0).

- When the game is over, the winner's name is displayed.

Using the preceding information and the IPO process, determine the data types and choose variable names as you go:

- What (new) outputs are requested, and what data types should they be? Current player score throughout the game (score1 and score2, both initialized to 0); points in hold area in case of a tie (holdPoints); and winner of game, either player1 or player2 unless the game ends in a tie (winner)

- What (new) inputs do you have available, and what data types should they be? Card played by each player for each hand, such as 2 to 10, J, Q, K, or A (cardName1 and cardName2)

- What (new) processing is required? Get players' cards for first hand, and convert card names to point count (cardPoints1 and cardPoints2)

In your pseudocode, after the line declaring the point goal variable (Declare Numeric pointGoal), enter these lines:

```
// current score for each player
Declare Numeric score1, score2
// points in hold area
Declare Numeric holdPoints
// winner of game
Declare String winner
// name of card played
Declare String cardName1, cardName2
// point values for cards played
Declare Numeric cardPoints1, cardPoints2
```

Next, initialize the variables for the players' scores and the hold points to 0. Press Enter to insert a blank line and type these lines:

```
// Initialize variables
score1 = 0;
score2 = 0;
holdPoints = 0;
```

Now enter the prompts for the first two cards played, and personalize the prompt by including the player's name. After the Display statement showing how many points the game is played to, press Enter to insert a blank line and type these lines:

```
// Ask for cards played in the first hand
Display "Enter card for " + player1 + ":"
Input cardName1
Display " Enter card for " + player2 + ":"
Input cardName2
```

Save the file again. It should look like the following:

```
Start

// Program name: War Game (Chapter 4)
// Purpose:
//    Keep score for the card game War, simplified version.
//    A point goal for the game is entered.
//    The user enters card values for two players each hand.
//    The values are compared, and the player with the
//    higher value wins the combined point value.
//    In case of a tie hand, the points are held while two
//    more card values are compared, until one player wins,
//    getting the points for those cards and all held cards.
//    The first player to reach the point goal wins.
// Author: Paul Addison
// Date last modified: 01-Sep-2011

    // Declare variables and constants
    // names of the players
    Declare String player1, player2
    // points needed to win
    Declare Numeric pointGoal
    // current score for each player
    Declare Numeric score1, score2
    // points in hold area
    Declare Numeric holdPoints
    // winner of game
    Declare String winner
    // name of card played
    Declare String cardName1, cardName2
    // point values for cards played
    Declare Numeric cardPoints1, cardPoints2

    // Initialize variables
    score1 = 0;
```

```
    score2 = 0;
    holdPoints = 0;
    // Welcome the user
    Display "Welcome to the Game of War!"

    // Ask for the names of the two players
    Display "Enter the name of the first player: "
    Input player1
    Display "Enter the name of the second player: "
    Input player2

    // Ask for the point goal
    Display "How many points will you play to? "
    Input pointGoal

    // Ask for cards played in the first hand
    Display "Enter card for " + player1 + ":"
    Input cardName1
    Display "Enter card for " + player2 + ":"
    Input cardName2

    // Display the data
    Display player1 + "plays: " + cardName1
    Display player2 + "plays: " + cardName2

    // Thank the user
    Display "Thank you for playing the game of War!"

Stop
```

Now you can make these changes in JavaScript. In Notepad, open the warGame.html file, and resave it as warGame-ch4.html. After the last constant (for the empty string), enter the statements corresponding to your pseudocode to declare the variables and add the lines to initialize the scores and hold points:

```
var score1, score2;        // current player scores
var holdPoints;            // points in hold area
var winner;                // winner of game
var cardName1, cardName2;  // name of card played
var cardPoints1, cardPoints2; // point values for cards

// Initialize variables
score1 = 0;
score2 = 0;
holdPoints = 0;
```

Finally, after the line displaying how many points the game is played to, press Enter to insert a blank line and type these lines:

```
// Ask for cards played in the first hand
cardName1 = prompt("Enter card for " + player1 + ":",ES);
cardName2 = prompt("Enter card for " + player2 + ":",ES);
```

Because you have successfully tested the display for the players'
names and the point goal, delete those lines. Test your new input
lines by pressing Enter to insert a blank line and typing these lines:

```
// Display the data
document.write(player1 + "plays: " + cardName1 + BR);
document.write(player2 + "plays: " + cardName2 + BR);
```

Save your file again, and try opening it in a browser. If it's not working
correctly, compare it with warGame-ch4-solution.html in your
student data files.

Now test your War Game program. If you enter the players' names as
Bert and Ernie, with a point limit of 100, and the first two cards as an
ace and a 2, your Web browser should look like Figure 4-16.

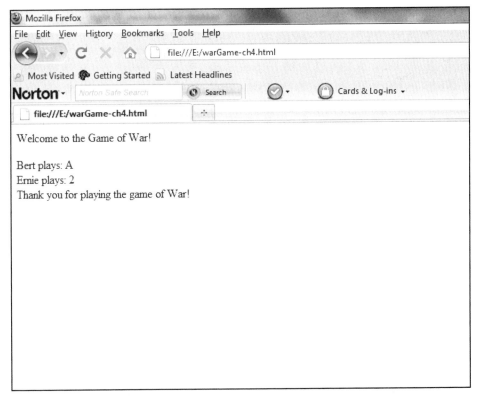

Figure 4-16　The warGame-ch4.html JavaScript program in a Web browser

The Selection Structure

In this chapter, you learn to:

- ◎ Define a Boolean expression
- ◎ Explain why a condition can have only two outcomes
- ◎ Define a selection structure
- ◎ Describe common relational operators and their functions
- ◎ Differentiate between a single-outcome and dual-outcome selection
- ◎ Describe the scope of a selection structure and how it's specified in pseudocode, flowcharts, and JavaScript
- ◎ Define a nested structure
- ◎ Design algorithms that evaluate several values for a variable
- ◎ Define and use the Case structure

"If you ain't wrong, you're right
If it ain't day, it's night
If you ain't sure, you might
Gotta be this or that."
—FROM THE SONG "GOTTA BE THIS OR THAT," LYRICS
BY SUNNY SKYLAR

The simple word "if" can make a world of difference. It's the foundation of the second control structure: selection. A **selection structure** evaluates a condition, which is an expression that's true or false. With a selection structure, your program can choose between alternate courses of action. You can instruct the computer to do one thing if the condition is true and another (or nothing at all) if the condition is false. Essentially, you're teaching the computer how to make decisions.

What makes programming selection structures easy is that there are no shades of gray between true and false. A condition is evaluated, and it evaluates to true or to false. There's no in between: It's gotta be this or that.

Conditions: Boolean Expressions

You use "if" expressions all the time in your daily life:

- If it's cold outside, you wear a coat.

- If you have enough cash, you can make a purchase.

- If you get a check in the mail, you endorse it and then deposit or cash it.

Computers can also use the word "if." You can tell a computer the following, for example:

- If an employee works more than 40 hours, pay time and a half on any hours over 40.

- If the balance goes below $100, send the customer a warning notice.

- If the password the user enters matches the stored password, allow the user access to the application.

Chapter 4 explained the first of the three control structures: sequence. This chapter discusses the second: selection. A selection structure depends on a **condition**, an expression describing the relationship between two values that's evaluated when it appears in program code. It evaluates to a true or false value. This kind of expression is called a **Boolean expression**, named after George Boole, who developed an extensive system of logic based on true and false conditions and their consequences. A condition expression uses one of the **relational operators** shown in Table 5-1.

Symbol	Meaning
<	Less than
>	Greater than
==	Equal to
<=	Less than or equal to
>=	Greater than or equal to
!=	Not equal to

Table 5-1   Relational operators

The two values being compared are usually two variables or a variable and a constant. (You could compare two constants, but the results would always be the same.) Evaluating an expression is like asking a question. Here are some examples:

- `age < 65`   Is the value of age less than 65?
- `hours > 40`   Is the value of hours greater than 40?
- `region == "Midwest"`   Is the value of region equal to "Midwest"?
- `status != "denied"`   Is the value of status not equal to "denied"?
- `quantity <= 10`   Is the value of quantity less than or equal to 10?
- `grade >= 90`   Is the value of grade greater than or equal to 90?

Use the double equals sign (==) when you're *testing* for the equality of two values. Use the single equals sign (=) in an assignment statement when you're making two values equal.

In many programming languages, and in the pseudocode in this book, the relational operator for testing whether two values are equal is a double equals sign (==). The single equals sign (=) is used in assignment statements. Don't get the two confused.

Comparing Values with `If`: The Single-Outcome Selection

The simplest selection structure is one in which an action is taken if the condition evaluates to true, but no action is taken if the condition evaluates to false. This structure is called the **single-outcome selection**. In pseudocode, a single-outcome selection consists of three parts:

- The word If, the condition expression, and the word Then
- The statement or statements to be performed (called the **scope** of the selection) if the condition is true; indented for readability
- The words End If lined up under the word If

Here are some examples of single-outcome selections. The following example means "If the value of age is greater than or equal to 65, set the value of discountRate to 0.10":

```
If age >= 65 Then
   discountRate = 0.10
End If
```

This example means "If the value of password is not bottomsUp, display the message Access denied.":

```
If password != "bottomsUp" Then
   Display "Access denied."
End If
```

Finally, this example means "If the value of numCorrect is equal to 3, set bonusPoints to 10 and display the message Congratulations! You win 10 bonus points.":

```
If numCorrect == 3 Then
   bonusPoints = 10
   Display "Congratulations! You win 10 bonus points."
End If
```

When creating a flowchart to represent selection structures, you use the diamond symbol for a condition expression. A question mark at the end of the expression emphasizes that the condition must be evaluated. Because there are only two possible evaluations of the expression—true or false—there are two exits from the diamond symbol, called **branches**, and they should be marked T and F. (You can also label them Y and N for yes and no.) The flowlines on the True side of the condition connect to the actions to take if the condition is true and make up the selection's T branch. In a single-outcome selection, no action is taken on the F branch. In a flowchart, the End If statement in pseudocode is represented by the round connector symbol.

Here are some flowchart segments for single-outcome selections. Figure 5-1 is the flowchart for the first pseudocode example, which sets discountRate to 0.10 if age is greater than or equal to 65.

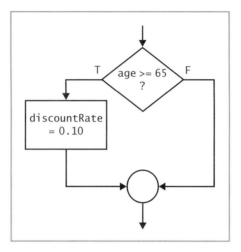

Figure 5-1 A flowchart segment for a single-outcome selection that tests the value of someone's age

Figure 5-2 is the flowchart for the second pseudocode example, which displays the message "Access denied." if password doesn't equal "bottomsUp".

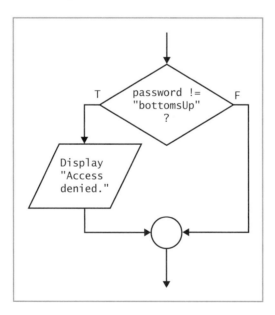

Figure 5-2 A flowchart segment for a single-outcome selection that tests the value of a password

Figure 5-3 is the flowchart for the third pseudocode example, which sets bonusPoints to 10 and displays the message "Congratulations! You win 10 bonus points." if numCorrect equals 3.

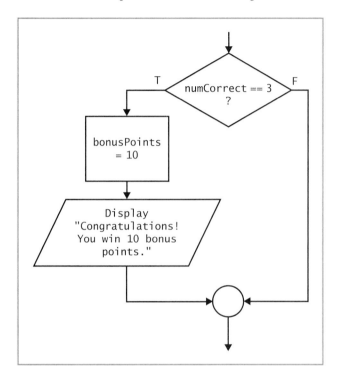

Figure 5-3   A flowchart segment for a single-outcome selection that tests the value of the number of correct items

In Figure 5-3, two statements are performed if the condition evaluates to true: an assignment statement setting the value of bonusPoints and a Display statement. However, it's still a single-outcome selection because nothing happens if the condition evaluates to false. What you have are two statements in sequence on the true side—in other words, a sequence structure within a selection structure.

A selection structure contained in a sequence structure is also possible. In the following example, a user is asked for a test score.

The program displays a "passing grade" message if the score is 60 or above, and then displays an end-of-program message:

```
Display "Enter a test score: "
Input testScore
If testScore >=60 Then
    Display "That is a passing grade."
End If
Display "End of program."
```

Figure 5-4 shows this example in flowchart form. Remember that Display and Input statements are combined into a single symbol in this book's flowcharts.

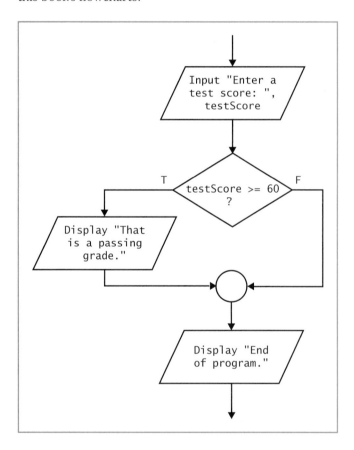

Figure 5-4 A flowchart segment for a selection in a sequence

Conditions: Boolean Expressions

Structures can contain other structures, and they can be contained in other structures. What they can't do is overlap. In both pseudocode and flowcharts, if the program is structured, the structures can be circled without crossing over each other. Figure 5-5 shows the preceding pseudocode example with the structures circled. The Display and Input statements are in sequence, the statements from If to End If make up a selection structure, and the last statement is in sequence.

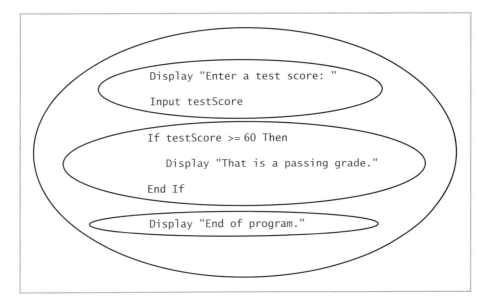

Display "Enter a test score: "

Input testScore

If testScore >= 60 Then

Display "That is a passing grade."

End If

Display "End of program."

Figure 5-5   A pseudocode example with the structures circled

Figure 5-6 shows a flowchart with the structures circled. The Display and Input statements are all in sequence, and the statements from If to End If make up a selection structure.

Structures can't overlap each other.

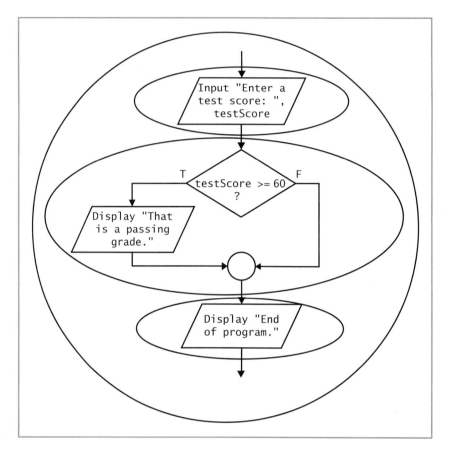

Figure 5-6   A flowchart example with the structures circled

Comparing Values with If and Else: The Dual-Outcome Selection

As you've learned, a single-outcome selection performs an action if the condition evaluates to true but does nothing if the condition is false. A **dual-outcome selection** performs one set of steps if the condition is true and a different set of steps if the condition is false. The keyword Else indicates the steps to be performed if the condition evaluates to false. It means the same as "otherwise." Here's a simple example in pseudocode that means "If the value of testScore is greater than or equal to 60, display the message "That is a passing grade."; otherwise, display "That is a failing grade." as the message.

```
If testScore >= 60 Then
    Display "That is a passing grade."
Else
    Display "That is a failing grade."
End If
```

Notice that the word Else aligns with the words If and End If, and Display statements are indented for readability. Figure 5-7 shows the same dual-outcome selection represented as a flowchart.

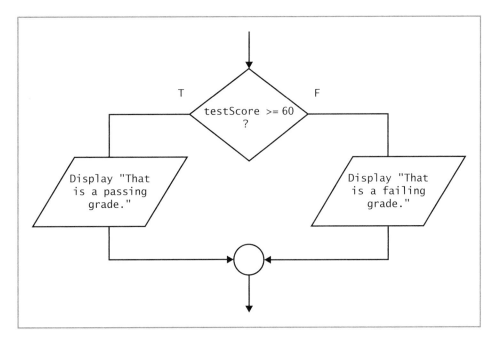

Figure 5-7 A flowchart for a dual-outcome selection

The flowlines join together after the actions on each side have been performed to indicate the end of the selection structure. The structure consists of the condition and any steps performed as a result of evaluating the condition.

As with single-outcome selections, the branches of a dual-outcome selection can consist of more than one statement. In the following example, an employee's gross pay is computed differently if the employee worked more than 40 hours during the week. Assume the values for hoursWorked and wageRate have already been input, and grossPay, regularPay, overtimeHours, and overtimePay have been declared as numeric:

Don't confuse a condition with a structure. A selection structure includes the condition as well as the steps taken as a result of the condition evaluating to true or false.

```
If hoursWorked > 40 Then
   overtimeHours = hoursWorked - 40
   overtimePay = overtimeHours * wageRate * 1.5
   regularPay = 40 * wageRate
   grossPay = regularPay + overtimePay
Else
   grossPay = hoursWorked * wageRate
End If
```

As you can see in Figure 5-8's flowchart, this example includes a sequence inside a selection structure.

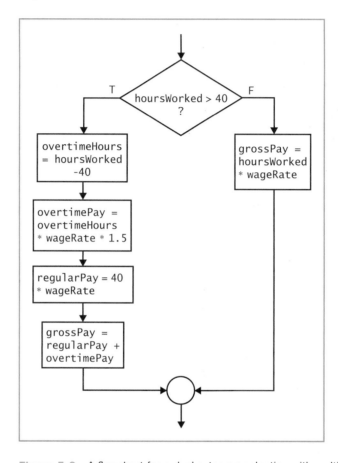

 As you design your programs, use structures as your building blocks.

Figure 5-8 A flowchart for a dual-outcome selection with multiple actions

The Selection Structure in JavaScript

 Make sure the beginning and end of your structures are clearly defined.

Knowing exactly which statements belong to a selection's scope is important. Pseudocode uses indentation and the keywords End If to define the scope. Flowcharts use flowlines that connect the actions to be performed on the true and false branches, and the flowlines meet at a connector symbol to indicate the end of the selection structure.

Now that you have seen how single-outcome and dual-outcome algorithms are designed with pseudocode and flowcharts, it's time to try them out in JavaScript. Here's how selection structures are written in JavaScript:

- The `if` and `else` keywords are lowercase.

- The `then` keyword isn't used.

- Conditions are placed inside parentheses.

- Braces (`{ }`) are used to define the scope of a selection's true and false branches. The opening brace marks the beginning of the scope, and the closing brace marks the end of the scope.

In this book's examples, the opening brace is placed on the same line as the keyword `if` or `else`, and all statements in the scope are indented. The closing brace lines up under the word `if`.

Take another look at the first single-outcome selection in this chapter:

```
If age >= 65 Then
    discountRate = 0.10
End If
```

Here's the JavaScript code for this algorithm:

```
if (age >= 65) {
    discountRate = 0.10;
}
```

Notice that a semicolon is added after the assignment statement setting `discountRate` to 0.10 but not after the line with the condition. That's because a condition is not a statement.

Converting a dual-outcome selection to JavaScript is similar. Here's the pseudocode for the previous example of a dual-outcome selection:

```
If testScore >= 60 Then
    Display "That is a passing grade."
Else
    Display "That is a failing grade."
End If
```

The JavaScript code for this algorithm is as follows:

```
if (testScore >= 60) {
    document.write("That is a passing grade.");
}
else {
    document.write("That is a failing grade.");
}
```

In JavaScript and other languages, you can omit the braces if the scope includes only a single statement. However, including braces for all selection structures is a good habit to get into because you don't have to remember to insert them later if you add

Don't put a semicolon after the condition in a selection structure; you should add one only after the statements that are part of the condition's scope. Using a semicolon after the condition ends the selection structure at that point, and statements following it are performed no matter what the evaluation of the condition is.

Notice the separate set of braces for the `if` statement and `else` statement. No separate set of braces is used to enclose the entire structure.

Use braces for all selection structures, even if the scope of the true or false branch consists of only one statement.

a statement to the scope of the true or false branch. In addition, your programs are easier to read if you're consistent in the way you write them.

Now take the example of the algorithm that computes overtime pay and make it into a complete pseudocode program.

PROGRAM 5-1 Pseudocode Program
overtimeCalculator.txt

Remember to add a blank line after the code section in each step.

1. Open a new document in Notepad, and save it as **overtimeCalculator.txt**.

2. Enter the usual documentation lines:

```
// Program name: Overtime Calculator
// Purpose: Calculate gross pay with overtime
// Author: Paul Addison
// Date last modified: 01-Sep-2011
```

3. Next, declare your variables:

```
Start
    Declare Numeric hoursWorked      // current
      balance
    Declare Numeric wageRate         // annual
      interest rate
    Declare Numeric grossPay         // interest
      amount
    Declare Numeric overtimeHours    // number of
      hours > 40
    Declare Numeric overtimePay      // pay for
      overtime hours
    Declare Numeric regularPay       // pay for first
      40 hours
```

4. Welcome the user and prompt for hours worked and wage rate:

```
// Welcome the user
// Ask for hours worked and wage rate
Display "Welcome to the overtime calculator!"
Display "Enter the number of hours worked: "
Input hoursWorked
Display "Enter the wage rate: "
Input wageRate
```

(continues)

(continued)

5. Include the dual-outcome selection developed earlier:

```
// Calculate gross pay
// Hours over 40 paid at time and a half
If hoursWorked > 40 Then
    overtimeHours = hoursWorked - 40
    overtimePay = overtimeHours * wageRate * 1.5
    regularPay = 40 * wageRate
    grossPay = regularPay + overtimePay
Else
    grossPay = hoursWorked * wageRate
End If
```

6. Display the gross pay:

```
// Display the result
Display "Gross pay: " + grossPay
```

7. Thank the user and end the program:

```
// Thank the user and end the program
Display "Thank you!"
Stop
```

8. Save the file again.

Next, you convert the program to JavaScript. Remember the following guidelines:

- Put parentheses around conditions.

- Use braces to mark the scope of the selection's true and false branches.

- Use constants as needed to make your code and the output easy to read.

- Use the toFixed() method to format the gross pay amount with two decimal places.

 Detective Work

Open a new document in Notepad, and save it as overtimeCalculator. html. Enter the JavaScript code, save the file again, and open it in a Web browser. Enter 45 for the number of hours worked and 15.50 for the wage. Your browser page should look like Figure 5-9. If the program doesn't run correctly, compare your code with overtimeCalculator-solution.html in your student data files.

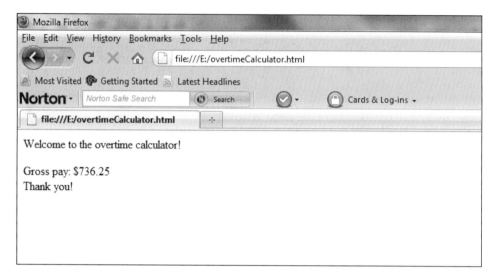

Figure 5-9   The overtimeCalculator.html program in a Web browser

Nested Selections

As you have learned, a structure can be contained inside another structure. You have seen examples of sequence structures inside selections and selections inside sequence structures. Selections can also be nested inside other selections. In some instances, a second condition must be evaluated before determining the correct programming steps. A selection contained in the scope of another selection is called a **nested selection**.

Suppose all students in grade 12 at a high school are to be selected for a field trip, but the boys are leaving on the 8:30 a.m. bus and the girls are leaving at 9:00 a.m. The algorithm must include the following:

- The first (or outer) selection structure asks whether the student's grade level is equal to 12. If not, no action is taken. This outer structure is a single-outcome selection.

- On the true branch of the selection, a second (or inner) selection determines the student's gender by asking the user to enter M for male or F for female. If M is entered, a message is displayed that the bus leaves at 8:30 a.m. If not, a message is displayed that the bus leaves at 9:00 a.m. The inner selection is a dual-outcome selection.

- The inner structure is enclosed by the outer structure and is, therefore, said to be nested.

The pseudocode looks like this:

```
If gradeLevel == 12 Then
   Display "Enter M for male, or F for female: "
   Input gender
   If gender == "M" Then
      Display "Your bus leaves at 8:30 a.m."
   Else
      Display "Your bus leaves at 9:00 a.m."
   End If
End If
```

The JavaScript code for this program segment is as follows:

```
if (gradeLevel == 12) {
   gender = prompt("Enter M for male, or F for female: ",ES);
   if (gender == "M") {
      document.write("Your bus leaves at 8:30 a.m." + BR);
   }
   else {
      document.write("Your bus leaves at 9:00 a.m." + BR);
   }
}
```

Notice in the JavaScript code that there's one set of braces for the overall selection, one set for the if branch for males, and one set for the else branch for non-males. In Figure 5-10's flowchart, the selection structure for the student's gender is contained in the true branch of the selection structure for the student's grade level.

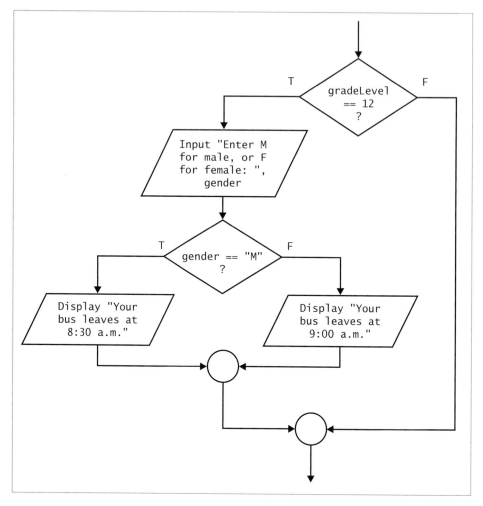

Figure 5-10   The flowchart for determining bus times by gender and grade level

Although there's no value between true and false for a single condition, you can have several different conditions you want to test for a variable. A grading scale, for example, might assign the following letter grades:

- A if the grade percentage is greater than or equal to 90

- B if it's greater than or equal to 80 and less than 90

- C if it's greater than or equal to 70 and less than 80

- D if it's greater than or equal to 60 and less than 70

- F if the grade percentage is less than 60

Logically, you can create this grading scale with several selection statements. After testing to see whether the percentage is 90 or higher, you can test to see whether it's *both* greater than or equal to 80 *and* less than 90. You would be testing two conditions for each of the B, C, and D grades. (You learn more about combining conditions in Chapter 7.)

However, testing for all five grades in this way is inefficient. Why? Because if the first condition is true, the grade is determined to be A. There's no need to test it again to see whether it's between 80 and 90, between 70 and 80, and so forth. Testing each condition separately requires evaluating each grade five times, even if the grade is determined with the first evaluation.

The efficient solution is testing the score for a value between 80 and 90 *only if* the first condition is false. If you know that the percentage isn't 90 or greater, you can test next to see whether it's 80 or greater. If so, the grade is B. If not, test to see whether it's 70 or greater, and so on. If grades happen to be distributed evenly and 1 of every 5 students receives an A, you have saved four comparisons for all those students.

Use your knowledge of programming to write efficient algorithms. Don't make the computer perform unnecessary steps by testing conditions after the outcomes are already known.

This solution can be accomplished with nested selections:

1. If the first condition is false, check to see whether the percentage is between 80 and 90. This check is a selection nested inside the first condition because it's part of the condition's false branch.

2. If the second condition is true, the grade B is assigned. If not, another selection is nested inside this condition's false branch to test whether the percentage is between 70 and 80.

3. If this third condition is true, the grade is a C. If not, the condition's false branch tests whether the percentage is between 60 and 70.

4. If this fourth condition is true, the grade is a D. If this condition evaluates to false, no more testing is needed; and the grade assigned is an F. This statement is placed under the last `Else`.

Nested selections, when written formally, require indentations for each new `Else`, and programs with several levels of nesting can be hard to follow. (You learn two ways of making code look neater shortly.) The pseudocode for this algorithm looks like this:

```
If gradePct >= 90 Then
    letterGrade = "A"
Else
    If gradePct >= 80 Then
        letterGrade = "B"
    Else
        If gradePct >= 70 Then
            letterGrade = "C"
```

```
            Else
                If gradePct >= 60 Then
                    letterGrade = "D"
                Else
                    letterGrade = "F"
                End If
            End If
        End If
    End If
```

Each false branch leads to another selection, until the grade percentage is checked for being 60 or greater. If it is, the grade D is assigned, and if not, an F is assigned. Note that all selections except the first are enclosed by the preceding selection. Figure 5-11 shows the flowchart for this pseudocode.

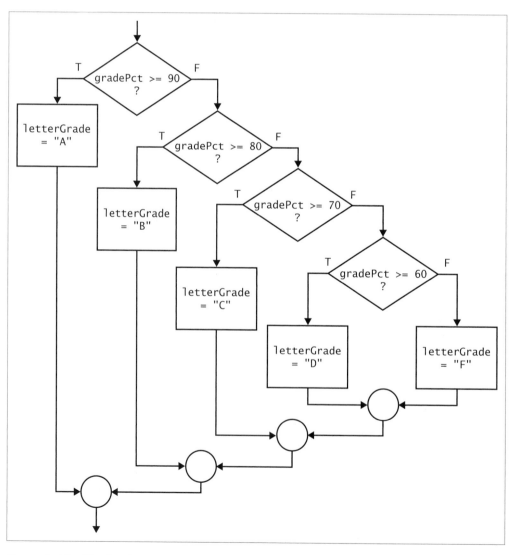

Figure 5-11   The flowchart for assigning letter grades

Streamlining Nested Selections: *Else If* and the *Case* Structure

Fortunately, developers of pseudocode and other programming languages recognized the awkwardness of having so many levels of indentation, so a variation is allowed that treats `Else If` as a single keyword that can be placed on one line. This variation doesn't require additional indents for each structure and or a closing `End If` for nested selection structures; an `End If` is required only for the outermost structure. As you can see, the pseudocode is much easier to read with this variation:

```
If gradePct >= 90 Then
    letterGrade = "A"
Else If gradePct >= 80 Then
    letterGrade = "B"
Else If gradePct >= 70 Then
    letterGrade = "C"
Else If gradePct >= 60 Then
    letterGrade = "D"
Else
    letterGrade = "F"
End If
```

JavaScript also allows using the keywords `else if` together and doesn't require nested braces around nested structures. Braces are used only for each scope in a condition. The JavaScript for the preceding pseudocode looks like this:

```
if (gradePct >= 90) {
    letterGrade = "A";
}
else if (gradePct >= 80) {
    letterGrade = "B";
}
else if (gradePct >= 70) {
    letterGrade = "C";
}
else if (gradePct >= 60) {
    letterGrade = "D";
}
else {
    letterGrade = "F";
}
```

For nested selections that test the same variable for different values, developers created the **Case structure**, which is actually a variation of the selection structure. A `Case` structure starts with the pseudocode keyword `Select`, followed by the name of the variable to test for equality with a variety of values, and ends with a colon. Each condition to test includes the keyword `Case`, followed by the value to match with the variable, and it ends with a colon. The last

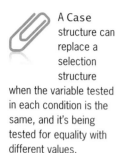

A Case structure can replace a selection structure when the variable tested in each condition is the same, and it's being tested for equality with different values.

Case statement, corresponding to the final Else in the previous pseudocode example, is called the Default case and catches all instances in which the value hasn't been matched yet.

In the following pseudocode example, the values 9, 10, 11, and 12 have been assigned to the variable gradeLevel to represent a student's grade level in school. A corresponding message is displayed based on the student's grade level. If no values match the data, a default message is displayed.

```
Select gradeLevel:
    Case 9:
        Display "You are a freshman."
    Case 10:
        Display "You are a sophomore."
    Case 11:
        Display "You are a junior."
    Case 12:
        Display "You are a senior."
    Default:
        Display "You are not in grades 9-12."
End Select
```

A Case structure also looks neater than a nested structure in a flow-chart (see Figure 5-12), with a single diamond symbol containing the variable being tested and a question mark. The processes for each tested value are placed in a single row, and the values next to flow-lines lead to the corresponding processes.

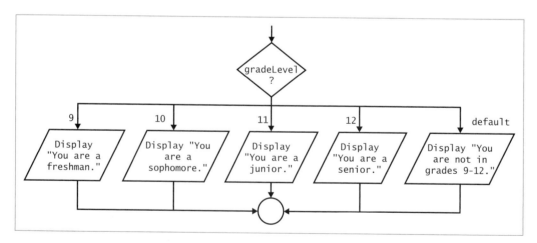

Figure 5-12   A flowchart for a Case structure

You can include multiple values when testing variables in a Case structure. The following pseudocode shows a more general version of the preceding algorithm. A message is displayed in which students in

184

grades 9, 10, 11, and 12 are considered to be in high school; students in grades 6, 7, and 8 are in middle school; and students in grades 1, 2, 3, 4, and 5 are in elementary school. (The values for a combined comparison can be in any order.)

```
Select gradeLevel:
   Case 9: Case 10: Case 11: Case 12:
      Display "You are in high school."
   Case 6: Case 7: Case 8:
      Display "You are in middle school."
   Case 1: Case 2: Case 3: Case 4: Case 5:
      Display "You are in elementary school."
   Default:
      Display "You are not in grades 1-12."
End Select
```

In some languages, including JavaScript, the Case structure can test only for equality of values, not inequalities using ranges of numbers. Therefore, the example of grades doesn't work in a JavaScript case structure. Also, a Case structure is limited in most languages to integers (whole numbers) and text characters, not decimal numbers.

In JavaScript, a Case structure starts with the keyword switch, and the name of the variable to test is enclosed in parentheses. The entire structure is enclosed in a set of braces. The scope for each condition doesn't have to be enclosed in a separate set of braces. However, before the next condition begins, you need to include the break command to exit the Case structure. Otherwise, the computer carries out *all* statements following the matching condition line.

In most languages, a Case structure uses the matching condition as an entry point to the structure, with all subsequent statements performed. In actuality, it's used most often when conditions are treated separately. The break command, which is an exception to structured programming principles, is the most efficient way to exit a Case structure.

The preceding example is written in JavaScript like this:

```
switch (gradeLevel)
{
   case 9: case 10: case 11: case 12:
      document.write("You are in high school.");
      break;
   case 6: case 7: case 8:
      document.write("You are in middle school.");
      break;
   case 1: case 2: case 3: case 4: case 5:
      document.write("You are in elementary school.");
      break;
   default:
      document.write("You are not in grades 1-12.");
}
```

The selection structure and its variations with Else If statements and Case structures are among the most powerful tools a programmer has. With them, you're instructing the computer on how to make decisions.

Programmer's Workshop

In this Programmer's Workshop, you create a customer ordering program for the small online store Bulk Is Best, which sells many items in large quantities from its warehouse in Idaho. This week, Bulk Is Best is having a sale on packages of paper towels. The price for a single six-roll package is $2.50, but if the customer orders six or more packages, the price per package goes down to $2.00. In addition, the customer enters the two-letter abbreviation for the state to which the order should be shipped. If the state is Idaho (abbreviated as "ID"), shipping is free, but shipping to any other state is $4.00.

Your task is to design a program that does the following:

- Welcomes the customer and asks for first and last name

- Asks the customer to enter the number of packages to be ordered

- Asks the customer to enter the two-letter state abbreviation

- Computes the cost of the order and displays the following:

  - Customer's name and state abbreviation

  - Number of packages ordered, price per package, and total package cost

  - Shipping cost

  - Total cost of the order

Discussion: Start with the IPO method:

- What outputs are requested?

  - Customer's name (string): `custName`

  - Package price (numeric): `pkgPrice`

  - Total package cost (numeric): `totPkgCost`

  - State to ship to (string): `state`

  - Shipping cost (numeric): `shipCost`

  - Total order cost (numeric): `totOrderCost`

- What inputs do you have available?

  - Customer's first and last name (string): `firstName`, `lastName`

  - State abbreviation (string): `state`

  - Number of packages ordered (numeric): `numPkgs`

- What processing is required?

  - Concatenate first and last name to create a single customer name.

  - Determine which package cost to use based on quantity ordered.

  - Determine which shipping cost to use based on the state abbreviation.

  - Calculate total package cost by multiplying quantity by package cost.

  - Add shipping cost to total package cost to get total order cost.

First, write the pseudocode program for calculating paper towel ordering for Bulk Is Best. Don't forget to add blank lines as usual to improve your program's readability.

1. Open a new document in Notepad, and save it as **bulkIsBestOrdering.txt**. Enter the documentation lines:

```
// Program name: Bulk Is Best Ordering
// Purpose: Take orders for packages
// of paper towels
//    Pricing is based on quantity ordered
//    Shipping cost is based on state
// Author: Paul Addison
// Date last modified: 01-Sep-2011
```

2. Start the program and declare your variables:

```
Start
    // Declare variables
    // # of packages ordered
    Declare Numeric numPkgs
    // cost of one package
    Declare Numeric pkgPrice
    // total cost of packages
    Declare Numeric totPkgCost
    // shipping cost
    Declare Numeric shipCost
    // total cost of order
    Declare Numeric totOrderCost
    // customer first name
    Declare String firstName
    // customer last name
    Declare String lastName
    // customer full name
    Declare String custName
    // state to be shipped to
    Declare String state
```

3. Welcome the user and prompt for name, number of packages, and state to ship to:

```
// Welcome the user
// Ask for ordering information
Display "Welcome to Bulk Is Best!"
Display "Please enter your first name: "
Input firstName
Display "Please enter your last name: "
Input lastName
Display "Enter the number of"
Display "paper towel packages: "
Input numPkgs
Display "Enter the state to ship to: "
Input state
```

4. Concatenate the customer's name, and compute the package price and shipping cost:

```
// Concatenate first and last name
custName = firstName + " " + lastName

// Compute per package price and shipping cost
If numPkgs >= 6 Then
    pkgPrice = 2.00
Else
   pkgPrice = 2.50
End If

If state == "ID" Then
    shipCost = 0.00
Else
    shipCost = 4.00
End If
```

5. Compute the totals and display the order information:

```
// Compute and display order totals
totPkgCost = pkgCost * numPkgs
totOrderCost = totPkgCost + shipCost
Display "Order Summary for " + custName
Display "Number packages ordered: " + numPkgs
Display "Price per package: " + pkgPrice
Display "Subtotal: " + totPkgCost
Display "Order will be shipped to: " + state
Display "Shipping cost: " + shipCost
Display "Order total: " + totOrderCost
```

6. Thank the user and end the program:

```
// Thank the user and end the program
Display "Thank you!"
Stop
```

7. Save the file again.

Detective Work

Now trying converting this pseudocode program to JavaScript. Open
a new document in Notepad, save it as bulkIsBestOrdering.html, and
enter the JavaScript code. Save the file again, and open it in a browser.
Enter Carmen for the first name, SanDiego for the last name, 22
for the number of packages, and FL for the state abbreviation. Your
browser page should look like Figure 5-13. You can compare your
code with bulkIsBestOrdering-solution.html in your student data files
if your program doesn't run correctly.

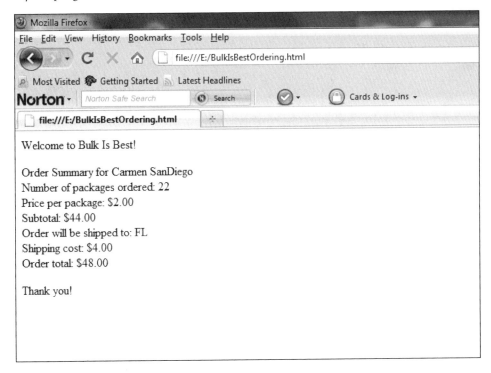

Figure 5-13   The bulkIsBestOrdering.html program in a Web browser

 **Object Lesson**

In the Object Lesson for this chapter, you design an order form for
MovieStream, which lets customers stream movies for instant viewing or download them for later viewing (up to 7 days after download).
MovieStream is offering a special on some classic movies this week:
$3.99 to stream the movie and $4.99 to download it.

This program is object-based, so in the <head> section of the HTML file, you create a constructor method for a MovieOrder class that contains variables for the movie title and movie price. The constructor method also sets the price to $3.99 or $4.99, depending on the delivery type requested. Therefore, this method needs to use a selection structure. It should also call a method for displaying information about an order.

In the <body> section of the HTML file, your program prompts the user to enter a number for the movie:

- 1 to order *Star Wars*

- 2 to order *E.T.*

- 3 to order *Raiders of the Lost Ark*

- If the user enters a different number, an "Invalid choice" message is displayed, and the movie title field is set to an empty string. (Data validation is discussed in more detail in Chapter 9.)

- If you want to put a line break in a JavaScript prompt, you need to use a special "newline" character that's different from the HTML tag because the prompt string is processed by JavaScript, not HTML. Declare a constant called NL, set it to "\n", and use it in the prompt. Here's the JavaScript code for this prompt:

```
// Get movie choice from user
choice = prompt("Enter 1 to order STAR WARS," + NL
    + "    2 for E.T., or" + NL
    + "    3 for RAIDERS OF THE LOST ARK",ES);
```

Based on the numbers entered, the program determines the movie name by using a selection structure. Next, the program asks the user for the delivery type:

- S to stream the movie

- D to download the movie for later viewing

Next, the program calls the constructor method to create an object for the movie order, sending it arguments for the movie title and the delivery type. Then it calls the method for displaying information about the order.

Start with a class diagram (see Figure 5-14). The constructor takes two arguments (for the movie title and delivery type).

MovieOrder
String movieName Numeric moviePrice
MovieOrder (String name, String deliv) displayInfo()

Figure 5-14   The class diagram for the `MovieOrder` class

Now you're ready to create the pseudocode for the MovieOrder class and the algorithm for prompting the user, creating the order, and displaying the information. Remember to add blank lines after the code section in each step.

1. Open a new document in Notepad, and save it as **MovieOrderClass.txt**. Enter the documentation lines:

    ```
    // Program name: Movie Order Class
    // Purpose: Create an order from MovieOrder class
    // Author: Paul Addison
    // Date last modified: 01-Sep-2011
    ```

2. Start the class definition and declare the class variables:

    ```
    Class MovieOrder
       // Variables
       String movieName      // title of movie
       Numeric moviePrice    // price of movie
    ```

3. Enter the constructor method and the method to display information, and then end the class definition:

    ```
    // Constructor method for movie order
    Constructor Method MovieOrder(String name, ↵
      String deliv)
        movieName = name
        If deliv == "S" Then
           moviePrice = 3.99
        Else
           moviePrice = 4.99
        End If
    End Method

    // Method to display information about order
    Method displayInfo()
        Display "Movie name: " + movieName
        Display "Price: " + moviePrice
    End Method
    End Class
    ```

4. Next, start the pseudocode section for creating a `MovieOrder` object by declaring variables and welcoming the user:

```
Start
    // Variables
    Numeric choice        // # of movie selection
    String movie          // name of movie
    String deliveryType   // delivery type (S or D)

    // Welcome the user
    Display "Welcome to MovieStream!"
```

5. Get the movie choice and delivery type from the user:

```
    // Get movie choice from user
    Display "Enter 1 to order STAR WARS,"
    Display "      2 for E.T., or"
    Display "      3 for RAIDERS OF THE LOST ARK"
    Input choice

    // Determine title
    If choice == 1 Then
        movie = "Star Wars"
    Else If choice == 2 Then
        movie = "E.T."
    Else If choice == 3 Then
        movie = "Raiders of the Lost Ark"
    Else
        movie = ""
        Display "Invalid choice."
    End If

    // Get delivery type from user
    Display "Enter S to stream movie"
    Display "or D to download: "
    Input deliveryType
```

6. Call the constructor method to create the object and the method to display information:

```
    // Call constructor method to create order
    // Call method to display movie name and price
    MovieOrder myOrder = new MovieOrder
    (movie, deliveryType)
    myOrder.displayInfo()
```

7. Thank the user and end the program:

```
    // Thank the user
    Display "Thank you!"
Stop
```

8. Save the file again.

Detective Work

Now try converting this pseudocode to JavaScript. Open a new document in Notepad, and save it as MovieOrderClass.html. Enter the JavaScript code, and refer back to the instructions given at the beginning of this Object Lesson if you need a reminder about using the NL constant in the prompt. When you're finished, save the file again, and open it in a browser for testing. Enter 3 for the movie selection and D for the delivery type. Your browser page should look like Figure 5-15. If your program doesn't run correctly, compare it with MovieOrderClass-solution.html in your student data files.

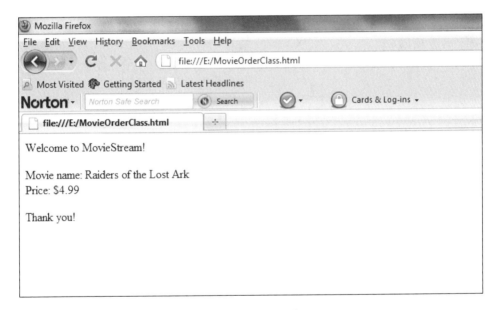

The MovieOrderClass.html file in a Web browser

Chapter Summary

- A condition is an expression that compares two values by using a relational operator.

- A Boolean expression is a condition that evaluates as true or false.

- A selection structure is made up of a Boolean expression, statements to be performed if it's evaluated as true, and (optionally) other statements to be performed if it's evaluated as false.

- There are six relational operators: less than (<), greater than (>), equal to (==), less than or equal to (<=), greater than or equal to (>=), and not equal to (!=).

- The true and false exits from a condition are called the selection's branches, and the steps to be performed make up the selection's scope.

- A single-outcome selection performs one action if the condition is true but doesn't perform any action if the condition is false.

- A dual-outcome selection performs one action if the condition is true and a different action if the condition is false.

- A branch of a selection can include another selection structure; this arrangement is called a nested selection.

- When an If statement is included in the Else branch of a selection, the words Else If can be combined on one line to reduce lines of code and indentation levels.

- A Case structure is a variation of the If/Else If structure, in which a single variable is tested for equality with many different values. In some languages, Case structures are limited to evaluating only equalities, not inequalities, and are limited to numeric integers and characters, not decimal numbers.

Key Terms

Boolean expression—A condition that can be evaluated as true or false.

branch—One of the two paths taken as a result of evaluating a condition; referred to as the true branch or false branch.

Case structure—A variation of the selection structure, in which a single variable is checked for equality against many different values.

condition—A statement comparing values, usually with a relational operator.

dual-outcome selection—A selection in which one or more statements are performed if the condition is true, and another statement or set of statements is performed if the condition is false.

nested selection—A selection contained entirely in the scope of another selection.

relational operator—A symbol used to compare two values.

scope—The statements that are performed as a result of the true or false evaluation of a condition.

selection structure—A control structure in which a condition is evaluated and one or more statements are performed as a result of the evaluation.

single-outcome selection—A selection in which one or more statements are performed if the condition is true, but no statements are performed if the condition is false.

Review Questions

True/False

1. A Boolean expression is a condition that can be evaluated as true or false. True or False?

2. Every statement using the keyword If must also include the keyword Else. True or False?

3. A single-outcome selection performs one or more statements if a condition is true but none if the condition is false. True or False?

4. A dual-outcome selection performs no statements if a condition is true but performs one or more statements if the condition is false. True or False?

5. Structures can overlap other structures, but they can't be contained completely in another structure. True or False?

6. Many languages allow placing Else If on one line, even though the If is really a nested selection. True or False?

7. A Case structure can be used when testing several different variables. True or False?

8. In all languages, a Case structure can test for a range of values by using one of the inequality relational operators. True or False?

9. You use a single equals sign (=) when you're assigning a value to a variable. True or False?

10. You use a double equals sign (==) when you're testing for the equality of two values. True or False?

Multiple Choice

1. How many resulting values are possible for evaluating a Boolean expression?

    a. 1

    b. 2

    c. 3

    d. unlimited

2. A selection in which statements are performed when the condition is true but aren't performed when the condition is false is called a _____ selection.

    a. single-outcome

    b. dual-outcome

    c. true-only

    d. simple

3. A selection in which one or more statements are performed when the condition is true and another statement or set of statements is performed when the condition is false is called a _____ selection.

    a. single-outcome

    b. dual-outcome

    c. true-only

    d. simple

4. Many languages allow treating the words `Else If` as a single keyword for which of the following reasons? (Choose all that apply.)

   a. reducing lines of code

   b. eliminating the need for multiple indentations

   c. eliminating the need for `End If` after each condition

   d. reducing processing time

5. A `Case` structure is a variation of which of the following?

   a. the single-outcome selection

   b. a series of sequential statements

   c. a series of nested `If/Else If` statements

   d. the `Display` and `Input` statements

6. When testing for the equality of two values in JavaScript, a condition uses which of the following?

   a. a single equals sign (=)

   b. a double equals sign (==)

   c. the "not equal to" operator (!=)

   d. the "less than or equal to" operator (<=)

7. A `Case` structure can test for equality of which of the following? (Choose all that apply.)

   a. integers

   b. text characters

   c. decimal numbers

   d. square roots

8. A selection structure contains which of the following? (Choose all that apply.)

   a. statements to be performed in both branches

   b. the keyword `If` and possibly `Else`

   c. a Boolean expression

   d. the scope of statements to be performed, depending on the condition's evaluation

9. A condition has _____ entry point(s) and _____ exit(s).

    a. 1, 1

    b. 1, 2

    c. 2, 1

    d. 2, 2

Discussion Questions

1. When should you use a single-outcome selection, and when should you use a dual-outcome selection?

2. What are the advantages of using an `If/Else If` statement rather than nested `If/Else` statements?

3. What can a series of `If/Else If` statements do that a `Case` structure can't do in some languages?

Hands-On Activities

Hands-On Activity 5-1

The manager of Guaranteed Gaskets has discovered a leak in the warehouse attic. It's raining, so he has placed a 25-liter bucket under the leak to catch the rain. He wants you to design a program to keep track of the amount of rain accumulated in the bucket as long as it's raining.

Every 10 minutes, you're to check the water level in the bucket and record it in the program. If the level is 20 liters or higher, the program should display a message reminding you to empty the bucket and put it back. Otherwise, the program should display a message reminding you to come back in 10 minutes and run the program again.

Using pseudocode, design a complete algorithm for displaying different messages based on the water level in the bucket. Save your pseudocode file as rainBucketMonitor.txt.

Hands-On Activity 5-2

The manager of Guaranteed Gaskets wants to see your program in action, so he asks you to develop it in JavaScript and show him how it works.

Convert the pseudocode program you wrote for Hands-On Activity 5-1 to JavaScript, and save the file as rainBucketMonitor.html.

Hands-On Activity 5-3

Design a complete algorithm that determines the sales tax on purchases under $1.00 for a state with a 7% sales tax rate. Display the sales tax amount if the number of cents entered was 99 or less; otherwise, display an error message.

Instead of multiplying the amount of the sale by 7% and rounding, use the following list to determine the exact amount of sales tax:

- 0 to 7 cents: no tax

- 8 to 21 cents: 1 cent tax

- 22 to 35 cents: 2 cents tax

- 36 to 49 cents: 3 cents tax

- 50 to 64 cents: 4 cents tax

- 65 to 78 cents: 5 cents tax

- 79 to 92 cents: 6 cents tax

- 93 to 99 cents: 7 cents tax

Hint: Because a Case structure can't handle ranges of numbers or inequalities in JavaScript, a series of If/Else If statements should be used. Have the user enter the number of cents with no decimal point.

Using pseudocode, design an algorithm for looking up the sales tax for amounts under $1.00. Save your pseudocode file as salesTaxLookup.txt.

Hands-On Activity 5-4

Use JavaScript to implement the algorithm in Hands-On Activity 5-3. Test your program, and use the list in Hands-On Activity 5-3 to see whether your program is computing the tax correctly. Save your JavaScript file as salesTaxLookup.html.

Adding a Selection Structure to It's War!

You're ready for one of the most important parts of the War card game: comparing card values to see who wins each hand. Now that you understand the selection structure, you can easily determine who wins each hand and add the cards' point values to the winning player's total.

Remember that values for the jack, queen, king, and ace are entered as J, Q, K, and A. As a result, before you can compare the points of each card played, you need to test whether the card values are J, Q, K, or A and convert them to their corresponding point values (11, 12, 13, and 14).

A quick review of the rules is in order here:

- The point values for cards 2 through 10 are the same as their face values. Face cards need to be converted to their point values. In pseudocode, a string is converted to a number with the `stringToNumber()` function.

- The player who wins the hand gets the combined point values of the cards played added to his or her total.

- If the card values are equal, the combined point values go into a holding area and stay there until the next hand that a player wins.

- As a result, whenever a player wins a hand, any points in the holding area should be added to the winning player's score, and the hold points should be reset to 0.

An `If/Else If` structure works nicely for this purpose. You can test first whether the card is a face card and convert it to its point value; otherwise, assign the card's face value as the point value.

Open your warGame-ch4.txt file from Chapter 4, and save it as warGame-ch5.txt. After the lines that display the cards played, insert a blank line and enter these lines:

```
// Convert jack, queen, king, or ace
// to points for the first player
If cardName1 == "J" Then
    cardPoints1 = 11
Else If cardName1 == "Q" Then
    cardPoints1 = 12
Else If cardName1 == "K" Then
    cardPoints1 = 13
Else If cardName1 == "A" Then
    cardPoints1 = 14
Else
    cardPoints1 = stringToNumber(cardName1)
End If

// Convert jack, queen, king, or ace
// to points for the second player
If cardName2 == "J" Then
    cardPoints2 = 11
Else If cardName2 == "Q" Then
    cardPoints2 = 12
```

Functions to convert strings to numbers and numbers to strings are discussed in more detail in Chapter 9.

```
    Else If cardName2 == "K" Then
        cardPoints2 = 13
    Else If cardName1 == "A" Then
        cardPoints2 = 14
    Else
        cardPoints2 = stringToNumber(cardName2)
    End If
```

Insert a blank lines, and then assign the combined points to the winning player (don't forget to add the hold points) or add them to the hold points if the card values are equal. Then display the current score and the points in the hold area. Enter the following lines:

```
// Compare cards
// Combined points and hold points go to winner
// In case of tie, combined points go into hold area

// Player 1 wins hand
If cardPoints1 > cardPoints2 Then
    score1 = score1 + cardPoints1 + cardPoints2 + ↵
      holdPoints
    holdPoints = 0

// Player 2 wins hand
Else If cardPoints2 > cardPoints1 Then
    score2 = score2 + cardPoints1 + cardPoints2 + ↵
      holdPoints
    holdPoints = 0

// Tie hand
Else
    holdPoints = holdPoints + cardPoints1 + cardPoints2
End If

// Display current score
Display "Current score:"
Display player1 + ": " + score1
Display player2 + ": " + score2
Display holdPoints + " points in hold area"
```

Save the file. It should look like warGame-ch5-solution.txt in your student data files.

Now you can make the changes in JavaScript. In Notepad, open the warGame-ch4.html file, and save it as warGame-ch5.html. After the line prompting the user for the second player's card, insert the following lines to convert the jack, queen, king, and ace to point values. Remember that the card name is entered as text, so you need to use the parseInt() function to convert the card name to the cardPoints variable.

```
// Convert jack, queen, king, or ace
// to points for the first player
if (cardName1 == "J") {
    cardPoints1 = 11;
}
```

```
else if (cardName1 == "Q") {
   cardPoints1 = 12;
}
else if (cardName1 == "K") {
   cardPoints1 = 13;
}
else if (cardName1 == "A") {
   cardPoints1 = 14;
}
else {
   cardPoints1 = parseInt(cardName1);
}

// Convert jack, queen, king, or ace
// to points for the second player
if (cardName2 == "J") {
   cardPoints2 = 11;
}
else if (cardName2 == "Q") {
   cardPoints2 = 12;
}
else if (cardName2 == "K") {
   cardPoints2 = 13;
}
else if (cardName2 == "A") {
   cardPoints2 = 14;
}
else {
   cardPoints2 = parseInt(cardName2);
}
```

Next, insert the code to compare values and assign the combined points to the winning player or to the hold area. Remember to clear the hold area if one of the players wins the hand:

```
// Compare cards
// Combined points and hold points go to winner
// In case of tie, combined points go into hold area

// Player 1 wins hand
if (cardPoints1 > cardPoints2) {
   score1 = score1 + cardPoints1 + cardPoints2 + holdPoints;
   holdPoints = 0;
}

// Player 2 wins hand
else if (cardPoints2 > cardPoints1) {
   score2 = score2 + cardPoints1 + cardPoints2 + holdPoints;
   holdPoints = 0;
}

// Tie hand
else {
   holdPoints = holdPoints + cardPoints1 + cardPoints2;
}
```

```
// Compare cards
// Combined points and hold points go to winner
// In case of tie, combined points go into hold area
if (cardPoints1 > cardPoints2) {        // player 1 wins hand
   score1 = score1 + cardPoints1 + cardPoints2 + holdPoints;
   holdPoints = 0;
}
else if (cardPoints2 > cardPoints1) {  // player 2 wins hand
   score2 = score2 + cardPoints1 + cardPoints2 + holdPoints;
   holdPoints = 0;
}
else {                                  // tie hand
   holdPoints = holdPoints + cardPoints1 + cardPoints2;
}
```

Finally, display the current score, including points in the hold area. Enter these lines:

```
// Display current score
document.write("Current score:" + BR);
document.write(player1 + ": " + score1 + BR);
document.write(player2 + ": " + score2 + BR);
document.write(holdPoints + " points in hold area" + BR);
```

Save the JavaScript file again. Your program should look like warGame-ch5-solution.html in your student data files.

Test your program in a browser. If you enter the players' names as Abe and Steve, the point goal as 10, and the cards played as a jack and a 3, your browser page should look like Figure 5-16.

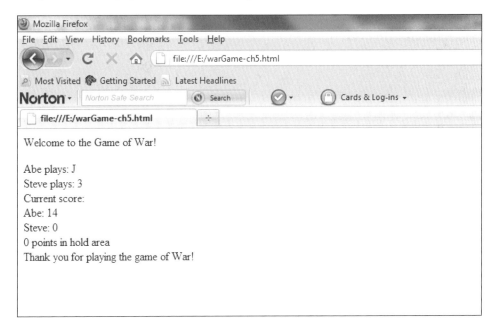

Figure 5-16   The warGame-ch5.html file in a Web browser

Now try it with the second player having a higher card, and make sure the point values and score are correct. Be sure to include values from 2 to 10 as well as J, Q, K, or A. Then try it with identical cards, and make sure the point values are correct and the combined points go into the hold area. Don't worry—you can't test your programs too much!

CHAPTER 6

The Repetition Structure

In this chapter, you learn to:

- ◎ Define the repetition structure and discuss advantages of looping

- ◎ Explain the three control elements of a loop

- ◎ Describe how a `While` loop works

- ◎ Define counters and how they're used in counter-controlled loops

- ◎ Define incrementing and decrementing and how they're used in loops

- ◎ Define sentinel values and explain their use in loops

- ◎ Explain the difference between pretest and posttest loops

- ◎ Describe the `Do While` loop and its difference from the `While` loop

- ◎ Describe the `For` loop, its advantages over the `While` loop, and when it's used

- ◎ Explain nested loops and give examples of when they're useful

- ◎ Define accumulators and show how they're used in loops

There was only one catch and that was Catch-22, which specified that a concern for one's safety in the face of dangers that were real and immediate was the process of a rational mind. "Orr" was crazy and could be grounded. All he had to do was ask; and as soon as he did, he would no longer be crazy and would have to fly more missions. Orr would be crazy to fly more missions and sane if he didn't, but if he was sane he had to fly them. If he flew them he was crazy and didn't have to, but if he didn't want to he was sane and had to. Yossarian was moved very deeply by the absolute simplicity of this clause of Catch-22 and let out a respectful whistle.

"That's some catch, that Catch-22," Yossarian observed.

"It's the best there is," Doc Daneeka agreed.

—FROM *CATCH-22* BY JOSEPH HELLER

In addition to the selection structure, the repetition structure (usually called a "loop") is one of the most powerful tools programmers have. Be warned, however: You must place an element in the loop that allows the computer to break out of it. Without this element, the computer has no way to get out of the loop. Failing to supply an "out" creates an infinite loop, and the only way to stop one is by terminating the task at the operating system level. This solution is inefficient and can have unintended side effects. For example, if your program is running in a browser with several windows open, and you have to terminate the browser program, all the browser windows might close.

After the computer is inside a loop, the only way to get out is by using the code inside the loop. If the code is outside the loop, the computer can't get to it, and the code outside the loop is never performed because the computer is stuck inside the loop. That's some catch, that Catch-22.

Controlling Loops: Initialization, Condition Evaluation, and Alteration

A computer can't think, but it can be programmed to act. It acts more quickly, accurately, and consistently than a person does, even when it's doing the same thing over and over. A computer never gets tired of performing the same task repeatedly.

Suppose you have a stack of 100 index cards, one for each customer of your business, and you write a program to input and display data from each card. Without the repetition structure, you would need to write 100 prompts and 100 print statements. However, with the repetition structure, you can write one prompt and one print statement and tell the computer to carry them out 100 times. Maybe you aren't sure exactly how many index cards you have. No problem! You can tell the computer to repeat the process until you tell it you're done.

The third control structure is the **repetition structure**, also called a loop. It's a section of programming instructions performed, perhaps repeatedly (and as many times as needed), as the result of a condition. Looping has the advantages of being able to do the following:

- Use one set of instructions to process multiple sets of data.

- Include selection structures to allow treating different data in varying ways, depending on the situation.

- Operate on known or unknown quantities.

The difference between a selection structure and a loop lies in the words "perhaps repeatedly" used in the definition. After the statements in a loop are performed, the condition is evaluated again; depending on the evaluation's outcome, the statements might be performed again. Each performance (or execution) of the statements in a loop is called an **iteration** of the loop.

For a loop to perform correctly, you need to set it up so that the condition for performing the statements is clear. As you learned in Chapter 5, a condition is most often a comparison of a variable with another value. In a loop, this variable is called the **loop variable**. You must be sure to include these three components in your loops:

- *Initialization*—An initial value is assigned to the loop variable.

- *Condition evaluation*—A condition is evaluated that determines whether the loop iterates.

- *Alteration*—The loop variable can be changed so that the condition is eventually evaluated differently and the loop can terminate.

Neglecting the third component can get you trapped in the **infinite loop** mentioned in the introduction—a loop that never stops. If the condition specifies repeating the loop as long as the condition is true, something has to happen inside the loop that eventually causes the condition to become false.

Loops are commonly used to perform a task a specified number of times, such as displaying the name "Beetlejuice" three times. What you need in this case is a **counter** representing the number of times the name has been displayed. A counter is numeric and often named index. In this example, because it represents the number of times "Beetlejuice" has already been displayed, it should be initialized to 0.

The condition specifies that statements in the loop should be performed as long as "Beetlejuice" hasn't been displayed three times. So as long as the value of index is still less than 3, the statements should be performed again.

In the loop itself, only two statements are needed: a statement to display the name "Beetlejuice" and a statement to add 1 to the value of index after each time the name is displayed. By adding to the value of index each time through the loop, the condition eventually evaluates to false. Adding to the value of a variable is known as **incrementing** the variable.

After all statements in the loop have been performed, program control returns to the condition again. When index equals 0, 1, or 2, the loop enters another iteration, but a value of 3 means "Beetlejuice" has been displayed three times, and the statements in the loop aren't performed again.

The While Loop: A Pretest Loop

The most common repetition structure is the **While loop**. It consists of three parts, containing the three components described previously:

- A loop variable is initialized before the loop starts.

- In the loop header, the word While is followed by a condition.

  - If the condition evaluates to true, statements in the loop body are performed up to the End While statement, and the condition is evaluated again.

  - If the condition evaluates to false, the statements aren't executed, the loop ends, and program control passes to the statement after the end of the loop (after the End While statement).

- Somewhere in the loop body, the loop variable is altered so that the condition eventually becomes false.

The loop for displaying "Beetlejuice" three times is stated like this in pseudocode:

```
Declare Numeric index = 0
While index < 3
    Display "Beetlejuice"
    index = index + 1
End While
```

Because the condition is evaluated before any statements are performed, the While loop is considered a **pretest loop**. As with a selection structure, in which statements in the scope of the If statement are indented, statements in the loop body are indented, and the End While lines up with the While for readability.

A flowchart for a While loop has similarities to the one for a selection structure. After the step initializing the loop variable, there's a condition with two exits, labeled T and F for true and false. The true branch contains the steps to display the message and increment the loop variable. After that, control returns to the condition. Eventually, index equals 3 (which is different from being less than 3), the false branch is taken, and the program proceeds to the next step. Look at the flowchart segment in Figure 6-1. The round connector symbol indicates the end of the loop.

The initialization statement is actually a sequential statement before the loop, not part of the loop. The loop consists of the While statement with the condition and all statements up to and including the End While statement.

209

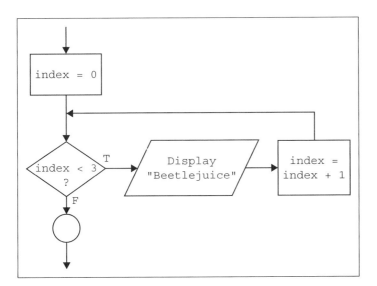

Figure 6-1   A flowchart segment for a While loop

Converting pseudocode to JavaScript is easier than converting a flowchart to JavaScript because flowcharts don't use the keywords If, Else, End If, While, or End While. You have to recognize structures by the relationship of conditions to the statements around them:

- If you have a condition leading to statements on the true branch (or on both the true and false branches), but the flowline doesn't go back to the condition, it's an If (or If/Else) statement.

- If you have a condition leading to statements on the true branch, and the flowline goes back to the condition, it's a While loop.

The `while` statement in JavaScript is similar to the `if` statement. The condition after the `while` keyword is enclosed in parentheses and followed by the opening brace ({) to indicate the beginning of statements in the loop body. The pseudocode keywords `End While` are replaced by the closing brace (}). The JavaScript for the previous algorithm looks like this:

```
var index = 0;
while (index < 3) {
    document.write("Beetlejuice ");
    index = index + 1;
}
```

The output from this example looks like the following:

```
Beetlejuice Beetlejuice Beetlejuice
```

Notice that the output appears on the same line because there's only a space after the name, not a line break. To change this display, you can declare the familiar BR constant and append it to the displayed name, as shown:

```
document.write("Beetlejuice" + BR);
```

Conditions, Counters, and Sentinel Values

Like a selection structure, a loop is controlled by a condition. When a loop is used to perform a task a specified number of times, the loop variable (the counter) is usually incremented by 1. However, you can increment a counter by any value. Suppose you want to display all odd numbers from 1 to 15. All you need to do is to initialize the loop variable to 1 and increment it by 2 each time, as shown in this example:

```
Declare Numeric oddNum = 1
While oddNum <= 15
    Display oddNum
    oddNum = oddNum + 2
End While
```

What's most important is making sure you include a statement inside the loop that eventually causes the condition to be evaluated as false.

You can also subtract values from a loop variable, which is called **decrementing**. For example, here's how you can count backward from 10 to 1:

```
Declare Numeric countDown = 10
While countdown > 0
    Display countDown
    countDown = countDown - 1
End While
```

Of course, you can also decrement the loop variable by values other than 1.

When using counters and loop variables that are incremented and decremented by a fixed amount, you can determine ahead of time how many times the loop should iterate. This kind of loop is called a **determinate loop**.

Sometimes, however, you don't know how many times a loop will iterate. Suppose a clerk has a stack of invoices to process. Instead of having to count the number of invoices ahead of time, you can have the program ask the clerk repeatedly whether there are more invoices to enter, and if the clerk answers "Y," the loop repeats. To do this, you can declare a variable named more, which indicates whether there are more invoices to enter and causes the loop to repeat. To get into the loop the first time, the program can ask whether there are any invoices to enter at this time. If not, the loop never executes. Inside the loop, after the invoice is processed, the program asks whether there are any more invoices to enter. The pseudocode looks like this:

```
Declare Numeric invoiceNum
Declare String more
Display "Do you have any invoices to enter (Y/N)? "
Input more
While more == "Y"
    Display "Enter the invoice number:"
    Input invoiceNum
    [more processing statements]
    Display "Do you have any more invoices to enter (Y/N)? "
    Input more
End While
```

Notice that the question about invoices to enter occurs twice. The first time is *before* the loop starts, as a way to determine whether to enter the loop the first time. It's called a **priming prompt** (like priming a pump to get it started). The question is asked again inside the loop, at the end, to determine whether to repeat the loop. This prompt is used with an **indeterminate loop**, meaning you don't know the number of iterations ahead of time.

There's also a technique that eliminates the need for the more variable. It involves using a special value called a **sentinel value**, entered in place of a valid data value to signal the end of input. The program "watches out" (as a sentinel does) for this special value, which must be one that can't be used as a valid data value.

In this example, if valid invoice numbers are always positive integers, a good choice for a sentinel value is -1. The prompt asks the clerk to enter an invoice number or enter -1 to quit. Besides eliminating the

You might think continue would be a good name for the loop control variable. However, continue is a reserved keyword in many languages, so it can't be used as a variable name.

Don't confuse indeterminate loops with infinite loops. With an indeterminate loop, you don't know the number of iterations ahead of time. An infinite loop is one that never ends.

Make sure the value you choose for a sentinel can't be used as a valid data value.

extra variable, a sentinel value eliminates the lines of code asking whether to continue, as shown in this example:

```
Declare Numeric invoiceNum
Display "Enter an invoice number or -1 to quit: "
Input invoiceNum
While invoiceNum != -1
    [more processing statements]
    Display "Enter another invoice number or -1 to quit: "
    Input invoiceNum
End While
```

Notice that this algorithm has three fewer statements than the previous one!

The Do While Loop: A Posttest Loop

The most common programming loops are While loops, in which the condition is evaluated before the first iteration. Sometimes, however, you want to perform statements in the loop body at least one time and use the condition only to determine whether to repeat the loop. The condition is evaluated *after* the loop body and is, therefore, called a **posttest loop**. The body of a posttest loop is always executed at least once.

The most common posttest loop is the **Do While loop**. The Do keyword is the first line of the loop, followed by indented statements in the loop body. The last line of the loop contains the While keyword followed by the condition. Here's an example of a loop that asks for two numbers, adds them and displays the result, and asks whether the user would like to do it again:

```
Do
    Display "Enter the first number: "
    Input num1
    Display "Enter the second number: "
    Input num2
    total = num1 + num2
    Display "Sum of the numbers: " + total
    Display "More numbers to add (Y/N)? "
    Input more
While more == "Y"
```

A flowchart for a Do While loop is similar to one for a While loop, except the condition occurs at the end of the statements instead of at the beginning (see Figure 6-2).

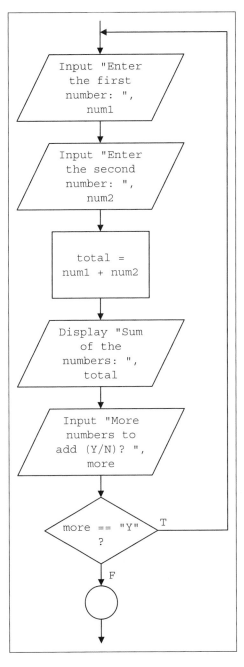

Figure 6-2 A flowchart segment for a Do While loop

Notice that the Do While loop has only one entrance and one exit. In a While loop, the condition is at the beginning, guarding the entry point to the loop. In a Do While loop, the condition guards the exit.

The condition in a loop should always be at the beginning (as in a While loop) or the end (as in a Do While loop), but never in the middle.

The JavaScript do while loop has some important differences from the while loop, besides placing the condition at the end of the loop body. The closing brace lines up with the do keyword and is followed *on the same line* by the keyword while, the condition in parentheses, and a semicolon. Because the condition appears at the end of a do while loop, the semicolon is placed at the end of the condition line. (Remember that you don't put a semicolon at the end of a condition line with a while loop.) The previous Do While loop converted to JavaScript looks like this:

> In a JavaScript while loop, there's no semicolon after the condition, which appears before the loop body, but in a JavaScript do while loop, there *is* a semicolon after the condition, which appears after the loop body.

```
do {
    num1 = prompt("Enter the first number:",ES);
    num1 = parseInt(num1);
    num2 = prompt("Enter the second number:",ES);
    num2 = parseInt(num2);
    total = num1 + num2;
    document.write("Sum of the numbers: " + total + BR);
    more = prompt("More numbers to add (Y/N)?",ES);
} while (more == "Y");
```

If you add the documentation, variable declarations, and comments to the preceding pseudocode loop example, you have a complete pseudocode program (also available as additionLoop.txt in your student data files):

```
// Program name: Addition Loop
// Purpose: Use a Do While loop to add numbers
// Author: Paul Addison
// Date last modified: 01-Sep-2011

Start
    // Declare variables
    Declare Numeric num1, num2    // numbers to add
    Declare Numeric total         // total of two numbers
    Declare String more           // more numbers to add?

    // Welcome the user, identify program
    Display "Welcome to this addition program."
    Display "It repeats until you choose to quit."

    // Start loop, prompt for two numbers
    Do
        Display "Enter the first number: "
        Input num1
        Display "Enter the second number: "
        Input num2

        // Add numbers and display total
        total = num1 + num2
        Display "Sum of the numbers: " + total
```

```
    // Ask whether to continue, end loop
    Display "More numbers to add (Y/N)? "
    Input more
  While more == "Y"

  // Thank the user and end the program
  Display "Thank you!"
Stop
```

PROGRAM 6-1 JavaScript Program additionLoop.html

Now convert the preceding pseudocode to a working JavaScript program. Remember to add a blank line after each code section to improve the readability of your program.

1. Open a new document in Notepad, and save it as **additionLoop.html**. Enter the opening HTML tags and documentation lines:

```
<html>
<body>
<script type="text/javascript">

// Program name: additionLoop.html
// Purpose: Use a do while loop to add numbers
// Author: Paul Addison
// Date last modified: 01-Sep-2011
```

2. Declare variables and constants, and welcome the user:

```
// Variables and constants
var num1, num2;        // numbers to add
var total;             // total of two numbers
var more;              // more numbers to add?
var ES = "";           // literal empty string
var BR = "<br />";     // HTML line break

// Welcome the user, identify program
document.write
("Welcome to this addition program." + BR);
document.write
("It repeats until you choose to quit." + BR);
```

3. Enter the following code for the loop:

```
// Start loop, prompt for two numbers
do {
    num1 = prompt("Enter the first number:",ES);
    num1 = parseInt(num1);
    num2 = prompt("Enter the second number:",ES);
    num2 = parseInt(num2);
```

(continues)

(continued)

```
// Add numbers and display total
total = num1 + num2;
document.write("Sum of the numbers:"↵
+ total + BR);

// Ask whether to continue, end loop
more = prompt("More numbers to add (Y/N)?",ES);
} while (more == "Y");
```

4. Thank the user and end the program:

```
// Thank the user and end the program
document.write("Thank you!" + BR);

</script>
</body>
</html>
```

5. Save the file again, and open it in a browser. Enter **56** and **78** for the first two numbers, answer **Y** to the first question about more numbers, enter **340** and **560** for the next two numbers, and answer **N** to the second question about more numbers. Your browser page should look like Figure 6-3.

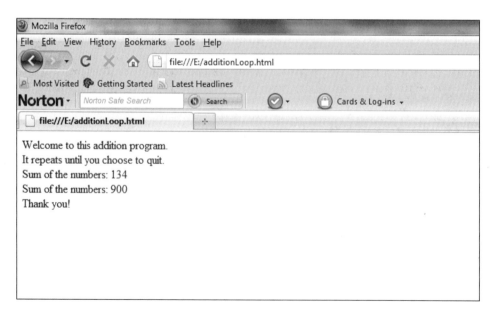

Figure 6-3 The additionLoop.html program in a Web browser

The For Loop: Combining Three Steps into One

You have learned that loops have three components: initialization, condition testing, and alteration. However, in While and Do While loops, the initialization and alteration components can sometimes be hard to find:

- In a While loop, the loop variable can be initialized at any place in the program before the condition. The alteration usually takes place near the end of the loop, which might be dozens of lines of code away from the top.

- In the Do While loop, the statement initializing the loop variable is usually the same statement that alters it. Both are found near the end of the loop.

A variation of the While loop was developed to combine all three loop control components and place them on the same line: the **For loop**. It allows anyone reading the code to see the factors controlling the loop easily. This structure is especially useful for counter-controlled loops, when you know the loop variable's starting and ending values and the increment amount in advance. The syntax of the For loop is as follows:

```
For loopIndex = m To n [Step x]
    [statements]
End For
```

This loop header consists of the For keyword, the loop index variable (*loopIndex*), an equals sign (as an assignment operator), the starting value (*m*), the To keyword, the ending value (*n*), and optionally the Step keyword and the increment's value (*x*). If no increment value is entered, it's assumed to be 1. The body of the loop follows, and the loop ends with the keywords End For. Notice that the ending value is included in the count (as though to say "while the loop variable is less than *or equal to* the ending value"). A For loop that prints "Happy Birthday!" 10 times looks like this in pseudocode:

```
For count = 1 To 10
  Display "Happy Birthday!"
End For
```

The equivalent While loop requires two extra lines—one for the initialization and one for the increment—that aren't required in the For loop:

```
count = 1
While count <= 10
    Display "Happy Birthday!"
    count = count + 1
End While
```

A For loop to display all even numbers from 0 to 100 uses the Step keyword because the increment is 2, as shown in this algorithm:

```
For evenNum = 0 To 100 Step 2
    Display evenNum
End For
```

To decrement the loop value, simply use a negative number for the Step value. This pseudocode counts down from 50 to 0 in increments of 5:

```
For skipByFive = 50 To 0 Step -5
    Display skipByFive
End For
```

Sometimes the number of loop iterations is known when the program runs but might be different every time. In this case, the user can be asked for the number, and this value can be used for the ending value of the For loop. In this example, a teacher wants to add student names to a class:

```
Display "Enter the number of student names to add: "
Input numStudents
For index = 1 to numStudents
    Display "Enter the name of Student # " + index
    Input studentName
End For
```

Before discussing the for loop in JavaScript, you should know about a shortcut that most languages have for incrementing a variable. In JavaScript, as well as in many other languages, the **increment operator** consists of two plus signs (++) appended to the variable name and causes the computer to add 1 to the variable's value. The **decrement operator** is two minus signs (--). If you want to add 1 to the value of index in JavaScript, for example, you can use this statement:

```
index++;
```

Here's the syntax of the JavaScript for loop:

```
for (loopIndex = m; loopIndex <= n; m++) {
    [loop body]
}
```

The JavaScript for loop header consists of the for keyword and parentheses enclosing these three parts:

- The loop variable, an equals sign as the assignment operator, and the starting value, followed by a semicolon

- The loop condition, which keeps the loop going as long the condition evaluates to true, followed by a semicolon

- The statement to increment or otherwise alter the loop variable

The braces enclose the loop body. The for loop is a pretest loop, so remember that there's no semicolon after the header.

PROGRAM 6-2 JavaScript Program numStudentsForLoop.html

Now try converting the preceding For loop pseudocode into a complete JavaScript program. Don't forget to add a blank line after each code section to improve your program's readability.

1. Open a new document in Notepad, and save it as **numStudentsForLoop.html**. Add the opening HTML tags and the documentation lines:

```
<html>
<body>
<script type="text/javascript">
// Program name: numStudentsForLoop.html
// Purpose: A for loop to enter student numbers
// Author: Paul Addison
// Date last modified: 01-Sep-2011
```

2. Declare variables and constants:

```
// Variables and constants
var numStudents;      // number of students to add
var index;            // for loop index
var studentName;      // name of each student
var ES = "";          // literal empty string
var BR = "<br />";    // HTML line break
var PA = "<p />";     // HTML paragraph break
```

3. Welcome the user to the program and prompt for the number of students to add:

```
// Identify program
document.write("Student name entry program."
 + PA);

// Prompt for number of students to add
numStudents = prompt
("Enter the number of student names to add:",ES);
```

4. Write the for loop:

```
// For loop asks for names of students
for (index = 1; index <= numStudents; index++) {
   studentName = prompt
("Enter the name of Student #" + index,ES);
}
```

(continues)

(continued)

5. Thank the user and end the program:

```
// Thank the user and end the program
document.write("Thank you!" + BR);

</script>
</body>
</html>
```

6. Save the file again, and open it in a browser. Enter **3** at the prompt. The program should ask you for three student names. The only output that's displayed, however, is the opening and closing messages to the user. The program doesn't display the names that have been entered.

Nested Loops

Loops can be nested just as selection structures can. In a **nested loop**, remember that the inner loop performs all its iterations for *every* iteration of the outer loop. On the second iteration of the outer loop, the inner loop starts over and performs all its iterations again.

In this example, a loop is used to display minutes and seconds. The minutes loop from 0 to 59, and inside this loop, the seconds loop from 0 to 59. The pseudocode looks like this:

```
For minutes = 0 to 59
    For seconds = 0 to 59
        Display minutes + ":" + seconds
    End For
End For
```

The output looks like this:

```
0:0
0:1
0:2
0:3
and so forth
```

After the seconds variable is displayed at 59 and incremented to 60, the inner loop doesn't repeat. Control passes to the outer loop's End For statement, the minutes variable is incremented to 1, and the inner loop starts over. The last two lines for 0 minutes and the first two iterations for 1 minute look like this:

```
0:58
0:59
1:0
1:1
```

This idea can be expanded easily to include hours, especially if you use military time, with the value of hours going from 0 to 23. The new loop then becomes the outer loop, and the loop for minutes is in the middle. The pseudocode looks like this:

```
For hours = 0 to 23
  For minutes = 0 to 59
    For seconds = 0 to 59
        Display hours + ":" + minutes + ":" + seconds
    End For
  End For
End For
```

The output looks like this:

```
0:0:0
0:0:1
0:0:2
and so forth
```

In this example, a company wants you to input quarterly sales figures for sales employees. You can use an outer loop for the salespeople and an inner loop for the four quarterly sales figures, as shown:

```
Display "Enter the number of salespeople: "
Input numSalespeople
For empIndex = 1 To numSalespeople
   For qtrIndex = 1 To 4
      Display empIndex + ", quarter " + qtrIndex
      Input salesAmt
   End For
End For
```

The nested for loops in the previous example look like this in JavaScript:

```
for (empIndex = 1; empIndex <= numSalespeople; empIndex++) {
   for (qtrIndex = 1; qtrIndex <= 4; qtrIndex++) {
     salesAmt = prompt(empIndex + " quarter " + qtrIndex,ES);
   }
}
```

Accumulators

Another common use for loops is adding to a total when the input amounts aren't known ahead of time. The total is called a "running total" or an **accumulator**.

Say the company you work for is collecting food cans for a charity drive. You're asked to write a program that inputs the number of cans each employee donates and adds it to the total. At the end of the program, the total number of cans is displayed.

You need one variable for the accumulator, representing the total number of cans collected, and it should be initialized to 0. As each new donation is entered, the number of cans is added to the total. Because you don't know ahead of time how many donations there will be, you're using an indeterminate loop with a sentinel value to be most efficient. Here's the pseudocode for this algorithm, and canned-FoodDrive.txt is also available in your student data files:

```
// Program name: Canned Food Drive
// Purpose: Use a loop to accumulate donations
// Author: Paul Addison
// Date last modified: 01-Sep-2011

Start
    // Declare variables
    Declare Numeric numCans          // cans for one donation
    Declare Numeric totalCans = 0   // total cans donated

    // Identify program and prompt for first donation
    Display "Canned Food Donation Program"
    Display "Enter # of cans (or -1 to quit): "
    Input numCans

    // Start loop, add cans to total, display running total
    While numCans != -1
        totalCans = totalCans + numCans
        Display "Total cans so far: " + totalCans

        // Prompt for next donation, end loop
        Display "Enter # of cans (or -1 to quit): "
        Input numCans
    End While

    // Display final total, thank user, end program
    Display "Total # of cans donated: " + totalCans
    Display "Thank you!"
Stop
```

 Detective Work

Try converting this pseudocode program to JavaScript and testing it. Open a new file in Notepad, and save it as cannedFoodDrive.html. Enter the code, save the file again, and open it in a browser. Enter the numbers 34, 79, and 145. Your output should look similar to Figure 6-4. If not, compare your file with cannedFoodDrive-solution.html in your student data files, and make any necessary corrections.

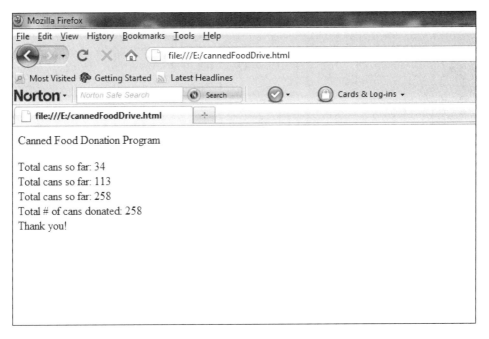

Figure 6-4   The cannedFoodDrive.html program in a Web browser

Using the Break and Continue Statements

In Chapter 5, you saw how the Break keyword was used in the Case structure. Because of the way the Case structure is designed, the matching condition is the starting point for the code to perform (such as a matching condition in an Else If condition). However, instead of the code stopping at the next condition (such as the next Else If), it continues all the way through the rest of the structure. The **Break statement** is the only way to prevent the rest of the code from being performed. This practice goes against the spirit, if not the letter, of structured programming principles, so it's not used often in this book. However, as a programmer, you should be aware of this tool, as long as you remember to use it sparingly.

The Break statement can also be used in a While or a Do While loop. It causes program control to skip immediately to the first statement after the end of the loop. As with the Case structure, it goes against structured programming principles. However, in some situations, a loop should be terminated early, but the programming alternative is clumsy—such as continuing normal processing in an Else clause.

For example, a shipping clerk is entering package information in a program that prints shipping labels, but for any packages over 50 pounds, the clerk is supposed to halt data input and report the package to the manager. Without the Break statement, the code might look like this:

```
Do
    Display "Enter the shipping tag number: "
    Input shipTagNum
    Display "Weigh the package and"
    Display "enter the shipping weight: "
    Input shipWeight
    If shipWeight > 50 Then
       Display "Please report this package"
       Display "to your manager immediately!"
    Else
       Display "Enter the destination state code: "
       Input destState
       Display "Enter the shipping priority code: "
       Input priorityCode
       Display "Enter the sender's state code: "
       Input senderState
       [additional processing statements]
    End If
    Display "Do you have more packages to ship (Y/N)? "
    Input again
While again == "Y"
```

The bulk of the processing for a normal shipment (when the package is 50 pounds or less) is contained in the Else clause of the If statement. This placement means indenting more lines, making it seem as though the rest of the processing is for an exceptional case. The same code with the Break statement looks a little cleaner:

```
Do
    Display "Enter the shipping tag number: "
    Input shipTagNum
    Display "Weigh the package and"
    Display "enter the shipping weight: "
    Input shipWeight
    If shipWeight > 50 Then
       Display "Please report this package"
       Display "to your manager immediately!"
       Break
    End If
    Display "Enter the destination state code: "
    Input destState
    Display "Enter the shipping priority code: "
    Input priorityCode
    Display "Enter the sender's state code: "
    Input senderState
    [additional processing statements]
    Display "Do you have more packages to ship? (Y/N) "
    Input again
While again == "Y"
```

A related command, the **Continue statement**, also breaks the normal flow of programming code. When it's used in a `While` or `Do While` loop, program control goes immediately to the *beginning* of the loop and starts a new iteration. It's used in similar situations as the `Break` statement, but instead of breaking out of the loop, the current case is simply put aside so that the loop can continue. Suppose the shipping clerk in the previous example is asked to set the package in the corner and start entering data for the next package. The `Continue` statement can be used as follows:

```
Do
    Display "Enter the shipping tag number: "
    Input shipTagNum
    Display "Weigh the package and"
    Display "enter the shipping weight: "
    Input shipWeight
    If shipWeight > 50 Then
        Display "Please set this package aside"
        Display "and start with the next one."
        Continue
    End If
    Display "Enter the destination state code: "
    Input destState
    Display "Enter the shipping priority code: "
    Input priorityCode
    Display "Enter the sender's state code: "
    Input senderState
    [additional processing statements]
    Display "Do you have more packages to ship? "
    Input again
While again == "Y"
```

Because **Break** and **Continue** statements go against structured programming principles, use them sparingly, if at all.

A loop is a powerful tool in a programmer's hands. Use the tool well, and don't get stuck in an infinite loop!

Programmer's Workshop

The manager of Frozen Rainbow Ice Cream, Jacqui Spratt, has been running a sales promotion for the past week, Monday through Friday. All her employees were given coupon booklets printed with their names to give to potential customers. During this week, when customers used a coupon to make a purchase, the employee's name, amount of purchase, and date were recorded. At the end of each day, the amounts for each employee for each day were totaled. You have a list of employee names and five daily coupon sales amounts for each employee.

Jacqui wants you to enter the daily totals for each employee in a program that computes and determines the following statistics:

- Total coupon purchases attributed to each employee

- Name of the employee with the highest coupon purchase total

- Total coupon purchases for all employees

The promotion might be repeated, so she doesn't want you to lock in the number of employees. However, you can specify that it's a five-day promotion. Here are some guidelines for your program:

- You don't need to retain every daily amount; just add it to the total for an employee. You need to set each employee's total to 0 before entering the daily amounts.

- You don't need to retain every employee's name, just the one with the highest total.

- You need an outer loop for employees and an inner loop for the five days of the promotion.

- You don't know the number of employees, so use a sentinel value for the outer loop. Remember that you need a priming prompt and a prompt at the end of the loop. In addition, you need to ask for the employee's name before the daily amounts, so the sentinel should be a string value that can't be confused with a name. Q for "quit" will work.

- You know the number of iterations for the inner loop, so a For loop is suitable.

Discussion: First, you create your algorithm in pseudocode, and then convert it to JavaScript and test it. Start with the IPO method:

- What outputs are requested?

  - Total coupon purchases attributed to each employee (numeric): empTot

  - Name of the employee with the highest sales (string): maxName

  - Total coupon sales for all employees (numeric): grandTot

- What inputs do you have available?

  - Employee name (string): empName

  - Daily coupon sales amounts (numeric): dailyAmt

- What processing is required?

  - Add daily amounts to total for each employee.

- After each employee's five amounts have been entered, display the employee's name and total.

- Keep track of the highest total by any employee (numeric): maxTot. To do this, initialize a variable for the maximum to 0, compare any new value with it, and replace the variable's value with the new value if it's higher.

- If the employee's total is the highest so far, retain this amount and the employee's name.

- After the numbers for all employees have been entered, display the grand total and the name of the employee with the highest total.

1. Open a new document in Notepad, and save it as **frozenRainbowPromotion.txt**. Your pseudocode should look something like the following:

```
// Program name: Frozen Rainbow Promotion
// Purpose: Compute stats for coupon purchases
//     attributed to employees for a 5-day period
// Author: Paul Addison
// Date last modified: 01-Sep-2011

Start
    // Declare variables
    Declare String empName
    // employee name
    Declare String maxName
    // employee with high total
    Declare Numeric dailyAmt
    // daily employee amounts
    Declare Numeric empTot
    // total employee purchases
    Declare Numeric maxTot = 0
    // highest employee total
    Declare Numeric grandTot = 0
    // total of all purchases
    Declare Numeric dayIndex
    // loop index for weekdays

    // Display program header,
    // prompt for first employee name
    Display "Frozen Rainbow Promotion Program"
    Display "Enter employee's name or Q to quit: "
    Input empName

    // Start the outer loop,
    // and set employee's total to 0
    While empName != "Q"
        empTot = 0
```

```
            // Start the inner loop,
            // prompt for daily amounts
            // Add each daily amount to total
            For dayIndex = 1 to 5
                Display "Enter the amount for day: " + ↵
        dayIndex
                Input dailyAmt
                empTot = empTot + dailyAmt
            End For

            // Display employee's name and total
            // Compare total with max total
            // If higher,
            // replace max total and employee's name
            // Add total to grand total
            Display empName + ": total is " + empTot
            If empTot > maxTot Then
                maxTot = empTot
                maxName = empName
            End If
            grandTot = grandTot + empTot

            // Prompt for next employee's name, end loop
            Display "Enter employee's name or Q to quit: "
            Input empName
        End While

        // Display grand total and display
        //    name and amount of highest employee
        Display "Grand total of coupon purchases: " ↵
    + grandTot
        Display "Employee with highest amount: " ↵
    + maxName
        Display "Highest amount: " + maxTot

        // Thank the user and exit the program
        Display "Frozen Rainbow thanks you!"
    Stop
```

2. Now convert the pseudocode to JavaScript. Save the file as **frozenRainbowPromotion.html**, and open it in a browser. Enter the following data:

- First employee: **Mandy Lifeboats**. Daily amounts: **15, 19, 22, 10, 20**

- Second employee: **Saul Teasnacks**. Daily amounts: **17, 12, 28, 15, 19**

- For the third employee, enter **Q** to quit the program. Your output should look similar to Figure 6-5. If your program doesn't produce the correct output, compare it with frozen-RainbowPromotion-solution.html in your student data files.

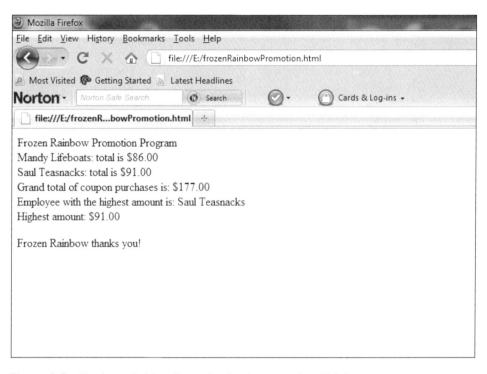

Figure 6-5   The frozenRainbowPromotion.html program in a Web browser

In this Programmer's Workshop, you have used a loop to accumulate amounts and determined the maximum amount by comparing each total with the current maximum. In the Object Lesson, you learn the difference between variables that each object gets and variables that occur only once for the class.

 **Object Lesson**

In this Object Lesson, you use a `While` loop to create new customer objects for QuickTunes, a company that sells songs, albums, and soundtracks for download. QuickTunes prides itself on quick purchases and fast download speeds after a customer has been entered into the system. Class definitions consist of instance variables assigned to each object that's created (instantiated) from the class; in other words, each instance of an object gets its own copy of each variable. However, some properties of classes occur only once for the class, not for each instance. In Chapter 3, you used the static constant `PI` from the `Math` class to help compute statistics for a circle. There's only one value for `PI` and no need to provide separate instances of it. An instance method is one that operates on a single object, not the whole class.

On some occasions, you might want to create your own static variables (used for the entire class, not each instance of a class). In this Object Lesson, you're creating new customer objects, and each customer is assigned a unique number. Instead of requiring the input operator to come up with a new number, you can have the class keep track of the next number to be assigned. Then each time a new customer object is created, a number is assigned to the new customer and incremented by 1. A static variable works well for this purpose. In the class diagram and pseudocode, the keyword `Static` is placed before the data type.

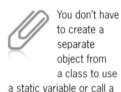

You don't have to create a separate object from a class to use a static variable or call a static method.

Along with a static variable, you need to create a static method that assigns the starting customer number to the static variable. When you increment the static variable, you can use the increment operator (++) explained previously. To call a static method in pseudocode, you use the keyword `Call`, the class name, a period (called a dot), the method name, and any arguments in parentheses. To call a static method named `setCustNum()` from the `QuickTunesCustomer` class, with the numeric argument `startNum`, your pseudocode statement should look like this:

`Call QuickTunesCustomer.setCustNum(startNum)`

After you create the `QuickTunesCustomer` class, you need to create a program to instantiate objects from this class. You can use any starting customer number supplied by the user. After you enter new customer information, you should call the constructor method to create the object, and then call the method to display information for the new customer. Also, your program should keep track of the number of new customers created. Use the increment operator for this variable, too.

The instance variables needed for the `QuickTunesCustomer` class are as follows:

- Customer number (numeric): `custNumber`
- Customer last name and first name (string): `custLastName`, `custFirstName`
- Customer street address, city, state, and zip code (string): `custStreetAddr`, `custCity`, `custState`, `custZip`

You also need a static variable to assign new customer numbers:

- Assigned customer number (numeric): `newCustNum`

Methods needed include the following:

- A constructor method named `QuickTunesCustomer()` (because constructor methods have the same name as the class) with arguments for last name, first name, street address, city, state, and zip code

- A static method to assign the starting customer number:
  setCustNum()

- An instance method to display all information for a customer:
  displayInfo()

Start by creating a class diagram with the class name, variables, and methods (see Figure 6-6).

QuickTunesCustomer
Numeric custNumber String custLastName, custFirstName String custStreetAddr String custCity, custState, custZip Static Numeric newCustNum
QuickTunesCustomer(String lName, String fName, String strAddr, String city, String state, String zip) Static setCustNum(Numeric startNum) displayInfo()

Figure 6-6 A class diagram for the QuickTunesCustomer class

Now you're ready to create the pseudocode for the QuickTunesCustomer class:

1. Open a new document in Notepad, and save it as **QuickTunesCustomerClass.txt**. Start by creating a class definition, including class variables, the constructor method, the static method to assign the starting customer number, and the instance method to display information:

```
// Program name: QuickTunesCustomer Class
// Purpose: Create class for QuickTunes customers
// Author: Paul Addison
// Date last modified: 01-Sep-2011

Class QuickTunesCustomer

    // Variables
    Numeric custNumber          // customer number
    String custLastName         // last name
    String custFirstName        // first name
    String custName             // concatenated name
    String custStreetAddr       // street address
    String custCity             // city
    String custState            // state
    String custZip              // zip code
    Static Numeric newCustNum   // number to assign

    // Constructor method for new customer
    Constructor Method QuickTunesCustomer ↵
```

```
(String lName, String fName, String strAddr, ↵
 String city, String state, String zip)
     // Assign customer # set by separate method
     // Increment # for next customer
     custNumber = newCustNum
     newCustNum++

     // Set values for other variables
     custLastName = lName
     custFirstName = fName
     custName = lName + " " + fName ↵
 // concatenate name
     custStreetAddr = strAddr
     custCity = city
     custState = state
     custZip = zip
  End Method

     // Method to set starting customer number
     Static Method setCustNum(Numeric startNum)
         newCustNum = startNum
     End Method

     // Method to display all customer information
     Method displayInfo()
         Display "Customer #: " + custNumber
         Display "Name: " + custName
         Display "Address: " + custStreetAddr
         Display "City, State, Zip: " + custCity + ↵
 "," + custState + " " + custZip
     End Method
End Class
```

2. Next, you write the pseudocode for creating customer objects, following these guidelines:

   - You need a loop to enter new customers. A While loop suits this purpose.

   - You don't know how many new customers will be created, so a sentinel value should be used.

   - The program should ask you to enter the first customer number to be assigned, and then the method to store this number should be called.

   - Use the same object name (newCust) for each new customer you create because you don't need to save the values for later use. In Chapter 8, you learn how to store multiple related values.

3. You need a variable to keep track of the number of new customers added, which can be incremented each time you

start a new iteration of the loop. Add a blank line at the end of the QuickTunesCustomerClass.txt file, and enter the pseudo-code for assigning the starting customer number and entering new customers. Save the file again when you're finished.

```
Start

    // Variables
    Declare Numeric startNum ↵
    // 1st customer #
    Declare String lastName, firstName ↵
    // customer name
    Declare String address ↵
    // street address
    Declare String city, state, zip ↵
    // more address info
    Declare Numeric numNewCusts = 0 ↵
    // # new customers

    // Program header
    Display "QuickTunes New Customer Program"

    // Get next customer number from user
    // Call method to set starting customer #
    Display "Enter starting customer number: "
    Input startNum
    Call QuickTunesCustomer.setCustNum(startNum)

    // Priming prompt for new customer or quit
    Display ↵
"Enter last name or Q to quit: "
    Input lastName

    // Start loop to process new customers
    // Increment number of new customers
    While lastName != "Q"
        numNewCusts++

        // Get new customer information
        Display "Enter customer's first name: "
        Input firstName
        Display "Enter customer's street address: "
        Input address
        Display "Enter customer's city: "
        Input city
        Display "Enter customer's state: "
        Input state
        Display "Enter customer's zip code: "
        Input zip

        // Call constructor
        // to create new customer record
        // Call method to display information
```

```
            QuickTunesCustomer newCust =↵
    new QuickTunesCustomer(lastName, ↵
    firstName, address, city, state, zip)
            Call newCust.displayInfo()

            // Prompt for new customer,
            // or quit and end loop
            Display "Enter last name or Q to quit: "
            Input lastName
    End While

            // Display number of new customers
            // Thank the user, quit the program
            Display "# of new customers added: " +↵
    numNewCusts
            Display "Thank you!"

    Stop
```

To convert these algorithms to JavaScript, remember that the class definition is included in the <head> section of the HTML file and the code for creating objects is in the <body> section. Here are some guidelines for JavaScript class and object programs:

- You don't have to declare instance variables separately in the <head> section. They're declared automatically when the constructor method is called. However, you should use the keyword this followed by a period to refer to an instance variable.

- Data types aren't needed in JavaScript.

- Be sure to link the constructor method to the instance method displayInfo() by using the keyword this.

- The static variable should be declared in the <head> section.

- When you call a static method in JavaScript, you don't need the class name; you need only the method name and any arguments.

- Constants declared in the <head> section are valid in the <body> section. The only local variables in JavaScript are the ones declared inside a function.

- When calling a constructor, the class name is used before the object name in pseudocode, but in JavaScript, you use the var keyword before the object name.

    4. Convert the pseudocode file to JavaScript, and save it as **QuickTunesCustomerClass.html**. Open the file in a browser, and run it with the data shown in Figure 6-7. If your program doesn't run correctly, compare it with QuickTunesCustomerClass-solution.html in your student data files.

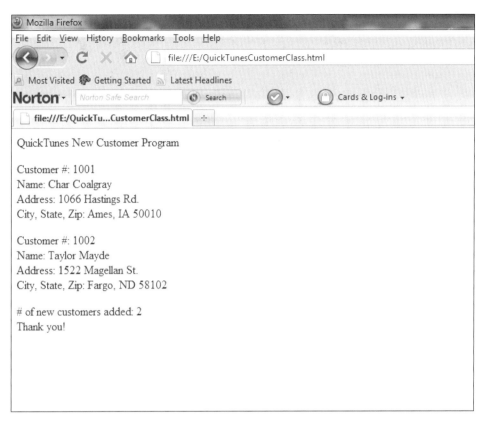

Figure 6-7   The QuickTunesCustomerClass.html program in a Web browser

In this Object Lesson, you have learned to use static variables and static methods in addition to the instance methods you've been using.

Chapter Summary

- The repetition structure (or loop) performs a set of steps based on evaluating a condition, and then evaluates the condition again and repeats the steps if the condition evaluates the same.

- Loops have three control elements: initialization of a loop variable, evaluation of a condition, and alteration of the loop variable.

- A While loop evaluates the condition before determining whether to perform statements in the loop body, making it a pretest loop; then it evaluates and optionally repeats the statements.

- In a determinate loop, when the number of iterations is known, a counter is used to keep track of the number of iterations.

- In a counter-controlled loop, the loop variable is incremented (added to) or decremented (subtracted from) by a fixed amount.

- In an indeterminate loop, a sentinel value is often used to signal the end of valid data input, precluding the need for an additional variable to indicate the end of input.

- A `Do While` loop performs statements in the loop body first, and then tests the condition and optionally repeats the statements, making it a posttest loop.

- A `For` loop is a variation of the `While` loop; it's a pretest loop that combines initialization, condition testing, and alteration in one line.

- Nested loops are useful when one variable changes multiple times for each iteration of another variable.

- An accumulator is a running total that's added to with each iteration of the loop.

Key Terms

accumulator—A loop variable to which amounts are added; also called a "running total."

`Break` **statement**—A statement in a case structure or loop that causes program control to skip immediately to the first statement after the end of the loop.

`Continue` **statement**—A statement in a case structure or loop that causes program control to go immediately to the *beginning* of the loop and start a new iteration.

counter—A loop variable used to represent the number of times a loop iterates.

decrement operator—The symbol -- appended to a variable name to indicate that the variable's value should be decreased by 1.

decrementing—Subtracting from the value of a loop variable.

determinate loop—A loop in which the number of iterations is known ahead of time.

`Do While` **loop**—A posttest loop that always performs statements in the loop body at least once, and then evaluates the condition to determine whether to repeat the loop.

`For` **loop**—A pretest loop (and a variation of the `While` loop) that combines the initialization, condition evaluation, and alteration into one line; it's especially useful for counter-controlled loops, when you know the loop variable's starting and ending values and the increment size in advance.

increment operator—The symbol ++ appended to a variable name to indicate that the variable's value should be increased by 1.

incrementing—Adding to the value of a loop variable.

indeterminate loop—A loop in which the number of iterations can't be determined ahead of time.

infinite loop—A loop that continues to repeat because nothing changes the evaluation of the loop condition.

iteration—One performance of the steps that make up a loop's body.

loop variable—A variable used in evaluating a loop's condition.

nested loop—A loop contained inside another loop.

posttest loop—A loop in which the condition is evaluated after the body of the loop.

pretest loop—A loop in which the condition is evaluated before performing any steps in the loop.

priming prompt—A prompt used before a loop starts to determine whether to enter it the first time.

repetition structure—A structure in which a set of statements is performed (and possibly repeated) based on the evaluation of a condition; also called a "loop."

sentinel value—A predefined value used to signal the end of valid data input in a loop.

`While` **loop**—A pretest loop that evaluates a condition, and then performs the steps in the loop body based on the evaluation.

Review Questions

True/False

1. If the condition of a `While` loop evaluates to false the first time, the statements in the loop body aren't performed. True or False?

2. Altering a loop variable causes an infinite loop. True or False?

3. A `While` loop is a posttest loop, and a `Do While` loop is a pretest loop. True or False?

4. A loop in which you know the number of iterations ahead of time is called an indeterminate loop. True or False?

5. A Do While loop performs the statements in the loop body first, and then evaluates the condition. True or False?

6. A For loop is a variation of the Do While loop. True or False?

7. The loop variable should be initialized inside the While loop. True or False?

8. A sentinel value is a special value used to signal the end of valid data input and stop a loop from repeating. True or False?

9. The body of a Do While loop is always performed at least once. True or False?

10. An accumulator doesn't need to be initialized before the loop starts. True or False?

Multiple Choice

1. The statements in the body of a While loop are performed _____.

    a. as long as the condition is true

    b. as long as the condition is false

    c. until the loop variable is altered

    d. infinitely

2. Where is the condition in a Do While loop placed?

    a. before the loop body

    b. after the loop body

    c. somewhere in the middle of the loop body

    d. both before and after the loop body

3. A For loop combines which of the following into one control statement?

    a. pretest, posttest, and nested loops

    b. flags, sentinels, and loop variables

    c. initialization, condition testing, and alteration

    d. And, Or, and Not

4. The prompt "Enter a score or -1 to quit: " is an example of using which of the following in a loop?

    a. accumulator

    b. sentinel value

    c. operator

    d. increment operator

5. A variable added to with each iteration of a loop is called which of the following? (Choose all that apply.)

    a. accumulator

    b. sentinel value

    c. counter

    d. increment operator

6. A variable that keeps track of the number of loop iterations is a(n) _____.

    a. accumulator

    b. counter

    c. subscript

    d. Boolean operator

7. Adding to the value of a variable is called _____.

    a. incrementing

    b. decrementing

    c. nesting

    d. evaluating

8. A loop contained inside another loop is called a(n) _____ loop.

    a. infinite

    b. nested

    c. closed

    d. enclosed

9. Which of these statements causes 1 to be added to the value of index? (Choose all that apply.)

    a. index = 1

    b. index = index + 1

    c. index + 1 = index

    d. index++

10. Which of the following keywords is used in a loop? (Choose all that apply.)

    a. While

    b. Do While

    c. If

    d. For

11. A Do While loop evaluates the condition _____ performing the loop body the first time.

    a. before

    b. when

    c. after

    d. except when

12. A loop in which you don't know the number of iterations ahead of time is called which of the following?

    a. determinate

    b. indeterminate

    c. infinite

    d. Boolean

Discussion Questions

1. When is a Do While loop more suitable than a While loop?

2. What are some examples of situations in which you could use a nested loop?

3. Why can't valid data values be used as sentinel values?

4. What might cause an infinite loop to occur?

Hands-On Activities

Hands-On Activity 6-1

Before your boss allows adjustable thermostats in the office suite, he must be convinced that major temperature variations occur in different offices and within each office on different days. You're to write a program that allows each employee to enter the temperature at noon on each of five days and displays the highest, lowest, and average (mean) temperatures.

Using pseudocode, design a complete algorithm that accepts five daily temperature readings and displays the highest, lowest, and average (mean) temperatures. Use a For loop to take the five readings. (*Hint*: Initialize the highest and lowest temperature variable to the first temperature that's read, and then compare other temperatures to see whether they're lower or higher.) Save your pseudocode file as tempStats.txt.

Hands-On Activity 6-2

Convert the algorithm in Hands-On Activity 6-1 to JavaScript. Use the parseFloat() method to convert your temperature input to a decimal number and display the average to one decimal place. Test your program, and check that the high, low, and average are being determined correctly. Save your JavaScript file as tempStats.html.

Hands-On Activity 6-3

The owner of Mack's Coffee Cove, Mack Swellhouse, has been advertising a one-day promotion, in which a customer gets coffee for half-price by filling out a customer survey card and depositing it in a box. The cards are timestamped when customers drop them into the box. Eventually, the owner will tally up responses to the questions, but for now, the cards should be grouped into categories by time of day (morning, afternoon, or evening). You are to write a program that asks for the card category for a batch of cards and the number of cards in the batch. The program will add up the totals during the input, and after all the cards have been entered, the program will display the totals in each category. *Hint*: You can use a selection to check the category inside the loop for user input.

Using pseudocode, design a complete algorithm for accumulating three totals and then calculating and displaying them. Save your pseudocode file as coffeeSurvey.txt.

Hands-On Activity 6-4

Convert the algorithm in Hands-On Activity 6-3 to JavaScript. Be sure to initialize your totals for the card categories to 0. Save your JavaScript file as coffeeSurvey.html.

Hands-On Activity 6-5

A staff psychologist has suggested a mental exercise of trying to think of sentences in reverse word order. She wants you to design an algorithm that tests the user's skill at this exercise. The user will type one word at a time into the program, in reverse order. When the input is done, the program will display those words in reverse, which should be the sentence in correct order.

Using pseudocode, design a complete algorithm that builds a sentence backward by asking the user to enter one word at a time, and then displays the words in reverse order with spaces between them. (*Hint*: Build a new sentence by concatenating each new word and a space to the *beginning* of the previously built sentence.) Save your pseudocode file as sentenceReverser.txt.

Hands-On Activity 6-6

Convert the algorithm in Hands-On Activity 6-5 to JavaScript and test it. If you enter the words `out! monkeys the let Teacher out, school's out, School's` the program should display `School's out, school's out, Teacher let the monkeys out!`. Save your JavaScript file as sentenceReverser.html.

CASE STUDY: Adding Loops to It's War!

Until now, your War program could play only one hand. Now that you understand loops, you can modify the program to play multiple hands. In fact, with this enhancement, you can play a complete game with correct scoring! In future chapters, you learn how to make this program more efficient and user friendly, but the game will be functional when you finish this section.

You have designed your program so far to play one hand and score it correctly. In the actual game, the players continue to play until the point goal has been reached. A loop is the perfect structure for this situation. If either player's score has reached or exceeded the point goal, the loop to play a hand should continue. Instead of comparing each player's score to the point goal, determining the higher player's score and comparing it with the point goal is simpler.

To find the higher player's score, you just need a selection structure after the points have been distributed for each hand. Open your warGame-ch5.txt pseudocode file in Notepad, and save it as warGame-ch6.txt. Add this line immediately after the last line in the section where you declare variables:

```
Declare Numeric highScore    // high score for While loop
```

After the last line of the section where you initialize variables, add the following line to control the loop:

```
highScore = 0
```

At the end of the section where you compare cards, right after the End If statement, add a blank line, and then this pseudocode:

```
// Determine high score for While loop
If score1 >= score2 Then
   highScore = score1
Else
   highScore = score2
End If
```

The beginning of the While loop goes just before you ask for the first player's card. Add a blank line after the line for entering the pointGoal variable, and then type these two lines as the beginning of the loop. Indent each line three spaces:

```
// While loop continues until point goal has been reached
While (highScore < pointGoal)
```

Of course, you need to end the loop. The loop ends right after the selection structure you just added to determine the value of highScore. Add a blank line after the End If line, and then enter these two lines. Indent each line three spaces:

```
// End loop
End While
```

Now that you can play the game until the point goal is reached, you can declare the winner. After the End While line, display the final score and insert a selection statement that determines and declares the winner.

Insert a blank line and then add these lines after the End While statement to determine the winner of the game. Indent each line three spaces:

```
// Display final score, then determine and display winner
Display "Final score:"
Display player1 + ": " + score1
Display player2 + ": " + score2
If score1 > score2 Then
   Display player1 + " is the winner!"
```

```
Else If score2 > score1 Then
   Display player2 + " is the winner!"
Else
   Display "The game has ended in a tie."
End If
```

This next step is for readability. Don't underestimate its importance! For every line of pseudocode between the `While` and the `End While` statements, add three more spaces at the beginning of each line to indent these statements. This indentation makes it clear that all these statements are contained in the body of the `While` loop.

Your complete pseudocode program should now look like this:

```
Start

// Program name: War Game (Chapter 6)
// Purpose:
//    Keep score for the card game War, simplified version.
//    A point goal for the game is entered.
//    The user enters card values for two players each hand.
//    The values are compared, and the player with the
//    higher value wins the combined point value.
//    In case of a tie hand, the points are held while two
//    more card values are compared, until one player wins,
//    getting the points for those cards and all held cards.
//    The first player to reach the point goal wins.
// Author: Paul Addison
// Date last modified: 01-Sep-2011

   // Declare variables and constants
   Declare String player1, player2 ↵
   // names of the players
   Declare Numeric pointGoal ↵
   // points needed to win
   Declare Numeric score1, score2 ↵
   // current player scores
   Declare Numeric holdPoints ↵
   // points in hold area
   Declare String winner ↵
   // winner of game
   Declare String cardName1, cardName2 ↵
   // name of card played
   Declare Numeric cardPoints1, cardPoints2 ↵
   // point values for cards
   Declare Numeric highScore ↵
   // high score for While loop

   // Initialize variables
   score1 = 0
   score2 = 0
   holdPoints = 0
   highScore = 0
```

```
// Welcome the user
Display "Welcome to the Game of War!"

// Ask for the names of the two players
Display "Enter the name of the first player: "
Input player1
Display "Enter the name of the second player: "
Input player2

// Ask for the point goal
Display "How many points will you play to? "
Input pointGoal

// While loop continues until point goal has been reached
While (highScore < pointGoal)

    // Ask for cards played in the first hand
    Display "Enter Player 1's card (2-10, J, Q, K, or A):"
    Input cardName1
    Display "Enter Player 2's card (2-10, J, Q, K, or A):"
    Input cardName2

    // Display the data
    Display player1 + "plays: " + cardName1
    Display player2 + "plays: " + cardName2

    // Convert jack, queen, king, or ace to points ↵
for the first player
    If cardName1 == "J" Then
        cardPoints1 = 11
    Else If cardName1 == "Q" Then
        cardPoints1 = 12
    Else If cardName1 == "K" Then
        cardPoints1 = 13
    Else If cardName1 == "A" Then
        cardPoints1 = 14
    Else
        cardPoints1 = stringToNumber(cardName1)
    End If

    // Convert jack, queen, king, or ace to points ↵
for the second player
    If cardName2 == "J" Then
        cardPoints2 = 11
    Else If cardName2 == "Q" Then
        cardPoints2 = 12
    Else If cardName2 == "K" Then
        cardPoints2 = 13
    Else If cardName1 == "A" Then
        cardPoints2 = 14
    Else
        cardPoints2 = stringToNumber(cardName2)
    End If
```

```
        // Compare cards; combined points and hold points↵
go to winner
        // In case of tie, combined points go into hold area
        If cardPoints1 > cardPoints2 Then↵
   // player 1 wins hand
            score1 = score1 + cardPoints1 + cardPoints2 +↵
holdPoints
            holdPoints = 0
        Else If cardPoints2 > cardPoints1 Then↵
   // player 2 wins hand
            score2 = score2 + cardPoints1 + cardPoints2 +↵
holdPoints
            holdPoints = 0
        Else              // tie hand
            holdPoints = holdPoints + cardPoints1 + cardPoints2
        End If

        // Determine high score for While loop
        If score1 >= score2 Then
            highScore = score1
        Else
            highScore = score2
        End If

    // End loop
    End While

    // Display final score, then determine and display winner
    Display "Final score:"
    Display player1 + ": " + score1
    Display player2 + ": " + score2
    If score1 > score2 Then
        Display player1 + " is the winner!"
    Else If score2 > score1 Then
        Display player2 + " is the winner!"
    Else
        Display "The game has ended in a tie."
    End If

    // Display current score
    Display "Current score:"
    Display player1 + ": " + score1
    Display player2 + ": " + score2
    Display holdPoints + " points in hold area"

    // Thank the user
    Display "Thank you for playing the game of War!"
Stop
```

Now you can make the equivalent changes to your JavaScript program. Save the warGame-ch6.txt file. Open the warGame-ch5.html file, and save it as warGame-ch6.html. Add JavaScript code to do the following:

- At the end of the variable declaration section, declare the highScore variable.

- At the end of the initialization section, initialize highScore to 0.

- Just before you prompt for the first player's card, insert the while loop comment and the loop header line. Make sure the while keyword is lowercase, include the condition in parentheses, and add the opening brace ({).

- Insert the code after the points have been distributed and the information has been displayed to determine the value of highScore. Remember to lowercase the if and else keywords, include the condition in parentheses, and use braces instead of the keywords Then and End If.

- Insert the end while comment line and closing brace (}) after the section you just entered for determining the high score.

- Insert the code to display the final score and determine the winner. Lowercase the if and else keywords, include the condition in parentheses, use braces instead of the keywords Then and End If.

- Indent all lines between the opening and closing braces of the while loop three spaces.

Save and run your program. If it doesn't run correctly, compare it with the warGame-ch6-solution.html file in your student data files. Your output should be similar to Figure 6-8, if you enter the following data:

- Names of players: Jack and Jill

- Cards played in this order: 4, K, Q, Q, 5, 6

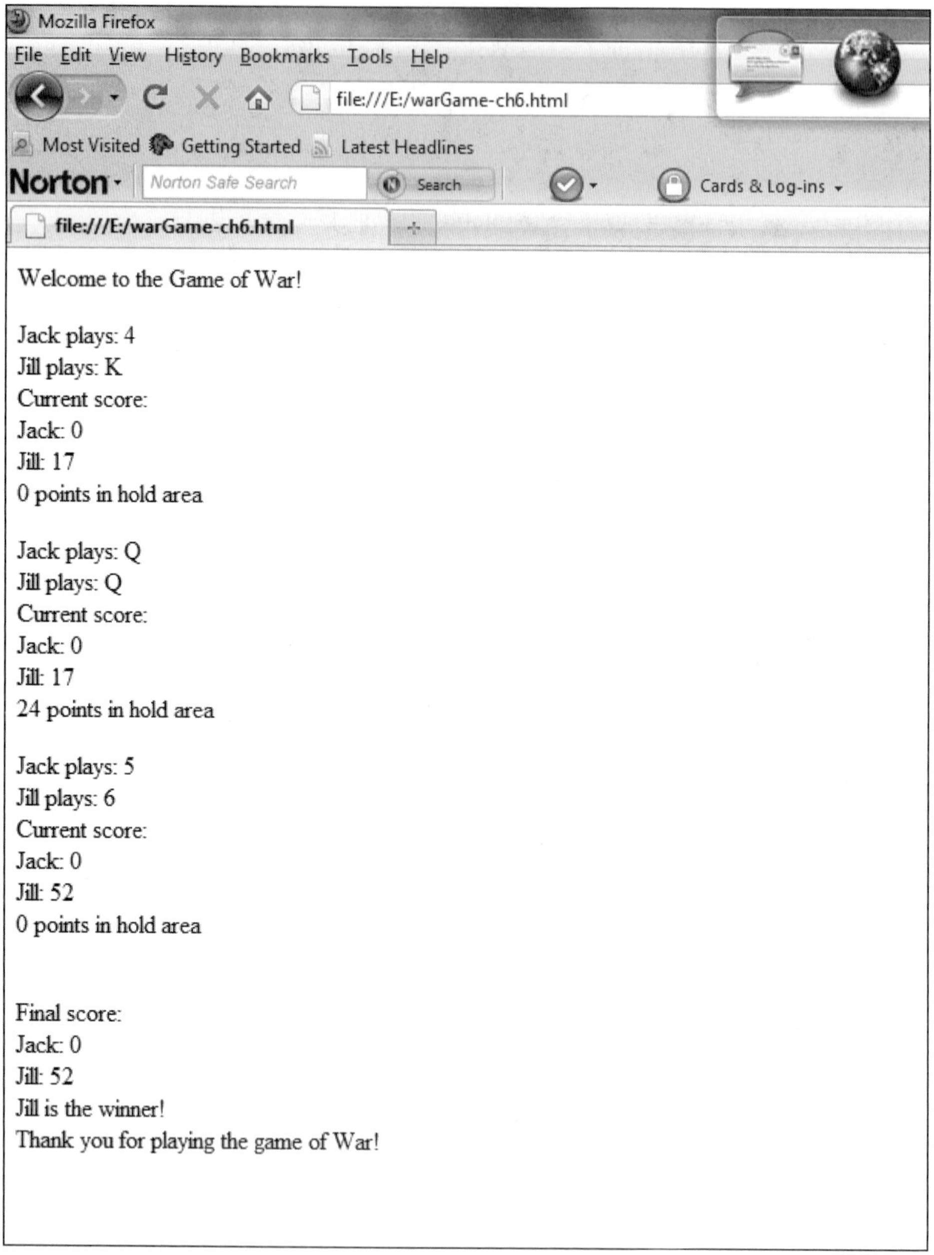

Mozilla Firefox

File Edit View History Bookmarks Tools Help

file:///E:/warGame-ch6.html

Most Visited   Getting Started   Latest Headlines

Norton ·   Norton Safe Search   Search   Cards & Log-ins ▾

file:///E:/warGame-ch6.html

Welcome to the Game of War!

Jack plays: 4
Jill plays: K
Current score:
Jack: 0
Jill: 17
0 points in hold area

Jack plays: Q
Jill plays: Q
Current score:
Jack: 0
Jill: 17
24 points in hold area

Jack plays: 5
Jill plays: 6
Current score:
Jack: 0
Jill: 52
0 points in hold area

Final score:
Jack: 0
Jill: 52
Jill is the winner!
Thank you for playing the game of War!

Figure 6-8   The warGame-ch6.html program in a Web browser

Complex Conditions

In this chapter, you learn to:

◎ Express complex conditions with Boolean values and logical operators

◎ Use truth tables, decision tables, and binary trees to specify conditions and their results

◎ Use the correct syntax for logical operators in JavaScript

◎ Explain how condition evaluation can be made more efficient with short-circuit evaluation

◎ Specify the order for performing multiple condition evaluations

◎ Determine whether complex conditions or nested conditions are most suitable

For every complex problem, there is an answer that is clear, simple, and wrong.

—H. L. MENCKEN

Life isn't always simple, and neither are programming situations. Determining whether to take a particular course of action can depend on several conditions, and deciding whether to repeat a section of code might depend on finding a certain combination of conditions. This chapter helps you learn how to express complex problems and choose the correct course of action based on what you need to accomplish.

Programmers tend to jump into coding and write several lines of code before testing them or rush through complex conditions without considering the consequences carefully. Writing clear and simple code should always be a programmer's goal, but not if your clear and simple code is wrong!

Describing Complex Conditions

Often two or more conditions are involved in a decision. When this happens, you have to describe the logical relationship between the conditions:

- A student makes the dean's list for taking 12 credit hours and having a grade point average of at least 3.5.

- A movie theater offers a discount to anyone who's under 6 years old or over 65.

- An employee gets a bonus vacation day for meeting a sales quota and not being absent for a three-month period.

One way to describe complex conditions is using Boolean variables, discussed next.

Boolean Variables

Until now, you have declared all variables in pseudocode as Numeric or String data types. String variables can be used to hold values such as "true" and "false" or "yes" and "no." However, a variable of a type that's defined to hold only true and false values is ideal for representing the result of evaluating a condition. This variable is called a **Boolean variable** (named after the same George Boole who developed logical concepts). From this point on, when you use a variable storing only true and false values, you declare it as a Boolean data type, like this:

```
Declare Boolean paymentIsOverdue
Declare Boolean seniorCitizen
```

This variable can be set to only true or false. In pseudocode, the words `True` and `False` are capitalized the same way other keywords are, as in these examples:

```
paymentIsOverdue = True
seniorCitizen = False
```

An advantage of the Boolean data type is that when testing a variable's value, a true value is assumed without having to state it. In other words, these two conditions are equivalent:

```
If paymentIsOverdue
If paymentIsOverdue == True
```

This assumption can make your code easier to read because it's more like natural language, as shown in this example:

```
If paymentIsOverdue Then
    lateFee = 4.00
End If
```

 When testing whether the value of a Boolean variable is true, you don't need to include the relational operator and the value (as in `== True`) in the condition. However, when testing to see whether a Boolean variable's value is false, you must include the `== False` or use the keyword `Not` in front of the variable (explained in the next section.) Also, if you're assigning a value to a Boolean variable, you need to include the assignment operator and the value `= True` or `= False`.

Logical Operators: And, Or, and Not

In Chapter 5, you learned about the six relational operators used to compare two values in a condition. However, sometimes a problem requires evaluating two or more conditions before a course of action can be determined, as in these examples:

- An employee is eligible for a discount on store items after working two months and having a perfect attendance record.

- A member of a DVD club gets a bonus rental after six rentals or three purchases.

- A student is eligible to apply for the dean's award if he or she hasn't won the award previously or been disqualified.

A **complex condition** occurs when two or more conditions have to be evaluated for an action to take place. Conditions are joined with the keyword `And` or `Or`, or a single condition can be negated with the keyword `Not`. These three keywords are known as **logical operators**.

For example, if you're buying a ticket for a movie, usually you need only enough money to cover the ticket price, and then you're allowed into the theater. However, if you're claiming a student discount, you might also have to show a student ID to get the reduced price. In this case, two conditions must be true to get the discount: having enough money for the ticket price *and* showing a student ID. You start by declaring two Boolean variables:

```
Declare Boolean personHasMoney
Declare Boolean showedID
```

For this example, both conditions must be true, so the And logical operator is used. In pseudocode, it's expressed by placing the keyword And between the two conditions:

```
If personHasMoney And showedID Then
    ticketPrice = discountPrice
End If
```

You might want to make it a dual-outcome selection and set the ticket price to the regular price if both conditions aren't true, as shown here:

```
If personHasMoney And showedID Then
    ticketPrice = discountPrice
Else
    ticketPrice = regularPrice
End If
```

Sometimes only one of two conditions needs to be true for a particular action to take place. In this situation, the Or logical operator is used. For example, a movie theater admits a customer free if he or she is under 2 years old *or* if he or she is 65 or older. You can express this condition as follows:

```
If age < 2 Or age >=65 Then
    admissionPrice = 0
Else
    admissionPrice = regularPrice
```

In this case, of course, both conditions can't be true at the same time, but often you have conditions in which one or the other or *both* conditions could be true. For example, say a hotel customer gets a 10% discount for showing a hotel club card or a travel club card. Even if the customer shows both cards, only one discount is given. Start by declaring two Boolean variables:

```
Declare Boolean showsHotelClubCard
Declare Boolean showsTravelClubCard
```

The algorithm for the condition is expressed like this:

```
If showsHotelClubCard Or showsTravelClubCard Then
    discount = 0.10
Else
    discount = 0.00
End If
```

The logical operators And and Or are called **binary logical operators** because they operate on two conditions, joining them into a combined condition. The Not operator, which is placed before a condition to negate it, is a **unary logical operator** because it operates on a single condition or a single combined condition. Suppose you want to specify that if a customer's balance doesn't fall below $200, a message is displayed that the account continues to earn interest, as shown:

```
If Not balance < 200 Then
    Display "Your account will continue to earn interest."
End If
```

Of course, with single conditions, you can use a relational operator (discussed in Chapter 5) and avoid the need for a logical operator. In this example with a relational operator, the selection statement has the same result as the previous one with the Not operator:

```
If balance >= 200 Then
    Display "Your account will continue to earn interest."
End If
```

If possible, avoiding the Not operator by stating the condition in a positive way is preferable because stating a condition is simpler than stating a condition and then negating it. You can also use the Not Equals relational operator (!=), as shown in this clear, direct selection statement:

```
If password != "sugarBear" Then
    Display "Sorry, incorrect password."
End If
```

Using the Not operator for this condition is somewhat awkward, although it can be done:

```
If Not password == "sugarBear" Then
    Display "Sorry, incorrect password."
End If
```

The Not operator is used more often when negating a combined condition, one that has already been joined with And or Or. Suppose the only legal country codes for an application are "USA", "MEX", and "CAN". You can state that if the country code is a mismatch for every code in the list, an error message should be displayed:

```
If code != "USA" And code != "MEX" And code != "CAN" Then
    Display "ERROR...invalid code."
```

However, an easier-to-understand solution might be stating that if the country code doesn't match any codes in the list, an error message should be displayed. The logic and the result are the same, but this way of stating the condition is closer to the way you would describe

Try to express conditions in the way that's easiest for you to understand.

it in English. When a combined condition is negated with the Not operator, it should be enclosed in parentheses to clarify that the logical operator applies to the entire condition, as shown:

```
If Not (code == "USA" Or code == "MEX" Or code == "CAN") Then
    Display "ERROR...invalid code."
End If
```

Detective Work

To get practice in using logical operators and complex conditions, try developing an algorithm for this situation: A customer of a travel agency is entitled to a free vacation if he or she meets these conditions:

- Has taken three or more vacations through the agency

- Has booked at least one hotel stay or at least one flight through the agency

- Has not canceled a reservation for a vacation, flight, or hotel

Start by determining some variables to use with this problem:

- Number of vacations (numeric): numVacations

- Number of hotel stays and flights booked (numeric): numHotelStays, numFlights

- Whether the customer has canceled vacations, flights, or hotels (Boolean): canVacations, canFlights, canHotels

- Whether the free vacation is awarded (Boolean): vacationAwarded

The following lines show how all three conditions are expressed:

```
numVacations >= 3
(numHotelStays >= 1 Or numFlights >= 1)
Not (canVacations Or canFlights Or canHotels)
```

Now see whether you can express the entire complex condition, including actions and the logical operators to join the conditions. Put the three conditions on separate lines for readability. Compare your answer with vacationAwarded.txt in your student data files.

Logic Development Tools

Programmers use a variety of tools to help them sort out complex logical situations and to make coding easier. These tools include truth tables, decision tables, and binary trees, discussed in the following sections.

Truth Tables

A **truth table** is a tool for expressing the results of combinations of conditions. When two conditions are joined by the logical And operator, both must be true for the combined condition to be true. If either or both conditions are false, the combined condition is false. Table 7-1 shows the truth table for the logical And operator. As you can see, the only way for a complex condition containing And to be evaluated as true is if both conditions are true. All other combinations result in the complex condition being evaluated as false.

Condition 1	Condition 2	Condition 1 And Condition 2
T	T	T
T	F	F
F	T	F
F	F	F

Table 7-1   Truth table for the logical And operator

When two conditions are joined by Or, the combined condition is true if one *or* both are true. Table 7-2 shows the truth table for the logical Or operator. The only way for the combined condition to be false is if both conditions are false and all other combinations result in the complex condition being evaluated as true.

Condition 1	Condition 2	Condition 1 Or Condition 2
T	T	T
T	F	T
F	T	T
F	F	F

Table 7-2   Truth table for the logical Or operator

When a single condition is negated by the logical Not operator, the result is the opposite of the result of evaluating the condition. Table 7-3 shows the truth table for the logical Not operator. Similarly, when a combined condition is negated, the result is the opposite of the condition's evaluation.

Condition 1	Not Condition 1
T	F
F	T

Table 7-3   Truth table for the logical Not operator

Some situations are more complicated than a combination of two conditions or the negation of a condition. Multiple outcomes might be possible, based on various combinations of different conditions. Imagine a customer applying to a bank for a loan. In this situation, the decision to approve the loan is based on three factors:

- Whether the customer's income is $40,000 or more

- Whether the customer has a credit score of 600 or more

- Whether the customer has had the same job for more than 12 months

This is the bank's policy on loan applications:

- If the customer's income is $40,000 or more, and the credit score is 600 or more, the loan is approved.

- If income is $40,000 or more, the credit score less than 600, and the customer has had the same job for more than 12 months, the loan is approved.

- If income is less than $40,000, the credit score is 600 or more, and the customer has had the same job for more than 12 months, the loan is approved.

- For any other combination of conditions, the loan is denied.

Setting up all these outcomes can require a rather complicated selection statement to dive into. Fortunately, some logic development tools are available to help you with this task: decision tables and binary trees.

Decision Tables

A **decision table** enables you to state all conditions relevant to a decision, the true and false combinations of these conditions, and the outcomes associated with each combination. Each condition must be stated as a Boolean condition, with only true and false possibilities as answers. The table is made up of rows and columns that meet in cells.

Because each condition can have two possibilities, the number of combinations of conditions is 2 raised to the power of the number of conditions. If there are two conditions, the number of possible combinations is 2^2, or 4 (TT, TF, FT, or FF). With three conditions, the number of possible combinations is 2^3, or 8 (TTT, TTF, TFT, TFF, FTT, FTF, FFT, or FFF). In the bank loan example, there are three conditions, so there are eight possibilities, and the outcome is whether the loan is approved.

The table should be divided horizontally into two major sections:

- The top section, labeled Conditions, has a row for each condition. In the first column, each condition is stated, and it can have only a true or false result.

- The bottom section, labeled Outcomes, has a row for each outcome. In the first column, each outcome is stated so that it's performed or not performed as a result of the conditions.

Each column after the first represents a unique combination of condition results:

- Each condition for the column is marked T or F.

- Each outcome cell for the column is marked with an X if the combination results in a "true" outcome, and the cell is left blank if the combination results in a "false" outcome.

Table 7-4 lists the conditions and outcomes for the bank loan decision.

Conditions								
Income >= 40000?								
Credit score >= 600?								
Months at job > 12?								
Outcomes								
Approve loan?								

Table 7-4 Decision table for a bank loan with three conditions and one outcome

Each condition has an equal number of T and F possibilities:

- Start with the first condition, and fill the columns with four Ts and four Fs (TTTTFFFF).

- For the next condition, alternate Ts and Fs in groups of two instead of four (TTFFTTFF).

- For the next condition, alternate Ts and Fs as shown: TFTFTFTF. The last condition always alternates possibilities in this way.

Table 7-5 shows the T and F possibilities filled in.

Conditions								
Income >= 40000?	T	T	T	T	F	F	F	F
Credit score >= 600?	T	T	F	F	T	T	F	F
Months at job > 12?	T	F	T	F	T	F	T	F
Outcomes								
Approve loan?								

Table 7-5   Decision table with T and F possibilities filled in

Look again at the combinations of conditions in which the loan is approved, and put an X in the "Approve loan?" row for these combinations, as Table 7-6 shows.

Conditions								
Income >= 40000?	T	T	T	T	F	F	F	F
Credit score >= 600?	T	T	F	F	T	T	F	F
Months at job > 12?	T	F	T	F	T	F	T	F
Outcomes								
Approve loan?	X	X	X		X			

Table 7-6   Decision table with outcomes marked

This decision table isn't complete yet. Although there are eight combinations of the three conditions, in some cases, one condition is irrelevant. For example, in the first two columns, if the income is $40,000 or more and the credit score is 600 or more, the loan is approved. It doesn't matter how many months the customer worked at the same job; this condition is irrelevant. In a decision table, you put a dash in cells containing irrelevant conditions and then merge the columns.

Notice also that in the last two columns, if the income is less than $40,000 and the credit score is less than 600, the loan is denied, and the number of months at the same job is again irrelevant. In the decision table, change the T and F for the columns corresponding to the irrelevant condition to dashes, as shown in Table 7-7.

Conditions								
Income >= 40000?	T	T	T	T	F	F	F	F
Credit score >= 600?	T	T	F	F	T	T	F	F
Months at job > 12?	-	-	T	F	T	F	-	-
Outcomes								
Approve loan?	X	X	X		X			

Table 7-7 Decision table with irrelevant conditions marked

The final step is to combine columns with irrelevant conditions into one. Then your table clearly shows the combinations that result in the loan being accepted or denied. Table 7-8 is the final decision table.

Conditions						
Income >= 40000?	T	T	T	F	F	F
Credit score >= 600?	T	F	F	T	T	F
Months at job > 12?	-	T	F	T	F	-
Outcomes						
Approve loan?	X	X		X		

Table 7-8 Decision table with irrelevant condition columns merged (final version)

Binary Trees

In Chapter 4, you learned that people who prefer to learn visually are often referred to as "right-brained" people. A method for indicating the outcome of combining conditions that appeals to right-brained people is a **binary tree**, which traces all combinations by starting with one condition and splitting into true and false paths. Each path leads to another condition that also splits into two paths. Each path leads to the next condition, and so on, until all possibilities have been represented and lead to their correct outcomes. If a condition is irrelevant at some point, it doesn't need to be split into true and false paths.

A binary tree can be drawn in a variety of ways, but one of the simplest is to use flowchart shapes: diamond boxes for conditions, flowlines labeled T and F for branches, and process rectangles for outcomes. Figure 7-1 shows a binary tree drawn with these shapes.

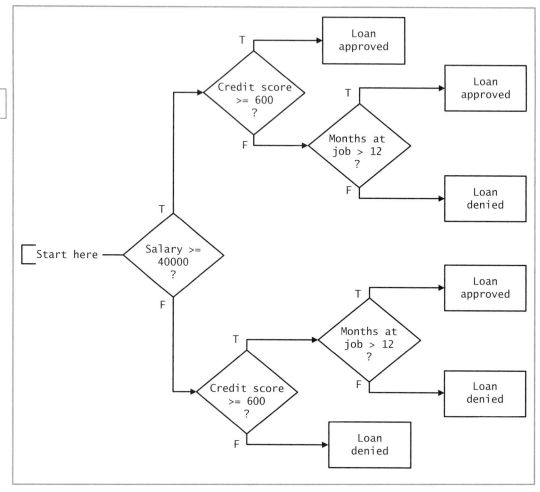

Figure 7-1 A binary tree showing the logic of the bank loan decision process

 Detective Work

Converting a decision table into a binary tree isn't difficult. Using standard flowchart symbols, start with the first condition and trace its true and false branches, representing each condition in a diamond. When you get to an outcome, place it in a process rectangle. Study the decision table in Table 7-9 first, and be sure you understand how each outcome is determined. You're analyzing a decision for this situation: A grade school is organizing a field trip to take students to see a movie, which is being shown at 4:00 p.m. and 7:00 p.m. on a weekday evening. Group A will see the 4:00 movie, Group B will see the 7:00 movie, and Group C won't be able to see the movie at all. Group assignment is based on these conditions:

- If the student has no after-school activities, he or she is assigned to Group A.

- If the student has after-school activities and has a parent's permission, he or she is assigned to Group B.

- If the student has after-school activities and doesn't have a parent's permission, he or she is assigned to Group C.

Conditions							
After-school activities?		T		T		F	
Parent's permission?		T		F		-	
Outcomes							
Assigned to Group A						X	
Assigned to Group B		X					
Assigned to Group C				X			

Table 7-9   Decision table for a field trip after merging irrelevant conditions

This table lists only two conditions. If the first condition evaluates as false, the outcome is determined, so the second condition is irrelevant, and the two columns are merged into one.

Now draw a diamond shape for the first condition, and follow the true and false branches. If the condition evaluates as false, you have reached the outcome. If it evaluates as true, you must go to the second condition, which determines the outcome. Your binary tree should look like Figure 7-2.

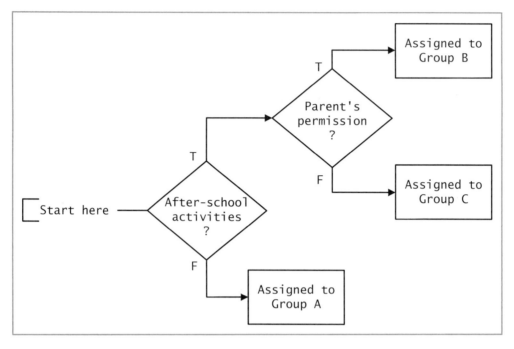

Figure 7-2   A binary tree showing the logic of the field trip selection process

Describing Complex Conditions in JavaScript

JavaScript, like most programming languages, includes logical operators for combining and negating conditions:

- The And operator is &&.
- The Or operator is | |.
- The Not operator is !.

As you've learned in previous chapters, conditions in JavaScript are enclosed in parentheses. The syntax for a complex condition with the And or Or logical operator is as follows:

```
if (condition1 logicalOperator condition2)
```

The selection's scope is similar to that of a simple condition and is enclosed between a pair of braces. For example, the following selection statement with the And operator displays a message if a person's age is from 18 to 65 years, using the BR constant for the line break:

```
// See whether age is between 18 and 65 inclusive
if (age >= 18 && age <= 65) {
   document.write("The age is between 18 and 65." + BR);
}
```

This next selection statement with the Or operator displays a message if a book is more than 10 days overdue or if the patron owes a fine:

```
// See whether book is more than 10 days overdue
// or whether a fine is owed
if (daysOverdue > 10 || fineOwed > 0.00) {
   document.write("Please call the library immediately!" + BR);
}
```

The following lines show the syntax for using the Not operator with a single condition and with a complex condition. Notice that with a complex condition, you need another set of parentheses to enclose the condition you're negating.

```
if(!single condition)
if (!(complex condition))
```

Continuing the library book example, you might want to negate the previous condition to send a message about their accounts to people who don't have overdue books or owe a fine. By negating the condition, you're selecting all the people you did *not* select before. When you negate a condition, often you're changing the message, too. Here's the previous selection but with a negated condition:

```
// If there is no book more than 10 days overdue
// or a fine owed, display a message of good standing
if (!(daysOverdue > 10 || fineOwed > 0.00)) {
   document.write("Your account is in good standing." + BR);
}
```

The following while loop prints an error message when the month entered isn't within the acceptable range of 1 to 12, using the ES constant for the empty string in the prompt. It's an example of data validation that keeps the user in the loop until a correct value is entered.

```
// Display error message while month is not within range
while (!(month >= 1 && month <= 12)) {
   month = prompt ⏎
("ERROR...Enter a number between 1 and 12",ES);
}
```

You learn more about data validation techniques in Chapter 9.

264

PROGRAM 7-1: Logical Operators Program

At this point, you have the tools to create a JavaScript program that uses the And, Or, and Not logical operators. In this step-by-step example, you create a program that asks for two integers and then uses logical operators to determine whether one or both are greater than 100. Start by designing an algorithm that asks the user for two integers and then performs the following actions:

- Use the And operator and display a message that both integers are greater than 100 or at least one number is less than 100.

- Use the Or operator and display a message that one integer is greater than 100 or neither integer is greater than 100.

- Use the Not operator and display a message that neither integer is greater than 100 or one integer is greater than 100. (*Hint:* Use Not to negate the combined condition in the Or selection, and switch the order of the resulting messages.)

To make it clear which selection is being performed, display AND: before the result of the And selection, OR: before the result of the Or selection, and NOT: before the result of the Not selection. Remember to add a blank line at the end of the code section in each step to improve the program's readability.

1. Open a new document in Notepad, and save it as **logicalOperators.txt**. Enter the following lines for the program documentation, the start of the pseudocode, and the variable declarations:

```
// Program name: Logical Operators
// Purpose: Use the logical operators And, Or, Not
// Author: Paul Addison
// Date last modified: 01-Sep-2011

Start

    // Declare variables
    Declare Integer num1, num2 // numbers to enter
```

2. Enter the code to welcome the user and prompt for the two numbers to enter:

```
// Welcome the user, prompt for two numbers
Display "Welcome to Logical Operators!"
Display "Enter the first number: "
```

(continues)

(continued)

```
Input num1
Display "Enter the second number: "
Input num2
```

3. Enter the code to use the And logical operator to test both numbers for being greater than 100:

```
// See whether both numbers are greater
// than 100, using And
Display "AND: "
If num1 > 100 And num2 > 100 Then
    Display "Both numbers are greater than 100."
Else
    Display "At least one number"
    Display "is less than or equal to 100."
End If
```

4. Enter the code to use the Or logical operator to test each number for being greater than 100:

```
// See whether either number
// is greater than 100, using Or
Display "OR: "
If num1 > 100 Or num2 > 100 Then
    Display "At least one number"
    Display "is greater than 100."
Else
    Display "Neither number is greater than 100."
End If
```

5. Enter the code to use the Not logical operator to test each number for being greater than 100:

```
// See whether either number
// is greater than 100, using Not
// The combined condition is negated,
// and the order of messages is switched
Display "NOT: "
If Not (num1 > 100 || num2 > 100) Then
    Display "Neither number is greater than 100."
Else
    Display "At least one number"
    Display "is greater than 100."
End If
```

6. Enter the code to thank the user and end the program:

```
// Thank the user and end the program
Display "Thank you!"
```

Stop

7. Save the file again.

Detective Work

Now try converting the preceding pseudocode to JavaScript. Open a new document in Notepad, and save it as logicalOperators.html. Remember that all conditions must be enclosed in parentheses, and you need two sets of parentheses with the Not operator. When you're finished, save the file again, and open it in a browser. Try running it with several different pairs of numbers, and see whether you get the correct responses. If you enter the numbers 55 and 120, your browser page should look like Figure 7-3. If your program doesn't run correctly, compare it with logicalOperators-solution.html in your student data files.

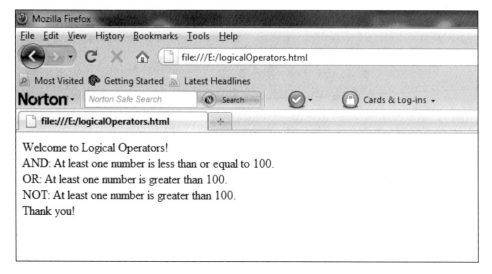

Figure 7-3 The logicalOperators.html program in a Web browser

Working with Complex Conditions

Now that you understand complex conditions, you can use a couple of techniques to help you express them more efficiently and clearly. One saves unnecessary programming steps by eliminating one of the evaluations, and the other ensures that evaluations are being made in the correct order.

Short-Circuit Evaluation

When two conditions joined by the logical And operator are evaluated, if the first one is false, there's no need for the computer to evaluate the second one. For this reason, many languages, including JavaScript, are designed to perform **short-circuit evaluation**. With this type of processing, if the first condition is false, the second one doesn't have to be evaluated, which speeds up processing the combined condition. A similar situation occurs with the logical Or operator. When two conditions are joined by Or, only one needs to be true for the combined condition to be true, so if the first condition evaluates as true, the second one isn't evaluated.

What implications does short-circuit evaluation have for programmers, besides saving some processing time? If you have two conditions and a good idea which one will evaluate as true and which one will evaluate as false, you can arrange the order of conditions so that it's more likely the first evaluation determines the outcome.

Suppose a pizza place keeps customer names in a database and offers an automatic 20% discount if a customer has placed six or more orders in the past month and the order total is $20 or more. Based on statistics the pizza place keeps, only 10% of its customers place six or more orders in a month, but 40% of orders total $20 or more. By placing the condition about number of orders first, all but 10% of the first evaluations are false, and the computer doesn't need to evaluate the second condition.

For example, if 100 customers place an order, the first condition is evaluated 100 times. However, only 10 are expected to be true, so the second condition needs to be evaluated only 10 times, resulting in a total of 110 evaluations:

```
If numOrdersInMonth >= 6 And orderTotal >= 20.00 Then
    discountAmt = orderTotal * 0.20
EndIf
```

If the condition about the order total were listed first, however, the second condition would have to be evaluated 40 times, for a total of 140 evaluations.

Often you don't know the likelihood of conditions evaluating as true or false, but if you do, you should use this information to your advantage and the computer's. If you're processing 100,000 customer orders, for instance, performing 30,000 extra evaluations can take up a considerable amount of time, even on a fast computer.

 If you have statistics on the expected frequency of condition evaluations, use them to make your program faster and more efficient.

Logical Operator Precedence: Use Parentheses

You might encounter a situation in which you have more than two conditions joined by one or more logical operators. For example, if you have three possible shipping code values (SF for "Shipped Final," SP for "Shipped Partial," and SB for "Shipped Back-Ordered"), your selection statement might be expressed like this:

```
If code == "SF" Or code == "SP" Or code == "SB" Then
    Display "Your order has been shipped."
End If
```

As long as the logical operators are identical, the same principle for using two conditions applies to three conditions. If any of the three conditions evaluates as true, the combined condition is also true. The order of conditions matters only for determining the outcome efficiently with the fewest evaluations, as discussed previously.

The same principle applies to the And operator. If three conditions must be true, you can express the selection as follows, assuming hasId, hasPrice, and allowedAdmittance have been declared as Boolean variables:

```
If hasID And age >= 17 And hasPrice Then
    allowedAdmittance = True
End If
```

However, if you mix the operators And, Or, and Not, the potential for error increases substantially. Logical operations have a specified order of precedence, just as arithmetic operations do. In JavaScript, for example, the And operator takes precedence over Or, but this precedence shouldn't be assumed for all programming languages. In the following example, anyone under age 12 or over 65 receives a $2.00 discount if he or she has a coupon. You might express the selection as shown (with hasCoupon declared as a Boolean variable):

```
If age < 12 Or age > 65 And hasCoupon Then
    discountAmt = 2.00
End If
```

You don't know how the computer will process the statement without parentheses. So does a person under age 12 need a coupon to get the discount? If the Or operator has precedence or if the evaluation is done left to right regardless of precedence, the first two conditions are evaluated together before the third condition. In the preceding example, the answer is yes.

If your policy is that a person in either age category needs a coupon, use parentheses as shown here to eliminate confusion:

```
If (age < 12 Or age > 65) And hasCoupon Then
    discountAmt = 2.00
End If
```

However, in the statement without parentheses, if the And operator has precedence and the second and third conditions are evaluated together first, the person under age 12 doesn't need a coupon to get the discount. This condition is expressed with parentheses as shown:

```
If age < 12 Or (age > 65 And hasCoupon) Then
    discountAmt = 2.00
End If
```

In either case, using parentheses overrides the normal operator precedence, ensuring that evaluations are made in the order you intend. Parentheses also make the code easier to read and understand, another good reason to use them.

Most languages, including JavaScript, Java, Visual Basic, and C#, give the And operator higher precedence than the Or operator. So in this example, if parentheses hadn't been used with the conditions, a person under 12 wouldn't need a coupon to get the discount.

Use parentheses to make your intentions clear to both the computer and the reader.

 ## Detective Work

Determine the answers to the following questions, based on the order of precedence of logical operators in the code examples.

Example 1: If a person has 3500 miles accumulated and is a frequent flyer member, what's the cost of the ticket?

```
If miles >= 6000 Or (miles > 3000 And frequentFlyer) Then
    ticketCost = 400.00
Else
    ticketCost = 600.00
End If
```

Example 2: If an employee has exempt status (E) and works 45 hours, will he or she earn any overtime pay?

```
If status != "E" And hoursWorked > 40 Then
    overtimePay = (hoursWorked - 40) * wageRate * 1.5
Else
    overtimePay = 0.00
End If
```

Example 3: Will a 15-year-old person with a membership card be given admittance status?

```
If (age >= 18 And age <= 65) Or ↵
  (personHasMemberCard Or age >= 16) Then
    admit = True
Else
    admit = False
End If
```

Complex Versus Nested Conditions

A complex condition is used when you need one action performed when the combined condition is true and another action performed when the combined condition is false. If the conditions lead to different outcomes when they're evaluated, it's better to nest them so that they're evaluated separately.

To see why nested conditions are preferable in some situations, take a look at a program with the following conditions:

- Customers have a status code of "P" for preferred or "R" for regular.

- Preferred customers get a 20% discount on orders of $50.00 or more and a 10% discount on all other orders.

- Regular customers get a 10% discount on orders of $50.00 or more and no discount on all other orders.

Using a complex condition for this program results in the following statements:

```
If status == "P" And orderTotal >= 50.00 Then
    discount = 0.20
Else If status == "P" And orderTotal < 50.00 Then
    discount = 0.10
Else If status == "R" And orderTotal >= 50.00 Then
    discount = 0.10
Else If status == "R" And orderTotal < 50.00 Then
    discount = 0.00
End If
```

Using the method you learned earlier for eliminating irrelevant conditions, you can omit the second and fourth order total comparisons because if the total isn't greater than or equal to 50, it must be less than 50:

```
If status == "P" And orderTotal >= 50.00 Then
    discount = 0.20
Else If status == "P" Then
    discount = 0.10
Else If status == "R" And orderTotal >= 50.00 Then
    discount = 0.10
Else If status == "R" Then
    discount = 0.00
End If
```

Even with this change, you're still testing the status value four times: twice for "P" and twice for "R". When one of the conditions in a complex condition is treated differently than the combined condition, nested conditions result in the clearest logic and the fewest comparisons, as shown in this recommended code:

```
If status == "P" Then
    If orderTotal >= 50.00 Then
        discount = 0.20
    Else
        discount = 0.10
    End If
Else If status == "R" Then
    If orderTotal >= 50.00 Then
        discount = 0.10
    Else
        discount = 0.00
    End If
End If
```

Programmer's Workshop

Not Quite Free Throws is a company that sells flying discs, boomerangs, and other throwable sports and game items. The company is having a special sale: Any customer who orders at least one flying disc and one boomerang or who orders three or more of either product gets free shipping for the order.

You have been asked to develop an algorithm to take a customer's order, compute the cost (including shipping), and display a message if the customer has earned free shipping. Here are the prices:

- Flying disc: $4.98

- Boomerang: $3.98

- Regular shipping: $5.00

Use the IPO method:

- What outputs are requested?

  - Total purchase amount (numeric): `totPurchase`

  - Shipping cost (numeric): `shippingCost`

  - Total order (numeric): `totOrder`

- What inputs do you have available?

  - Number of discs and boomerangs ordered (numeric) `numDiscs` and `numBooms`

  - Price for flying discs (constant): `DISC_PRICE`

  - Price for boomerangs (constant): `BOOM_PRICE`

  - Regular shipping cost (constant): `REG_SHIP`

- What processing is required?

  - Calculate the total purchase amount by multiplying the number of discs ordered by the disc price, multiplying the number of boomerangs ordered by the boomerang price, and adding them.

  - Determine whether the customer gets free shipping and display a message if true.

  - Calculate the total order amount by adding the total purchase amount and the shipping cost.

Develop the pseudocode first. Don't forget to add a blank line after the section of code in each step.

1. Open a new document in Notepad, and save it as **notQuiteFreeThrows.txt**. Enter the lines for the program documentation, the start of the pseudocode, and the variable declarations:

```
// Program name: Not Quite Free Throws
// Purpose: Calculate orders for a sale
// on flying discs and boomerangs
// Author: Paul Addison
// Date last modified: 01-Sep-2011

Start
    // Declare variables
    Declare Numeric totPurchase    // total purchase
    Declare Numeric shippingCost   // shipping cost
    Declare Numeric totOrder       // total order
    Declare Numeric numDiscs       // # flying discs
    Declare Numeric numBooms       // # boomerangs
    // Declare constants for prices and rates
    Constant Numeric DISC_PRICE = 4.98 // disc price
    Constant Numeric BOOM_PRICE = 3.98 ⏎
      // boomerang price
    Constant Numeric REG_SHIP = 5.00 ⏎
      // shipping rate
```

2. Display the program header, prompt for the number of discs and boomerangs, and calculate the total purchase amount:

```
    // Display program header,
    // get number of discs and boomerangs
    Display "Not Quite Free Throws Sale"
    Display "We are ready to take your order!"
    Display "How many flying discs do you want? "
    Input numDiscs
    Display "How many boomerangs do you want? "
    Input numBooms

    // Calculate total purchase amount
    totPurchase = (numDiscs * DISC_PRICE) + ⏎
      (numBooms * BOOM_PRICE)
```

3. Use a complex condition to determine whether the customer gets free shipping:

```
    // Determine whether customer gets free shipping
    If (numDiscs >= 1 And numBooms >= 1) Or ⏎
      (numDiscs >= 3 Or numBooms >= 3) Then
        shippingCost = 0.00
        Display "Congratulations! Shipping is free!"
    Else
        shippingCost = REG_SHIP
    End If
```

4. Calculate and display the order details and total:

```
// Calculate and display order details, total
totOrder = totPurchase + shippingCost
Display "Total Purchase Amount: " + totPurchase
Display "Shipping Cost: " + shippingCost
Display "Total Order: " + totOrder
```

5. Thank the user, and exit the program:

```
// Thank the user and exit the program
Display "Thanks for shopping here!"
Stop
```

6. Save the file again.

Detective Work

The manager of Not Quite Free Throws asks you to convert the program to JavaScript and test it. Open a new document in Notepad, and save it as notQuiteFreeThrows.html. Enter the JavaScript code, and when you're finished, save the file again, and open it in a browser. Test the program by entering 2 for the number of flying discs and 1 for the number of boomerangs. Your browser page should look something like Figure 7-4. If the program doesn't work correctly, compare it with notQuiteFreeThrows-solution.html in your student data files.

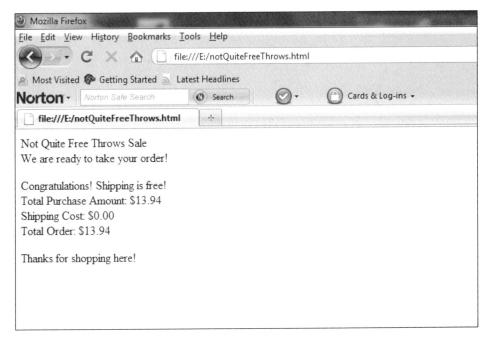

Figure 7-4   The notQuiteFreeThrows.html program in a Web browser

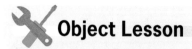

Object Lesson

In this Object Lesson, you create a form to simulate a slot machine. Slot machines use random numbers to generate patterns, with certain patterns worth prizes of different values. So for this form, you need a system to generate random numbers within a specific range.

In this game, when the user clicks a Play Slots button, a function is called to generate a random number for each of three slot boxes and place the name of a fruit—CHERRY, LEMON, ORANGE, LIME, or BANANA—in each box. The program then checks to see whether three of a kind (a jackpot) or two of a kind were selected and displays a corresponding message or the message "No prize."

The Math class in JavaScript has the random() method, which generates a random decimal number between 0 and 1 (greater than or equal to 0 and less than 1). Here's one way to use it:

```
// generate a random number between 0 and 1
var randomNum = Math.random();
document.write(randomNum);
```

Say this method generates the output 0.9584548893756453. This information might not be useful for your program's purposes, but you can get a larger number by multiplying the result by an integer, such as 10. The following example shows multiplying the number random() generates by 10 to get a number that's greater than or equal to 0 and less than 10:

```
// generate a random number between 0 and 10
var randomNum = Math.random() * 10;
document.write(randomNum);
```

Multiplying by 10 changes the generated random number to 9.584548893756453. The set of possible numbers resulting from this process ranges from 0. 000000000000000 to 9.999999999999999 (rounded off). However, you want a set of whole numbers from 1 to 10, so there are two more steps in the process:

- Taking just the integer portion of the number, which leaves you with a set of whole numbers from 0 to 9

- Adding 1 to the number

The Math method floor() returns a number's integer portion. Think of a decimal number as being in a room. The floor is the nearest whole number less than or equal to the decimal number, and the ceiling is the nearest whole number greater than the decimal number. (The Math method ceil() returns the next higher whole number.) Applying this method to the random number that's generated looks like this:

```
// generate a random integer between 0 and 9
var randomNum = Math.random() * 10;
randomNum = Math.floor(randomNum);
document.write(randomNum);
```

Using the same random number generated in the previous example, the output is 9. The floor() method applied to a random number that's multiplied by 10 generates an integer from 0 to 9. To change it to a number from 1 to 10, just add 1 to the result, as shown in this example:

```
// generate a random integer between 1 and 10
var randomNum = Math.random() * 10;
randomNum = Math.floor(randomNum)+ 1;
document.write(randomNum);
```

So to generate a random integer from 1 to n, multiply a random number by n with the random() method, find the integer portion with the floor() method, and add 1.

Here are some guidelines for creating the program for this Object Lesson:

- Remember that in JavaScript, methods are called functions.

- The form should have three text boxes to hold the names of fruits, a Play Slots button to generate the action, and a text box to display the result. Name the form SlotForm, name the text boxes box1, box2, box3, and result, and name the button play.

- The function that's called should generate three random integers from 1 to 5 and put the corresponding fruit names in the text boxes. JavaScript's switch statement works well for this purpose.

- The function should test to see whether there are three of a kind, two of a kind, or no matches and display the corresponding message in the result text box.

1. Open a new file in Notepad, enter the following heading information, and save the file as **slotMachine.html**. Because you're using a function, you need a <head> section in the HTML file:

```
<html>
<head>
<script type="text/javascript">

// Program name: slotMachine.html
// Purpose: Create a form
//    to simulate a slot machine.
// Author: Paul Addison
// Date last modified: 01-Sep-2011
```

2. Declare variables and constants:

```
// Variables
var random1, random2, random3;    // box numbers
// Text constants for slot boxes
var TEXT_CHERRY = "CHERRY";       // cherry box
var TEXT_LEMON = "LEMON";         // lemon box
var TEXT_ORANGE = "ORANGE";       // orange box
var TEXT_LIME = "LIME";           // lime box
var TEXT_BANANA = "BANANA";       // banana box
// Text constants for possible results
var RESULT_JACKPOT = "3 of a kind! JACKPOT!";
var RESULT_2KIND = "2 of a kind!";
var RESULT_NOPRIZE = "No prize";
```

3. Create the JavaScript function for generating a random number between 1 and 5 and displaying the corresponding fruit name in the first text box. Start with the comments for the function's purpose. Notice that the closing function brace is missing at this point.

```
// This function generates three random numbers
// from 1 to 5
// It puts the words Cherry, Lemon, Orange,
// Lime, or Banana in the slot boxes
// It then checks whether 3 of a kind or
// 2 of a kind were selected.

function playSlots() {
    // Generate random numbers, put text in boxes
    random1 = Math.floor(Math.random()*5) + 1
    switch(random1) {
        case 1:
            document.SlotForm.box1.value =↵
            TEXT_CHERRY;
            break;
        case 2:
            document.SlotForm.box1.value =↵
            TEXT_LEMON;
            break;
        case 3:
            document.SlotForm.box1.value =↵
            TEXT_ORANGE;
            break;
        case 4:
            document.SlotForm.box1.value =↵
            TEXT_LIME;
            break;
        case 5:
            document.SlotForm.box1.value =↵
            TEXT_BANANA;
            break;
    }
```

4. Create similar `switch` statements for the second and third text boxes:

```
random2 = Math.floor(Math.random()*5) + 1
switch(random2) {
    case 1:
        document.SlotForm.box2.value = ↵
         TEXT_CHERRY;
        break;
    case 2:
        document.SlotForm.box2.value = ↵
         TEXT_LEMON;
        break;
    case 3:
        document.SlotForm.box2.value = ↵
         TEXT_ORANGE;
        break;
    case 4:
        document.SlotForm.box2.value = ↵
         TEXT_LIME;
        break;
    case 5:
        document.SlotForm.box2.value = ↵
         TEXT_BANANA;
        break;
}
random3 = Math.floor(Math.random()*5) + 1
switch(random3) {
    case 1:
        document.SlotForm.box3.value = ↵
         TEXT_CHERRY;
        break;
    case 2:
        document.SlotForm.box3.value = ↵
         TEXT_LEMON;
        break;
    case 3:
        document.SlotForm.box3.value = ↵
         TEXT_ORANGE;
        break;
    case 4:
        document.SlotForm.box3.value = ↵
         TEXT_LIME;
        break;
    case 5:
        document.SlotForm.box3.value = ↵
         TEXT_BANANA;
        break;
}
```

5. Use a selection statement to see whether there are three of a kind or two of a kind, and then display the corresponding message in the result text box. Next, end the function with the closing brace, and end the <script> and <head> sections:

```
// Check for 3 of a kind or 2 of a kind
if (random1 == random2 && random1 == random3) {
    document.SlotForm.result.value =
      RESULT_JACKPOT;
}
else if (random1 == random2 ||
  random1 == random3 || random2 == random3) {
    document.SlotForm.result.value =
      RESULT_2KIND;
}
else {
    document.SlotForm.result.value =
      RESULT_NOPRIZE;
}
}

</script>
</head>
```

6. In the <body> section, create your form with the three text boxes for the slots, a Play Slots button, and a result text box. This code also specifies the form's color and heading:

```
<body bgcolor="Salmon">
<h2>It's Your Money Slots</h2>
<form name="SlotForm" action="">

<input type="text" name="box1" value="Box1"
  size="10">
<input type="text" name="box2" value="Box2"
  size="10">
<input type="text" name="box3" value="Box3"
  size="10"><p />

<input type="button" name="play"
  value="Play Slots" onclick="playSlots()" /><p />

<input type="text" name="result" value=""
  size="24">

</form>
</body>
</html>
```

7. Save the file again. When you run the program in a Web browser, it should look similar to Figure 7-5.

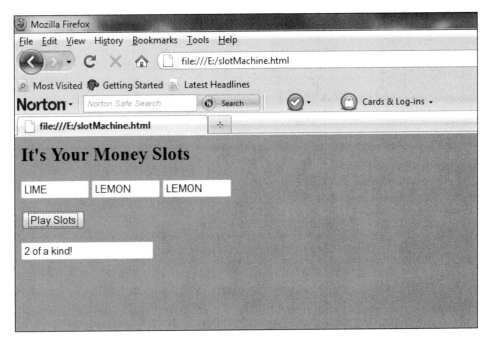

Figure 7-5   The slotMachine.html program in a Web browser

Chapter Summary

- Boolean variables can be used to represent evaluating a condition.

- Multiple conditions can be combined with the logical operators And, Or, and Not.

- A combined condition using And is true if both conditions are true.

- A combined condition using Or is true if at least one condition is true.

- The Not operator negates a condition or a combined condition.

- A truth table lists the results of logical operators used with relational conditions.

- A decision table specifies the correct outcomes for combinations of several conditions.

- A binary tree shows the same outcomes as a decision table but starts with a single condition and branches to others.

- JavaScript uses special symbols for logical operators: && for And, || for Or, and ! for Not.

- With short-circuit evaluation, conditions aren't evaluated if the outcome of a combined condition has already been determined. This method of evaluation saves processing time.

- When multiple logical operators are used, the And operator usually takes precedence over Or, but parentheses can be used in the condition statement to override the default precedence and for clarity.

- Complex conditions should be used when there's one outcome for a combined condition, and nested conditions should be used when any condition has different outcomes for true and false evaluations.

Key Terms

binary logical operator—A logical operator that's applied to two conditions (includes And and Or).

binary tree—A graphical representation of a decision table; typically uses flowchart shapes to indicate conditions and true and false paths.

Boolean variable—A variable that can hold only "true" or "false" values.

complex condition—A situation in which two or more conditions have to be evaluated for an action to take place.

decision table—A chart listing all combinations of conditions and their outcomes.

logical operators—The keywords And, Or, and Not, which are used to combine two relational conditions.

short-circuit evaluation—A process that doesn't evaluate the second condition of a combined condition if evaluation of the first condition determines the outcome.

truth table—A table that shows the outcome of logical operators on multiple conditions.

unary logical operator—A logical operator that's applied to one condition (includes Not).

Review Questions

True/False

1. If either of two conditions joined by And is true, the combined condition is always true. True or False?

2. If either of two conditions joined by Or is false, the combined condition is always false. True or False?

3. If a single condition is false, applying the Not operator makes it true. True or False?

4. If a decision table contains four conditions, the number of possible combinations of evaluations is 12. True or False?

5. If the first of two conditions joined by And is true, the second isn't evaluated because of short-circuit evaluation. True or False?

6. If the first of two conditions joined by Or is false, the second one needs to be evaluated. True or False?

7. If x is given the value 5, the evaluation of the combined condition x > 10 Or x < 20 is True. True or False?

8. Nesting is always preferable to complex conditions. True or False?

Multiple Choice

1. What is the process that doesn't evaluate a condition if the outcome has been determined?

    a. Boolean

    b. concatenation

    c. relational

    d. short-circuit evaluation

2. Which of the following is a tool for specifying complex conditions? (Choose all that apply.)

    a. decision table

    b. binary tree

    c. pseudocode program

    d. truth table

3. If both conditions joined by Or are false, the combined condition is _____.

    a. true

    b. false

    c. evaluated again

    d. caught in an infinite loop

4. If one condition of a combined condition has separate outcomes for true and false, which of the following should be done?

   a. Use the And operator.

   b. Use the Or operator.

   c. Nest the conditions.

   d. Use the Not operator.

5. If the first of two conditions joined by And is false, which of the following is true?

   a. The second condition doesn't need to be evaluated.

   b. The second condition must be evaluated.

   c. The second condition is always true.

   d. The second condition is always false.

6. The condition Not x < 3 is identical to which of the following?

   a. x > 3

   b. x >= 3

   c. x <= 3

   d. x == 3

7. When the number 8.6 is changed to 8, what method has been used?

   a. round()

   b. floor()

   c. ceil()

   d. sqrt()

8. When the number 8.6 is changed to 9, what methods might have been used? (Choose all that apply.)

   a. round()

   b. floor()

   c. ceil()

   d. sqrt()

Discussion Questions

1. What order takes precedence when using And and Or?

2. How can you be sure that combined conditions are evaluated in a specific order?

3. What are the differences between a decision table and a binary tree?

4. When should multiple conditions be combined, and when should they be nested?

Hands-On Activities

Hands-On Activity 7-1

UpperCrust College has an admissions procedure based on a student's total SAT score, whether either parent is an alumnus, and the family income. This procedure is summarized as follows:

- If the student's SAT score is 1400 or higher, the student is accepted.

- If the student's SAT score is 1200 or higher and at least one parent is an alumnus, the student is accepted.

- If the student's SAT score is 1200 or higher and the family income is $100,000 or more, the student is accepted.

- If the student is accepted and the family income is less than $100,000, the student is granted a scholarship.

Create a decision table showing the four conditions (a score of 1400 or higher, a score of 1200 or higher, an alumnus parent, and a family income of $100,000 or more) and the two outcomes (whether the student is accepted and whether the student gets a scholarship). Be sure to identify and eliminate columns with irrelevant conditions, but remember that a condition is irrelevant only if all outcomes are the same when the condition is eliminated. Use a word-processing program to create this decision table, and save the file as upperCrustAdmissions.doc (or another word-processing format).

Hands-On Activity 7-2

Based on the decision table created for Hands-On Activity 7-1, use Notepad to create a pseudocode program that asks the user for SAT score, alumnus status for at least one parent, and the family income.

The program should display a message stating whether the student is admitted, and if so, whether the student is granted a scholarship. Save the file as upperCrustAdmissions.txt.

Hands-On Activity 7-3

Convert the pseudocode program created for Hands-On Activity 7-2 to JavaScript, and test your program. Save the file as upperCrustAdmissions.html.

Hands-On Activity 7-4

A student's grade in a class is based on a percentage for classwork and for attendance, according to this policy:

- Any student with more than five absences fails the class, regardless of percentage.

- A student with two or fewer absences gets 3% added to the percentage.

- The grading scale, after being adjusted for attendance, is 90 to 100 = A, 80 to 89.9 = B, 70 to 79.9 = C, 60 to 69.9 = D, and below 60 = F.

Use Notepad to write a pseudocode program that allows a student to enter a percentage and the number of absences, and then displays the grade and an explanation if any adjustments were made. Save the file as gradeReporter.txt.

Hands-On Activity 7-5

Convert the pseudocode program created for Hands-On Activity 7-4 to JavaScript, and test your program. Save the file as gradeReporter.html.

CASE STUDY: Using a Complex Condition in It's War!

In this version of the card game War, play continues until one player reaches the point goal. Until now, you had to test for this condition in two steps:

- You created the highScore variable and set it equal to the leading player's score at the end of each hand.

- The while loop condition checked to see whether the high score had reached or passed the point goal.

With a complex condition, you can eliminate the unnecessary variable `highScore` and express the loop condition more directly. Open your pseudocode file warGame-ch6.txt, and save it as warGame-ch7.txt. You no longer need the `highScore` variable, so remove the following line from your variable declarations:

```
Declare Numeric highScore      // high score for While loop
```

Remove this line that initializes `highScore` to 0:

```
highScore = 0
```

In Chapter 6, you set up the `While` loop to continue as long as the higher player's score was less than the point goal, using this condition:

```
While (highScore < pointGoal)
```

Replace the `While` loop condition with the following complex condition that compares the players' scores directly with the point goal. Play continues as long as both players' scores are less than the point goal.

```
While (score1 < pointGoal And score2 < pointGoal)
```

Now you can eliminate the entire selection that compares the players' scores to determine the high score. Find and remove these lines:

```
// Determine high score for While loop
If score1 >= score2 Then
   highScore = score1
Else
   highScore = score2
End If
```

Save the pseudocode file. Open your JavaScript file warGame-ch6. html, and save it as warGame-ch7.html. Make the same changes to the JavaScript file as you did to the pseudocode file. The new condition line for the `while` loop is as follows:

```
while (score1 < pointGoal && score2 < pointGoal) {
```

Test your program to make sure it works correctly. Compare your program with warGame-ch7-solution.html in your student data files, if necessary. If your two players are named Bonnie and Clyde, the point goal is 30, and they play the following cards, your output should look like Figure 7-6.

- Bonnie: 2, Clyde: A

- Bonnie: Q, Clyde: Q

- Bonnie: 10, Clyde: 9

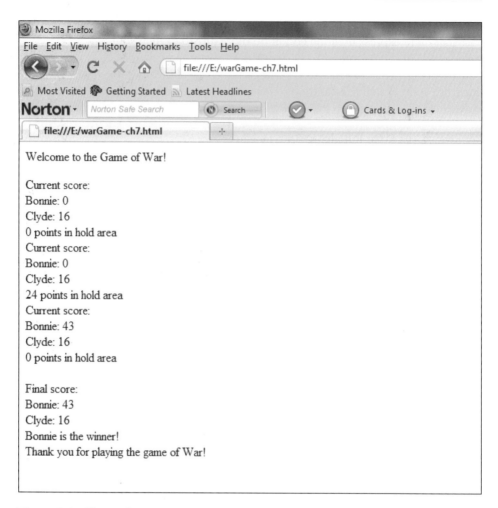

Figure 7-6   The warGame-ch7.html program in a Web browser

CHAPTER 8

Modules and Functions

In this chapter, you learn to:

◎ Explain the purpose of modular programming and functions

◎ Describe how modular programming works with a top-down design methodology

◎ Define global and local variables and their implications for writing functions

◎ Create flowcharts for calling and defining modules

◎ Use modules with and without arguments and modules that do and do not return values

◎ Define passing arguments by value and passing arguments by reference

◎ Define and contrast syntax errors and logic errors

◎ Explain module cohesion and coupling

As long as machines were the largest item in the budget, the programming profession could get away with its clumsy techniques.

—EDSGER W. DIJKSTRA, FROM "THE HUMBLE PROGRAMMER," THE ACM TURING LECTURE, 1972

Structured programming, the method for creating all programs from sequence, selection, and repetition structures, is about clarity. You shouldn't have to read through an entire program to understand its purpose and what each section does. You've learned in previous chapters that using comments consistently is one way to make your programs clear. Another way is using modules in your program. A **module** is simply a section of a program that performs a specific task. Instead of listing all the code in the main program, your main program calls the module. This way, others who use your program get an overview of what the module does from its name and accompanying comments and can go to the module code to see the details.

Structured programming developed as a methodology after many years of what Edsger Dijkstra refers to as "clumsy techniques." Clumsy programming involves code that repeats throughout a program, long modules without any apparent organization, and use of the infamous GOTO statement. This chapter helps you become a less clumsy programmer, and what can be wrong with that?

Modular Programming and Top-Down Design

Top-down design is a well-tested means of program design. It's used to create a program's overall outline and describe tasks to be accomplished, and then details of these tasks are refined later. For example, a typical group of tasks in data processing results in these steps:

- Open data files and declare and initialize variables.

- Read and process records until the end of input.

- Display totals, compute statistics, and close data files.

Until now, all your pseudocode programs have begun with the keyword Start and ended with the keyword Stop, and all program code has been contained between these keywords. When you use an additional module, the code between the Start and Stop keywords is called the **main module**, and the additional module is placed outside the main module, with its statements performed only when the main module calls it, as shown in the bolded line:

```
Start
    Call housekeeping()
    While moreInput == "Y"
        Call processRecord()
    End While
    Call finishUp()
Stop
```

Modules can call other modules.

For this example of a payroll input program, an additional module needed is housekeeping(), which consists of declaring and initializing variables, displaying a welcome message, and printing report headings. The steps for printing report headings can even be a separate module named reportHeadings(), as shown:

```
Module housekeeping()
    // Declare variables
    Declare String lastName        // employee last name
    Declare String firstName       // first name
    Declare Numeric hours          // hours worked
    Declare Numeric wage           // wage rate
    Declare Numeric deductions     // total deductions
    Declare Numeric grossPay       // gross pay
    Declare Numeric netPay         // net pay
    Declare String moreInput = "Y"  // sentinel to continue
                                   // >= 1 record assumed
    Declare Numeric numEmps = 0    // count of employees

    // Welcome the user
    Display "Big Time Payroll Input Program"

    // Print report headings
    Call reportHeadings()
End Module
```

At some point, you need to develop the reportHeadings() module. It might consist of inserting a blank line, printing three lines, inserting another blank line, printing column headings, and inserting one more blank line. The pseudocode looks like this:

```
Module reportHeadings()
    // Print headings
    Print
    Print "        Big Time Entertainment Company"
    Print "         Payroll Report for May, 2011"
    Print "              (By Department)"
    Print
    Print "LAST     FIRST     GROSS     DEDUCTIONS     NET"
    Print
End Module
```

In this example, the report's output is meant to go to a printer, so the Print keyword is used instead of Display, which causes output to go to the screen.

When output is meant for the screen, use the Display keyword. When it's meant for a printer, use Print.

To continue the top-down design process, you would write the pseudocode for the processRecord() and finishUp() modules. Their content, of course, depends on the program's needs. The processRecord() module might get the input, do the calculations, and print the data for each record to be processed. Here's an example:

```
Module processRecord()
    // Increment record count and get input
    numEmps = numEmps + 1
```

```
        Display "Enter employee's first name: "
        Input firstName
        Display "Enter employee's last name: "
        Input lastName
        Display "Enter # of hours worked: "
        Input hoursWorked
        Display "Enter the wage rate: "
        Input wageRate
        Display "Enter total deductions: "
        Input deductions

        // Calculate gross and net pay
        grossPay = hoursWorked * wageRate
        netPay = grossPay - deductions

        // Print data line on report
        Print lastName + " " + firstName + " " + ↵
    grossPay + " " + deductions + " " + netPay

        // Ask whether there is more input
        Display "Do you have more data to input (Y/N)? "
        Input moreInput
End Module
```

Notice that the module doesn't contain a loop to process each record. The loop is in the main module, which continues as long as the moreInput variable equals "Y".

Finally, you have the finishUp() module to code. It counts the numbers of employees but doesn't keep any other statistics, so it's a short module:

```
Module finishUp()
    // Print blank line and record count
    Print
    Print "Total # of employees processed: " + numEmps

    // Thank the user and end the program
    Display "End of program. Thank you!"
End Module
```

Modularizing a Program

Suppose you have a program that asks the user to enter a customer's name and address and then prints mailing labels for this customer. If the entire program is contained in the main module, it would look something like this:

```
// Program name: Label Maker
// Purpose: Use a While loop to print mailing labels
// Author: Paul Addison
// Date last modified: 01-Sep-2011
```

```
Start
   // Declare variables
   Declare String more = "Y"
   Declare String lastName       // customer last name
   Declare String firstName      // first name
   Declare String streetAddr     // street address
   Declare String city           // city
   Declare String state          // state abbreviation
   Declare String zip            // zip code
   Declare Numeric numLabels     // number of labels to print
   Declare Numeric index         // loop index for labels

   // Welcome user, ask for customer info
   Display "Handy-Dandy Label Maker Program"
   While more == "Y"
      Display "Enter the customer's last name: "
      Input lastName
      Display "Enter the customer's first name: "
      Input firstName
      Display "Enter the customer's street address: "
      Input streetAddr
      Display "Enter the customer's city: "
      Input city
      Display "Enter the customer's state abbreviation: "
      Input state
      Display "Enter the customer's zip code: "
      Input zip
      Display "How many labels would you like printed? "
      Input numLabels

      // Print labels for customer (include a blank line)
      For index = 1 to numLabels
         Display firstName + " " + lastName
         Display streetAddr
         Display city + ", " + state + " " + zip
         Display
      End For

      // Ask if user wants to continue
      Display "Continue (Y/N)? "
      Input more
   End While

   // Thank user, end program
   Display "Thank you!"
Stop
```

Most of this program consists of the details of getting and printing customer information on mailing labels. This section (all the variables and prompts for the customer's name and address and the loop variable with the code for printing the labels) can be removed from the main module easily and put into a separate module, given a name, and called from the main module.

Modules are named in much the same way as variables, and camel casing is normally used: The names start with a lowercase letter and can contain letters, digits, hyphens, and underscores but no spaces. The module name is followed by parentheses to enclose any arguments that need to be sent to the module. (You learned about sending arguments to methods in Chapter 2.)

The previous program example creates mailing labels, so you might name the new module makeLabels(). All the code for creating labels can be moved to the new module and replaced by a single statement to call the new module. The new main module looks like this, with the call to the new module bolded:

```
// Program name: Label Maker
// Purpose: Use a While loop to print mailing labels
// Author: Paul Addison
// Date last modified: 01-Sep-2011

Start
    // Declare variables
    Declare String more = "Y"

    // Welcome user, call label module
    Display "Handy-Dandy Label Maker Program"
    While more == "Y"
        Call makeLabels()

        // Ask if user wants to continue
        Display "Continue (Y/N)? "
        Input more
    End While

    // Thank user, end program
    Display "Thank you! "
Stop
```

The rest of the code goes in the makeLabels() module. Instead of the keywords Start and Stop, a module starts with the keyword Module and the module name with parentheses. The last line of the module is End Module, and all code belonging to the module goes between these keywords. The following code for this module is placed after the main module code:

```
Module makeLabels()
    // Declare variables
    Declare String lastName      // customer last name
    Declare String firstName     // first name
    Declare String streetAddr    // street address
    Declare String city          // city
    Declare String state         // state abbreviation
    Declare String zip           // zip code
    Declare Numeric numLabels     // number of labels to print
    Declare Numeric index        // loop index for labels
```

```
    // Ask for customer info
    Display "Enter the customer's last name: "
    Input lastName
    Display "Enter the customer's first name: "
    Input firstName
    Display "Enter the customer's street address: "
    Input streetAddr
    Display "Enter the customer's city: "
    Input city
    Display "Enter the customer's state abbreviation: "
    Input state
    Display "Enter the customer's zip code: "
    Input zip
    Display "How many labels would you like printed? "
    Input numLabels

    // Print labels for customer (include a blank line)
    For index = 1 to numLabels
        Print firstName + " " + lastName
        Print streetAddr
        Print city + ", " + state + " " + zip
        Print
    End For
End Module
```

By reading the code for this program, you can see in the main module that the program creates mailing labels as long as the user wants to continue. If you want to see the details of printing labels, the code is available in the makeLabels() module.

When a module is called, the computer begins performing the steps in it and returns to the main module only after the called module has finished. The module issuing the call to another module is paused temporarily.

Global and Local Variables and Scope

In many languages, variables declared in a module are available only while that module is being performed. These variables are said to be "local" to the module. In the makeLabels() module, for example, the variables for the customer's name and address and the loop variable for printing labels aren't needed in the main program, so they're declared in the makeLabels() module.

Local variables are created when a module is called and exist only while statements in the module are performed. When the End Module statement is encountered, local variables are no longer in use or accessible by the program. In this way, the operating system can use the memory space for local variables for other purposes.

In Chapter 4, you learned that a selection structure's scope consists of the statements performed as the result of a condition's evaluation. With modular programming, a variable's scope is the section of program code in which a variable can be accessed. In general, a local variable's scope is the module where it's declared. For example, in the following code, the displayName() module can't print the person's name because the name variable is declared in the getInput() module, which is outside the displayName() module's scope:

```
Start
    Call getInput()
    Call displayName()
Stop

Module getInput()
    Declare String name
    Display "Enter your name: "
    Input name
End Module

Module displayName()
    Display "Your name is: " + name
End Module
```

To make the name variable available to both modules, it needs to be declared as a global variable or passed between modules as an argument. **Global variables** are available to all modules in the program. In most programming languages, global variables are declared explicitly as global or declared in the main module outside any other modules. In this book, the second method is used—considering variables declared in the main module to be global.

Using the preceding program again, you can make name a global variable and, therefore, available to both modules by making the following changes:

```
Start
    Declare String name
    Call getInput()
    Call displayName()
Stop

Module getInput()
    Display "Enter your name"
    Input name
End Module

Module displayName()
    Display "Your name is: " + name
End Module
```

Programming languages define global variables in different ways, but in general, variables are assumed to be local unless they're declared as global. You might wonder why all variables aren't declared as global. Although the idea of local variables might sound overly restrictive, these variables actually have an advantage for programmers. Many programs are so large that programmers work independently on different modules. By using local variables, programmers working on a module don't have to worry about what variable names are used in the main module or any other module. All variables declared in separate modules are local and can't be affected by other modules. Even if two variables in different modules happen to have the same name, they're stored in different memory locations, and the statements affecting one don't affect the other.

What happens if a module uses a local variable with the same name as a main module variable, which is assumed to be global? In this case, the variable declared locally is used. To see how variables in different modules are completely independent of each other, take a look at the following example of a program that calls the displayStars() module to display a row of asterisks. The main module uses a variable named num for the number of times the displayStars() module is called and a loop variable named index. The displayStars() module also uses a variable named num for the number of asterisks displayed in each row and a loop variable named index.

```
// Program name: Character Art
// Purpose: Display patterns of keyboard characters
// Author: Paul Addison
// Date last modified: 01-Sep-2011

Start
   // Declare variables
   Declare Numeric num        // # rows to display
   Declare Numeric index      // loop variable

   // Display program heading, ask for # of rows
   Display "Character Art program."
   Display "Display rows of keyboard characters."
   Display "The character is the asterisk, *."
   Display "You choose the length of each row."
   Display
   Display "How many rows do you want? "
   Input num

   // Call the module for # of rows
   For index = 1 to num
      Call displayStars()
   End For

   // Thank the user and end the program
   Display "Thank you!"
Stop

Module displayStars()
   // Declare variables
   Declare Numeric num        // # asterisks in a row
   Declare Numeric index      // loop variable
```

```
// Ask for number of asterisks, display
// The num and index variables are local
Display
Display "How many asterisks in this row? "
Input num
For index = 1 to num
   Display "*"
End For
End Module
```

If the user wants to display three rows and specifies rows of 10, 15, and 20 asterisks, the program interaction looks like the following. (User responses are bolded.)

```
Character Art program.
Display rows of keyboard characters.
The character is the asterisk, *.
```

You choose the length of each row.

```
How many rows do you want? 3

How many asterisks in this row? 10
**********

How many asterisks in this row? 15
***************

How many asterisks in this row? 20
********************
Thank you!
```

The variables num and index in the main module are used to determine how many times the displayStars() module is called. Inside the displayStars() module, these variables are used to determine how many asterisks are displayed in each row.

Flowcharting Modules

The flowchart shape for a called module is a rectangle with stripes, which indicates a predefined process. The text inside the rectangle contains the command Call displayStars() or the name of the module you're calling. Remember that a For loop is depicted like a While loop in a flowchart, with initialization and incrementing as separate steps.

Until now, you have been creating flowcharts only for program segments, not complete programs. To make flowcharts easier to read, some groups of activities are summarized in single shapes, such as a process rectangle that says "Declare variables" or an input/output parallelogram that says "Display headings." Off to the side of these shapes are annotations, which list variables or headings in open-ended boxes. Figure 8-1 shows the main module for the Character Art program.

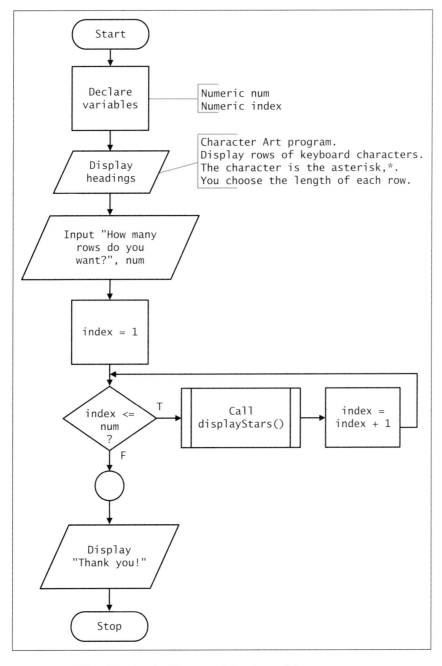

Figure 8-1 Flowchart for the Character Art main module

The called module, displayStars(), has its own flowchart in which the terminating symbols contain the same text as the module's pseudocode: Module displayStars() and End Module (see Figure 8-2). Otherwise, the flowchart is the same as though it had been for the main module.

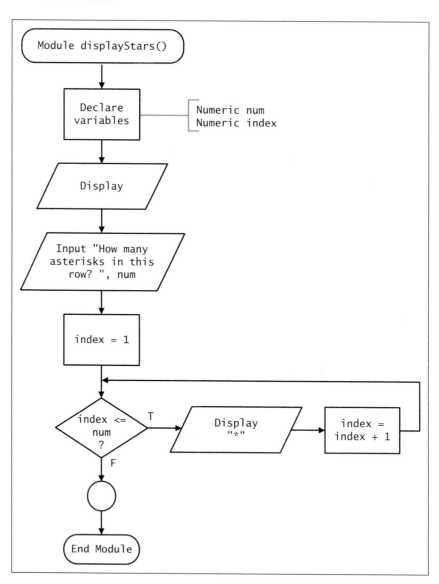

Figure 8-2   Flowchart for the displayStars() module of the Character Art program

Modules in JavaScript

Terminology in different programming languages isn't always consistent. For example, functions have been described in this chapter as modules that return a value to the place in the program that called it. However, JavaScript uses the term "function" for all modules, whether they return a value or not. Modules that return values are discussed later in "Functions: Modules That Return Values."

In Chapter 3, you used JavaScript constructor functions to create objects, and in the Object Lesson, you used them to call functions in response to button clicks. Recall that functions are placed in the <head> section of the HTML file and are called from the <body> section. Therefore, writing a JavaScript program with functions is the reverse of writing a pseudocode algorithm: Modules appear first as functions in the <head> section, followed by the main module in the <body> section. Remember the following guidelines:

- The function body is enclosed between opening and closing braces, and so is the loop body.

- The <head> and the <body> sections of the HTML file have their own <script> sections.

- The call to a function doesn't need the keyword Call; just use the function's name.

PROGRAM 8-1: JavaScript Program characterArt.html

You can write the Character Art program in JavaScript by creating the <head> section with the displayStars() module written as a function. Then close the <head> section, start the <body> section, and write the JavaScript code for the pseudocode's main module. Remember to add a blank line after the code section in each step.

1. Open a new document in Notepad, and save it as **characterArt.html**. Enter the HTML tags and the documentation lines:

```
<html>
<head>
<script type="text/javascript">

// Program name: characterArt.html
// Purpose: Display patterns of keyboard characters
```

(continues)

(continued)

```
// Author: Paul Addison
// Date last modified: 01-Sep-2011
```

2. Enter the code for the JavaScript function to display a row of stars, and end the `<head>` section:

```
function displayStars() {
    // Declare variables and constants
    var num;              // # asterisks in a row
    var index;            // loop variable
    var BR = "<br />";    // HTML line break
    var ES = "";          // empty string for prompt

    // Ask for number of asterisks
    // Display them horizontally
    document.write(BR);
    num = prompt
("How many asterisks in this row?",ES);

    for (index = 1; index <= num; index++) {
        document.write("*");
    }
}

</script>
</head>
```

3. Start the `<body>` section, and declare local variables and constants:

```
<body>
<script type="text/javascript">

// Declare variables and constants
var num;              // # rows to display
var index;            // loop variable
var BR = "<br />";    // HTML line break
var ES = "";          // empty string for prompt
```

4. Display the program heading and ask for the number of rows the user wants:

```
// Display program heading, ask for # of rows
document.write("Character Art program." + BR);
document.write
("Display rows of keyboard characters." + BR);
document.write
("The character is the asterisk, *." + BR);
document.write
("You choose the length of each row." + BR);
num = prompt("How many rows do you want?",ES);
```

(continues)

(continued)

5. Use a `for` loop to call the function once for each row:

```
// Call the function for # of rows
for (index = 1; index <= num; index++) {
    displayStars();
}
```

6. Thank the user and end the program:

```
// Thank the user, end the program
document.write(BR + "Thank you!" + BR);

</script>
</body>
</html>
```

7. Save the file, and open it in a browser. If you enter **3** for the number of rows and **10**, **15**, and **20** for the number of asterisks in each row, your output should look like Figure 8-3.

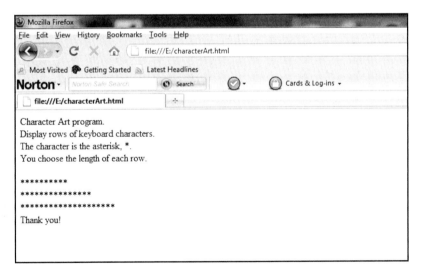

Figure 8-3   The characterArt.html program in a Web browser

Modules That Require Arguments

Global variables are one way to make variables available to other modules. However, if a module has to look up variables outside its own scope, this process takes extra time and requires programmers to be aware of all other variables being used in the program. An efficient way of providing data to modules and still allowing the use of local variables is to pass the data as an argument.

For example, a module that doubles a number needs to know which number to double. This number can be sent as an argument. Arguments are values represented as constants or variables, which are enclosed in the parentheses following the module name in the `Call` statement. If you want to call a module named `double()` to double the number 4, for example, you put the 4 inside the parentheses, as shown:

```
Call double(4)
```

If you have a variable containing the value 4, you can enclose the variable name in the parentheses, like this:

```
Declare Numeric someNumber = 4
Call double(someNumber)
```

A module created to receive an argument must be specifically designed to do so. Inside the parentheses for the module header, you must declare the data type of the value to be received and assign a local variable name. This data type and variable pair is called a parameter.

The parameter in parentheses essentially declares a local variable, which can be used anywhere in the module, and the variable is initialized to the argument's value when the module is called. Here's an example of a program that asks the user for a number and calls a module named `double()`, which takes the argument, doubles the value, and displays the result:

```
// Program name: Number Doubler
// Purpose: Call a module to double a number
// Author: Paul Addison
// Date last modified: 01-Sep-2011

Start
    // Declare variables
    Declare Numeric someNum      // number to double

    // Welcome user, ask for number to double
    Display "Welcome to the Number Doubler!"
    Display
    Display "Enter the number to double: "
    Input someNum

    // Call module to double the number
    Call double(someNum)

    // Thank the user and end the program
    Display "Thank you!"
Stop

Module double(Numeric num)
    // Declare variables
    Declare Numeric result    // result of doubling

    // Compute and display result, end module
    result = num * 2
```

> Data sent when a module is called is an argument; a parameter consists of the data type and variable pair to receive the data.

```
   Display "Your number doubled is: " + result
End Module
```

When this program runs, if the user enters 512 as the number to double, the interaction would look like the following. (User input is bolded.)

```
Welcome to the Number Doubler!

Enter the number to double: 512
Your number doubled is: 1024
Thank you!
```

PROGRAM 8-2: JavaScript Program numberDoubler.html

To create a JavaScript program from the preceding pseudocode program, remember that data types don't need to be declared in function parameters. Don't forget to add a blank line after the code section in each step to improve your program's readability.

1. Open a new document in Notepad, and save it as **numberDoubler.html**. Enter the HTML tags for a JavaScript file and the documentation lines:

```
<html>
<head>
<script type="text/javascript">

// Program name: numberDoubler.html
// Purpose: Call a function to double a number
// Author: Paul Addison
// Date last modified: 01-Sep-2011
```

2. Enter the code for the function to double the number sent as an argument, and end the `<head>` section:

```
function double(num) {
   // Declare variables
   var result;          // result of doubling
   var BR = "<br />";   // HTML line break

   // Compute and display result, end function
   result = num * 2;
   document.write ↵
("Your number doubled is: " + result + BR);
}

</script>
</head>
```

(continues)

(continued)

3. Start the `<body>` section, and declare local variables:

```
<body>
<script type="text/javascript">

// Declare variables
var someNum;           // number to double
var BR = "<br />";     // HTML line break
var ES = "";           // empty string for prompt
```

4. Welcome the user, prompt for the number to double, and call the `double()` module, including the argument:

```
// Welcome user, ask for the number to double
document.write ↵
("Welcome to the Number Doubler!" + BR);
someNum = prompt("Enter the number to double:",ES);

// Call function to double the number
double(someNum);
```

5. Thank the user, and end the program:

```
// Thank the user and end the program
document.write("Thank you!" + BR);

</script>
</body>
</html>
```

6. Save the file again. To test your program, open the file in a browser, and enter some numbers for the program to double. Figure 8-4 shows an example.

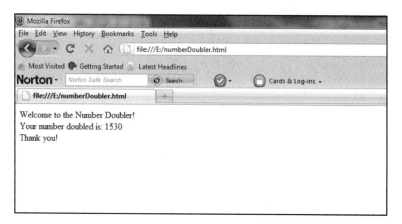

Figure 8-4 The numberDoubler.html program in a Web browser

In the preceding example, data is passed to a module or function by sending its value to the module, where a local variable is initialized to the argument's value. This process is known as **passing by value**.

Another way of passing an argument to a module is "passing by reference." In this process, the variable's actual memory address is sent to the module, and the parameter variable is the same location in memory as the variable in the calling module. The result is that even if the parameter variable has a different name, it's actually "pointing" to the same place in memory and can, therefore, change the variable's value in the calling module. In procedural programming, passing by reference (discussed in Chapter 10 on arrays) is far less common than passing by value.

Passing Multiple Arguments

Modules can be designed to accept more than one argument. As a matter of fact, it's common for a module to have two or three arguments sent to it. For example, you might want to compute the interest for a savings account based on three factors: principal (initial amount), annual interest rate, and period for which interest is computed. A call to this module might look like the following:

```
Declare Numeric principal = 1000.00   // $1000 principal
Declare Numeric annualRate = 0.025    // 2.5% annual interest
Declare Numeric numYears = 0.75       // 9 months period
Call calcInterest(principal, annualRate, numYears)
```

The `calcInterest()` module needs to be defined with three numeric parameters to accept the three arguments. Parameters must match the arguments sent to them in number, data type, and order. If the wrong number of arguments is sent or if the data types don't match, for example, the computer can detect and declare a **syntax error**, which occurs when the language's rules are violated. However, sending arguments in the wrong order, such as mixing up the annual interest rate and the number of years (resulting in a 75% interest rate for 2.5% of a year in the previous example), is a logic error. A **logic error** occurs when the wrong instruction is given to the computer for solving a problem. The syntax is correct, so the computer can process the instruction, but it isn't the correct instruction.

Parameters and arguments must match in number, data type, and order.

Each parameter in the module header must include the data type and a local variable name. Typically, parameter variable names are shorter than variable names in the main module to indicate their temporary nature. The `calcInterest()` module might look like this:

```
Module calcInterest(Numeric prin, Numeric rate, Numeric yrs)
   Declare Numeric interest
   interest = prin * rate * yrs
   Display "The amount of interest earned is: $" + interest
End Module
```

The values of the three arguments from the main module (`principal`, `annualRate`, and `numYears`) are used to initialize the parameter variables, and the body of the module does the computation—in this case, displaying the result in the module. (You learn about returning a value to the calling module later in "Functions: Modules That Return Values.") Any additional local variables needed can be defined in the module. An `End Module` statement marks the end of the module.

You can also have arguments of different data types. The following module displays a message (sent as a `String` argument) a specific number of times (sent as a `Numeric` argument). The arguments must be received in the called module in the same order they're sent from the calling module.

```
Declare String message
Declare Numeric numTimes
Display "What message would you like displayed? "
Input message
Display "How many times would you like it displayed? "
Input numTimes
Call displayMessage(message, numTimes)
```

The code for the called module might look like this:

```
Module displayMessage(String msg, Numeric times)
    Declare Numeric index
    For index = 1 to times
        Display msg
    End For
End Module
```

The number of arguments allowed when calling a module is limited for a practical reason rather than a technical reason. If you have more than five or six arguments in a single module, you might consider breaking it up into two modules with two or three arguments sent to each one to improve your program's readability.

Functions: Modules That Return Values

Many modules do their work without the main (or calling) module needing to know anything about the module's results. Modules used for displaying information, for example, don't usually need to send anything back to the main module. However, if data is needed, such as the result of a calculation, the module can send a **return value** back to the calling module, where it's usually assigned to a variable or used in a display statement or calculation.

As stated, in many programming languages, modules that return values are often called functions. When you call a module by using an argument, you're sending data *to* the module. Functions return values by sending data *back* to the calling module. Although multiple arguments can be sent to modules and functions, a function can return only one value.

Functions can't return more than one value.

You have already used modules that return values. In Chapter 3, you used the following Math method (another name for a module) to calculate a number's square root:

```
someSqRoot = Math.sqrt(someNum);
```

You sent it an argument (someNum), and the sqrt() method calculated the square root and returned the value to the calling statement, where it was stored in the someSqRoot variable. It's a prewritten method of the Math object, along with random(), max(), min(), and many others, but you can write your own functions, too. You might want a function that takes a series of numbers and averages them (calculates the numeric mean), for example. You could write a function that asks the user for two numbers, and then calculates and returns the average. However, you can make the function work for any quantity of numbers by asking the user how many numbers are to be entered or by using a sentinel value to end the input. By making your function flexible in this manner, you can use it several times throughout the program.

Design your modules and functions to be capable of being used in more than one way.

Because a function returns a value to the calling program, the data type of the returned value must be declared by declaring the function itself to be a particular data type. If the function returns a number, for example, it's declared with a Numeric data type. If it returns a string, it's declared as a function with a String data type.

In pseudocode, a function is written much like a module, except the keyword Function is used, followed by the data type, the function name, and the parentheses (with or without parameters to accept arguments). Also, a Return statement is used at the end of the function declaration that includes the value to be sent back to the calling module. When the function is called, the keyword Call isn't needed; instead, an assignment statement calls the function and assigns the returned value to the variable on the left side of the equals sign.

PROGRAM 8-3: Pseudocode Program scoreAverager.txt

In this example, the function you're developing to average an unknown quantity of numbers is declared a Numeric function; however, it doesn't need to accept any arguments because all the input can be done inside the function. After all, matching the number of arguments to the number of parameters in the function is difficult if you don't know how many numbers are going to be averaged. The user is asked how many numbers to input. (Using a sentinel value presents a problem, unless valid input values are restricted. If any number can be input, what sentinel value could be used?)

For this pseudocode program, you code the function first, and then add the main module that calls it later. As usual, add a blank line after each code section, and insert a few blank lines at the beginning so that you have a spot to add the main module later.

1. Open a new document in Notepad, and save it as **scoreAverager.txt**. Enter the function header and declare variables:

```
Function Numeric average()
    // Declare variables
    Declare Numeric inputNum    // number entered
    Declare Numeric quantity    // # numbers input
    Declare Numeric total = 0   // accumulated total
    Declare Numeric index       // loop variable
    Declare Numeric avg         // avg of numbers
```

2. Ask the user how many numbers to average:

```
    // Ask user how many numbers to input
    Display "How many numbers will you input? "
    Input quantity
```

3. Use a For loop to get numbers from the user, and add them to the total:

```
    // Loop for input, accumulate total
    For index = 1 to quantity
        Display "Enter number " + index + ":"
        Input inputNum
        total = total + inputNum
    End For
```

4. Compute the average and return the value to the main module, and then end the function:

```
    // Compute and return average, end function
    avg = total / quantity
```

(continues)

(continued)

```
    Return avg
End Function
```

5. Now you can write the main module that calls the function. The function is called twice to average scores for homework assignments and quizzes. Go back to the top of the file where you left a blank spot, and insert the documentation lines:

```
// Program name: Score Averager
// Purpose: Call the average() function
//    to calculate a mean
// Author: Paul Addison
// Date last modified: 01-Sep-2011
```

6. Start the pseudocode for the main module, declare variables, and welcome the user:

```
Start
    // Declare variables
    Declare Numeric hwAvg      // avg homework scores
    Declare Numeric quizAvg    // avg quiz scores

    // Welcome user
    Display "This program calculates the average"
    Display "for any quantity of numbers."
```

7. Prompt the user to enter homework scores, call the `average()` function, and display the returned result:

```
    // Call function for homework average
    // and display the result
    Display "First, enter homework scores: "
    hwAvg = average()
    Display "Average homework score: " + hwAvg
```

8. Next, prompt the user to enter quiz scores, call the `average()` function, and display the returned result:

```
    // Call function for quiz average
    // and display the result
    Display "Next, enter quiz scores: "
    quizAvg = average()
    Display "Average quiz score: " + quizAvg
```

9. Thank the user, and end the program:

```
    // Thank the user and end the program
    Display "Thank you for using this program."
Stop
```

10. Save the file again.

Detective Work

To convert the program to JavaScript, remember to define the function in the <head> section. Open a new document in Notepad, and save it as scoreAverager.html. Enter your JavaScript code, and then test the program by opening it in a browser. If it doesn't run correctly, compare it with scoreAverager-solution.html in your student data files. Figure 8-5 shows an example of the program in a Web browser.

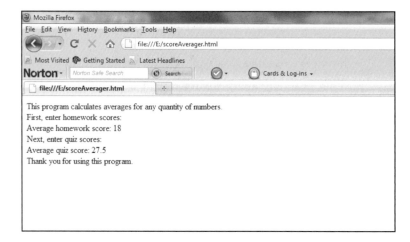

Figure 8-5   The scoreAverager.html program in a Web browser

The following example calls a function to get input and sends a prompt as the argument to the function. Therefore, input for each variable can be done with one line of code in the main module (the function call) instead of two (Display and Input statements).

```
Start
   Declare String username
   Declare String lastName, firstName

   username = getInput("Enter your username: ")
   lastName = getInput("Enter your last name: ")
   firstName = getInput("Enter your first name: ")
Stop

Function String getInput(String prompt)
   Declare returnString
   Display prompt
   Input returnString
   Return returnString
End Function
```

Module Efficiency: Cohesion and Coupling

How do you know whether to turn a few steps of a program into a module or just write the code for the steps in the main module? How do you know whether to pass an argument or just let the module take care of the input? How do you know when to have a module return a value or just display the result in the module?

Two concepts can be helpful in answering these questions: cohesion and coupling. **Cohesion** is the measure of the degree to which all statements and variables in the module relate to one purpose. The function for determining an average in the previous example has strong cohesion because everything in it is related to getting the numbers needed from the user and calculating the average. It doesn't mix the average calculation with statements about homework or quiz scores because the function is designed to be used for any situation in which you need an average. Designing a module for flexibility includes not limiting its use to a specific situation. The module also doesn't contain any code about low scores, high scores, or people's names. It just contains steps to compute the average. The higher a module's cohesion, the better because it has a single purpose and can be used whenever you need code for that purpose.

Coupling is the degree to which a module depends on other modules to do its work. If the average() function relied on global variables instead of arguments, it would be highly coupled with the main module. Likewise, if a function requires more than three or four arguments, it relies more heavily on the module calling it. High coupling limits a module's flexibility, so the lower the coupling factor, the better.

Modularizing a program makes it more efficient by including highly cohesive code and calling another module for each separate task. At first glance, the following example looks like a well-designed program, with numerous module calls in the main module and few details:

```
Start
    Declare Numeric num1, num2   // input numbers
    Declare Numeric result       // result of operation
    Display "Enter the first number: "
    Input num1
    Display "Enter the second number: "
    Input num2
    result = addNums(num1, num2)
    Call displayResult("sum", result)
    result = subtractNums(num1, num2)
    Call displayResult("difference", result)
    result = multiplyNums(num1, num2)
    Call displayResult("product", result)
```

```
        result = divideNums(num1, num2)
        Call displayResult("quotient", result)
    Stop

    Function Numeric addNums(Numeric a, Numeric b)
        Numeric sum = a + b
        Return sum
    End Function

    Function Numeric subtractNums(Numeric a, Numeric b)
        Numeric diff = a - b
        Return diff
    End Function

    Function Numeric multiplyNums(Numeric a, Numeric b)
        Numeric prod = a * b
        Return prod
    End Function

    Function Numeric divideNums(Numeric a, Numeric b)
        Numeric quot = a / b
        Return quot
        End Function

    Module displayResult(String keyword, Numeric num)
        Display "The " + keyword + " of the numbers is " + num
    End Module
```

However, notice that performing all arithmetic and display functions in the main module doesn't require additional lines of code in this module and doesn't require all the code of the four functions and the one module, as shown here:

```
Start
    Declare Numeric num1, num2  // input numbers
    Declare Numeric result      // result of operation
    Display "Enter the first number: "
    Input num1
    Display "Enter the second number: "
    Input num2
    result = num1 + num2
    Display "The sum of the numbers is " + result
    result = num1 - num2
    Display "The difference of the numbers is " + result
    result = num1 * num2
    Display "The product of the numbers is " + result
    result = num1 / num2
    Display "The quotient of the numbers is " + result
Stop
```

A certain amount of computing power is required to call a module. The calling module is paused, and the code for the called module runs. When the called module is completed, the steps in the calling module resume. In other words, you might be "overmodularizing" your code if you write a separate module for every task.

Common sense and a rule of thumb come in handy when deciding whether to use modules. For example, the `prompt()` command in JavaScript is actually a function, so there's no need to write your own function for getting input from the user and calling it each time you want the user to enter a value, even though it would be a highly cohesive function. The `prompt()` function *is* the function you need.

Similarly, writing modules with only two to three lines of code probably cost more computer overhead than just having those two to three statements in the program where they're used. A good rule of thumb is that if you have more than five to six statements that are closely related to the same purpose (high cohesion) and have the potential of being used in more than one place in your program (low coupling), you should consider turning these statements into a module.

Modularization has these advantages:

- The main module is easier to understand yet still gives the "big picture" of what's happening.

- Programmers can work on separate modules for efficiency without having to worry about variable names used in other modules.

- Modules can be reused in a program.

 Programmer's Workshop

Dicey Games is a company that develops computer games. Les Play, the chief gaming officer, has asked you to develop a short program that asks a user to guess a random number from 1 to 10 that the computer generates. After each guess, the program tells the user whether the guess was high, low, or correct. If the user guesses it in three or fewer tries, he or she wins; otherwise, the computer wins.

The program is to use modules or functions to do the following:

- Generate a random number from 1 to 10.

- Compare each user's guess with the random number and report high, low, or correct.

- Report who won (the user or the computer).

Use the IPO method:

- What outputs are requested? A message stating the guess is high, low, or correct and a message indicating the winner of the game

- What inputs do you have available? A random number generated by the computer (numeric), `winningNum`, and the user's guess (numeric), `userGuess`

- What processing is required?

  - Call a `Math` method to generate a random number.

  - Call a module to determine whether a correct guess has been made (string `correct`).

  - Compare each user's guess with the random number up to three times or until the user guesses correctly.

  - Call a module to determine the winner.

Discussion: As you learned in Chapter 7's Object Lesson, the `random()` method of the `Math` class in JavaScript returns a random decimal number between 0 and 1. So to generate a random integer between 1 and the number *n*, the call is `Math.floor(Math.random()*n) + 1`. However, in pseudocode, a random number can be called with this syntax:

```
variable = Random(low number, high number)
```

The module to compare the guess with the correct number should accept both numbers as arguments. A Boolean variable indicates whether a correct guess has been made.

1. Open a new document in Notepad, and save it as **numberGuesser.txt**. Start with the documentation lines:

```
// Program name: Number Guesser
// Purpose: User tries to guess a random number
//    between 1 and 10 in three or fewer guesses
// Author: Paul Addison
// Date last modified: 01-Sep-2011
```

2. Start the program, and declare variables:

```
Start
    // Declare variables
    Declare Numeric winningNum        // winning #
    Declare Numeric userGuess         // user's guess
    Declare Numeric index             // loop index
    Declare Boolean correct = False   // guess
```

3. Generate the random number that the user tries to guess:

```
    // Call Math method to generate random number
    winningNum = Random(1,10)
```

4. Set up a `While` loop to get user guesses. The loop continues until the user has made three guesses or makes a correct guess.

```
// Loop up to three times to get user's guess
index = 1
While index <= 3 And Not correct
    Display "Guess the number: "
    Input userGuess
```

5. Call the module for comparing the user's guess with the winning number and returning a true or false result:

```
// Call module to compare guess with
// winning number and increment index
correct = compareNums(userGuess, winningNum)
index = index + 1
End While
```

6. Call the module to display the winner of the game, and end the main module:

```
// Report winner based on correct variable,
// thank user, and end program
Display "The winning number was " + winningNum
Call reportWinner(correct)
Display "Thank you!"
Stop
```

7. Define the function that compares two numbers and returns a true or false result:

```
Function Boolean compareNums ↵
(Numeric guess, Numeric win)
    Declare Boolean result
    If guess == win Then
        result = True
    Else
        result = False
        If guess < win Then
            Display "Your guess was low."
        Else
            Display "Your guess was high."
        End If
    End If
    Return result
End Function
```

8. Define the module that displays a message based on whether the user won:

```
Module reportWinner(Boolean itIsUser)
    If itIsUser Then
```

```
        Display "Congratulations! You won!"
    Else
        Display "Sorry. Better luck next time."
    End If
End Module
```

9. Save the file again.

Detective Work

Les wants to try the game himself, so he asks you to create a JavaScript program for him to use. Open a new document in Notepad, save it as numberGuesser.html, and convert the preceding pseudocode to JavaScript. Test the program by opening it in a browser. If it doesn't seem to be working correctly, compare it with numberGuesser-solution.html in your student data files. In Figure 8-6, the winning number is 1, and the three guesses are 10, 5, and 1.

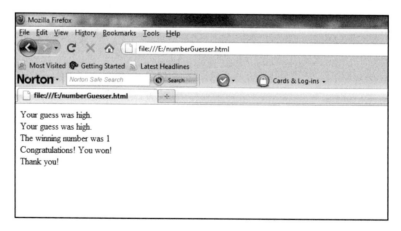

Figure 8-6   The numberGuesser.html program in a Web browser

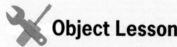

Object Lesson

In object-oriented programming, class modules are called methods, whether they return a value to the calling module or not. In a pseudo-code class definition, if a method doesn't return a value, the method header starts with the method name, as shown:

```
displayInfo()
```

If it does return a value, the data type is listed before the method name, like this:

```
Numeric computeRentalCost(Numeric games)
```

In this Object Lesson, you create a shoe rental system for Lanes Galore, a bowling alley. The system consists of a ShoeRental class, which includes the following attributes:

- Shoe ID (numeric code from 1000 to 9999)

- Shoe size (numeric)

- Renter's first and last names (string)

- Date of rental (string, format MM/DD/YYYY)

- Time of rental (string, format HH:MM, using a 24-hour clock)

- Number of games bowled (numeric)

- Cost of rental (numeric, based on $2 per game bowled)

Your program should have a constructor method for each rental that asks for the preceding information, except the cost of rental, which is a separate method called by the constructor. The cost-of-rental method asks how many games will be played, computes the cost, and returns it to the constructor. You design the program by creating a class diagram and pseudocode, and then develop the program in JavaScript.

1. Using pencil and paper, create a class diagram for the ShoeRental class (see Figure 8-7).

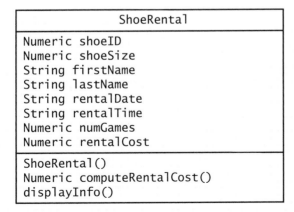

ShoeRental
Numeric shoeID Numeric shoeSize String firstName String lastName String rentalDate String rentalTime Numeric numGames Numeric rentalCost
ShoeRental() Numeric computeRentalCost() displayInfo()

Figure 8-7   Class diagram for the ShoeRental class

2. Now create the pseudocode for the Shoe Rental Class program. Open a new document in Notepad, and save it as **ShoeRentalClass.txt**. Start with the documentation lines:

```
// Program name: Shoe Rental Class
// Purpose: Pseudocode for creating a
// ShoeRental class
// Author: Paul Addison
// Date last modified: 01-Sep-2011
```

3. Start the class definition, and declare the class variables:

```
Class ShoeRental

    // Variables
    Numeric shoeID      // ID# (1000 to 9999)
    Numeric shoeSize    // shoe size
    String firstName    // first name of renter
    String lastName     // last name of renter
    String rentalDate   // rent date (MM/DD/YYYY)
    String rentalTime   // rent time (HH:MM, 24-hr)
    Numeric numGames    // number of games bowled
    Numeric rentalCost  // rental cost ($2 per game)
```

4. Enter the code for the constructor method, which prompts the user for each input field:

```
// Constructor method for shoe rental
Constructor Method ShoeRental()
    Display "Enter the shoe ID number: "
    Input shoeID
    Display "Enter the shoe size: "
    Input shoeSize
    Display "Enter renter's first name: "
    Input firstName
    Display "Enter renter's last name: "
    Input lastName
    Display "Enter date (MM/DD/YYYY): "
    Input rentalDate
    Display "Enter time (HH:MM): "
    Input rentalTime
    Display "How many games is renter bowling? "
    Input numGames
    rentalCost = computeRentalCost(numGames)
End Method
```

5. Enter the code for the method that computes the rental cost:

```
// Method to compute rental cost
Numeric computeRentalCost(Numeric games)
    Constant Numeric COST_PER_GAME = 2
    Declare Numeric cost
    cost = games * COST_PER_GAME
    Return cost
End Method
```

```
    // Method to display info
    displayInfo()
        Display "Renter's name: " ↵
  + firstName + " " + lastName
        Display "Shoe ID: " + shoeID
        Display "Shoe size: " + shoeSize
        Display "Rental date: " + rentalDate
        Display "Rental time: " + rentalTime
        Display "Number of games bowled: " + numGames
        Display "Cost of rental: " + rentalCost
    End Method

  End Class
```

6. Now develop the pseudocode for the main module. First, start the program and welcome the user:

```
Start

    // Welcome the user
    Display "Welcome to Lanes Galore Shoe Rentals"
```

7. Call the constructor module to create the next customer and the method to display information:

```
// Rent a pair of shoes to a customer
ShoeRental nextCustomer = new ShoeRental()
nextCustomer.displayInfo()
```

8. Thank the user, and end the main module:

```
    // Thank the user
    Display "Thank you!"

Stop
```

9. Save the file again.

 Detective Work

Now convert the pseudocode program to JavaScript. Remember that the constructor and other methods are called "functions" in JavaScript and go in the <head> section of the HTML file. Open a new document in Notepad, save it as ShoeRentalClass.html, and enter the JavaScript code.

Test the program by opening it in a browser. If you enter the following data, your browser page should look like Figure 8-8: Renter's name, Carl LaFong; Shoe ID, 12345; Shoe size, 10.5; Rental date, 09/01/2011; Rental time, 13:30; Number of games bowled, 3. If your program doesn't work correctly, compare it with ShoeRentalClass-solution.html in your student data files.

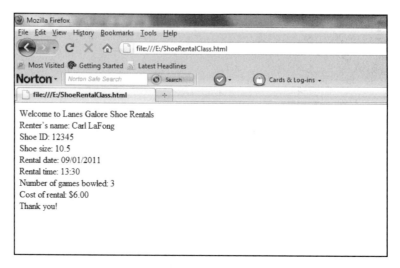

Figure 8-8 The ShoeRentalClass.html program in a Web browser

Chapter Summary

- Modules can make a program's overall purpose clearer and still allow finding details easily.

- Modules can perform useful, reusable tasks in a program.

- A program can be modularized by creating modules from sections of code that perform single tasks.

- Variables can be declared locally in modules without conflicting with other variables.

- Global variables can be used in all modules of a program.

- In flowcharts, a module call is represented by a rectangle with stripes, and a module has its own flowchart.

- Some modules need data, called arguments, sent to them.

- Modules written to accept arguments do so with parameters that match the arguments' number, data type, and order.

- Functions are usually defined as modules that return values.

- In JavaScript, modules are called functions, whether they return a value or not. In object-oriented programming, modules are called methods, whether they return a value to the calling module or not.

- Cohesion is the measure of the degree to which all statements and variables in a module relate to one purpose—in other words, the module's internal consistency. The more a module relates to a specific task, the higher its cohesion.

- Coupling is the degree to which a module depends on other modules to do its work.

Key Terms

cohesion—The measure of the degree to which all statements and variables in the module relate to one purpose.

coupling—The degree to which a module depends on other modules to do its work.

global variables—Variables that are available to all modules in a program.

local variables—Variables created when a module is called; their use is limited to the module in which they're declared.

logic error—An error resulting from giving incorrect instructions to the computer for solving a problem.

main module—The section of a program that's performed first.

module—A section of program code that performs a specific task.

passing by value—Sending the value of a variable or constant to a module, where a local variable is initialized to the argument's value.

return value—A value sent back to the calling module from a called module.

syntax error—An error that occurs when a language's rules are violated, such as a misspelled keyword or incorrect punctuation.

top-down design—This well-tested means of program design is used to develop a program's overall outline and describe tasks to be accomplished first, and then details of these tasks are refined later.

Review Questions

True/False

1. The main module in a program can call a maximum of three other modules. True or False?

2. A module defined by a programmer can call other programmer-defined modules. True or False?

3. When an argument is sent to a module, the data type must be declared in the calling statement. True or False?

4. The number, data types, and order of arguments must match those of parameters in the module being called. True or False?

5. Modules can't declare local variables other than the ones defined as parameters. True or False?

6. A module can be called with multiple arguments. True or False?

7. A module can be called with arguments of different data types. True or False?

8. The value a function returns must be compatible with the variable receiving it as the result of a function call. True or False?

9. A function can return at most one value. True or False?

10. High coupling and low cohesion are usually preferred in modules. True or False?

Multiple Choice

1. What is the purpose of a module? (Choose all that apply.)
    a. to make sections of code reusable
    b. to remove the details of a task from the main module
    c. sometimes to calculate and return a value
    d. to speed up execution time

2. Data sent to a module when calling it is referred to as which of the following?
    a. parameter
    b. argument
    c. constant
    d. constructor

3. A parameter defined in a module must include which of the following? (Choose all that apply.)

    a. data type

    b. new set of parentheses

    c. local variable name

    d. closing bracket

4. Arguments sent to a module must match parameters defined in the module in which of the following ways? (Choose all that apply.)

    a. alphabetical order

    b. number

    c. data type

    d. order

5. Modules that return values to their calling modules are usually referred to as _____.

    a. arguments

    b. parameters

    c. functions

    d. global modules

6. Which of the following flowchart symbols is used to depict calling a module?

    a. decision box diamond

    b. rectangle with stripes

    c. input/output parallelogram

    d. flowline

7. When a module is called, the module that called it is _____.

    a. paused temporarily

    b. terminated permanently

    c. erased

    d. caught in an infinite loop

8. If all the statements in a module relate to a specific task, the module has high _____.

    a. cohesion

    b. coupling

    c. vulnerability

    d. overhead

9. A module that depends on data and conditions from another module has high _____.

    a. cohesion

    b. coupling

    c. vulnerability

    d. overhead

Discussion Questions

1. How do you decide when to create a module from a section of program code?

2. What are some advantages of modularized programs for a programmer?

3. What are some possible drawbacks of overly modularized programs?

Hands-On Activities

Hands-On Activity 8-1

Design a pseudocode program that asks the user for two numbers, and then sends these two numbers as arguments to four arithmetic functions: addition, multiplication, division, and modulus (the remainder after dividing one number by the other). The functions should return the values to the calling module, where they're displayed. (*Note*: The modulus operator is %.) Use Notepad to create the program, and save the file as numberFunctions.txt.

Hands-On Activity 8-2

Convert the pseudocode file in Hands-On Activity 8-1 to JavaScript, and test your program. Save the file as numberFunctions.html.

Hands-On Activity 8-3

Create a pseudocode program that asks the user to enter an integer number from 1 to 20, and then calls a function to compute the factorial of this number. A factorial is the product of an integer times each smaller integer down to 1. For example, the factorial of 5 is 5 * 4 * 3 * 2 * 1 and has the value 120. Use Notepad to create the program, and save the file as factorial.txt. (*Hint*: Set a result variable to 1, and then use a For loop that multiplies the result variable by every number from the given number down to 1.)

Hands-On Activity 8-4

Convert the pseudocode file in Hands-On Activity 8-3 to JavaScript, and test your program. Save the file as factorial.html.

CASE STUDY: Modularizing the Code for It's War!

In this chapter, you make your simulation of the card game War easier to understand and eliminate several lines of code. After the two players' cards are entered, the program runs through a selection structure with If and Else If to determine the point value of each player's card. Because the purpose of these two sections is identical, just applied to different players, the section to convert a card name to its correct point value is an ideal candidate for modularization. Open your pseudocode file warGame-ch7.txt, and save it as warGame-ch8.txt.

After the Stop statement at the end of the program, press Enter twice to add a blank line, and type the header for a function named convertCard(), which takes a string argument called cardName. Add another blank line, and then declare a variable called cardPoints, which is eventually returned to the main module.

```
Function Numeric convertCard(String cardName)

// Declare variables
   Declare Numeric cardPoints
```

Now cut the entire If/Else If structure under the comment "Convert jack, queen, king, or ace to points for the first player," and paste it under the variable declaration you just typed. Change all occurrences of cardName1 to cardName and all occurrences of cardPoints1 to cardPoints. Remember: You're creating one function that can be called for both players. The code should look like this:

```
If cardName == "J" Then
   cardPoints = 11
Else If cardName == "Q" Then
   cardPoints = 12
```

```
Else If cardName == "K" Then
    cardPoints = 13
Else If cardName == "A" Then
    cardPoints = 14
Else
    cardPoints = stringToNumber(cardName)
End If
```

Next, add a statement to return the value of cardPoints to the main module and end the function:

```
Return cardPoints
```

```
End Function
```

Now it's time to clean up the main module. You already cut the If/Else If section under the first player. Insert the call to the function that sends this player's card (cardName1) and receives the points (cardPoints1):

```
cardPoints1 = convertCard(cardName1)
```

Next, delete all code that converts the second player's card name to points, and replace it with the call to convert the card name to points:

```
cardPoints2 = convertCard(cardName2)
```

Save the file again. Your pseudocode program is now cleaner and leaner.

Now it's time to do the same thing to your JavaScript program. Open the JavaScript file warGame-ch7.html, and save it as warGame-ch8.html. You're writing the first function for this program, so you need to insert a <head> section. After the <html> line at the beginning, insert the <head> and <script> tags:

```
<head>
<script type="text/javascript">
```

It's a good idea to have program documentation at the beginning for easier access, so delete the entire comment section and paste it after the new <script> tag for the <head> section, as shown:

```
// Program name: War Game (Chapter 8)
// Purpose:
//    Keep score for the card game War, simplified version.
//    A point goal for the game is entered.
//    The user enters card values for two players each hand.
//    The values are compared, and the player with the
//    higher value wins the combined point value.
//    In case of a tie hand, the points are held while two
//    more card values are compared, until one player wins,
//    getting the points for those cards and all held cards.
//    The first player to reach the point goal wins.
// Author: Paul Addison
// Date last modified: 01-Sep-2011
```

Now make the same changes you did with the pseudocode. Add a function header for the convertCard() function, declare the cardPoints variable, delete the section that converts the first player's card name to points, and paste it under the new variable declaration. Be sure to include opening and closing braces for the function and return the cardPoints value:

```
function convertCard(cardName) {
    // Declare variables
    var cardPoints;

    if (cardName == "J") {
        cardPoints = 11;
    }
    else if (cardName == "Q") {
        cardPoints = 12;
    }
    else if (cardName == "K") {
        cardPoints = 13;
    }
    else if (cardName == "A") {
        cardPoints = 14;
    }
    else {
        cardPoints = parseInt(cardName);
    }
    return cardPoints;
}
```

Under the comment for converting the first player's card, insert the line to call the function:

```
cardPoints1 = convertCard(cardName1);
```

Then replace the whole if/else if section under the comment for converting the second player's card with the line to call the function and convert that card to points:

```
cardPoints2 = convertCard(cardName2);
```

Save your JavaScript file again, and test it. (The output should be identical to the previous version because you didn't make changes to the input or display, so a screenshot isn't included in this chapter.) If the program doesn't run correctly, compare it with warGame-ch8-solution.html in your student data files. It should perform the same as the previous version, and you're using just one section of code to do the conversion for both players!

CHAPTER 9

Menus and Data Validation

In this chapter, you learn to:

◎ Differentiate between interactive and noninteractive programs

◎ Describe the elements of a menu system

◎ Explain how menus and functions work together

◎ Design a validation loop that minimizes user errors during input

◎ Ensure that valid menu choices are made

◎ Explain the use of data validation methods

◎ Use exception handling in addition to immediate error handling

◎ Design and use multilevel menus

Mistakes are a part of being human. Appreciate your mistakes for what they are: precious life lessons that can only be learned the hard way. Unless it's a fatal mistake, which, at least, others can learn from.

—AL FRANKEN, *OH, THE THINGS I KNOW*, 2003

To err is human, but to really foul things up you need a computer.

—PAUL ERLICH, BIOLOGIST AND EDUCATOR

A common acronym in the computer field is GIGO, standing for "garbage in, garbage out." It means that if bad data is entered in the system, the system produces bad data as output. As a programmer, you'll make mistakes, but it's your job to test your programs thoroughly before releasing them to the public.

However, *your* mistakes are only part of the problem. Users can and will make many mistakes when running your programs. Another part of your job is to design your programs in such a way that if users do make mistakes, you inform them immediately and clearly so that they can correct them. If users continue to make mistakes, your program should be designed to stop in a manner that prevents good data from being lost or corrupted. This design feature is sometimes called "bullet-proofing" your programs. Programs that can handle all kinds of user errors without allowing damage are called robust. Programs that can do it immediately, correctly, and smoothly are called elegant.

Two methods for reducing user input errors are providing menus for users to help ensure correct choices and validating data to help ensure correct data input.

Interactive Versus Noninteractive Programs

In the early days of data processing, computer operators often spent a lot of time preparing input data files by keying punch cards. These files were then verified against paper reports to ensure that no errors occurred during processing that might cause the program to halt and result in corrupted data files. After data files were verified, they were often processed at night, when the computer's resources weren't busy handling dozens of system users during business hours. This method of processing data from an input file is called **batch processing**, with the input file considered the batch.

What kinds of mistakes could cause the program to quit or corrupt the files? As an example, if a user enters the letter O instead of the number 0, resulting in the value 259.1O, the computer can't use the numeric value correctly in any calculation. The transaction would be incorrect, and any subtotals, totals, averages, or other statistics would be incorrect because of this one mistake.

Today's processing environment usually includes a database, and updates are typically done at the time of the transaction instead of waiting until evening. With advances in computing power, systems don't require most users to log off so that resources are available for data processing. Transaction processing is done immediately, so it's referred to as **interactive processing** or real-time processing.

When a person is requesting the transaction and being notified of the results, the program is said to be "interactive."

Imagine the problems of a noninteractive system for concert ticket reservations. If updates weren't run until the evening, you would run the risk of selling tickets for the same seat multiple times. You might also have to divide tickets among several local sites, which would limit the number available at each site and possibly deny customers a purchase even if seats were available.

If users are allowed to authorize transactions, you must make sure they can get what they want easily and accurately and ensure that the database (or whatever system you're using) records the transaction correctly.

Single-Level Menus

A menu system limits the choices a user can make so that only valid options are processed. The simplest menu system displays a number of user choices and processes the one the user selects. If the user is expected to make only one choice and then quit, a selection structure can be used.

For example, you have an algorithm that asks the user to deposit money in an account, withdraw money from the account, or inquire about the balance. (Assume the correct account has already been accessed and the current balance is available.) Typically, a single character or digit is entered to select a menu item. Either is acceptable, but if you specify entering a character, you should accept both upper-case and lowercase input. To do this, you can include the toUpper() function, which converts any input to uppercase. This converted input can then be compared with an uppercase value, as shown:

> When prompting users to enter a character, allow uppercase or lowercase input.

```
// Display choices, ask for user input
Display "Enter D for deposit, W for withdrawal,"
Display "or I for inquiry: "
Input menuChoice
menuChoice = toUpper(menuChoice)

// Process menu
If menuChoice == "D" Then
   Display "Enter the amount of the deposit: "
   Input depositAmt
   currentBalance = currentBalance + depositAmt
   Display "Your new balance is: " + currentBalance
Else If menuChoice == "W" Then
   Display "Enter the amount of the withdrawal: "
   Input withdrawalAmt
   currentBalance = currentBalance - withdrawalAmt
   Display "Your new balance is: " + currentBalance
```

```
Else If menuChoice == "I" Then
   Display "Your current balance is: " + currentBalance
End If
```

Notice that if the user doesn't enter a valid choice (D, W, or I), nothing happens. If the user enters an invalid letter, no error message is displayed, and there's no chance for the user to enter a valid choice without running the program again.

When you use a menu system, the most common model is a menu that stays onscreen to use repeatedly, instead of a menu that allows users to make only one choice. To create a menu that's used more than once, a repetition structure that encloses the selection structure is more suitable, and you can also add a choice for the user to exit the menu. As a form of data validation, you should display an error message if the user doesn't enter a valid choice (including the exit choice).

The following pseudocode for a menu using a repetition structure has more choices than the previous example, so the characters users can enter are lined up vertically in the Display statements to make them easier to see. Because the prompt for displaying the menu appears before the start of the loop (a priming prompt, discussed in Chapter 6), this code must be repeated just before the End While at the end of the loop, as shown:

```
// Display choices, ask for user input
Display "Enter D for deposit,"
Display "     W for withdrawal,"
Display "     I for inquiry,"
Display "  or X to exit the menu: "
Input menuChoice
menuChoice = toUpper(menuChoice)

// Process menu until user enters X
While menuChoice != "X"
   If menuChoice == "D" Then
      Display "Enter the amount of the deposit: "
      Input depositAmt
      currentBalance = currentBalance + depositAmt
      Display "Your new balance is: " + currentBalance
   Else If menuChoice == "W" Then
      Display "Enter the amount of the withdrawal: "
      Input withdrawalAmt
      currentBalance = currentBalance - withdrawalAmt
      Display "Your new balance is: " + currentBalance
   Else If menuChoice == "I" Then
      Display "Your current balance is: " + currentBalance
   Else
      Display "ERROR: Enter D, W, I, or X: "
   End If

   // Display choices, ask for user input
   Display "Enter D for deposit,"
```

```
        Display "      W for withdrawal,"
        Display "      I for inquiry,"
        Display "   or X to exit the menu: "
        Input menuChoice
        menuChoice = toUpper(menuChoice)
End While
```

If you replace the While loop with a Do While loop, as shown in the following example, you don't have to prompt the user twice:

```
// Process menu until user enters X
Do
    // Display choices, ask for user input
    Display "Enter D for deposit,"
    Display "      W for withdrawal,"
    Display "      I for inquiry,"
    Display "   or X to exit the menu: "
    Input menuChoice
    menuChoice = toUpper(menuChoice)

    If menuChoice == "D" Then
        Display "Enter the amount of the deposit: "
        Input depositAmt
        currentBalance = currentBalance + depositAmt
        Display "Your new balance is: " + currentBalance
    Else If menuChoice == "W" Then
        Display "Enter the amount of the withdrawal: "
        Input withdrawalAmt
        currentBalance = currentBalance - withdrawalAmt
        Display "Your new balance is: " + currentBalance
    Else If menuChoice == "I" Then
        Display "Your current balance is: " + currentBalance
    Else If menuChoice != "X" Then
        Display "ERROR: Enter D, W, I, or X. "
    End If
While menuChoice != "X"
```

Menus, Functions, and Stubs

In Chapter 8, you learned that a module or function is suitable when you have a series of highly cohesive statements that can be used in more than one place in a program. In a menu with several items, a module or function can also be useful for the lines of code to display the menu and get the user's choice. Using the same bank account example, the following module produces a value the main program needs, so a function is called for. The displayMenu() function returns the string value the user inputs in response to the prompt. The variable is created in the function, and its value is passed back in the Return statement.

```
// Function to display choices, ask for user input
Function String displayMenu()
    Declare String selection
    Display "Enter D for deposit,"
```

```
   Display "      W for withdrawal,"
   Display "      I for inquiry,"
   Display "   or X to exit the menu: "
   Input selection
   Return selection
End Function
```

In the main module, the preceding code is replaced by this line:

```
menuChoice = displayMenu()
```

The processing steps for each menu choice are also candidates for modules or functions because the deposit and withdrawal choices are cohesive tasks. The account balance is changed by both tasks, but the deposit and withdrawal amounts are temporary. Therefore, the account balance can be sent as an argument and returned as a value, with the variable for the transaction amount being prompted for inside the module (called "local to the function").

Should you make the processing for inquiring about the balance a separate module? After all, it's just one line of code. However, you need to consider the program's consistency as well as the amount of code a task involves when you're making decisions about when to use modules. Because you're turning all other processing tasks into modules, consistency should take precedence.

Consistency is important for good programming design and readability.

The inquiry module doesn't need to return a value, but it can accept the account balance as an argument. Here are the three processing functions and modules:

```
// Deposit function
Function Numeric deposit(Numeric balance)
   Declare Numeric transAmt
   Display "Enter the amount of the deposit: "
   Input transAmt
   balance = balance + transAmt
   Display "Your new balance is: " + balance
   Return balance
End Function

// Withdrawal function
Function Numeric withdrawal(Numeric balance)
   Declare Numeric transAmt
   Display "Enter the amount of the withdrawal: "
   Input transAmt
   balance = balance - transAmt
   Display "Your new balance is: " + balance
   Return balance
End Function

// Inquiry module
Module Void inquiry(Numeric balance)
   Display "Your current balance is: " + balance
End Module
```

The selection part of the main module now looks like this:

```
If menuChoice == "D" Then
    currentBalance = deposit(currentBalance)
Else If menuChoice == "W" Then
    currentBalance = withdrawal(currentBalance)
Else If menuChoice == "I" Then
    Call inquiry(currentBalance)
Else If menuChoice != "X" Then
    Display "ERROR: Enter D, W, I, or X. "
End If
```

Because you aren't using a data file with existing accounts and balances, this algorithm requires starting all accounts with a balance of 0. You can find the complete pseudocode for a working algorithm in bankAccountMenu.txt in your student data files for this chapter.

In JavaScript, the `toUpperCase()` function is called by using the *object.method*() format, as shown:

`menuChoice = menuChoice.toUpperCase();`

When converting the preceding pseudocode to JavaScript, keep these points in mind:

- Remember that functions are listed first in the <head> section.

- Constants are declared in the <head> section before any function definitions so that they're available to the <head> section.

Starting in this chapter, error messages are displayed in a JavaScript **alert box**, a pop-up box that requires the user to click OK before proceeding. The syntax of this function is as follows:

`alert(string message);`

Informational messages, such as account balances, are still displayed by using `document.write()`.

PROGRAM 9-1 JavaScript Program bankAccountMenu.html

Remember to add a blank line after the code section in each step to improve your program's readability.

1. Open a new document in Notepad, and save the file as **bankAccountMenu.html.**

2. Enter the HTML tags for a JavaScript program and the documentation lines.

(continues)

(continued)

```
<html>
<head>
<script type="text/javascript">

// Program name: bankAccountMenu.html
// Purpose: Use a menu system to process
// bank account transactions
// Author: Paul Addison
// Date last modified: 01-Sep-2011
```

3. Declare the usual constants:

```
// Declare constants for <head> section
var ES = "";         // empty string
var BR = "<br />";   // HTML line break
```

4. Enter the code for the `deposit()` and `withdrawal()` functions:

```
// Deposit function
function deposit(balance) {
    var transAmt;
    transAmt = ↵
 prompt("Enter the amount of the deposit:",ES);
    transAmt = parseFloat(transAmt);
    balance = balance + transAmt;
    document.write("Your new balance is: $" + ↵
 balance.toFixed(2) + BR);
    return balance;
}

// Withdrawal function
function withdrawal(balance) {
    var transAmt;
    transAmt = ↵
 prompt("Enter the amount of the withdrawal:",ES);
    transAmt = parseFloat(transAmt);
    balance = balance - transAmt;
    document.write("Your new balance is: $" + ↵
 balance.toFixed(2) + BR);
    return balance;
}
```

5. Enter the code for the `inquiry()` function and the tags for the end of the `<head>` section:

```
// Inquiry function
function inquiry(balance) {
    document.write("Your current balance is: $" + ↵
 balance.toFixed(2) + BR);
}
```

(continues)

(continued)

```
</script>
</head>
```

6. Enter the code to start the <body> section and declare variables and constants:

```
<body>
<script type="text/javascript">

// Declare variables and constants for <body>
var menuChoice;                    // user's menu choice
var currentBalance = 0.00; // current acct balance
var BR = "<br />";                 // HTML line break
var PA = "<p />";                  // HTML paragraph
var NL = "\n";                     // newline character
```

7. Welcome the user, start the loop, display the menu, and get the user's choice:

```
// Welcome the user
document.write ↵
("Welcome to the Bank Account Menu program!" + PA);

do {
    // Display choices, ask for user input,
    // convert to uppercase
    menuChoice = prompt("Enter D for deposit," + NL
        + "   W for withdrawal," + NL
        + "   I for inquiry, or" + NL
        + "   X to exit the menu:",ES);
    menuChoice = menuChoice.toUpperCase();
```

8. Process the user's choice by calling the matching function. Display an error message if the input is invalid, and then close the loop:

```
    if (menuChoice == "D") {
        currentBalance = deposit(currentBalance);
    }
    else if (menuChoice == "W") {
        currentBalance = withdrawal(currentBalance);
    }
    else if (menuChoice == "I") {
        inquiry(currentBalance);
    }
    else if (menuChoice != "X") {
        alert("ERROR: Enter D, W, I, or X." + BR);
    }
} while (menuChoice != "X");
```

(continues)

(continued)

9. Thank the user, and end the program:

```
// Thank the user and end the program
document.write("Thank you!" + BR);

</script>
</body>
</html>
```

10. Save the file again, and open it in a browser. Your account starts at 0. To test the program, try making inquiries and entering deposits and withdrawals. Figure 9-1 shows what your browser page looks like if you make a deposit of $100, a withdrawal of $25, and an inquiry, and then exit the program.

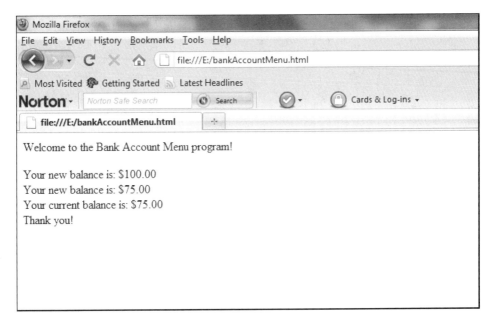

Figure 9-1   The bankAccountMenu.html program in a Web browser

When modules and functions are used as menu-processing choices, you can design a menu system easily by using the top-down method of program design. With this method, you can give the module a name for testing purposes, and then fill in the details for performing the task later. A module is sometimes called a **black box** because those looking at the module don't need to know what it contains internally, as long as they know the module's purpose and how to use it.

For purposes of testing, you can create a temporary module for each menu choice by just adding a display statement with a message such as "In Shipping module". This temporary module is called a **stub**, and it serves as a placeholder in your program until you develop the code. It enables you to test your program so that you can make sure the module is called correctly.

For example, you're creating a menu for a word game. You know what games will be included but haven't written the code for them yet. Still, you can test the menu. To make sure modules are called correctly, you can design each module as a stub, including a simple one-line display indicating that the program has indeed found the module, as shown:

```
// Program name: Word Game Menu
// Purpose: Uses a menu system to play
// different word games
// Author: Paul Addison
// Date last modified: 01-Sep-2011

Start
    // Declare variables
    Declare Numeric menuChoice

    // Loop until user exits menu
    Do
        // Call function to display menu
        // and get user selection
        menuChoice = displayMenu()
        If menuChoice == 1 Then
            playCryptogram()
        Else If menuChoice == 2 Then
            playAnagram()
        Else If menuChoice == 3 Then
            playWordSearch()
        Else If menuChoice != 9 Then
            Display "Invalid selection."
            Display "Please enter 1, 2, 3, or 9: "
        End If
    While menuChoice != 9
Stop

// Display menu function
Function Numeric displayMenu()
    // Declare variables, display menu, get selection
    Declare Numeric choice
    Display "Enter 1 to play Cryptogram,"
    Display "      2 to play Anagram,"
    Display "      3 to play Word Search,"
    Display "   or 9 to exit this menu. "
    Input choice
    Return choice
End Function
```

```
// Cryptogram module (stub)
Module playCryptogram()
    Display "Playing Cryptogram!"
End Module

// Anagram module (stub)
Module playAnagram()
    Display "Playing Anagram!"
End Module

// Word Search module (stub)
Module playWordSearch()
    Display "Playing Word Search!"
End Module
```

As you know, the Case structure is a variation of the If/Else If
structure and can be used if your programming language supports it.
The menu portion of the preceding code can be written like this:

```
// Loop until user exits menu
Do
    // Call function to display menu
    // and get user selection
    menuChoice = displayMenu()
    Select menuChoice:
        Case 1:
            playCryptogram()
        Case 2:
            playAnagram()
        Case 3:
            playWordSearch()
        Case 9:
            Display    // no action taken but a valid choice
        Default:
            Display "Invalid selection."
            Display "Please enter 1, 2, 3, or 9: "
While menuChoice != 9
```

Like all modular program development, developing a menu system
this way keeps the control section (the menu itself) separated from
the content section (the modules), making it easier to develop and
improve both sections.

Validation Loops

One of the simplest and most common methods to ensure that users
enter correct data is called a **validation loop**. Immediately after the user
makes a selection or enters input, the program checks to see that the data
is acceptable. If it isn't, the user is prompted again to enter an acceptable
value, normally with a hint or a list of acceptable values. A loop is used
because if the user enters incorrect data a second or third time, it's a way
to make sure valid data is entered before the program proceeds.

In a small business, even if employees are allowed to work overtime, there might be a policy limiting total hours a week to 80. Your program prompts the user for input, followed by a validation loop that repeats until an acceptable value is entered:

```
// Declare variables
Declare Numeric numHours    // number of hours worked

// Prompt for number of hours
Display "Enter number of hours worked or -1 to quit: "
Input numHours

// Verify number of hours
While numHours < -1 Or numHours > 80
   Display "ERROR: The number must be from 0 to 80 or -1."
   Display "Enter number of hours worked or -1 to quit: "
   Input numHours
End While
```

If an acceptable value is entered the first time, the loop body isn't entered. However, after it's entered, the user stays in the loop until a number between -1 and 80 is entered. The condition in the `While` statement specifies an invalid condition that requires attention.

Sometimes an entry needs to match a predetermined set of valid values. For example, you might have status codes of S for shipped, I for invoiced, and O for ordered. You can state the `While` condition so that the loop body is entered if the input doesn't match any of the predetermined valid values, as shown:

```
// Declare variables
Declare String statusCode    // status code for order

// Prompt for status code
Display "Enter the status code for the order: "
Input statusCode

// Verify status code
While statusCode != "S" And statusCode != "I" ↵
 And statusCode != "O"
   Display "ERROR: The status code must be S, I, or O."
   Display "Enter the status code for the order: "
   Input statusCode
End While
```

Progressive Error Messages

You might discover that users tend to make the same mistakes with your program, even when you repeatedly display an error message with the correct information. One technique for "breaking the bottleneck" is to display increasingly severe messages if the user continues to make mistakes. After, say, the third incorrect entry, the message can be worded more strongly, and after the sixth incorrect entry, the user can be instructed to see a manager or seek other professional help. (Be careful how you word this message, however!) To include a count of the number of incorrect entries, the previous pseudocode can be rewritten as shown:

```
// Declare variables
Declare String statusCode        // status code for order
Declare Numeric numErrors = 0    // count of user errors
// Prompt for status code
Display "Enter the status code for the order: "
Input statusCode

// Verify status code
While statusCode != "S" And statusCode != "I" ↵
 And statusCode != "O"
    numErrors = numErrors + 1
    If numErrors <= 3 Then
       Display "ERROR: The status code must be S, I, or O."
    Else If numErrors <=6 Then
          Display ↵
   "ERROR: You entered a status code of: " + statusCode
          Display ↵
   "The only valid status codes are S, I, or O."
    Else
       Display "ERROR: You have repeatedly entered"
       Display "invalid status codes."
       Display "Please see your manager about"
       Display "valid status codes before continuing."
    End If
    Display "Enter the status code for the order: "
    Input statusCode
End While
```

Code to verify the correctness of entries is yet another candidate for a module or function. If you add three status codes (for example, B, R, and P for back-ordered, reordered, and partial), the code in the main module begins to look cluttered. In this example, you can write a function named isValidStatusCode() to return True if the code is valid and False if not:

```
// Function to verify status code
Function Boolean isValidStatusCode(String code)
    If code != "S" And code != "I" And code != "O" ↵
   And code != "B" And code != "R" And code != "P" Then
       Display ↵
   "ERROR: The status code must be S, I, O, B, R, or P."
       Return False
Else
    Return True
End Function
```

The code in the main module looks like this:

```
// Prompt for status code
Display "Enter the status code for the order: "
Input statusCode

// Verify status code
While Not isValidStatusCode(statusCode)
    Display "Enter the status code for the order: "
    Input statusCode
End While
```

Types of Data Validation

In the preceding section, you checked to see whether a value was within an accepted range (0 to 80) and whether it matched specific values (status codes S, I, or D). These checks are only two of the many types of data validation you can perform. Others include the following:

- Data type

- Presence of data

- Logical relationships of data

Text data (data of the String type) consists of almost anything the user can type at the keyboard. Many languages have functions for use with text data to see whether its contents can be converted to another data type, usually Numeric. In the following examples, str refers to string data entered by the user, and num represents a numeric value. Functions that operate on strings are called **string manipulation functions**. Some of these functions include the following:

- isNumeric(str)—Returns True if the text can be converted to a number

- isLetter(str)—Returns True if all characters in the string are letters of the alphabet

JavaScript has a function called isNaN() that returns a True value if a string can't be converted to a number; the "NaN" stands for "not a number."

If you know the string can be converted correctly, most languages have conversion functions that do the work for you. Testing data before converting it is important because programs can "crash" (stop running abruptly) if they encounter a data error. Data conversion functions include the following:

- stringToNumber(str)—Converts a string to a numeric value

- numberToString(num)—Converts a number to a string value

In JavaScript, the `parseInt()` and `parseFloat()` functions perform these two conversions. JavaScript converts a number to a string format automatically if the number needs to be displayed as text.

To show how this type of data validation works, the following pseudocode performs a test on data that's supposed to be numeric:

Test your data before converting it to help prevent programs from crashing.

```
// Declare variables
Declare String userInput
Declare Numeric wageRate

// Ask for wage rate
Display "Enter the wage rate: "
Input userInput

// Verify that input is numeric
While Not isNumeric(userInput)
   Display "Please enter a numeric value. "
   Display "Enter the wage rate: "
   Input userInput
End While

// Convert to a number
wageRate = stringToNumber(userInput)
```

Most programming languages have other string manipulation functions or methods that can help you validate string input. Two of the most common in pseudocode are used to return the length of a string and a substring of characters from the string:

- `length(str)`—Returns the number of characters in a string (the string length)

- `substring(str, start, numChars)`—Returns a substring of the original string, starting with the position specified by the `start` argument and including the number of characters specified by `numChars`. Remember that the first position in a string is considered position 0.

For example, say the string variable `storeName` has been set to the value "Goodness Grocery", and your program contains the following statements:

```
storeNameLength = length(storeName)
storeAbbr1 = substring(storeName,0,4)
storeAbbr2 = substring(storeName,9,3)
```

After these statements are performed, the numeric variable `storeNameLength` has the value 16, and the string variables `storeAbbr1` and `storeAbbr2` have the values "Good" and "Gro". Figure 9-2 shows these function calls.

Figure 9-2   The `length()` and `substring()` functions applied to a string

The JavaScript equivalents of these functions are the `length` property and the `substr()` method:

- `str.length`—The string is named first followed by a dot and the keyword `length`, with no parentheses.

Depending on the programming language, arguments to functions differ in number, order, and meaning, especially in string manipulation functions. The second numeric argument for string functions might specify the number of characters to include, the last character to include, or sometimes the first character *not* to include. Always check the definitions of functions for the language you're using.

- `str.substr(start, numChars)`—The string is named first followed by a dot, the keyword `substr`, and the two numeric arguments in parentheses.

The previous pseudocode functions are implemented in JavaScript like this:

```
storeNameLength = storeName.length;
storeAbbr1 = storeName.substr(0,4);
storeAbbr2 = storeName.substr(9,3);
```

 Although functions, methods, and properties can yield the same results, their syntax differs. Function calls start with the function name and are followed by the arguments (which can be constants or variables) in parentheses. Method calls start with the object name and are followed by a dot, the method name, and parentheses for enclosing arguments. Properties of objects are formatted similarly—object name, dot, and property name—but have no parentheses because there are no arguments to be sent. In pseudocode, strings are treated as variables, so the `length()` and `substr()` examples shown in pseudocode are functions. In JavaScript, strings are objects, so `length` is a property and `substr()` is a method.

You can use string manipulation functions to check every character in a string, a process sometimes called **traversing** a string. For example, you can set up a loop to check the length of a string and use the `substring()` function to extract one character at a time. The following algorithm is used to count the number of times the uppercase letter A appears in a sentence:

```
// Declare variables
Declare String sentence      // sentence user enters
Declare Numeric numA = 0     // number of times A occurs
Declare String char1         // single character in sentence
Declare Numeric index        // loop index
Declare Numeric sentLen      // length of sentence

// Get sentence from user
Display "Enter a sentence: "
Input sentence
```

```
// Traverse sentence, count occurrences of letter A
sentLen = length(sentence)
For index = 0 to sentLen - 1
    char1 = substring(sentence, index, 1)
    If char1 == "A" Then
        numA = numA + 1
    End If
End For

// Display result
Display "Number of times A occurs: " + numA
```

You can also use relational operators to check whether a character is within a certain range because the 26 uppercase letters, the 26 lowercase letters, and the 10 digits are consecutive in the ASCII and Unicode character sets. To check that a character is an uppercase letter, for example, you can see whether it's "between" the letters A and Z in the character set by using >= "A" and <= "Z". To count the number of uppercase letters in a sentence, you need to modify the preceding algorithm just slightly:

```
// Declare variables
Declare String sentence        // sentence user enters
Declare Numeric numUpper = 0   // # of uppercase letters
Declare String char1           // single character in sentence
Declare Numeric index          // loop index

// Get sentence from user
Display "Enter a sentence: "
Input sentence

// Traverse sentence, count occurrences of uppercase letters
For index = 0 to length(sentence) - 1
    char1 = substring(sentence, index, 1)
    If char1 >= "A" And char1 <= "Z" Then
        numUpper = numUpper + 1
    End If
End For

// Display result
Display "Number of uppercase letters: " + numUpper
```

Another type of validation is checking for the presence of data. This task is fairly easy because you can set the value of an empty string for a data field, and if the user doesn't enter anything, the field still contains the empty string. In this example, the program asks for a customer ID number:

```
// Declare variables
Declare String customerID = ""

// Ask for Customer ID
Display "Enter the customer ID: "
Input customerID
```

In some programming languages, when a user presses Enter without typing anything, the input variable's value is set to a constant called NULL. Instead of checking for an empty string, you check to see whether the variable equals NULL.

```
// Verify presence of customer ID
While customerID == ""
    Display "This is a required field."
    Display "Enter the customer ID: "
    Input customerID
End While
```

A third type of data validation concerns logical relationships between two pieces of data, as in the following examples:

- The day of the month shouldn't be less than 1 or greater than the number of days in the month.

- A loan-out date (for a book or DVD, for example) shouldn't be later than the due date.

- A five-digit zip code field shouldn't be included if the country code isn't USA.

You can write your own validation functions with some basic knowledge of functions already available to you. Many languages have a date validation function, but you can easily write one that checks to see whether the date is in the correct format. If you require dates in the format mm/dd/yyyy, you can write a function called isValidDateFormat(str) that returns True if the date is entered in this format and False if it isn't. For example, the following function checks that the month and day entries are two characters and the year is four characters. It also checks that the month is between 1 and 12 and the day is between 1 and 31. (It doesn't check the number of days in a particular month or whether the year is a leap year.)

You can use the substring() function explained earlier to look for certain characters in specific positions, such as the slash (/) in a date:

```
// Date validation function
Function Boolean isValidDateFormat(String str)

    // Declare variables
    Declare String mm, dd, yyyy       // month, day, year
    Declare Boolean result = True     // valid date format

    // Check that length of string is 10
    If length(str) != 10 Then
        result = False
    End If

    // Check that third and sixth characters are slashes
    If substring(str,2,1) != "/" Or ↵
 substring(str,5,1) != "/" Then
        result = False
    End If
```

```
   // Separate string into parts
   // Check that all entries are numeric
   mm = substring(str,0,2)      // month
   dd = substring(str,3,2)      // day
   yyyy = substring(str,6,4)    // year
   If Not isNumeric(mm) Or Not isNumeric(dd) ↵
 Or Not isNumeric(yyyy) Then
       result = False
   End If

   // Check that month is between 1 and 12
   // and day is between 1 and 31
   If (mm < 1 Or mm > 12) Or (dd < 1 Or dd > 31) Then
       result = False
   End If

   Return result
End Function
```

Exception Handling

Anticipating user errors in a program is always a good practice, but adding data validation code at every point in the program where input occurs takes a lot of code and a lot of time. To provide another method for detecting data input errors (known as "exceptions") when they occur in a program, a concept called **exception handling** was developed along with object-oriented programming. Several exceptions are defined in programming languages and detected automatically by the operating system when they occur during runtime. Exception handling works like this:

- The programmer writes code that should run when a particular type of exception is detected. This code is put in a Catch block, one for each type of anticipated exception. Typical exception types are "invalid format" and "attempted division by zero."

- To test whether the Catch block works, the programmer puts statements that might cause a particular type of error in a Try block.

- When an error is detected, a signal is created, which is an action called "throwing" an exception. At this point, any Catch blocks associated with the Try block are activated to check whether the exception that was thrown matches the exception specified in the Catch block. If so, the code in the Catch block runs.

In the following example of a Try block, if the user enters input that's not a number in response to the prompt, a NumberFormatException error is thrown:

```
Try
    Display "Enter a number: "
    Input num1
End Try
```

The following Catch block takes action if an exception of the NumberFormatException type is detected. The parameter ex is the name of the exception thrown; it's actually an object with properties, such as a descriptive message.

```
Catch(NumberFormatException ex)
    Display "You did not enter a valid number."
End Catch
```

The Try block containing the "test" statement and its associated Catch block can be in the module where the exception occurred or in the module that called the module where the exception occurred. If there's no Try/Catch block combination in the module where the exception was thrown, the program passes the exception back to the module that called it to see whether it contains a Try/Catch block combination and, if applicable, passes the exception to the module that called it. The program continues passing the exception, and if there's no Try/Catch block in any module all the way up to the main module, the exception is passed to the operating system, and the program typically crashes.

The names for exceptions differ with each language.

In the following example, a module asks for two numbers and checks for two exceptions: "invalid format" and "attempted division by zero." Notice that the exception names in the Catch parameters are used like data types.

```
Module divideNums()
    // Declare variables
    Declare Numeric numerator      // numerator
    Declare Numeric denominator    // denominator
    Declare Numeric quotient       // quotient

    Try
        Display "Enter the numerator: "
        Input numerator
        Display "Enter the denominator: "
        Input denominator

        quotient = numerator / denominator
        Display "The quotient is: " + quotient
    End Try
```

```
    Catch(InvalidFormatException ex)
        Display "You did not enter a valid number."
        Display "Please try again."
    End Catch

    Catch(AttemptedDivisionByZeroException ex)
        Display "You cannot enter zero (0) as a denominator."
        Display "Please try again."
    End Catch
End Module
```

If the user enters a nonnumeric character for the variable numerator or denominator, an InvalidFormatException exception is thrown because the variables were declared as numeric, and the first Catch block is performed. If both values are numeric but the second one is 0, an AttemptedDivisionByZeroException exception is thrown at the line that tries to do the division, and the second Catch block is performed.

The Try and Catch blocks could also have been placed in a main module that calls the divideNums() module, as shown in the following example. If the program finds no Try/Catch block combination in the module where they occurred, the exception is passed back to the main module, and the Catch block code is performed at that point.

```
Start
    Try
        Call divideNums()
    End Try

    Catch(InvalidFormatException ex)
        Display "You did not enter a valid number."
        Display "Please try again."
    End Catch

    Catch(AttemptedDivisionByZeroException ex)
        Display "You cannot enter zero (0) as a denominator."
        Display "Please try again."
    End Catch
Stop

Module divideNums()
    // Declare variables
    Declare Numeric numerator      // number for division
    Declare Numeric denominator    // number for division
    Declare Numeric quotient       // answer

    Display "Enter the numerator: "
    Input numerator
    Display "Enter the denominator: "
    Input denominator

    quotient = numerator / denominator
    Display "The quotient is: " + quotient
End Module
```

You aren't limited to predefined exception types, however. In most languages, you can throw an exception you define. The simplest type is a message. Because these programmer-defined exceptions aren't known in the programming language, you can test for the exception's value and proceed accordingly.

The following example shows how to define your own exceptions for out-of-range values. If the number is out of range, an exception is thrown. The Display statement indicating correct input is performed only if an exception isn't thrown. In this pseudocode, a generic exception (that is, one without a name) is thrown by using the keyword Throw followed by the error message as a string literal. The exception is caught in a Catch block with a string parameter (ex) to receive the error message. The string is then tested for different values to determine what kind of error occurred.

PROGRAM 9-2 Pseudocode Program
rangeExceptions.txt

Don't forget to add a blank line after the code section in each step.

1. Open a new document in Notepad, and save it as **rangeExceptions.txt**. First, start with the module code:

```
Module rangeExceptions()
    // Declare variables
    Declare Numeric num1    // number for testing

    Try
        Display "Enter a number between 1 and 100: "
        Input num1
        If num1 < 1 Then
            Throw "Out of Range Low"
        Else If num1 > 100 Then
            Throw "Out of Range High"
        End If
        Display "Number is in the correct range."
    End Try

    Catch(String ex)
        If ex == "Out of Range Low" Then
            Display "The number entered is too low."
        Else If ex == "Out of Range High" Then
            Display "The number entered is too high."
        End If
    End Catch
End Module
```

(continues)

(continued)

2. To turn this module into a usable program, insert a main module at the beginning with a loop that prompts the user to enter a number and asks whether the user wants to continue:

```
// Program name: Range Exceptions
// Purpose: Throw and catch out-of-range errors
// Author: Paul Addison
// Date last modified: 01-Sep-2011

Start
    // Declare variables
    Declare String more = "Y"

    // Program heading
    Display "This program tests numbers in a range."

    While toUpper(more) == "Y"
        Call rangeExceptions()
        Display "Test another number? "
        Input more
    End While

    // Thank user
    Display "Thank you."
Stop
```

3. Save the file again.

JavaScript also has try, catch, and throw capabilities. The throw statement should be accompanied by an error message, which isn't enclosed in parentheses. The catch block checks to see what the error message is before proceeding.

 ## Detective Work

Now try converting the preceding pseudocode to JavaScript. Remember that a module is a function in JavaScript, and you need to add a <body> section with its own <script> section to call the module. The only statement you need in this <script> section is rangeExceptions();. When you run the program, test it by entering values that are in range (such as 40 and 100) and out of range (for example, –50 and 200). Your browser page should look like Figure 9-3. If your program doesn't run correctly, compare it with rangeExceptions-solution.html in your student data files.

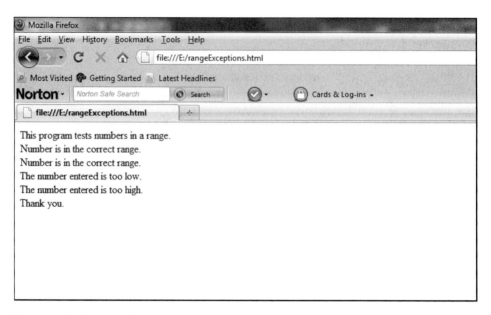

Figure 9-3   The rangeExceptions.html program in a Web browser

Using Multilevel Menus

You know that modules can call other modules. In a similar way, a menu choice from the main module can also consist of a menu, referred to as a **submenu**. A **multilevel menu** presents a main menu, and then leads users to submenus. It can be designed without using modules, but top-down design is easier when you use modules as a starting point for designing a menu.

For example, the top-level menu in a small business might divide data-processing applications into two major areas: Customer Service and Order Processing. Selecting Customer Service takes the user to a submenu with the choices Add New Customer, Change Customer Information, and Delete Customer. The Order Processing selection takes the user to a submenu with the choices Placing an Order, Invoicing, and Shipping. Because there are only two menu choices plus a choice to exit the application, menu choices are displayed in the main module, instead of calling a separate module.

PROGRAM 9-3 Pseudocode Program companyMenu.txt

Don't forget to add a blank line after the code section in each step.

1. First, you write the pseudocode for the main module. Open a new document in Notepad, and save it as **companyMenu.txt**. Enter the following code:

```
// Program name: Company Menu
// Purpose: A menu system for customer service
// and order processing
// Author: Paul Addison
// Date last modified: 01-Sep-2011

Start
    // Declare variables
    Declare String menuChoice

    // Loop until user exits menu
    Do
        // Display menu
        Display "Enter C for Customer Service menu,"
        Display "     O for Order Processing menu,"
        Display "  or Q to Quit this program: "
        Input menuChoice
        menuChoice = toUpper(menuChoice)

        // Call requested submenu or exit program
        If menuChoice == "C" Then
            customerServiceMenu()
        Else If menuChoice == "O" Then
            orderProcessingMenu()
        Else If menuChoice != "Q" Then
            Display "Invalid selection:"
            Display "Enter C, O, or Q: "
        End If
    While menuChoice != "Q"

    // Say goodbye and end program
    Display "Goodbye!"
Stop
```

2. The next level is the two submenus: Customer Service and Order Processing. You can design these submenus in a similar manner, except that exiting these submenus takes the user back to the main menu instead of exiting the program.

(continues)

(continued)

```
// Customer Service menu
Module customerServiceMenu()
    // Declare variables
    Declare String subMenuChoice

    // Loop until user exits submenu
    Do
        // Display submenu
        Display "Enter A to Add a new customer,"
        Display "      C to Change customer info,"
        Display "      D to Delete a customer, or"
        Display "      Q to Quit this submenu: "
        Input subMenuChoice
        subMenuChoice = toUpper(subMenuChoice)

        // Process submenu choice
        If subMenuChoice == "A" Then
            addCustomer()
        Else If subMenuChoice == "C" Then
            changeCustomer()
        Else If subMenuChoice == "D" Then
            deleteCustomer()
        Else If subMenuChoice != "Q" Then
            Display "Invalid selection:"
            Display "Enter A, C, D, or Q. "
    While subMenuChoice != "Q"
End Module

// Order Processing menu
Module orderProcessingMenu()
    // Declare variables
    Declare String subMenuChoice

    // Loop until user exits submenu
    Do
        // Display submenu
        Display "Enter P for Placing an order,"
        Display "      I for Invoicing,"
        Display "      S for Shipping, or"
        Display "      Q to Quit this submenu: "
        Input subMenuChoice
        subMenuChoice = toUpper(subMenuChoice)

        // Process submenu choice
        If subMenuChoice == "P" Then
            placeOrder()
        Else If subMenuChoice == "I" Then
            invoiceOrder()
        Else If subMenuChoice == "S" Then
            shipOrder()
```

(continues)

(continued)

```
    Else If subMenuChoice != "Q" Then
        Display "Invalid selection:"
        Display "Enter P, I, S, or Q. "
    While subMenuChoice != "Q"
End Module
```

3. For now, you can create stubs for the three choices in each submenu:

```
// Add Customer Record module (stub)
Module addCustomer()
    Display "In Add Customer module"
End Module

// Change Customer Record module (stub)
Module changeCustomer()
    Display "In Change Customer module"
End Module

// Delete Customer Record module (stub)
Module deleteCustomer()
    Display "In Delete Customer module"
End Module

// Ordering module (stub)
Module placeOrder()
    Display "In Place order module"
End Module

// Invoicing module (stub)
Module invoiceOrder()
    Display "In Invoicing module"
End Module

// Shipping module (stub)
Module shipOrder()
    Display "In Shipping module"
End Module
```

4. Save the file again.

 Detective Work

Converting this pseudocode with modules to JavaScript is easy, as long as you keep these rules in mind:

- Modules are coded as functions in JavaScript and placed in the <head> section.

356

- Conditions are enclosed in parentheses.

- Keywords (such as if, else, do, and while) are lowercase in JavaScript.

- You should convert user input to uppercase by using JavaScript's string.toUpperCase() method to reduce the number of conditions needed.

- In a do-while loop in JavaScript, the closing brace is followed by the keyword while, the condition, and a semicolon.

Open a new document in Notepad, and save it as companyMenu.html. Enter your JavaScript code, and then save the file again. Open it in a browser, and then test the program to see whether it calls all menus and submenus correctly. If it doesn't work as expected, compare your JavaScript file with companyMenu-solution.html in your student data files.

Hierarchy Charts

You learned in Chapter 8 that modules can call other modules, and the menu programs in this chapter are examples of this procedure. A graphical tool called a **hierarchy chart** can help you keep track of which modules call other modules. It's useful for seeing a program's overall structure as well as providing a guide for making changes. For example, if you decide to change the spelling of a module name, the hierarchy chart shows you all the modules where you called the module with the spelling change, so you can make sure you change the spelling in the module call. Figure 9-4 shows a hierarchy chart for the Company Menu program.

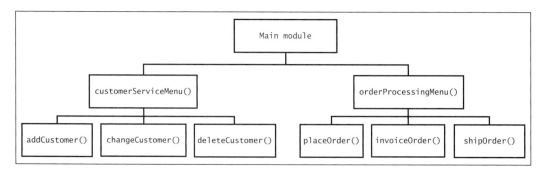

Figure 9-4   A hierarchy chart for the Company Menu program

In the Programmer's Workshop, you create some games with a multilevel menu.

Programmer's Workshop

Your local school board has asked you to develop interactive games involving arithmetic and geometry for students. They want it to be an integrated program, so the main menu should have choices for students to play arithmetic games, play geography games, or exit the program. For now, the Arithmetic menu choice should take users to a submenu with two choices (Addition and Subtraction), and the Geography menu choice should take them to a submenu with two choices (Guess the Country and Name the Capital).

Discussion:

- In arithmetic games, random numbers can be generated within a certain range.

- In the Programmer's Workshop in Chapter 8, you learned the syntax for generating a random number in pseudocode and in JavaScript.

- For the geography games, you can also use random numbers to choose between pairs of cities and countries or cities and states.

First, draw a hierarchy chart to keep track of which modules call other modules (see Figure 9-5 for an example):

- The main module calls the `displayMenu()`, `arithmeticMenu()`, and `geographyMenu()` modules.

- The `arithmeticMenu()` module calls `playAddition()` and `playSubtraction()`.

- The `geographyMenu()` module calls `playGuessTheCountry()` and `playNameTheCapital()`.

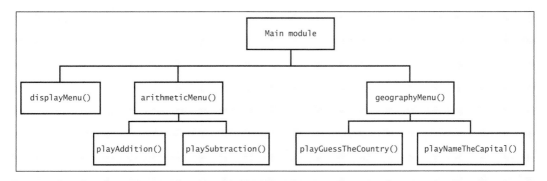

Figure 9-5   A hierarchy chart for the School Game program

Now use the IPO process:

- What outputs are requested?

  - The correct answer to each question (numeric `correctSum` and `correctDiff` for the arithmetic games and string `correctCapital` and `correctCountry` for the geography games)

  - A message stating whether the user's guess was correct (a string literal)

- What inputs are available?

  - The user's menu selections (string `menuChoice` and `subMenuChoice`)

  - Random numbers for arithmetic games (numeric `num1` and `num2`)

  - City and country for the Guess the Country game (string `city` and `correctCountry`)

  - City and country for the Name the Capital game (string `country` and `correctCapital`)

- What processing is required?

  - Generate random numbers for arithmetic games, compute correct sum or difference, compare user's guess with the correct answer, display the correct answer, display a message indicating whether the user was correct.

  - Generate random numbers for city and country pair in geography games, compare user's guess with the correct answer, display the correct answer, display a message indicating whether the user was correct.

  1. Open a new document in Notepad, and save it as **schoolGameMenu.txt**. Start with the usual comment lines, declare variables, and then add the function to display the main menu:

```
// Program name: School Game Menu
// Purpose: Uses a menu system to play games
// in arithmetic and geography
// Author: Paul Addison
// Date last modified: 01-Sep-2011

Start
    // Declare variables
    Declare String menuChoice    // user's selection
```

```
// Display program heading
Display "School Games Menu"

// Loop until user exits menu
Do
    // Call function to display menu, get user
    // selection, and convert to uppercase
    menuChoice = displayMenu()
    menuChoice = toUpper(menuChoice)
    If menuChoice == "A" Then
        arithmeticMenu()
    Else If menuChoice == "G" Then
        geographyMenu()
    Else If menuChoice != "X" Then
        Display "Invalid selection:"
        Display "Please enter A, G, or X: "
    End If
While menuChoice != "X"

// Say goodbye and end program
Display "Goodbye!"
Stop

// Display menu function
Function String displayMenu()
    // Declare variables, display menu,
    // get selection
    Declare String choice
    Display "Enter A to play Arithmetic games,"
    Display "     G to play Geography games,"
    Display "  or X to exit this program. "
    Input choice
    Return choice
End Function
```

2. Develop the arithmeticMenu() and geographyMenu() modules. When users exit these menus, they return to the main menu.

```
// Arithmetic menu module
Module arithmeticMenu()
    // Declare variables
    Declare String subMenuChoice

    // Loop until user exits this menu
    // and returns to main menu
    Do
        // Call function to display submenu, get
        // user selection, and convert to uppercase
        subMenuChoice = displayArithmeticMenu()
        subMenuChoice = toUpper(subMenuChoice)
        If subMenuChoice == "A" Then
            playAddition()
```

```
            Else If subMenuChoice == "S" Then
                playSubtraction()
            Else If subMenuChoice != "X" Then
                Display "Invalid selection:"
                Display "Enter A, S, or X: "
            End If
        While subMenuChoice != "X"
End Module


// Function to display Arithmetic menu
Function String displayArithmeticMenu()
    // Declare variables, display menu,
    // get selection
    Declare String choice
    Display "Enter A for Addition,"
    Display "      S for Subtraction,"
    Display "  or X to exit this menu: "
    Input choice
    Return choice
End Function


// Geography menu module
Module geographyMenu()
    // Declare variables
    Declare String subMenuChoice

    // Loop until user exits this menu
    // and returns to main menu
    Do
        // Call function to display submenu, get
        // user selection, and convert to uppercase
        subMenuChoice = displayGeographyMenu()
        subMenuChoice = toUpper(subMenuChoice)
        If subMenuChoice == "G" Then
            playGuessTheCountry()
        Else If subMenuChoice == "N" Then
            playNameTheCapital()
        Else If subMenuChoice != "X" Then
            Display "Invalid selection:"
            Display "Please enter G, N, or X: "
        End If
    While subMenuChoice != "X"
End Module


// Function to display Geography menu
Function String displayGeographyMenu()
    // Declare variables, display menu,
    // get selection
    Declare String choice
    Display "Enter G to play Guess the Country,"
    Display "      N to play Name the Capital,"
    Display "  or X to exit this menu. "
```

```
      Input choice
      Return choice
   End Function
```

3. Now enter the pseudocode for the arithmetic and geography games:

```
// Addition module
Module playAddition()
   // Declare variables
   Declare Numeric num1, num2    // random numbers
   Declare Numeric correctSum    // correct answer
   Declare Numeric userGuess     // user's guess

   // Get numbers, compute correct sum
   num1 = Random(1,100)
   num2 = Random(1,100)
   correctSum = num1 + num2

   // Prompt user for sum and
   //   compare with correct answer
   // Display result and correct answer
   //   if user is wrong
   Display "What is " + num1 + " + " + num2 + "? "
   Input userGuess
   If userGuess == correctSum Then
      Display "That is correct!"
   Else
      Display "Sorry. The correct answer is " +↵
 correctSum
   End If
End Module

// Subtraction module
Module playSubtraction()
   // Declare variables
   Declare Numeric num1, num2    // random numbers
   Declare Numeric temp          // swap variable
   Declare Numeric correctDiff   // correct answer
   Declare Numeric userGuess     // user's guess

   // Get numbers, swap if second number is higher
   //   to keep answer from being negative
   // Compute correct difference
   num1 = Random(1,100)
   num2 = Random(1,100)
   If num2 > num1 Then
      temp = num1
      num1 = num2
      num2 = temp
   End If
   correctDiff = num1 - num2
```

```
        // Prompt user for difference and
        //   compare with correct answer
        // Display result and correct answer
        //   if user is wrong
        Display "What is " num1 + " - " + num2 + "? "
        Input userGuess
        If userGuess == correctDiff Then
            Display "That is correct!"
        Else
            Display "Sorry. The correct answer is " +↵
    correctDiff
        End If
End Module

    // Guess the Country module
    Module playGuessTheCountry()
        // Declare variables
        Declare String city               // city clue
        Declare String correctCountry     // right answer
        Declare String userGuess          // user's guess
        Declare Numeric randomNum         // selection

        // Use random number to select city and country
        randomNum = Random(1,5)
        Select randomNum
        Case 1:
            city = "Hamburg"
            correctCountry = "GERMANY"
        Case 2:
            city = "Osaka"
            correctCountry = "JAPAN"
        Case 3:
            city = "Liverpool"
            correctCountry = "ENGLAND"
        Case 4:
            city = "Rio de Janeiro"
            correctCountry = "BRAZIL"
        Case 5:
            city = "Mombasa"
            correctCountry = "KENYA"
        End Select

        // Display city name, ask for country
        // Convert user's guess to uppercase
        Display "In what country is " + city +↵
    " located? "
        Input userGuess
        userGuess = toUpper(userGuess)
        If userGuess == correctCountry Then
            Display "That is correct!"
```

```
      Else
         Display "Sorry. The correct answer is " +↵
   correctCountry
      End If
End Module

// Name the Capital module
Module playNameTheCapital()
   // Declare variables
   Declare String country          // country clue
   Declare String correctCapital   // right answer
   Declare String userGuess        // user's guess
   Declare Numeric randomNum       // selection

   // Use random number to select
   //    country and capital
   randomNum = Random(1,5)
   Select randomNum
      Case 1:
         country = "Afghanistan"
         correctCapital = "KABUL"
      Case 2:
         country = "Austria"
         correctCapital = "VIENNA"
      Case 3:
         country = "Canada"
         correctCapital = "OTTAWA"
      Case 4:
         country = "Finland"
         correctCapital = "HELSINKI"
      Case 5:
         country = "Portugal"
         correctCapital = "LISBON"
   End Select

   // Display country name, ask for capital
   // Convert user's guess to uppercase
   Display "What is the capital of " +↵
   country + "? "
   Input userGuess
   userGuess = toUpper(userGuess)
   If userGuess == correctCapital Then
      Display "That is correct!"
   Else
      Display "Sorry. The correct answer is " +↵
   correctCapital
   End If
End Module
```

4. Save the file again.

Detective Work

Now convert the pseudocode program to JavaScript. Open a new document in Notepad, and save it as schoolGameMenu.html. Enter the JavaScript code, and then test the program by opening it in a browser. If it doesn't run correctly, compare your code with schoolGameMenu-solution.html in your student data files. Figure 9-6 shows the browser page with all four games played (Addition, Subtraction, Guess the Country, and Name the Capital). The first and third questions were answered correctly, and the second and fourth were answered incorrectly.

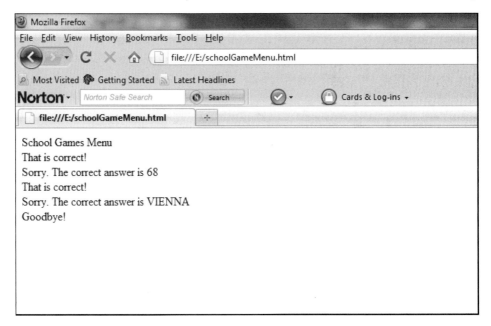

Figure 9-6   The schoolGameMenu.html program in a Web browser

In the Programmer's Workshop, you created a multilevel menu and validated user input. In the Object Lesson, you use a function to validate data entered in an HTML form.

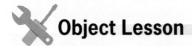

Object Lesson

In this Object Lesson, you create a customer inquiry form for Sounds Right, a sound equipment rental company. This form should work as follows:

- The customer enters name, address, and e-mail information.

- The program verifies all fields for the presence of data.

- The state field is verified for length and converted to uppercase if necessary.

- The zip code field is verified for length and data type.

- The e-mail address is verified for inclusion of the @ sign and a period.

- The program displays the user-entered information if it's correct; if it's not, the program displays error messages.

JavaScript has a built-in method, indexOf(), that takes a character as an argument and returns the position in a string where the character occurs or -1 if the character isn't found. One way to validate an e-mail address is to see whether the character @ occurs in the string. If the return value isn't 0 or greater, the character doesn't exist and the e-mail address is invalid.

As mentioned earlier, JavaScript also has the Boolean function isNaN(), which returns true if the string argument can't be converted to a number. You can use this method to determine whether all five characters in the zip code are digits.

1. First, draw the form on paper so that you can see what labels, text boxes, and buttons you need (see Figure 9-7 for an example). This step makes writing the HTML code for creating the form easier.

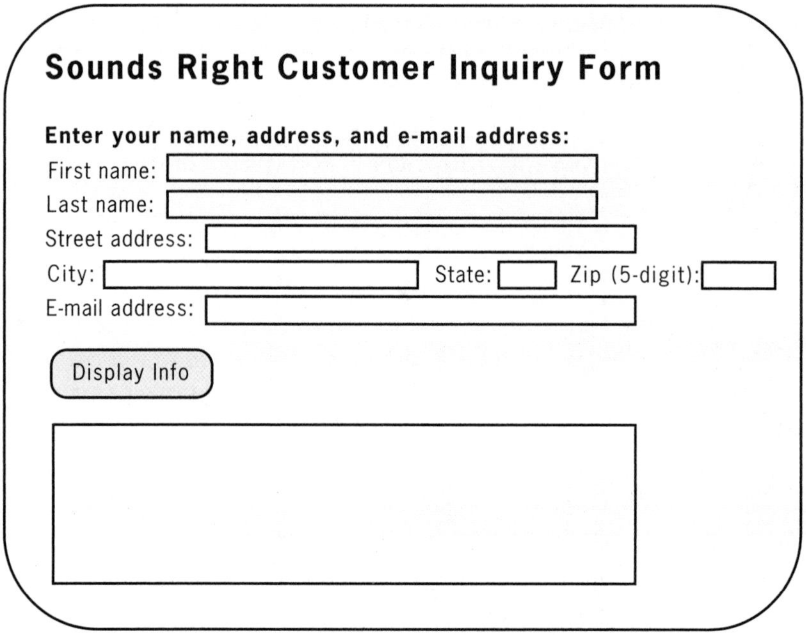

Sounds Right Customer Inquiry Form

Enter your name, address, and e-mail address:
First name: [   ]
Last name: [   ]
Street address: [   ]
City: [   ] State: [   ] Zip (5-digit): [   ]
E-mail address: [   ]

(Display Info)

[   ]

Figure 9-7   Drawing the Sounds Right Customer Inquiry form

2. Open a new document in Notepad, and save it as **soundsRightInfoForm.html.** Enter the following code to create the form in HTML in the <body> section. The text box at the bottom is read-only; it's where the program displays error messages or validated input. Notice that no JavaScript is needed in the form. When the Display Info button is clicked, the displayInfo() function is called.

```html
<html>

<body bgcolor="WhiteSmoke">
<h2>Sounds Right Customer Inquiry Form</h2>
<form name="InfoForm" action="">

<strong>Enter your name, address, and e-mail
  address:</strong><br />
First name:<input type="text" name="firstName"
  value="" size="40"><br />
Last name:<input type="text" name="lastName"
  value="" size="40"><br />
Street address:<input type="text"
  name="streetAddress" value="" size="40"><br />
City:<input type="text" name="city"
  value="" size="30">
State:<input type="text" name="state"
  value="" size="2">
Zip (5-digit):<input type="text" name="zip"
  value="" size="5"><br />
E-mail address:<input type="text" name="email"
  value="" size="40"><p />
<input type="button" name="displayButton"
  value="Display Info" onclick="displayInfo()" /><p />
<textarea name="fullInfo" readonly="true" value=""
  rows="8" cols="50" /></textarea><br />

</form>
</body>
</html>
```

3. Now enter the following JavaScript code in the <head> section; it includes the displayInfo() function to validate data. Remember to include the documentation comments. Place this code after the <html> tag and before the <body> tag in the code from Step 2.

```html
<head>
<script type="text/javascript">

// Program name: soundsRightInfoForm.html
// Purpose: Creates a customer inquiry form
```

```
//    for Sounds Right
//    and calls a function to verify the data.
// Author: Paul Addison
// Date last modified: 01-Sep-2011

// Variables and constants
var NL = "\n";    // newline character

// This function verifies and displays customer
// information, including
// the name and e-mail address of the customer,
// along with a heading and a thank-you line.
function displayInfo() {
   var firstName =
 document.InfoForm.firstName.value;
   var lastName =
 document.InfoForm.lastName.value;
   var streetAddress =
 document.InfoForm.streetAddress.value;
   var city =
 document.InfoForm.city.value;
   var state =
 document.InfoForm.state.value;
   var zip =
 document.InfoForm.zip.value;
   var email =
 document.InfoForm.email.value;
   var errMsg = "";

   // Check for presence of name and address fields
   // Check for length of credit card number

   if (firstName.length <= 0)
errMsg = errMsg + "First name required." + NL;
   if (lastName.length <= 0)
errMsg = errMsg + "Last name required." + NL;
   if (streetAddress.length <= 0)
errMsg = errMsg + "Street address required." + NL;
   if (city.length <= 0)
errMsg = errMsg + "City required." + NL;
   if (state.length != 2) errMsg = errMsg +
"State code must be two letters." + NL;
   if (zip.length != 5)
errMsg = errMsg + "5-digit zip code required." + NL;
   if (isNaN(zip)) errMsg = errMsg +
"Zip code must include only digits." + NL;
   if (email.indexOf("@") <= 0)   errMsg = errMsg +
"Invalid e-mail address." + NL;
   if (email.indexOf(".") <= 0) errMsg = errMsg +
"Invalid e-mail address." + NL;
```

```
            if (errMsg.length > 0) {
                document.InfoForm.fullInfo.value = errMsg;
            }
            else {
                document.InfoForm.fullInfo.value = ↵
        "HERE IS YOUR INFORMATION:" + NL + NL
                + "YOUR NAME: " + firstName + " " + ↵
        lastName + NL
                + "ADDRESS: " + streetAddress + NL
                + "CITY, STATE, ZIP: " + city + ", " + ↵
        state + " " + zip + NL
                + "E-MAIL ADDRESS: " + email + NL + NL
                + "Thank you for your interest!";
            }
        }

    </script>
    </head>
```

4. Save the file again, and open it in a browser. Figure 9-8 shows the browser page when a four-letter state abbreviation was entered, the zip code contained the letter S instead of the digit 5, and the e-mail address contained a dot where the @ symbol should have been used.

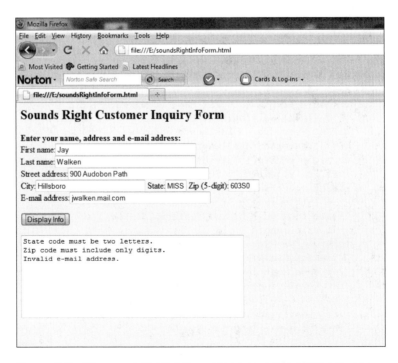

Figure 9-8   The soundsRightInfoForm.html program in a Web browser

Chapter Summary

- Interactive processing requires that programmers validate all data input and design programs so that users must correct any invalid data immediately.

- Menus are lists of choices for users and limit users' input to valid choices.

- Single-level menus go directly to the selected application; multilevel menus have a main menu and one or more submenus.

- Creating menus works well with top-down design, with each menu choice represented by a module or function call.

- A module without all its code developed is called a stub.

- Menus are often represented as `While` loops that keep repeating until users enter the value to exit the menu. If an invalid menu selection is made, an error message is displayed.

- A validation loop checks for user input immediately and repeats until valid data is entered.

- Progressive error messages can be used to display more strongly worded messages if the user continues to enter invalid data.

- Types of data validation include data type, presence, range, and logical relationships.

- Exception handling is a method of catching data input without having to write error-checking code at every input line.

- Menus can be designed with multiple levels, in which choices in one menu lead to a submenu.

Key Terms

alert box—A JavaScript pop-up box that requires user acknowledgement before proceeding.

batch processing—A method in which data is processed noninteractively, requiring prior data validation.

black box—The term for a module in which the contents don't need to be known by the programmer; it emphasizes that knowing how to use the module is more important than knowing the module's details.

exception handling—In object-oriented programming, a method that allows for errors to be detected without having to write error-checking code at every point of input.

hierarchy chart—A graphical description of the relation between modules in a program; shows which modules call other modules.

interactive processing—Processing performed when the user requests it; also called "real-time processing."

multilevel menu—A menu with choices that lead to other menus, called submenus. *See also* submenu.

string manipulation functions—Functions that operate exclusively on strings to determine properties such as whether they contain certain characters or can be converted to a number.

stub—A temporary module without its code developed yet; used to test a program to make sure the module is called correctly.

submenu—A menu called by another menu, used for uncluttering the main menu and grouping functions.

traversing—The process of examining all the characters in a string.

validation loop—A loop that checks for valid input and repeats until valid input has been entered.

Review Questions

True/False

1. Batch processing is also referred to as interactive processing. True or False?

2. Data validation should be performed immediately after user input so that errors can be corrected as soon as possible. True or False?

3. A "black box" is a text box in which a user enters data. True or False?

4. A stub is a module without all its code developed that's used as a placeholder when designing menus or developing modules. True or False?

5. A validation loop usually uses the keyword For to check for invalid input. True or False?

6. User choices can be grouped into menus and submenus. True or False?

7. Users should be required to enter menu choices in uppercase only. True or False?

8. An alert box is a JavaScript pop-up box for displaying error messages. True or False?

9. A programmer can define exceptions and "throw" them in a program. True or False?

10. A Catch block is used to detect the kind of error and handle it so that the program doesn't crash. True or False?

Multiple Choice

1. A program is said to be robust if it _____.

   a. contains a lot of code

   b. can handle many kinds of user errors without crashing

   c. runs quickly

   d. contains many submenus

2. In a multilevel menu system, a main menu selection _____. (Choose all that apply.)

   a. can terminate the program

   b. can lead to a submenu

   c. doesn't allow the user to exit the program

   d. requires numeric input only

3. Which of the following is a recommended way to allow users to enter choices in uppercase or lowercase letters?

   a. Convert the input to uppercase and compare it with an uppercase value.

   b. Keep the user in a validation loop until the correct letter case is used for data entry.

   c. Require the user to press the Caps Lock key for data input.

   d. Use the Or keyword to check all input for uppercase or lowercase letters.

4. Do While loops work well with menus for which of the following reasons?

   a. They combine initialization, condition testing, and alteration.

   b. They process data faster than While loops.

   c. Only one prompt is needed for the menu selection.

   d. They call submenus to perform the menu selections.

5. A programmer can design a menu system and create a(n) _____ for a module before writing all the code for it.

   a. variable

   b. argument

   c. stub

   d. exception

6. A _____ keeps prompting the user until valid data is entered.

   a. black box

   b. batch input method

   c. case statement

   d. validation loop

7. Which of the following demonstrates data validation? (Choose all that apply.)

   a. checking whether data has been entered in a field

   b. checking for the correct data type

   c. checking whether a loan-out date is before a return due date

   d. checking whether a value is within an acceptable range

8. Which of the following demonstrates data validation for logical relationships?

   a. checking whether data has been entered in a field

   b. checking for the correct data type

   c. checking whether a loan-out date is before a return due date

   d. checking whether a value is within an acceptable range

9. In object-oriented programming, code where a user might enter invalid data is placed in a _____.

   a. Try block

   b. Catch block

   c. Throw statement

   d. submenu

10. Which of the following tests for the kind of exception thrown?

    a. Try block

    b. Catch block

    c. Throw statement

    d. submenu

Discussion Questions

1. What does GIGO stand for, and what does it mean for programmers?

2. Why is a data validation loop preferred over a selection statement for validating data?

3. How does exception handling differ from a data validation loop?

Hands-On Activities

Hands-On Activity 9-1

Design a pseudocode program that asks the user for a username with at least eight characters, beginning with a letter and including at least one digit. Next, write a validation loop to ensure that these conditions have been met, and continue to prompt the user until a valid username has been entered. (*Hint*: You can use the functions substring(), isLetter(), and isNumeric() to validate the input.) Use Notepad to create the program, and save the file as usernameValidator.txt.

Hands-On Activity 9-2

Convert your pseudocode file from Hands-On Activity 9-1 to JavaScript, and test your program. Save the file as usernameValidator.html.

Hands-On Activity 9-3

Create a pseudocode program with a single-level menu that asks the user to choose from two activities—count the words in a sentence or spell a sentence backward—or exit the menu. The main module should call modules to display the menu and get the user's choice, play the word-counting activity, and play the backward-spelling activity. *Hints*: To count words in a sentence, count the number of spaces by traversing the sentence with a For loop and the substr() function. The number of words is one more than the number of spaces. To spell a sentence backward, create a new string that starts with the original sentence's ending character, and work backward. Use Notepad to create the program, and save the file as wordGames.txt.

Hands-On Activity 9-4

Convert your pseudocode file from Hands-On Activity 9-3 to JavaScript, and test your program. Save the file as wordGames.html.

CASE STUDY: Adding Data Validation to It's War!

At this point, your War game allows playing cards of any value. Try it! Enter 100 for one player's card and −99 for the other player's card. So clearly, you need to build some data validation into the program. If the user enters anything other than 2 to 10, J, Q, K, or A, the program should display an error message. (In JavaScript, error messages are displayed in an alert box.)

In Notepad, open the file warGame-ch8.txt, and save it as warGame-ch9.txt. In the convertCard() function, after the If/Else If structure ends and before the Return statement, enter the following selection structure. It states that if the value isn't between 2 and 14, set the point value to -1. This value is used in the main module as an error indicator.

```
// Validate input value
If Not (cardPoints >= 2 And cardPoints <= 14) Then
    cardPoints = -1
    Display "ERROR...card must be 2-10, J, Q, K, or A."
End If
```

The Not operator is used because this statement not only catches numeric values outside the correct range, but also catches nonnumeric values.

In the main module, you're currently asking for both players' cards and then converting the card names to point values. A principle of good data validation is catching errors as soon as possible, so first, you should place the conversion function call for each player immediately after the input statement for the player. Cut and paste the conversion comments and calls after the input statement for each player so that your code looks like this:

```
// Ask for first player's card
Display "Enter Player 1's card (2-10, J, Q, K, or A): "
Input cardName1

// Convert jack, queen, king, or ace to points
// for the first player
cardPoints1 = convertCard(cardName1)

// Ask for second player's card
Display "Enter Player 2's card (2-10, J, Q, K, or A): "
Input cardName2

// Convert jack, queen, king, or ace to points
// for the second player
cardPoints2 = convertCard(cardName2)
```

Before the lines where you ask for the second player's card, insert the following validation loop, which checks whether the conversion function returns a -1 value and keeps prompting the user for correct input:

```
// Validate input for first player
While cardPoints1 == -1
   Display "Enter Player 1's card (2-10, J, Q, K, or A): "
   Input cardName1
   cardPoints1 = convertCard(cardName1)
End While
```

Insert a similar validation loop after the second player's card is converted:

```
// Validate input for second player
While cardPoints2 == -1
   Display "Enter Player 2's card (2-10, J, Q, K, or A): "
   Input cardName2
   cardPoints2 = convertCard(cardName2)
End While
```

Save the file again. Next, open the JavaScript file warGame-ch8.html, save it as warGame-ch9.html, and make similar changes. First, in the convertCard() function in the <head> section, just before the return statement, insert this selection structure:

```
// Validate input value; return -1 if invalid
if (!(cardPoints >= 2 && cardPoints <= 14)) {
     cardPoints = -1;
     alert("ERROR...card must be 2-10, J, Q, K, or A.");
}
```

In the <body> section, move the line calling the conversion function for each player (along with its comment) directly after the line prompting for the player's input so that your input section looks like this:

```
// Ask for first player's card
cardName1 = prompt("Enter card for " + player1 + ":",ES);

// Convert jack, queen, king, or ace to points
// for the first player
cardPoints1 = convertCard(cardName1);

// Ask for second player's card
cardName2 = prompt("Enter card for " + player2 + ":",ES);

// Convert jack, queen, king, or ace to points
// for the second player
cardPoints2 = convertCard(cardName2);
```

After the line calling the convertCard() function for the first player, insert this validation loop:

```
// Validate input for first player
while (cardPoints1 == -1) {
    cardName1 = prompt("Enter card for " + player1 + ":",ES);
    cardPoints1 = convertCard(cardName1);
}
```

After the line calling the convertCard() function for the second player, insert this validation loop:

```
// Validate input for second player
while (cardPoints2 == -1) {
    cardName2 = prompt("Enter card for " + player2 + ":",ES);
    cardPoints2 = convertCard(cardName2);
}
```

Save the file again, and run it. If you enter a card value lower than 2 or greater than 14 or a nonnumeric value other than J, Q, K, or A, an alert box should pop up with an error message. Figure 9-9 shows the error message that's displayed if an invalid card is entered. Your program might not catch every error a user makes, but it should ensure that correct card values are entered for the game to proceed.

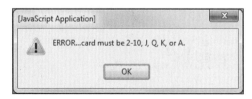

Figure 9-9   The error message displayed if an invalid card is entered

CHAPTER 10

Arrays

In this chapter, you learn to:

- ◎ Define an array and describe how to create one
- ◎ Describe how to load an array directly and interactively
- ◎ Explain how a For loop can be used to traverse an array
- ◎ Explain how to search an array sequentially for a specified value
- ◎ Explain how to improve the efficiency of a search
- ◎ Write a binary search algorithm
- ◎ Define parallel arrays and how they're used
- ◎ Define multidimensional arrays and describe how to code them

A guy walks into a bar and asks the bartender why all the cabs are lined up in a 4-by-4 grid on the street in front of the bar, and each one has a number painted on it in square brackets. The bartender, who is a programmer, replies, "It's because life is a cab array, old chum. Life is a cab array."

—PAUL ADDISON

Information processing often involves dealing with hundreds or thousands of data items. If you need a piece of data only once to print it or add a value to a total, for example, you can use the same variable name for each new piece of data input. However, if you need to retain each piece of information throughout the program, you need a separate variable name for each piece of data entered. This chapter discusses a way of handling a large number of similar variables.

What Is an Array?

To keep track of 2000 customer numbers, you could create variables ranging from `custNumber0001` to `custNumber2000`, but you would also have to write 2000 statements every time you want to use each customer number. You would also have to create 2000 variables for all the last names, first names, addresses, and other data as well as 2000 statements to use each variable.

The solution for keeping multiple occurrences of similar variables is an **array**. An array is a collection of variables called **elements**, each with the same name and data type. These elements are distinguished from one another by a unique index called a **subscript**, which is usually enclosed in square brackets immediately after the array name.

Array subscripts are numbered with nonnegative integers (whole numbers) starting with 0, so the first element of an array named `custNumber` is referred to as `custNumber[0]`. Like other variables, an array must be declared with a data type, but the number of elements it contains (its size) is also declared. For example, you can define a numeric array named `custNumber` with 10 elements like this:

```
Declare Numeric custNumber[10]
```

Loading Arrays Directly or Interactively

Declaring an array, like declaring a variable, doesn't necessarily give it a value. Although some programming languages automatically initialize numeric variables to 0 and string variables to NULL, you shouldn't rely on the language to **load** your array. You should initialize it yourself with a default value or provide a method for loading the array with correct values. An array that has been loaded with data values is said to be "populated."

For example, if you want to load five customer numbers into the `custNumber` array, you can do so with five direct assignment statements, as shown:

```
// Load custNumber array
custNumber[0] = 10001
custNumber[1] = 10643
```

```
custNumber[2] = 10922
custNumber[3] = 11532
custNumber[4] = 11765
```

Arrays can also be loaded in the same statement you use to declare them, as shown in this example.

```
Declare String vegetables[] = "asparagus", "beans", "carrots"
```

In this case, the number of elements doesn't need to be stated unless you want to create more elements than the ones assigned and leave some elements without assigned values. Without the number included in the brackets, the number of elements is equal to the number of values assigned. In the preceding example, three values are listed, so the array has three elements. The first value is assigned to vegetables[0], the second is assigned to vegetables[1], and the third is assigned to vegetables[2].

Loading Arrays Interactively with For Loops

Because arrays have consecutive integer subscripts, a For loop is an excellent tool for traversing an array. The loop counter, or index, can be used as the array subscript. For example, if you want to set all customer numbers in the custNumber array to 0 until the actual values are assigned, you can do that easily with a For loop.

Because the first element has a subscript of 0, the subscripts for an array of 10 elements range from 0 to 9. Using a constant, such as SIZE, to represent the number of elements is recommended, and subscripts for the array then range from 0 to SIZE - 1. In a program using an array, you'll likely refer to the array's size many times. By using a constant for the array's size, if you want to change the size later, you have to do it in only one place. The following For loop works even if you change the value of SIZE:

```
Declare Constant SIZE = 10
Declare Numeric custNumber[SIZE]
Declare Numeric index
For index = 0 to SIZE - 1
   custNumber[index] = 0
End For
```

You can also set up an interactive program that allows users to enter the numbers for loading the array. This method makes use of a For loop, too:

```
// Loop for a user to enter customer IDs
Declare index
For index = 0 to SIZE - 1
   Display "Enter the customer ID for subscript " + index
   Input custNumber[index]
End For
```

If data entry workers aren't aware that array subscripts start at 0, you might want to display each index incremented by 1 so that the element numbers displayed start at 1, even though they're stored in the array with the subscript starting at 0.

If your data entry workers aren't programmers, however, they might be confused by the term "subscript" used in the prompt and by the numbering starting with 0. If so, you can add 1 to the subscript number that's displayed for users so that the numbering appears to start at 1:

```
// Loop for a user to enter customer IDs,
// starting with 1
Declare index
For index = 0 to SIZE - 1
   Display "Enter the ID for Customer #" + (index + 1)
   Input custNumber[index]
End For
```

What if you don't want to fill the entire array with customer numbers because you want to leave room for future growth? To do that, initialize the array to a value such as 0, and then add new customer numbers starting at the beginning of the array. When you want to add a new customer number, look for the first customer number with a value of 0 and enter the new number there. The following algorithm uses a `While` loop that does nothing except bypass non-zero customer numbers:

```
// Enter a new customer number
// Array was originally initialized to 0
// Customer numbers are entered from the first element
// Find first location of a 0 value,
//    and enter new customer number
Declare index = 0
While custNumber[index] != 0
   index++
End While
Display "Enter the new customer number: "
Input custNumber[index]
Display "New customer entered at subscript: " + index
```

Arrays in JavaScript

JavaScript arrays are objects created (instantiated) with the keyword new. The argument to the array constructor is sent in parentheses, although the elements are referred to by using subscripts in square brackets. For example, the following statement creates an array of five book titles:

```
var bookTitles = new Array(5);
```

The preferred method, as in pseudocode, is declaring a variable to be used like a named constant for the array size and using it in the array declaration, like this:

```
var SIZE = 5;
var bookTitles;
bookTitles = new Array(SIZE);
```

In JavaScript, an array can be declared and instantiated in one statement, as shown:

```
var bookTitles = new Array(SIZE);
```

PROGRAM 10-1 JavaScript Program bookTitles.html

Create a program that prompts users to enter five book titles in an array and then displays the titles. Don't forget to add a blank line after the code section in each step.

1. Open a new document in Notepad, and save it as **bookTitles.html**. Enter the following code, starting with the HTML tags and documentation lines:

```
<html>
<body>
<script type="text/javascript">

// Program name: bookTitles.html
// Purpose: Creates an array for users to enter
//    five book titles and displays the titles
// Author: Paul Addison
// Date last modified: 01-Sep-2011
```

2. Next, declare variables and constants and create the array:

```
// Declare variables and constants
var SIZE = 5;          // size of array
var bookTitles;        // array for book titles
var index;             // loop index
var ES = "";           // empty string
var BR = "<br />";     // HTML line break

// Create book title array
bookTitles = new Array(SIZE);
```

3. Use a `for` loop to prompt the user to enter book titles, and number the books by adding 1 to the subscript:

```
// Prompt user to enter book titles
for (index = 0; index < SIZE; index++) {
   bookTitles[index] = prompt ↵
("Enter title for book #" + (index + 1) + ↵
":",ES);
}
```

(continues)

(continued)

4. Use another `for` loop to display the titles:

```
// Display book titles
document.write("Book titles entered:" + BR + BR);
for (index = 0; index < SIZE; index++) {
    document.write(bookTitles[index] + BR);
}
```

5. Thank the user and end the program:

```
// Thank the user and end the program
document.write("Thank you." + BR);
</script>
</body>
</html>
```

6. Save the file again, and open it in a browser. Your output should look similar to Figure 10-1.

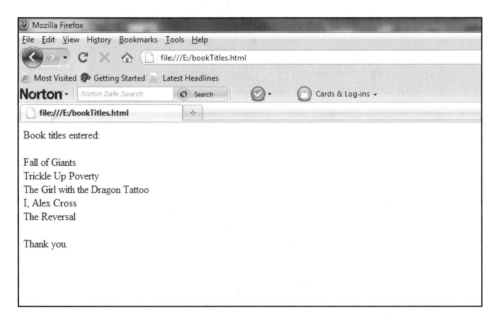

Figure 10-1   The bookTitles.html program in a Web browser

To access all elements in an array, often you traverse it from the lowest subscript to the highest with a `for` loop that ranges from 0 to SIZE - 1, which might be the order in which values were entered. Sometimes, however, you might want to list elements in reverse order, starting with the most recent value entered and going backward. If an array can be traversed in order with a `for` loop, it can be traversed backward, too. All you need to do is start the loop with the highest subscript and subtract 1 from the index each time through the loop, as shown:

```
// Display book titles in reverse order
document.write("Book titles entered:" + BR + BR);
for (index = SIZE - 1; index >= 0; index--) {
    document.write(bookTitles[index] + BR);
}
```

Shorthand Notation for Incrementing and Decrementing

In Chapter 6, you learned that a shorthand notation for incrementing a variable is *variable*++. To increment the variable num by 1, for instance, you use num++, and to decrement it by 1, you use the notation num--. Many languages, including JavaScript, Java, and the family of C languages, also have shorthand notations for incrementing and decrementing variables by values other than 1. For example, the += operator means to add the value on the right of the operator to the value of the variable on the left of the operator. In other words, to add 5 to the variable num, you can use this statement:

```
num = num + 5
```

With the += operator, however, you can express this statement as follows; it reads "num plus equals 5":

```
num += 5
```

Similarly, the -= operator decrements the variable to its left by the value on its right. So to decrement num by 2, you can use this statement:

```
num = num - 2
```

With the -= operator, however, you can express it as shown; it reads "num minus equals 2":

```
num -= 2
```

You can use these increment and decrement operators to create a sampling of elements in an array. Suppose the array size is more than 20 elements, and you want to see the titles of only one-fifth of the books. You can set up a for loop in JavaScript to look at every fifth book, as shown:

```
// Display the title of every fifth book entered
document.write("Sampling of book titles entered:" + BR);
for (index = 0; index < SIZE; index += 5) {
    document.write(bookTitles[index] + BR);
}
```

In the previous example, you wanted to list one-fifth of the book titles, so the increment, or interval, was 5. Now suppose you want to see 10 book titles from an array. To do this, divide the array size by 10, like this:

```
// Compute interval
var interval = Math.floor(SIZE / 10);

// Display 10 titles evenly distributed
document.write("Sample of 10 book titles:" + BR);
for (index = 0; index < SIZE; index += interval) {
    document.write(bookTitles[index] + BR);
}
```

Searching Arrays

So far, you have learned how to set up arrays, load them with values, and display them. Another useful feature is being able to search for a particular value in an array. Using the custNumber array defined earlier, suppose you want to know whether a particular customer number exists in the array. You can choose different search algorithms and use techniques to make the search more efficient.

Sequential Searches

A **sequential search** is the simplest search algorithm, although it's not necessarily the fastest or most efficient. You simply start from the beginning of the array and compare each element's value with the value you're trying to match, as shown in this example:

```
// Prompt for customer number, search array for matches
Declare Numeric searchValue
Declare Numeric index = 0
Display "Enter the customer number you're looking for: "
Input searchValue

For index = 0 to SIZE - 1
   If custNumber[index] == searchValue Then
      Display "Match found at subscript: " + index
   End If
End For
```

What happens if you go through the entire array without finding a match? You should inform users of this result. However, displaying "Sorry, no match found" as the Else clause of the If statement constitutes a logic error because if a match is found for 1 element of 1000, 999 "no match" messages are displayed for the remaining elements that don't match.

One solution is introducing a Boolean variable called found that indicates whether a match has been found. It's initialized to False and set to True if a match is found. After the loop ends, if the value of found is still False, you can display a "not found" message, as shown in this example:

```
// Prompt for customer number, search array for match
Declare Numeric searchValue
Declare Numeric index
Declare Boolean found = False
Display "Enter the customer number you're looking for: "
Input searchValue

For index = 0 to SIZE - 1
   If custNumber[index] == searchValue Then
      found = True
      Display "Match found at subscript: " + index
   End If
End For

If Not found Then
   Display "Sorry, no match found."
End If
```

Sometimes you need to look for multiple matches. For example, you might want a list of test scores greater than 90 or a list of negative account balances. The following example selects customers whose last name begins with the letter A. The array is named custNames, and each name is listed in the format *Lastname, Firstname*.

```
// For loop to select names starting with A
Declare String thisName         // single name from array
Declare String firstLetter      // 1st letter of last name
For index = 0 to SIZE - 1
   thisName = custNames[index]              // get one name
   firstLetter = substring(thisName,0,1)   // get 1st letter
   If firstLetter == "A" Then
      Display thisName
   End If
End For
```

Improving Search Efficiency

In the previous example, you needed to go through the entire array to find all names beginning with A, unless you knew the array was sorted. In this case, you can exit the loop as soon as you find a name starting with a letter that has a higher ASCII value than A.

When you need to find only one match, however, it's a waste of time and resources to continue comparing values if a match has been found. In the earlier example of trying to find a single match with a customer number, you should exit the loop after the match is found. If the array has 1000 customer numbers and a match is found at the second element, the For loop, as it's written now, still checks the next 998 elements, even though a match has already been found.

If a match is found, the loop shouldn't need to iterate again. To address this problem, the found variable can be used to terminate the loop *before* reaching the end of the array. You can have two conditions and continue searching only as long as more elements remain in the array and a match hasn't been found yet.

This point about efficiency brings up a limitation of the For loop: It's designed for counter-controlled loops, in which only one condition is used to determine when to quit. The For loop's syntax doesn't make it easy to use multiple conditions, so with multiple conditions, a While loop is clearer, as shown in this example:

```
// Prompt for customer number, search array for match
Declare Numeric searchValue
Declare Numeric index = 0
Declare Boolean found = False
Display "Enter the customer number you're looking for: "
Input searchValue

While index < SIZE And Not found
    If custNumber[index] == searchValue Then
        found = True
        Display "Match found at subscript: " + index
    End If
End While

If Not found Then
    Display "Sorry, no match found."
End If
```

This algorithm is more efficient now because it doesn't make unnecessary comparisons after finding a match.

When an array has already been sorted and you're looking for only a single match, search algorithms other than a sequential search are more efficient, even with a Boolean flag for an early exit. By adding a variable to track the number of comparisons, you can confirm the number of comparisons the algorithm made. An easy way to create a sorted array is to increment the value of each element as you increment the subscript. If you want an array with numbers ranging from 1 to 5,000,000, you can make each element's value 1 higher than the subscript, as shown in this JavaScript example:

```
// Declare variables
var SIZE = 5000000;
var numberArray = new Array(SIZE);
var index;

// Populate the array with integers in ascending order
for (index = 0; index < SIZE; index++) {
    numberArray[index] = index + 1;
}
```

Detective Work

Now try creating a sequential search algorithm in JavaScript, using the following guidelines:

- The program sets up an array of five million elements and populates it with the numbers 1 through 5,000,000 in order. Incrementing the subscript by 1 each time through the loop sorts the array.

- A variable named numComparisons is incremented each time a comparison is performed, and the final number of comparisons is displayed after the match is found or it's determined that the search value doesn't exist in the array.

Open a new document in Notepad, and save it as sequentialSearch.html. Enter the JavaScript code to create an array named numberArray with 5,000,000 elements and populate it with the numbers 1 through 5,000,000. Prompt the user for a number in this range, and then have the program search the array for a match and display the subscript where the match was found and the number of comparisons or display a message that the number wasn't found. Save the file again, and then open it in a browser. If you enter the number 7500, the output should be similar to Figure 10-2. If your program doesn't run or the output is incorrect, check your code against sequentialSearch-solution.html in your student data files.

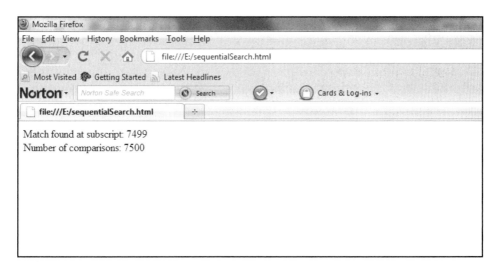

Figure 10-2   The sequentialSearch.html program in a Web browser

Binary Searches

A search algorithm that's more efficient on large arrays—meaning it requires far fewer comparisons—is a **binary search**, which checks whether the search value is lower or higher than an element in the

A binary search doesn't work unless values in the array have been sorted first.

array, adjusting the limits of the array's searchable area with each comparison. Note that values in the array must be sorted before a binary search can work because if the search value is less than the array value it's compared with, the rest of the array from that element on is eliminated from the remainder of the search.

Here's how a binary search operates: Two variables are set as low and high pointers (endpoints) to the array's outer limits or boundaries. The midpoint between the low and high pointers is determined, and the search value is compared with the element at the midpoint.

Because the array is known to be in order, if the value found at the midpoint is greater than the search value, the second half of the array can be eliminated from the search. This is done by resetting the high pointer to the current index position minus 1 (meaning the value at the current position is found to be higher than the search value).

Next, the midpoint of the array's remaining half is determined, and the search value is compared with this value. If the value at the midpoint is lower than the search value, the low pointer is reset to the current index position plus 1. Then half of the array's original half is eliminated from the search.

Figure 10-3 shows how half the searchable array is eliminated after each comparison. In this example, an array of 2001 elements (with subscripts numbered 0 to 2000) contains numbers that are identical to their subscripts. The user has entered 1375 as the number to search for. With each comparison, either a match with the search value is found, or half the remaining array is eliminated from the search.

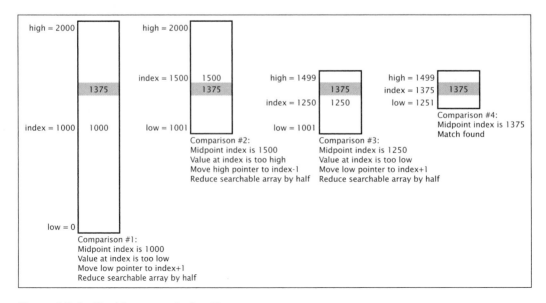

Figure 10-3 The binary search algorithm

The following algorithm searches for a movie title in a sorted array named movieTitles. (The binarySearch.txt file is also available in your student data files.) The array has already been declared and populated, and the movie titles are sorted in alphabetical order. To ensure that a match is found when the title is spelled correctly, whether the user entered it in uppercase or lowercase, both the search value and the movie title being compared are converted to uppercase letters (by using toUpper()) for the comparison.

```
// Program Name: Binary Search
// Purpose: Search an array of movie titles for a match
// Author: Paul Addison
// Date last modified: 01-Sep-2011

Start

    // Declare variables
    Declare Constant SIZE = 200          // array size
    Declare String movieTitles[SIZE]     // array of movie titles
    Declare Numeric index                // array index
    Declare String searchValue           // movie to find
    Declare Numeric low, high            // search endpoints
    Declare Boolean found                // indicates a match

    // Ask user for search value
    Display "What movie title are you searching for? "
    Input searchValue
    searchValue = toUpper(searchValue)

    // Begin binary search
    // Set found to false, set endpoints to array boundaries,
    // and compute midpoint
    found = False
    low = 0
    high = SIZE

    // Loop continues as long as there's a searchable area
    // (low < high) and a match hasn't been found
    While low <= high And Not found
        index = (low + high) / 2
        If toUpper(movieTitles[index]) == searchValue Then
            found = True
            Display "Match found at subscript: " + index
        Else
            If toUpper(movieTitles[index]) > searchValue Then
                high = index - 1
            Else
                low = index + 1
            End If
        End If
    End While
```

```
If Not found Then
    Display "Sorry, no match found."
End If
```

Stop

Figure 10-4 shows the flowchart for a binary search, including the `While` loop and the selection that checks for no match.

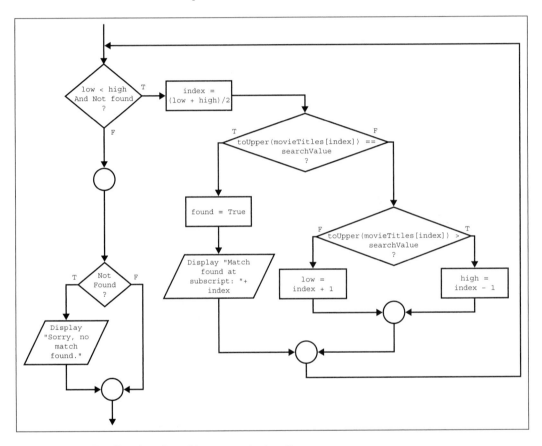

Figure 10-4 The flowchart for a binary search algorithm

 Detective Work

How much more efficient is a binary search than a sequential search? To see for yourself, change the JavaScript `numberArray` example you created earlier to use a binary search and find out how many comparisons are required. To write this program, use the following guidelines:

- Use the same array, `numberArray`, you used for the sequential search program.

- To calculate the midpoint of the searchable part of the array, add the low and high pointers (initially set to 0 and SIZE), divide the total by 2, and get the integer part of the total by using the Math.floor() method.

- When a comparison is made and the search value isn't found, the searchable part of the array is cut in half this way:

  - If the array value at the index position is higher than the search value, the high pointer is reset to the current index position minus 1.

  - If the array value at the index position is lower than the search value, the low pointer is reset to the current index position plus 1.

- When the low pointer is no longer less than or equal to the high pointer, the searchable part of the array has been eliminated, which means a match hasn't been found.

Open a new document in Notepad, and save it as binarySearch.html. Enter your JavaScript code, save the file again, and then open it in a browser. If you search for the number 7500, as you did in the sequential search, your output should look like Figure 10-5. If your program doesn't work or the output is incorrect, compare it with binarySearch-solution.html in your student data files. Notice the difference in the number of comparisons needed for these two searches: The sequential search took 7500 comparisons to find a match, and the binary search took only 21!

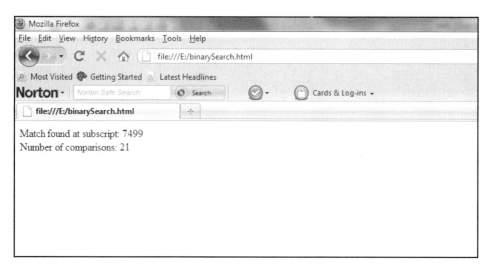

Figure 10-5   The binarySearch.html program in a Web browser

In the Programmer's Workshop, you learn to use a timer as another way to compare the efficiency of sequential and binary searches.

Parallel Arrays

An array has a single name and data type, unlike a database record that has several different fields. In an array of employee numbers, for example, the employee number doesn't tell you anything else about the employee, such as his or her first name and last name.

However, you can set up a **parallel array** for each employee data item. Parallel arrays use a common subscript to relate data fields. For example, you can have arrays for empNumber, empLastName, and empFirstName. The first employee's number is entered in array element empNumber[0], and his or her last and first names are entered in empLastName[0] and empFirstName[0]. The following pseudocode declares three parallel arrays, initializes them, and asks the user to enter the employee number, last name, and first name for all current employees:

```
// Declare three arrays and initialize them
Declare Constant SIZE = 1000
Declare Numeric empNumber[SIZE]
Declare String empLastName[SIZE], empFirstName[SIZE]
Declare Numeric index
Declare String moreInput = "Y"
For index = 0 to SIZE - 1
    empNumber[index] = 0
    empLastName[index] = ""
    empFirstName[index] = ""
End For

// Prompt user to enter employee information
index = 0
While moreInput == "Y"
    Display "Employee at subscript: " + index
    Display "Enter the employee number: "
    Input empNumber[index]
    Display "Enter the employee's last name: "
    Input empLastName[index]
    Display "Enter the employee's first name: "
    Input empFirstName[index]
    Display "Another employee to input? (Y/N) "
    Input moreInput
    moreInput = toUpper(moreInput)
    index++
End While
```

As with a single array, if you want to add more employees later, you can simply add a loop that bypasses all records in which the employee number isn't 0, and then use the For loop in the preceding pseudocode to begin entering employee information. At any time, you can display employee information from the three arrays by displaying elements with the same subscript, as long as the employee number isn't 0, like this:

```
// Display employee information
Declare Numeric index = 0
While empNumber[index] != 0
    Display "Employee #" + empNumber[index]
    + ", Last name: " + empLastName[index]
    + ", First name: " + empFirstName[index]
    index++
End While
```

You can search any of the arrays for a match with the data you have, and then use the subscript where the match is found to display information from the other arrays. Suppose you know that the employee's last name is Hoover, but his first name is Bill, and you don't know whether he's listed as Bill or William. You can search the empLastName array and list all records matching Hoover, as shown:

```
// Prompt for last name, search array for matches
Declare String searchValue      // employee to search for
Declare Numeric index = 0       // array index
Declare Boolean found = False   // indicates a match

Display "Enter the last name of the employee to find: "
Input searchValue

For index = 0 to SIZE - 1
    If empLastName == searchValue Then
        found = True
        Display "Match found at subscript: " + index
        Display "Employee number: " + empNumber[index]
        Display "Employee name: " + empFirstName[index] + " " + ↵
  empLastName[index]
    End If
End For

If Not found Then
    Display "Sorry, match not found."
End If
```

As another example of using parallel arrays, you might know the employee number but don't know whether the employee still exists in the array. Presumably, employee numbers are unique, so you would expect no match or at most one match. Your algorithm might start out like this:

```
// Prompt for employee number, search array for match
Declare Numeric searchValue
Declare Numeric index
Declare Boolean found = False
```

In this search, you don't want to quit at the first match. In arrays where values are expected to occur only once (such as ID numbers), a search normally ends when a single match is found. In arrays that might have multiple occurrences of values, such as an array of last names in a parallel array, a search normally lists all matches, along with values from other parallel arrays.

```
Display "Enter the employee number you're looking for: "
Input searchValue

index = 0
While index < SIZE And Not found
    If empNumber[index] == searchValue Then
        found = True
        Display "Match found at subscript: " + index
        Display "Employee name: " + empFirstName[index] + ↵
 " " + empLastName[index]
    End If
    index++
End While

If Not found Then
    Display "Sorry, match not found."
End If
```

Multidimensional Arrays

An array can be thought of as a list of variables, each numbered with its subscript. You can also think of arrays in two, three, or more dimensions. These arrays are called **multidimensional arrays**. Like one-dimensional arrays, they have a single name and data type, but they use two or more subscripts to identify a particular element.

Visualizing a two-dimensional array isn't difficult. Think of it as a grid of rows and columns, similar to a spreadsheet. A two-dimensional array has two subscripts. The first subscript represents a row, and the second subscript represents a column. Remember that both subscripts start numbering with 0, so the upper-left element in the grid is represented with the subscripts [0,0].

Say you're setting up an array to contain daily temperatures for three weeks. The rows represent the three weeks (numbered 0 through 2), and the columns represent the days of each week (numbered 0 through 6). Figure 10-6 shows how a two-dimensional array uses the first subscript for the row number and the second subscript for the column number.

[0,0]	[0,1]	[0,2]	[0,3]	[0,4]	[0,5]	[0,6]
[1,0]	[1,1]	[1,2]	[1,3]	[1,4]	[1,5]	[1,6]
[2,0]	[2,1]	[2,2]	[2,3]	[2,4]	[2,5]	[2,6]

Figure 10-6   Subscripts in a two-dimensional array

A For loop works well to traverse a one-dimensional array, but nested For loops are ideal for traversing two-dimensional arrays, with the outer loops covering the rows and the inner loops covering the columns in each row. The following pseudocode declares, populates, and displays this array; it's also available in your student data files as 2DtempArray.txt:

```
// Program Name: 2-D Temperature Array
// Purpose: Create and populate a 2-D array for temperatures
//    Rows represent weeks
//    Columns represent days of the week
// Author: Paul Addison
// Date last modified: 01-Sep-2011

Start
   // Declare variables
   Declare Constant WEEKS = 3       // # of weeks (rows)
   Declare Constant DAYS = 7        // # of days (columns)
   Declare Numeric temps[WEEKS,DAYS] // 2-D array of temps
   Declare Numeric weekIndex        // index for week
   Declare Numeric dayIndex         // index for day

   // Prompt user to populate array
   For weekIndex = 0 to WEEKS - 1
      For dayIndex = 0 to DAYS - 1
         Display "Enter the temperature for Week " ↵
+ (weekIndex + 1) + ", Day " + (dayIndex + 1)
         Input temps[weekIndex,dayIndex]
      End For
   End For

   // Display array
   For weekIndex = 0 to WEEKS - 1
      Display "Temperatures for Week " + (weekIndex + 1) ↵
+ ": "
      For dayIndex = 0 to DAYS - 1
         Display temps[weekIndex,dayIndex] + " "
      End For
      Display
   End For
Stop
```

Two-Dimensional Arrays in JavaScript

Most languages support arrays of two and more dimensions, but in JavaScript, arrays are objects, and two-dimensional arrays are implemented by making each array element contain an array object of its own. Essentially, a two-dimensional array in JavaScript is an array of arrays, so separate brackets for each subscript are required, as in [0][0]. To assign values to a 2-D array in JavaScript, create a one-dimensional array as usual, and then add a for loop that sets each array element to an array of its own.

Languages that support two-dimensional arrays usually include both subscripts separated by a comma in a single set of brackets, as in [0,0], as this book does for pseudocode. Languages in which arrays are objects, including JavaScript, implement a two-dimensional array as an array of arrays, so separate brackets must be used for the two subscripts. JavaScript uses this notation for the first element of a two-dimensional array: [0][0].

For example, four people are playing six games of golf and want to keep track of their golf scores. You can set up a two-dimensional array with the four rows representing the players and the six columns representing the six games. First, a one-dimensional array called scores is declared with four elements for the rows. Then a for loop assigns each element as an array with six elements for the columns:

```
// Declare variables
var ROWS = 4;
var COLUMNS = 6;

// Declare first dimension of the array
var scores = new Array(ROWS);

// Declare second dimension of the array
// Each ROWS element is an array of COLUMNS
for (index = 0; index < ROWS; index++) {
    scores[index] = new Array(COLUMNS);
}
```

If a two-dimensional array is organized in rows and columns, its values can be displayed row by row for easy readability. The following code displays the values of the scores array with a space between each value and a label identifying each row. It also adds 1 to each row number to make it easier for nonprogrammers to understand:

```
var rowIndex, colIndex        // row and column indexes
// Display array contents row by row
for (rowIndex = 0; rowIndex < ROWS; rowIndex++) {
    document.write("Row #" + (rowIndex + 1) + ": ");
    for (colIndex = 0; colIndex < COLUMNS; colIndex++) {
        document.write(scores[rowIndex][colIndex] + " ");
    }
}
```

 ## Detective Work

Now try converting the temps array shown previously in pseudocode to a JavaScript two-dimensional array, with rows representing weeks and columns representing days of the week. Open a new document in Notepad, and save it as 2DtempArray.html. Enter the JavaScript code, save the file again, and open it in a browser. The program should prompt you for temperatures for three weeks and seven days each week. Your output should look similar to Figure 10-7. If your program doesn't work correctly or the output is incorrect, check your code against 2DtempArray-solution.html in your student data files.

Mozilla Firefox

File Edit View History Bookmarks Tools Help

C X ⌂ file:///E:/2DtempArray.html

Most Visited Getting Started Latest Headlines

Norton · | Norton Safe Search | Search | ✓ · | Cards & Log-ins ▾

file:///E:/2DtempArray.html

Temperatures for Week 1: 68 69 75 77 76 69 65
Temperatures for Week 2: 58 60 62 61 69 76 74
Temperatures for Week 3: 72 82 80 75 73 68 66

Figure 10-7   The 2DtempArray.html program in a Web browser

Arrays of Three Dimensions or More

If a two-dimensional array can be thought of as a spreadsheet, you
can think of a three-dimensional array as a workbook containing
multiple spreadsheet pages, with each page containing a grid of rows
and columns. Each element is referenced by three subscripts: one for
the page, one for the row, and one for the column. As the programmer, you can decide which subscript represents which dimension, but
normally, programmers work from larger units to more specific, so it
makes logical sense to have the first subscript represent the page and
the second and third subscripts represent the row and column (see
Figure 10-8). For example, to locate an element in the quantity array
on the second page and in the first row and third column, you use the
reference quantity[1,0,2].

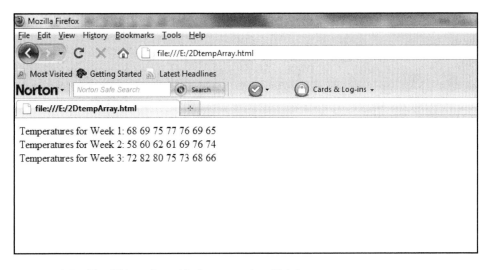

Figure 10-8   A three-dimensional array

In most programming languages, creating arrays of three dimensions or more is technically no more difficult than creating a two-dimensional array; each new dimension is added in much the same way the second one was added. However, after three dimensions, arrays are more difficult to visualize. It helps to remember that subscripts represent levels of organization, and with four or more dimensions, visualizing the array isn't as important as understanding what each subscript represents. For example, you have a four-dimensional array named cityPopulation with the following organizational scheme:

- The first subscript indicates the region (0=Northwest, 1=Southwest, and so on)

- The second subscript indicates the state (in the Northwest, 0=Washington, 1=Oregon, and so on)

- The third subscript indicates the county (in Washington, 0=Adams, 1=Asotin, and so on)

- The fourth subscript indicates the city (in Adams County, 0=Othello, 1=Ritzville, and so on)

Using this scheme, the reference to the population in Ritzville is cityPopulation[0,0,0,1]. As this example shows, arrays can be used to store thousands of variables in memory that programmers can access easily.

Programmer's Workshop

In this Programmer's Workshop, you learn a new way to evaluate the comparative efficiency of your programs: using JavaScript methods to create a timer and measuring the length of time a task takes. For example, when you instantiate an object from the JavaScript Date class, as in the following statement, the object contains the time of creation, including year, month, day, hour, minutes, seconds, and milliseconds. (It actually contains the number of milliseconds since January 1, 1970, and other date fields, such as year, month, day, and day of the week, can be computed from this number.)

```
var d1 = new Date();
```

By declaring a Date object just before you begin a task and declaring another as soon as you complete the task, you have two time markers in milliseconds. If you subtract the first time marker from the second, you can compute how much time has elapsed. Modern computers are so fast that many tasks can be completed in under 1 millisecond, so you create a program that performs a division problem six million times to get to a length of time greater than a millisecond. Without a task like this to pass the time, the number of milliseconds between two events is typically 0; however, this loop takes enough computer time that the second time reading is later than the first, and the difference in milliseconds is greater than 0.

Start by creating a simple program that uses a timer. The program works like this: Two date variables are instantiated. The first, d1, is created just before the loop with the division problem. The second, d2, is created just after the loop is finished. Then the difference between the two variables is computed and displayed.

1. Open a new document in Notepad, and save it as **timer.html**. Add the starting HTML tags and program documentation lines, and declare variables:

```
<html>
<body>
<script type="text/javascript">

// Program name: timer.html
// Purpose: Use Date objects to calculate
//    elapsed time in milliseconds
// Author: Paul Addison
// Date last modified: 01-Sep-2011

// Declare variables
var index;    // loop index
var x;        // variable for division problem
var d1, d2;   // date variables
```

2. Create a Date object, run a loop that takes more than a millisecond to complete, and then create another Date object:

```
// Set starting time
d1 = new Date();

// Loop to pass time
for (index = 0; index < 6000000; index++) {
    x = 123.456789 / 987.654321;
}

// Set ending time
var d2 = new Date();
```

3. Compute the elapsed time from the difference in the date variables' values, and then display it:

```
// Compute and display elapsed time
var diff = d2 - d1;
document.write("Difference in time is: " + diff +
    " milliseconds");
```

4. End the program:

```
</script>
</body>
</html>
```

Now that you know how to use a timer, you can create a program to compare sequential and binary searches in two ways: by counting the number of comparisons made to find a number in a sorted array and by computing the elapsed time for each search. Use the same array you used in the sequential search and binary search programs.

First, use the IPO process:

- What outputs are requested?
  - The number of comparisons required to find a match or determine there's no match (numeric numComparisons)
  - The number of milliseconds each search takes (numeric diff)
- What inputs do you have available?
  - An array of numbers from 1 to 5,000,000 (numeric numberArray)
  - Date and time information from the computer (Date objects d1 and d2)
  - Number to search for from the user (numeric searchNumber)
- What processing is required?
  - Get the number to search for from the user.
  - Create a starting Date object.
  - Perform a sequential search and count the number of comparisons.
  - Create an ending Date object and compute the elapsed time.
  - Display the elapsed time and number of comparisons.

- Get another starting Date object.

- Perform a binary search and count the number of comparisons.

- Create another ending Date object and compute the elapsed time.

- Display the elapsed time and number of comparisons.

1. Open a new document in Notepad, and save it as **searchComparison.html**. Enter the HTML tags and documentation lines, and declare variables:

```
<html>
<body>
<script type="text/javascript">

// Program name: searchComparison.html
// Purpose: Compare timings for sequential
//    and binary searches
// Author: Paul Addison
// Date last modified: 01-Sep-2011

// Declare variables
var SIZE = 5000000;    // array size
var index;             // array index
var found = false;     // match found?
var numberArray;       // number array
var searchNumber;      // number to find
var numComparisons;    // # of comparisons
var d1, d2, diff;      // date/time
var low, high;         // search endpoints
var BR = "<br />";     // HTML line break
var ES = "";           // empty string
```

2. Instantiate the array, populate it with the numbers 1 through 5,000,000, and prompt the user for the number to search for:

```
// Instantiate array
numberArray = new Array(SIZE);

// Populate array with integers
for (index = 0; index < SIZE; index++) {
   numberArray[index] = index + 1;
}

// Prompt for number to search for
searchNumber = prompt ↵
("Enter a number between 1 and 5000000:",ES);
index = 0;
```

3. Next, add the sequential search. Create a Date object for the timer just before the search starts and another one as soon as a match is found or it's determined there's no match:

```
// Sequential search
numComparisons = 0;
d1 = new Date();

// Search until end of array or match found
while(index < SIZE && (!found)) {
    numComparisons++;
    if (numberArray[index] == searchNumber) {
        d2 = new Date();
        found = true;
        document.write
("Match found at subscript: " + index + "." + BR);
    }
    index++;
}
if (!found) {
    d2 = new Date();
    document.write("Sorry, no match found.")
}
```

4. Compute and display the elapsed time and number of comparisons for the sequential search:

```
// Compute and display elapsed time
//    and number of comparisons
diff = d2 - d1;
document.write
("Sequential search: # of milliseconds: " +
 diff + BR);
document.write("Number of comparisons: " +
 numComparisons + BR + BR);
```

5. Next, add the binary search. Create a Date object for the timer just before the search starts and another one as soon as a match is found or it's determined there's no match:

```
// Binary search
found = false;
low = 0;
high = SIZE;
index = Math.floor((low + high) / 2);
numComparisons = 0;
d1 = new Date();
```

```
// Search until endpoints meet or match is found
while(low <= high && (!found)) {
   numComparisons++;
   if (numberArray[index] == searchNumber) {
      d2 = new Date();
      found = true;
      document.write("Match found at subscript: " + ↵
 index + "." + BR);
    }
    else {
       if (numberArray[index] > searchNumber) {
          high = index - 1;
       }
       else {
          low = index + 1;
       }
       index = Math.floor((low + high) / 2);
    }
}
if (!found) {
   d2 = new Date();
   document.write("Sorry, no match found.")
}
```

6. Compute and display the elapsed time and number of comparisons for the binary search:

```
// Compute and display elapsed time
//    and number of comparisons
diff = d2 - d1;
document.write("Binary search: # of milliseconds: " ↵
 + diff + BR);
document.write("Number of comparisons: " + ↵
 numComparisons + BR + BR);
```

7. Add the HTML tags to end the program:

```
</script>
</body>
</html>
```

8. Save the file again, and open it in a browser. Compare the two search methods by seeing which one takes less time and which one requires fewer comparisons. Figure 10-9 shows an example of the program's output.

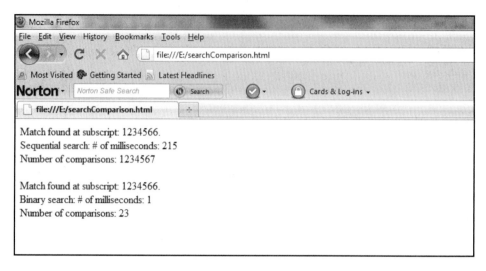

Figure 10-9 The searchComparison.html program in a Web browser

In the Programmer's Workshop, you used arrays to compare search times and number of comparisons for two search algorithms, sequential and binary. In the Object Lesson, you use arrays as a searching method for finding flight information.

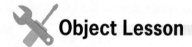 **Object Lesson**

RedEye Airlines has flights only between midnight and 6:00 a.m. In this Object Lesson, you create a form to search for and display flight information for RedEye Airlines and use parallel arrays to hold the information. Your program should meet the following specifications:

- Parallel arrays are set up for starting city, destination city, flight number, and price per person.

- There are five cities, and each has one flight to each of the other four cities every night (20 flights total).

- The form contains drop-down boxes for selecting the starting city or the destination city.

- Next to the drop-down boxes are Find Flights From and Find Flights To buttons.

- Clicking the buttons activates an array search for matches for the selected city, and information on each matching flight is displayed in a text box at the bottom of the form.

The parallel arrays have one element for each flight:

- The `startCity` array contains the starting city.
- The `endCity` array contains the ending city.
- The `flightNumber` array contains the flight number.
- The `pricePerPerson` array contains the price per person.

Discussion:

- When the user selects a city, your program is looking for all matches, not just one, so a sequential search is used, and your search algorithm should traverse the entire array.
- The arrays need to be loaded when the program starts, not when the user clicks a button, so a short script is needed in the `<body>` section with a statement calling the function to load the arrays.
- The function that loads the arrays can assign values in the declaration statement, so the number of array elements doesn't have to be specified.

1. Using paper and pencil, draw the form so that you can see what labels, text boxes, and buttons you need (using Figure 10-10 as a guideline). This step makes writing the HTML code to create the form easier.

Figure 10-10   The RedEye Airlines form

2. Open a new document in Notepad, and save it as **redEyeAirlines.html**. First, you create the form in HTML so that you can test whether it works before adding functions; notice that no JavaScript is needed to create the form. The text box at the bottom for displaying flight information is read-only. When the user clicks one of the buttons, the searchArray() function is called with an argument indicating whether the user is searching for flights from or to the selected city. Enter the following code, save the file again, and open it in a browser to make sure that the form is displayed correctly.

```html
<html>

<body bgcolor="Salmon">
<h2>RedEye Airlines Flight Information Form</h2>

<form name="InfoForm" action="">

<p>
Select your starting city:<br />
<select name="startingCity">
   <option value="ATLANTA">Atlanta (GA)</option>
   <option value="CLEVELAND">Cleveland (OH)</option>
   <option value="INDIANAPOLIS">Indianapolis (IN) ↵
</option>
   <option value="LOUISVILLE">Louisville (KY) ↵
</option>
   <option value="MEMPHIS">Memphis (TN)</option>
</select>
</p>

<p>
Select your destination city:<br />
<select name="endingCity">
   <option value="ATLANTA">Atlanta (GA)</option>
   <option value="CLEVELAND">Cleveland (OH)</option>
   <option value="INDIANAPOLIS">Indianapolis (IN) ↵
</option>
   <option value="LOUISVILLE">Louisville (KY) ↵
</option>
   <option value="MEMPHIS">Memphis (TN)</option>
</select>
</p>

<input type="button" name="goButton" value= ↵
"Find Flights" onclick='searchArray()' /><p />

<textarea name="flightBox" readonly="true" ↵
 value="" rows="6" cols="80" /></textarea><p />
```

```
</form>
</body>
</html>
```

3. Now you can add the JavaScript code in the <head> section for the documentation lines, the variables and constants needed, and the function to set up the arrays. You need to declare the arrays outside the loadArrays() function so that they're available later to the function that searches the arrays. Place this code after the <html> tag and before the <body> tag you added in Step 2; these lines (not bolded) are reproduced in the following code to help you with placement:

```html
<html>
<head>
<script type="text/javascript">

// Program name: redEyeAirlines.html
// Purpose: Creates a reservation form
//    searchable by city
// Author: Paul Addison
// Date last modified: 01-Sep-2011

// Variables and constants
var NL = "\n";          // newline character
var SIZE = 20;          // size of flight arrays
var index;              // index for loops
var fromCityName;       // selected from city
var toCityName;         // selected to city
var startCity;          // starting city array
var endCity;            // ending city array
var flightNumber;       // flight numbers array
var pricePerPerson;     // price array

function loadArrays() {
   startCity = new Array
   ("Atlanta", "Atlanta", "Atlanta", "Atlanta",
    "Cleveland", "Cleveland", "Cleveland",
    "Cleveland", "Indianapolis", "Indianapolis",
    "Indianapolis", "Indianapolis", "Louisville",
    "Louisville", "Louisville", "Louisville",
    "Memphis", "Memphis", "Memphis", "Memphis");

   endCity = new Array
   ("Cleveland", "Indianapolis", "Louisville",
    "Memphis", "Indianapolis", "Louisville",
    "Memphis", "Atlanta", "Louisville", "Memphis",
    "Atlanta", "Cleveland", "Memphis", "Atlanta",
    "Cleveland", "Indianapolis", "Atlanta",
    "Cleveland", "Indianapolis", "Louisville");
```

```
flightNumber = new Array
    ("RE103", "RE105", "RE107", "RE109",
     "RE305", "RE307", "RE309", "RE301",
     "RE507", "RE509", "RE501", "RE503",
     "RE709", "RE701", "RE703", "RE705",
     "RE901", "RE903", "RE905", "RE907");

pricePerPerson = new Array
    (110.00, 100.00, 90.00, 80.00,
     75.00, 90.00, 110.00, 120.00,
     65.00, 80.00, 120.00, 75.00,
     65.00, 90.00, 90.00, 65.00,
     80.00, 110.00, 80.00, 65.00);
}
</script>
</head>

<body bgcolor="Salmon">
```

4. Next, add the function to search the array. Insert this code before the `</script>` tag you added in Step 3, and don't forget to add a blank line before beginning the function:

```
function searchArray() {
    document.InfoForm.flightBox.value = ↵
"WELCOME TO REDEYE AIRLINES: " + ↵
"All flights leave at 2:00 am" + NL + NL;

    fromCityName = ↵
document.InfoForm.startingCity.value;
    toCityName = ↵
document.InfoForm.endingCity.value;
    if (fromCityName == toCityName) {
        document.InfoForm.flightBox.value += ↵
"Starting and destination city can't be the same." ↵
+ NL;

    for (index = 0; index < SIZE; index++) {
        if ((startCity[index].toUpperCase() == ↵
fromCityName) &&
            (endCity[index].toUpperCase() == ↵
toCityName)) {

            document.InfoForm.flightBox.value +=
            startCity[index] + " TO " +
            endCity[index] + ", Flight # " +
            flightNumber[index] +
            ", Price per person: $" +
            pricePerPerson[index].toFixed(2) + NL;
        }
    }
}
```

5. In the \<body> section, right after the closing \</h2> tag for the form heading (the lines that aren't bold), insert a short JavaScript section that calls the function to load the arrays:

```
<body bgcolor="Salmon">
<h2>RedEye Airlines Flight Information Form</h2>

<script type="text/javascript">
    loadArrays();
</script>
```

6. Save the file again, and open it in a browser. If your starting city is Atlanta and you select flights to Indianapolis, your browser page should look Figure 10-11.

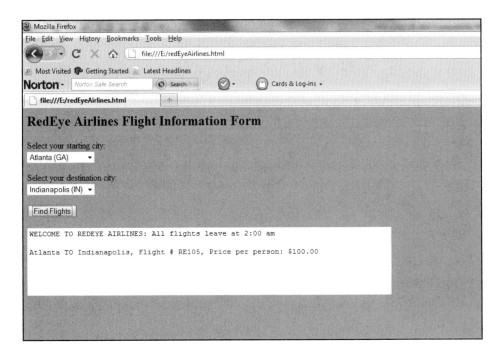

Figure 10-11   The redEyeAirlines.html program in a Web browser

Chapter Summary

- An array is a collection of related variables with the same name and data type, distinguished from one another by a unique index called a subscript.

- Array subscripts are numbered starting with 0, so the highest subscript is 1 less than the number of elements in the array.

- Arrays are most easily accessed, or traversed, by using For loops, in which the loop index serves as the varying array subscript.

- Arrays can be loaded directly with assignment statements or by including element values in the declaration statement. They can also be loaded interactively with input from the user.

- JavaScript arrays are objects created with the new keyword.

- The increment and decrement operators += and -= are shortcut notations for adding a value to or subtracting a value from a variable.

- Arrays can be searched sequentially or with a binary search, which reduces the array's searchable area by half after each comparison.

- A search for a single match can be made more efficient by terminating the search after a match is found.

- Parallel arrays use a common subscript to relate separate fields of information.

- Multidimensional arrays use two or more subscripts to reference a single array element.

Key Terms

array—A collection of related variables with a common name and data type, distinguished from one another by a unique index called a subscript. *See also* subscript.

binary search—An algorithm for looking through an array that reduces the array's searchable area by half after each comparison.

element—A single variable in an array.

load—Assign values to array elements.

multidimensional array—An array that requires two or more subscripts to reference a single array element.

parallel arrays—Two or more arrays that use a common subscript to relate separate fields of information.

sequential search—The process of examining the elements of an array in order, looking for a match for a specific value.

subscript—A nonnegative integer used to identify an element in an array.

Review Questions

True/False

1. An array can contain variables of different data types. True or False?

2. An array subscript is a number that can contain decimal places. True or False?

3. Array elements must be assigned values in the same statement in which they're declared. True or False?

4. A For loop can be used to access array elements, with the loop index used as the array subscript. True or False?

5. A sequential search moves through an array in order, looking for a match with a specific value. True or False?

6. When looking for a single match in an array, the search should terminate when the first match is found. True or False?

7. A binary search looks at only half of an array to find a match. True or False?

8. Parallel arrays contain the same data values in elements with the same subscripts. True or False?

9. In a two-dimensional array, subscripts can be used to represent rows and columns. True or False?

10. A five-dimensional array needs five subscripts to reference a single element. True or False?

Multiple Choice

1. If the variable first has the value 0 and the constant SIZE has the value 10, how do you reference the first element in the itemPrice array? (Choose all that apply.)

    a. itemPrice[0]

    b. itemPrice[1]

    c. itemPrice[first]

    d. itemPrice[SIZE]

2. In an array named department declared with the constant SIZE set to 10 and representing the number of elements, how do you reference the last element in the array? (Choose all that apply.)

    a. department[SIZE]

    b. department[SIZE - 1]

    c. department[10]

    d. department[9]

3. An array declared with the JavaScript statement
    var cost = new Array (12.00, 24.00); contains how many elements?

    a. 0

    b. 1

    c. 2

    d. can't be determined

4. Which of the following is a search algorithm that starts at the beginning of an array and moves through it in order?

    a. sequential search

    b. selection search

    c. insertion search

    d. binary search

5. Binary searches can be performed only on arrays that are
   _____.

   a. numeric

   b. string

   c. sorted

   d. object-oriented

6. When using a For loop to traverse an array, the loop variable
   can be used as the array _____.

   a. search value

   b. sentinel

   c. subscript

   d. terminator

7. Arrays in which related data fields have the same subscript are
   called which of the following?

   a. numeric arrays

   b. sequential arrays

   c. binary arrays

   d. parallel arrays

8. When looking for a single matching value in an array, the
   search should do which of the following?

   a. look through every element in the array

   b. perform a sequential search in all cases

   c. terminate after a match has been found

   d. display an error message for each nonmatching
      element

9. A multidimensional array has a single what? (Choose all
   that apply.)

   a. data type

   b. value

   c. subscript

   d. name

10. A three-dimensional array can be pictured as containing rows, columns, and _____.

    a.   cells

    b.   pages

    c.   loops

    d.   regions

Discussion Questions

1. How can a set of parallel arrays be used as a kind of database?

2. What are two ways to measure the efficiency of a search algorithm?

3. How are parallel arrays and multidimensional arrays different?

4. Why is loading an array after creating it a good idea?

Hands-On Activities

Hands-On Activity 10-1

Write a pseudocode program that creates an array, prompts the user to enter five cities, and displays the array's contents. The array contains five elements. Use a For loop to prompt the user to enter cities, and then use another For loop to display the contents. Save the file as cityArray.txt.

Hands-On Activity 10-2

Convert the algorithm you wrote for Hands-On Activity 10-1 to a JavaScript program, and test your program. Save the file as cityArray.html.

Hands-On Activity 10-3

Write a pseudocode program that creates an array of 500 elements and loads it with each value equal to the subscript's square, and then write a sequential search algorithm to see whether a number is a perfect square. Use a loop to load the array. Prompt the user for a value less than 250,000, and use another loop to search the array. Save the file as squaresArraySequential.txt.

Hands-On Activity 10-4

Convert the algorithm you wrote for Hands-On Activity 10-3
to a JavaScript program, and test your program. Save the file as
squaresArraySequential.html.

Hands-On Activity 10-5

Modify the pseudocode program in Hands-On Activity 10-3 to
perform a binary search. Save the file as squaresArrayBinary.txt.

Hands-On Activity 10-6

Modify the JavaScript program in Hands-On Activity 10-4 to perform
a binary search. Save the file as squaresArrayBinary.html.

CASE STUDY: Algorithm Development for It's War!

There's no case study project for this chapter. After learning about
building programs in Chapter 11, you use arrays to write a new
automated version of the War card game.

Building Programs

In this chapter, you learn to:

- ◎ Look for the main purpose of a program

- ◎ Design programs by matching structures and tools to the problems to be solved

- ◎ Determine whether a program fits the typical data-processing model

- ◎ Apply programming tools to new situations

- ◎ Use top-down design and module refinement to develop complete programs

- ◎ Use thorough program-testing techniques

- ◎ Design comprehensive data to test a program

There's a story about three bricklayers who were working side by side when each was asked, "What are you doing?" The first answered, "I am laying bricks." The second replied, "I am feeding my family." The third said, "I am building a great cathedral."

—ATTRIBUTED TO THE *RULE OF ST. BENEDICT*, ABOUT 530 A.D.

Throughout this book, you have been building a set of programming skills as tools you can use in different situations. "The right tool for the right job" is a common saying but a good one. However, being a skilled programmer is more than simply applying tools to tasks. It's being able to see a program's purpose and understand it in its entirety. This chapter helps you build cathedrals, not just lay bricks.

Seeing the Big Picture

In Chapter 1, you learned that programming involves skills and techniques that enable you to solve a problem with a computer. By now, you have had enough experience with developing algorithms and writing programs to begin recognizing the types of problems to be solved. Before writing any program, you should ask, "What's the purpose of the program?" Possible answers can include the following, and a program might involve all these tasks:

- Performing calculations

- Calculating statistics

- Generating reports

- Processing orders

Another thing to look for is the program's overall "shape," or pattern. A common pattern from the early days of computers and data processing is the three-part program, expressed like this:

1. Prepare (declare and initialize variables, display headings and messages)

2. Process data (until end of input)

3. Finish up (display totals, summaries, and closing messages)

Often these parts can be performed as modules. Preparation tasks, referred to as **housekeeping**, are performed once. The **processing module** is repeated for each instance of input data. The **finish-up module**, like housekeeping tasks, is performed once. Written as pseudocode with modules, a standard program can be written like this:

```
Call housekeeping()
While Not End-of-Input
   Call processData()
End While
Call finishUp()
```

The choice of calling modules, instead of writing code in the main module, depends on factors such as the program's length and whether modules need to share large amounts of data. Still, the pattern is a common one for programming as well as many aspects of daily life: Prepare to do something, do it completely, and clean up afterward. Take a look at programs you have written throughout this book and see how often this pattern appears.

Matching Tools and Techniques with Problems

In addition to seeing the big picture, you need to recognize what tools to use for solving specific problems in the programs you write. So far, you have learned about many programming tools and techniques and been guided through many examples of their use. One purpose of this chapter is to help you determine which tools and techniques are right for different situations. Of course, there might be other ways to solve a problem, but it's important to know what works well. Keep these points in mind:

- Programs are built with a combination of the three control structures: sequence, selection, and repetition.

- Module calls can be put in place, and their code can be developed later.

Example 1: A clerk needs a program to total the number of books donated for a book sale. A stack of cards listing the number of books each donor contributes is available.

Solution discussion:

- What structure do you need for the input? The number of books donated needs to be entered for each donor, so a loop is suitable.

- What kind of loop should be used? The number of input items isn't specified, so a sentinel value can be used to end the loop. You can use a While loop with a priming prompt or a Do While loop that processes the number only if it doesn't equal the sentinel value.

- How do you total the number of books donated? An accumulator variable (discussed in Chapter 6) is needed.

- Note that the shortcut operator += is used in the following pseudocode. By now, you should be able to use shortcuts (explained in Chapter 10) in both pseudocode and JavaScript.

The following pseudocode shows a possible solution for Example 1. A loop is used to prompt the user for the number of books each person donates, an accumulator is used to total the books, and a sentinel value is used to end the loop.

```
// Declare variables
Declare Numeric numBooks      // # of books for a donation
Declare Numeric totBooks = 0  // accumulator variable
```

```
// Priming prompt
Display "Enter number of books donated or -1 to quit: "
Input numBooks

// Loop until sentinel is entered
While numBooks != -1
   totBooks += numBooks
   Display "Enter number of books donated or -1 to quit: "
   Input numBooks
End While

// Display total
Display "Total number of books donated: " + totBooks
```

Example 2: The amount of rainfall for each day in April is to be entered and displayed along with each day's percentage of the month's total rainfall.

Solution discussion:

- What structure do you need for the input? Several items (rainfall amounts) need to be entered, so a loop is suitable.

- What kind of loop should be used? The number of inputs is known, so a For loop can be used.

- How can the percentage of the total month's rainfall be displayed? To display each day's percentage of total rainfall, the total amount must be known when the daily amount is displayed. This requirement suggests using an array, where the daily rainfall amounts can be stored in an accumulator variable until the total is computed, and then displayed along with their corresponding percentages.

- Note that array subscripts (explained in Chapter 10) are adjusted to match the day of the month by adding 1 each time they're displayed.

The following pseudocode is a possible solution for Example 2. It uses a For loop to prompt for and accumulate the rainfall for each day and a second For loop to compute and display each day's percentage of the month's rainfall along with the actual rainfall amount.

```
// Declare variables
Declare Constant DAYS = 30       // # of days in month
Declare Numeric rainAmt[DAYS]    // rainfall amt array
Declare Numeric totRainAmt = 0   // total for month
Declare Numeric index            // For loop index
Declare Numeric rainPct          // % of month's rainfall

// Get daily rainfall amounts
For index = 0 to DAYS - 1   // loop for # of days in month
   Display "Enter rainfall amount for April " + (index + 1)
   Input rainAmt[index]
   totRainAmt += rainAmt[index]
End For
```

```
// Calculate percentage for each day and display with amount
Display "April      Rainfall      % of Total"   // heading
For index = 0 to DAYS - 1
   rainPct = rainAmt[index] / totRainAmt
   Display (index + 1) + "      " + rainAmt[index] + ↵
   "      " + rainPct
End For
```

Uses for Control Structures and Other Tools

As a programmer, you have a variety of tools to use in problem solving. The following list summarizes uses for control structures and other tools you have learned about in this book:

- *Sequence structures*—The simplest control structure, used when statements are to be performed in order.

- *Selection structures*—Used when a choice must be made between two or more courses of action, based on evaluation of a condition.

- *Repetition structures*—Used when an action might need to be taken multiple times.

- *Modules and functions*—Used to make programs easier to manage and to provide reusable code.

- *Classes and objects*—Used in many programming languages to focus on objects rather than procedures.

- *Graphical user interfaces (GUIs)*—Used to create an attractive environment for users that's easier to use than a command-line interface.

- *Pseudocode*—Used to develop the steps of an algorithm without being tied to a specific language. It focuses more on the logic of a problem than on syntax rules.

- *Flowcharts*—Used to represent an algorithm's steps graphically.

- *IPO charts*—Used to list the inputs, processing steps, and outputs needed to solve a problem.

- *Truth tables*—Used to list the logical results of combining two or more conditions.

- *Decision tables*—Used to specify the actions to take for combinations of logical conditions.

- *Binary trees*—Used to represent in graphical form the outcomes of combining logical conditions.

- *Hierarchy charts*—Used to show the names of modules and their relationships to each other.

- *Menus*—Used to give users choices of possible valid actions.

- *Data validation*—Used to prevent or reduce user input errors.

- *Arrays*—Used to keep lists of similar variables in memory throughout the run of a program.

There are many other tools, such as loops (`While`, `Do While`, and `For`) and special types of variables (counters, loop indexes, sentinels, accumulators, and subscripts). As you use these tools more often, you'll recognize which one works best in certain situations.

Be on the lookout for patterns, too. If you need odd or even numbers for an application, for example, you can use a `For` loop that increments or decrements in steps of 2. If certain parts of your code have a special meaning, such as the first two letters of a job code variable representing a department (`AP123` representing Accounts Payable, for example), you can use the string manipulation function `substring()` to test what department a job code belongs to.

Of course, programs are made up of combinations of structures and tools. In the solution for Example 1, a series of sequential steps was followed by a loop to get input, and the solution ended with a sequential step to display output. The solution for Example 2 included sequential steps, a loop to get input, a sequential step to display headings, and another loop for output.

Example 3: Students' scores in a class are entered as percentages. The program is to display a letter grade when the percentage is input and display cumulative totals for the number of As, Bs, Cs, Ds, and Fs earned. The program should also check for invalid input.

Solution discussion:

- What structure do you need for the input? Several items (students' scores) need to be entered, so a loop is suitable.

- What kind of loop should be used? The number of inputs isn't known, so a sentinel value can be used with a `While` loop or `Do While` loop.

- How are letter grades determined? A series of `If/Else If` statements can be used.

- How should you count the number of occurrences of each letter grade? An accumulator for each letter grade should be incremented when the letter grade is determined. (Alternatively, parallel arrays could be used: one for the number of occurrences and one for the letter grades.)

The following pseudocode is a possible solution for Example 3. A Do While loop asks the user for a score of 0 to 100 or a sentinel value of –1 to quit. If/Else If statements determine the letter grade and increment the accumulator for the grade. When the loop ends, the totals for each grade are displayed.

```
// Declare variables
Declare Numeric numA = 0    // number of As earned
Declare Numeric numB = 0    // number of Bs earned
Declare Numeric numC = 0    // number of Cs earned
Declare Numeric numD = 0    // number of Ds earned
Declare Numeric numF = 0    // number of Fs earned
Declare Numeric score       // score
Declare Numeric index       // loop index

// Loop until sentinel value -1 entered
Do
   Display "Enter a student score (0-100) or -1 to quit: "
   Input score

   // Validate input
   While score < -1 Or score > 100
      Display "ERROR...enter 0-100 or -1 to quit: "
      Input score
   End While

   // Process score, increment accumulator
   If score >= 90 Then
      Display "Grade earned: A"
      numA++
   Else If score >= 80 Then
      Display "Grade earned: B"
      numB++
   Else If score >= 70 Then
      Display "Grade earned: C"
      numC++
   Else If score >= 60 Then
      Display "Grade earned: D"
      numD++
   Else
      Display "Grade earned: F"
      numF++
While score != -1

// Display number of each grade earned
Display "Number of A grades earned: " + numA
Display "Number of B grades earned: " + numB
Display "Number of C grades earned: " + numC
Display "Number of D grades earned: " + numD
Display "Number of F grades earned: " + numF
```

Applying Tools to New Situations

Sometimes you need to consider several aspects of a problem before you can outline an algorithm, and you should examine each aspect before choosing specific steps. Take, for example, shuffling a deck of cards and dealing all the cards to two players. Some aspects to consider include the following:

- How will the deck be represented?

- How will the point values of cards be determined?

- How will the value of players' hands be stored?

- How will shuffling be simulated?

- How will cards be distributed to players?

A simple way to represent a deck of cards is as a one-dimensional array of 52 elements, with each element containing the card's name and suit, such as "2C" for the two of clubs and "JD" for the jack of diamonds. A two-dimensional array could be used, with rows representing suits and columns representing card names, but you'd need additional programming steps to match specific rows with specific suits. A one-dimensional array is easier to implement and code.

There are at least two possibilities for determining card values. You can use an If/Else If or Case selection structure to examine the first character of the card name and match it with a card value ("2"=2, "J"=11, and so forth). Another possibility is using a parallel array for card values matched to card names so that the subscript where the card name is found holds the card's value in the other array. Both methods involve a search (through If/Else If conditions or the card name array), so the only difference is in the way the card values are assigned: one by an assignment statement and one by a parallel array.

The players' hands can be stored as arrays. An important question is whether (and if so, how) the players' hands should be replenished. Do they draw from the deck? Do they win cards played in a hand? If an array is used, you need a system to keep track of the next card to be played (such as a variable representing the next subscript) and the next available subscript for adding a new card to a player's hand, which can also be represented by a variable.

Shuffling calls for a random number generator (described in Chapter 8). If your deck array has subscripts for 52 cards, you can generate a random number from 0 to 51 and assign that card to one of the players. How do you keep track of whether a card has already been assigned, however? You can use a parallel array for tracking assigned values, like this:

- All 52 elements of a Boolean array called cardAssigned can be initialized to False.

- Each time a random number is generated for a card from the deck, the parallel array cardAssigned is checked:

  - If the cardAssigned array still holds the value False at the subscript for the card, meaning the card is available, it can be changed to True, and this card is then copied to one player's hand.

  - If the cardAssigned array has already been changed to True, another random number must be generated, with the process repeating until all cards have been assigned to one player or another.

Because both players get the same number of cards, you set up a single For loop with the loop index ranging from 0 to half the number of cards to be dealt. In the loop, two cards are assigned, one to each player, using the loop index as the subscript. In other words, if all 52 cards are to be dealt, a For loop that executes 26 times assigns cards to both players, using subscript 0 the first time, 1 the second time, and so on. When the loop ends, each player has 26 cards randomly assigned from the deck, with subscripts from 0 to 25.

Based on this discussion, you can develop the following algorithm for shuffling and dealing a deck of 52 cards to two players:

```
// Declare variables and constants
Declare Numeric DECK_SIZE = 52        // # of cards in deck
Declare Numeric index                 // array index
Declare Numeric deckSubscript         // card assigned?
Declare Numeric numPlayerCards1 = 0   // # cards, player 1
Declare Numeric numPlayerCards2 = 0   // # cards, player 2

// Create card deck array, array of card deck points,
// and array of assigned cards
Declare String cardDeck[] =
   "2C", "3C", "4C", "5C", "6C", "7C", "8C", "9C", "10C",
   "JC", "QC", "KC", "AC", "2D", "3D", "4D", "5D", "6D",
   "7D", "8D", "9D", "10D", "JD", "QD", "KD", "AD", "2H",
   "3H", "4H", "5H", "6H", "7H", "8H", "9H", "10H", "JH",
   "QH", "KH", "AH", "2S", "3S", "4S", "5S", "6S", "7S",
   "8S", "9S", "10S", "JS", "QS", "KS", "AS"

// Create a parallel array to track assigned cards
// Initialize values to False
Declare Boolean cardAssigned[DECK_SIZE]
For index = 0 to DECK_SIZE - 1
   cardAssigned[index] = False
End For
```

```
// Create array of cards for each player's hand
Declare String playerDeck1[DECK_SIZE]
Declare String playerDeck2[DECK_SIZE]

// Initialize player decks
For index = 0 to (DECK_SIZE / 2) - 1
   // Choose random card until an unassigned one is found
   Do
      deckSubscript = Random(0, DECK_SIZE - 1)
   While cardAssigned[deckSubscript]

   // Deal card to player 1, mark as assigned
   playerDeck1[index] = cardDeck[deckSubscript]
   numPlayerCards1++
   cardAssigned[deckSubscript] = True

   // Choose random card until an unassigned one is found
   Do
      deckSubscript = Random(0, DECK_SIZE - 1)
   While cardAssigned[deckSubscript]

   // Deal card to player 2, mark as assigned
   playerDeck2[index] = cardDeck[deckSubscript]
   numPlayerCards2++
   cardAssigned[deckSubscript] = True
End For
```

Top-Down Design and Stubs

The concept of top-down design works especially well with menu programs, as you learned in Chapter 9. Menus can be written cleanly when each selection calls a module, which is refined in a later step.

Example 4: In a program with statistics activities, the user should have a choice of repeatedly calculating statistics—including sum, product, maximum, minimum, and average—on sets of numbers.

Solution discussion:

- What structure do you need for the input? The user needs to be able to make repeated choices, so a menu is suitable. (A repeating menu is implemented in a loop. Do While loops work well because you want the menu displayed at least once.) Menus usually use sentinel values to exit.

- How should the statistics activities be coded? The steps can be done in the scope of an If/Else If structure. However, modules can be used efficiently to display the menu and process the user's choices.

The following pseudocode is a possible solution for Example 4. It uses a menu that calls a function to get the menu selection.

```
Start
    // Declare variables
    Declare String menuChoice

    // Loop until user selects exit option
    Do
        // Display menu, get choice
        menuChoice = getMenuChoice()

        // Process choices
        If menuChoice == "A" Then
            Call addNumbers()
        Else If menuChoice == "M" Then
            Call multiplyNumbers()
        Else If menuChoice == "X" Then
            Call getMax()
        Else If menuChoice == "N" Then
            Call getMin()
        Else If menuChoice == "V" Then
            Call getAverage()
    While menuChoice != "Q"
Stop

// Function to display menu and get choice
Function String getMenuChoice()

    // Declare variable
    Declare String choice

    // Display menu
    Display "Statistics Menu"
    Display "Enter "A" to Add numbers,"
    Display "      "M" to Multiply numbers,"
    Display "      "X" to get the maXimum,"
    Display "      "N" to get the miNimum,"
    Display "      "V" to get the aVerage, or"
    Display "      "Q" to Quit this program: "

    // Get, validate, and return user choice
    Input choice
    choice = toUpper(choice)
    While choice != "Q" And Not (choice == "A" Or
        choice == "M" Or choice == "X" Or
        choice == "N" Or choice == "V")
        Display "ERROR...enter A, M, X, N, V,"
        Display "or Q to quit: "
        Input choice
    End While
    Return choice
End Function
```

To test your program logic at this point, you can simply write the five menu functions as stubs, which ensures that the program can call each module correctly:

```
// Module to add numbers
Module addNumbers()
    Display "In addNumbers()"
End Module

// Module to multiply numbers
Module multiplyNumbers()
    Display "In multiplyNumbers()"
End Module

// Module to find maximum of numbers
Module getMax()
    Display "In getMax()"
End Module

// Module to find minimum of numbers
Module getMin()
    Display "In getMin()"
End Module

// Module to find average of numbers
Module getAverage()
    Display "In getAverage()"
End Module
```

After you know the menu is working correctly, you can change the stubs to full-fledged modules by writing code for them. Because all numeric values are acceptable as valid data, a separate variable (moreInput) is used instead of a sentinel value to indicate whether there's more input. For the getMax() and getMin() functions, the first value entered is set as the initial maximum and minimum, and other values entered are compared with them, as shown in the following pseudocode:

```
// Module to add numbers
Module addNumbers()

    // Declare input variables
    Declare String moreInput = "Y"   // text input to continue
    Declare Numeric inputNum          // input number
    Declare Numeric sum = 0           // accumulator

    // Loop until sentinel is entered
    While toUpper(moreInput) == "Y"

        // Get a number
        // (assume user wants to enter at least one)
        Display "Enter a number: "
        Input inputNum
        sum += inputNum
```

```
            // Check for more input
            Display "Another (Y/N)? "
            Input moreInput
        End While

        // Display sum
        Display "The sum of the numbers is: " + sum
    End Module
```

```
// Module to multiply numbers
Module multiplyNumbers()

    // Declare input variables
    Declare String moreInput = "Y"    // text input to continue
    Declare Numeric inputNum          // input number
    Declare Numeric product = 1       // running total

    // Loop until sentinel is entered
    While toUpper(moreInput) == "Y"

        // Get a number
        // (assume user wants to enter at least one)
        Display "Enter a number: "
        Input inputNum
        product = product * inputNum

        // Check for more input
        Display "Another (Y/N)? "
        Input moreInput
    End While

    // Display product
    Display "The product of the numbers is: " + product
End Module

// Module to find maximum of numbers
Module getMax()

    // Declare input variables
    Declare String moreInput = "Y"    // text input to continue
    Declare Boolean firstInput        // first value flag
    Declare Numeric inputNum          // input number
    Declare Numeric highest           // current highest

    // Set first input flag to true
    firstInput = True

    // Loop until sentinel is entered
    While toUpper(moreInput) == "Y"

        // Get a number
        // (assume user wants to enter at least one)
        Display "Enter a number: "
        Input inputNum
```

```
      // If first input, set max to this value
      If firstInput Then
         highest = inputNum
         firstInput = False
      End If

      // Replace max value if current number is higher
      If inputNum > highest Then
         highest = inputNum
      End If

      // Check for more input
      Display "Another (Y/N)? "
      Input moreInput
   End While

   // Display maximum
   Display "The highest number you entered is: " + highest
End Module

// Module to find minimum of numbers
Module getMin()

   // Declare input variables
   Declare String moreInput = "Y"    // text input to continue
   Declare Boolean firstInput        // first value flag
   Declare Numeric inputNum          // input number
   Declare Numeric lowest            // current lowest

   // Set first input flag to true
   firstInput = True

   // Loop until sentinel is entered
   While toUpper(moreInput) == "Y"

      // Get a number
      // (assume user wants to enter at least one)
      Display "Enter a number: "
      Input inputNum

      // If first input, set min to this value
      If firstInput Then
         lowest = inputNum
         firstInput = False
      End If

      // Replace min value if current number is lower
      If inputNum < lowest Then
         lowest = inputNum
      End If

      // Check for more input
      Display "Another (Y/N)? "
      Input moreInput
   End While
```

```
    // Display minimum
    Display "The lowest number you entered is: " + lowest
End Module

// Module to find average of numbers
Module getAverage()

    // Declare input variables
    Declare String moreInput = "Y"    // text input to continue
    Declare Numeric inputNum           // input number
    Declare Numeric sum                // running total
    Declare Numeric count = 0          // count of input values
    Declare Numeric average            // calculated average

    // Loop until sentinel is entered
    While toUpper(moreInput) == "Y"

        // Get a number
        // (assume user wants to enter at least one)
        Display "Enter a number: "
        Input inputNum
        sum += inputNum
        count++

        // Check for more input
        Display "Another (Y/N)? "
        Input moreInput
    End While

    // Calculate and display average
    average = sum / count
    Display "The average of the numbers is: " + average
End Module
```

In the previous examples, programming tools were used to solve problems. The next example calls for a logic development tool: a decision table (discussed in Chapter 7).

Example 5: A college dormitory holds an annual euchre (a card game) tournament. You're writing a program that determines who's allowed to play in the euchre tournament, based on three factors: whether the student is a senior, whether the student has lived in the dormitory for longer than the current year, and whether the student's grade point average is 2.0 or higher. All seniors are allowed to play. Others are allowed to play if they have lived in the dormitory for longer than the current year, unless their grade point average is less than 2.0.

Solution discussion: The combination of conditions calls for a decision table or binary tree. A decision table is usually written in two stages: first, the table with all combinations of conditions and outcomes listed, and then the final version with irrelevant conditions eliminated. Table 11-1 is the decision table with all combinations listed.

Conditions								
Class = senior?	T	T	T	T	F	F	F	F
Lived in dorm for longer than current year?	T	T	F	F	T	T	F	F
GPA >= 2.0?	T	F	T	F	T	F	T	F
Outcomes								
Allowed to play	X	X	X	X	X			

Table 11-1   Decision table for allowing a student to play in the tournament

All seniors are allowed to play, so when the first condition is true, the other two are irrelevant. Also, if the student isn't a senior and hasn't lived in the dorm for longer than a year, the third condition is irrelevant. Table 11-2 is the decision table with all irrelevant conditions eliminated.

Conditions				
Class = senior?	T	F	F	F
Lived in dorm for longer than current year?	-	T	T	F
GPA >= 2.0?	-	T	F	-
Outcomes				
Allowed to play	X	X		

Table 11-2   Decision table for allowing a student to play in the tournament (final)

Thorough Program Testing and Comprehensive Data Sets

Top-down design is a well-proven method for a development plan. A comprehensive project is developed with main modules that are refined (often as smaller modules) until further refinement is no longer necessary. However, modules must be tested by themselves and with other modules to make sure they perform correctly and handle data input errors without crashing. With this approach, you test a module's code thoroughly for accuracy and efficiency, using all kinds of data. You examine how data is input, processed, output, and stored and consider whether other ways of handling these tasks might require fewer steps, take less processing power, and present fewer opportunities for errors.

One way of testing programs is to develop data that includes as many possible variations as you can think of. Data values created for the purpose of testing program logic are called **data sets**. For example, if your program is supposed to accept test scores from 0 to 100, test it with data that includes values such as -1, 0, 1, 99, 100, and 101. This method is sometimes referred to as "testing at the borders," with the borders being the limits of the values that result in a condition evaluating to true or false. In addition, if you use the comparison < 100 instead of <= 100 in this example, your code won't include the value 100. Data sets should include values before, at, and after the values named in conditions. Doing so helps you determine whether you're selecting the exact values you want.

You should also include checking for nonnumeric data and empty or null data. For example, what does your program do when the user enters the letters O or I for the digits 0 or 1? What does your program do when the user presses Enter or clicks OK or Cancel without entering any data? As mentioned in Chapter 9, your program should be robust enough to detect all errors without crashing and elegant enough to handle them in a way that allows users to correct errors and move ahead.

Always check reference materials and help information for any programming language you use to find the answers to these questions. An excellent Web site for learning about JavaScript (and trying it on your own) is the W3Schools Online Web Tutorials at *www.w3schools. com*. If you search for "illegal number javascript," for example, you find a link to JavaScript's isNaN() function (NaN stands for "not a number"), which checks to see whether a numeric value is illegal. If you search for "null javascript," you find a link to information about the null value that you can use to test for nonentry of values in JavaScript. Here are the different possibilities when a user is prompted to enter a number, for instance:

- If the user enters a valid number and presses Enter or clicks OK, the text variable contains the digits, and the value converted to a number is a valid number.

- If the user enters an invalid number and presses Enter or clicks OK, the text variable contains digits and is considered NaN, and the value converted to a number is considered NaN.

- If the user presses Enter or clicks OK in a prompt box without entering a value, the text variable is considered an empty string, the equivalent of "". The value converted to a number is considered NaN.

- If the user clicks Cancel, whether a value has been entered or not, the text variable is considered null, and the value converted to a number is considered NaN.

PROGRAM 11-1 JavaScript Program nullTester.html

Because many of the messages start with the same words—"JavaScript says the variable ="—a constant is used to represent these repeated words. Remember to add a blank line after the code section in each step.

1. Open a new document in Notepad, and save it as **nullTester.html**. Enter the program documentation lines and declare variable and constants:

```
<html>
<body>
<script type="text/javascript">

// Program name: nullTester.html
// Purpose: Handles a user entering null data
// Author: Paul Addison
// Date last modified: 01-Sep-2011

// Declare variables and constants
var userInputText;    // user input
var userInputNum;     // input converted to number
var ES = "";          // literal empty string
var BR = "<br />";    // HTML line break
var MSG = "JavaScript says the variable = ";
                      // message text constant
```

2. Get the user input and test it for a null value, an empty string, and whether it's NaN (not a number):

```
// Get input and test it as entered
userInputText = prompt ↵
  ("Enter a number and press Enter:",ES);
document.write ↵
  ("You entered: " + userInputText + BR);

if (userInputText == null) {
   document.write(MSG + "null" + BR);
}

if (userInputText == ES) {
   document.write(MSG + "an empty string" + BR);
}

if (isNaN(userInputText)) {
   document.write(MSG + "NaN" + BR);
}
```

(continues)

(continued)

3. Convert the input to a number, and see whether JavaScript recognizes it as a number, a null value, an empty string, or an NaN value. Then end the program.

```
// Convert input to a number and test it
userInputNum = parseFloat(userInputText);
document.write ↵
("Your entry converted to a number is: " ↵
 + userInputNum + BR);

if (userInputNum == null) {
    document.write(MSG + "null" + BR);
}

if (userInputNum == ES) {
    document.write(MSG + "an empty string" + BR);
}

if (isNaN (userInputNum)) {
    document.write(MSG + "NaN" + BR);
}

</script>
</body>
</html>
```

4. Save the file again, and open it in a browser. Try running the program in these ways, and take note of what happens:

   - Enter a valid number and press **Enter** or click **OK**.

   - Enter an invalid number (text characters) and press **Enter** or click **OK**.

   - Press **Enter** without typing any input.

   - Click **OK** without typing any input.

   - Click **Cancel** without typing any input.

   If the program doesn't run correctly, compare your code with nullTester.html in your student data files.

Besides testing a module's internal contents, thorough testing checks a module's interaction with other modules by trying all kinds of argument values when a module calls other modules. You can try sending arguments with incorrect data types, arguments out of order, and the wrong number of arguments, for example. Make sure your program can handle anything a user might "throw" at it by using techniques for handling exceptions (covered in Chapter 9).

Field Testing

Software engineering is concerned with methods, best practices, and tools for professional software development. When a company sells software to businesses, industry, or the public, code testing and data validation are essential. A software company's reputation is on the line when a product goes to market, so testing of any software product must be thorough and accurate.

In addition to testing every line of code and anticipating every conceivable user action, software testing should simulate the actual conditions of real-world business. In your testing, you might be loading an array of 20 records, but in the real world, the array might need to be loaded with 20,000 records. Inefficient use of memory and wasted processing steps might not be noticeable with a small number of records, but they can have a major effect with large numbers of records or users. So you should always check for whether memory is being used efficiently and whether any processing steps are unnecessary.

Field testing involves running a program in an environment set up to simulate real-world operating conditions. It's often done with employees who will be using the program eventually. The data files used to test the program aren't actual production files and are usually kept on separate drives or folders where they can be analyzed for accuracy. Other factors measured during field testing include processing time and throughput (the number of records processed in a given time period). Users testing the program are often surveyed for their opinions and suggestions about the program and its interface.

As a beginning programmer, it will probably be a while before you're testing software under "industrial-strength" conditions. However, there are several ways you can ensure that the programs you write now are as good as they can be:

- *Comments*—Give your code to other programmers and ask for their reactions to the comments, not to the code. Do they have a general sense of what the program does? Do they understand what specific sections of the program are accomplishing, even if they don't read the code? Your comments should be understandable without others having to inspect the code.

- *Understandability*—Let other people run your program and ask for their comments. Is the program easy to learn and use? Are the instructions clear? Did they know what they were supposed to do at different points in the program? You'll be surprised at the constructive suggestions you can get from other people.

- *Bullet-proof testing*—Let other people run your program and challenge them to "break" it. Suggest that they enter values they know are invalid, and see whether your program not only keeps running, but also handles errors correctly.

As with any business report or resume you write, any program you write should be checked and tested carefully. Your company's reputation for quality software and your own reputation as a quality programmer rely on writing programs that produce correct results efficiently, are easy to use, and don't crash under normal operating conditions.

Programmer's Workshop

In this Programmer's Workshop, you write an algorithm and a JavaScript program to find the mode of numbers that a user enters. The mode is the number occurring most often in a group of numbers. (If more than one number occurs the maximum number of times, each of these numbers is a mode; if no number occurs more than once, there's no mode for that data set.) In this program, the user needs to know ahead of time how many numbers to enter, but the numbers can be of any value. When all numbers are entered, the program reports which number occurred most often and how many times it occurred.

Discussion:

- What kind of structure should be used for the input? There are repeated inputs, so a loop is needed, and because the user specifies how many numbers will be entered, a For loop can be used.

- How should the numbers be stored without knowing the values ahead of time? An array can be used to store numbers that are entered, but how can you store the frequency of these numbers occurring? Use two parallel arrays: one for the numbers being stored (numbersEntered) and one for the frequency of each number's occurrence (frequency). If a number is entered more than once, it's found in the numbersEntered array, and its parallel entry in the frequency array is incremented.

- If the values had to be within a limited range, the arrays could be preset with a number of elements encompassing all numbers in this range. However, the values aren't limited, and setting up an array with millions of elements is impractical. Instead, the arrays can be created each time a new number is found. Each time a number is entered, it's checked against existing numbers in the numbersEntered array. If the number is found, the parallel element in the frequency array is incremented. If it isn't found, the number is added to the numbersEntered array, and the parallel element in the frequency array is set to 1.

- A variable (uniqueNums) is needed to keep track of the subscript of the last element entered in the numbersEntered array. The loop to search the array of existing numbers should run from 0 to this last number, but the loop shouldn't run before the first number is entered. To do this, set the initial value of uniqueNums to −1 and increment it each time a new unique number is entered.

- After all numbers have been entered, the frequency array is searched for the maximum value. The parallel element in the numbersEntered array is the number occurring most.

Don't forget to add blank lines as usual to improve your program's readability.

1. Open a new document in Notepad, and save it as **modeFinder.txt**. Enter the documentation lines and declare the variables:

```
// Program name: Mode Finder
// Purpose: Find the number occurring most often
//    in a series of numbers. Use parallel arrays,
//    one for numbers entered and one for frequency
//    of each number.
// Author: Paul Addison
// Date last modified: 01-Sep-2011

Start
   // Declare variables
   Declare Numeric inputNum       // number entered
   Declare Numeric numEntries     // # of entries
   Declare Numeric uniqueNums     // last unique #
   Declare Numeric count          // loop counter
   Declare Numeric index          // array index
   Declare Boolean found          // number found?
   Declare Numeric maxFrequency   // highest freq
   Declare Numeric maxLocation    // max location
   Declare Numeric freq           // single freq
   Declare Numeric numModes       // count of modes
```

2. Next, initialize the subscript for the unique numbers array, ask the user how many numbers are being entered, and set up the parallel arrays:

```
// Initialize subscript for unique numbers
uniqueNums = -1

// Ask user how many entries there will be
Display "How many numbers will you enter? "
Input numEntries

// Declare arrays for numbers entered
//   and frequencies of occurrence
Declare Numeric numbersEntered[numEntries]
Declare Numeric frequency[numEntries]
```

3. Start the For loop to get the next input number from the user:

```
// Get user input
For count = 0 to numEntries - 1
    Display "Enter a number: "
    Input inputNum
```

4. Now search the array of existing numbers for a match with the current number entered. If it's found, increment the frequency for this number.

```
// See whether number has been entered
// If so, increment count in frequency array
found = False
For index = 0 to uniqueNums
    If inputNum == numbersEntered[index] Then
        frequency[index]++
        found = True
    End If
End For
```

5. If the number isn't found, add it to the array of numbers and set the number's frequency to 1. It's also the end of the For loop for user input.

```
// If not found, add to numbersEntered array
//   and set frequency of new number to 1
If Not found Then
    uniqueNums++
    numbersEntered[uniqueNums] = inputNum
    frequency[uniqueNums] = 1
End If
End For
```

6. Now that the input is finished, search the `frequency` array to find the highest number, and note the location:

```
// Go through frequency array
// Find location of maximum occurrences
// The number stored in the numbersEntered
//   array at that location is the mode
maxFrequency = 0
For index = 0 to uniqueNums
   If frequency[index] > maxFrequency Then
      maxFrequency = frequency[index]
      maxLocation = index
   End If
End For
```

7. Search the `frequency` array again to see whether there are instances of no modes or multiple modes:

```
// Go through frequency array again
// If maxFrequency occurs > 1 time,
//   there is > 1 mode
numModes = 0
For index = 0 to uniqueNums
   If frequency[index] == maxFrequency Then
      numModes++
   End If
End For
```

8. Next, display the mode. If no number occurred more than once, there's no mode. If `numModes` has a value greater than 1, more than one number is occurring the maximum number of times, meaning there are multiple modes. Otherwise, enter the number occurring most often and the number of times it occurred.

```
// Display mode
// If maxFrequency <= 1, there is no mode
// If numModes > 1, report all multiple modes
// Otherwise, report the single mode
If maxFrequency <= 1 Then
   Display "There is no mode."
   Display "No number occurred more than once."
Else If numModes > 1 Then
   Display "There are multiple modes."
   For index = 0 to uniqueNums
      freq = frequency[index]
      If freq == maxFrequency Then
         Display numbersEntered[index] + ↵
" occurred " + freq + " times."
      End If
   Next For
Else
```

```
        Display "The mode is: " +↵
numbersEntered[maxLocation]
        Display "Number of times occurring: " +↵
maxFrequency
    End If
```

9. Thank the user and end the program:

```
    // Thank the user and end the program
    Display "Thank you."
Stop
```

10. Save the file again.

Detective Work

Now convert the pseudocode program to JavaScript. Open a new document in Notepad, and save it as modeFinder.html. Enter your code, save the file again, and then open the file in a browser. If your program doesn't work correctly when trying the data given in the following examples, compare it with modeFinder-solution.html in your student data files. If you enter the numbers 32, 44, 12, 32, 55, and 22, the program output should look like Figure 11-1.

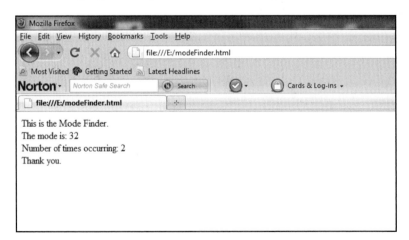

Figure 11-1 The modeFinder.html program with one mode

To see what happens when there's no mode, enter the numbers 4, 6, 3, 2, 9, 7, and 5. Your output should look like Figure 11-2.

Figure 11-2   The modeFinder.html program with no mode

To see an example of multiple modes, enter the numbers 101, 125, 115, 125, and 101. Your output should look like Figure 11-3.

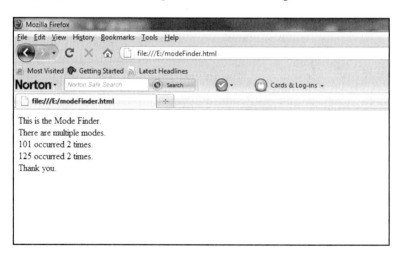

Figure 11-3   The modeFinder.html program with multiple modes

In this Programmer's Workshop, you used arrays and loops to determine which numbers were entered most often. In the Object Lesson, you use your knowledge of forms and arrays to set up a mailing list database.

Object Lesson

Hi-Tech Investments wants a form developed for a short mailing list that includes its top two dozen customers. It will be loaded with 24 names, cities, and states, but the user can change them while the program is running.

Program specifications are as follows:

- Buttons labeled First, Previous, Next, and Last are used to display records in the form.

- The form includes a text box where users can enter a record number and a Go To button to display the record.

- When a field in a record is changed, the new value is stored in the array. (*Note*: JavaScript doesn't allow writing to text files, so the changes won't be permanent.)

Discussion:

- Parallel arrays are set up for last name, first name, city, and state.

- The form is loaded with names and addresses from the array.

- Data validation should be done so that a record with a subscript less than 0 or higher than the highest subscript can't be displayed, and if the user enters a nontext or empty record number, the first record is displayed.

- A function should be called to load arrays when the HTML page is opened, so a short script is needed in the <body> section with a statement calling the function to load the arrays.

- A function to load the correct record in the form should be called when any button (First, Previous, Next, Last, or Go To) is clicked and when the arrays are first loaded.

- A function to change field values in the arrays should be called whenever a value is changed in a text box. (You can do this by associating an onchange event with the text box.)

1. First, draw the form on paper so that you can see what labels, text boxes, and buttons you need (see Figure 11-4 for an example). This step makes writing the HTML code for the form easier.

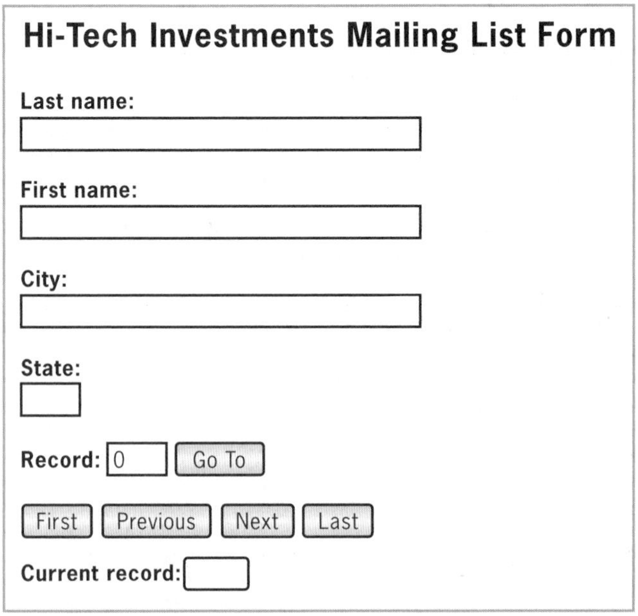

Hi-Tech Investments Mailing List Form

Last name:

[   ]

First name:

[   ]

City:

[   ]

State:

[   ]

Record: [0   ] [Go To]

[First] [Previous] [Next] [Last]

Current record:[   ]

Figure 11-4   The Hi-Tech Investments Mailing List form

2. Open a new document in Notepad, and save it as
    hiTechMailingListForm.html. Enter the following code to cre-
    ate the form in HTML in the <body> section. You start with
    the <html> tag so that you can test whether the form works
    before adding the functions. Notice the following points
    about the code:

    - Text boxes include an onclick event that calls a function to
      set the array for the current field to the text box's current
      value. The function has two arguments: the name of the
      field and the current value.

    - Special argument values are used for the Previous, Next,
      and Last button calls to the loadForm() function, which are
      handled in the function. The First button displays record 0,
      as does the Go To button.

    - The loadArrays() function is called after the form is dis-
      played because the onchange event would erase the values
      loaded when the form is first displayed.

    ```
    <html>

    <body bgcolor="LightCyan">
    <h2>Hi-Tech Investments Mailing List Form</h2>
    ```

```html
<form name="Mail" action="">

<strong>Last name:</strong><br />
<input type="text" name="lastName" value=""
 size="40" onchange="changeField('lastName',
this.value)"/><p />
<strong>First name:</strong><br />
<input type="text" name="firstName" value=""
 size="40" onchange="changeField('firstName',
this.value)"/><p />
<strong>City:</strong><br />
<input type="text" name="city" value="" size="40"
 onchange="changeField('city',this.value)"/><p />
<strong>State:</strong><br />
<input type="text" name="state" value="" size="2"
 onchange="changeField('state',this.value)"/><p />

<strong>Record: </strong>
<input type="text" name="subscript" value="0"
 size="2"/>
<input type="button" value="Go To" onclick=
"loadForm(document.Mail.subscript.value)">
 <p />

<input type="button" value="First"
 onclick="loadForm(0)">
<input type="button" value="Previous"
 onclick="loadForm(-2)">
<input type="button" value="Next"
 onclick="loadForm(-1)">
<input type="button" value="Last"
 onclick="loadForm(-3)"><br />

<strong>Current record: </strong>
<input type="text" name="message" readonly=
 "readonly" value="" size="3"/><p />

<script type="text/javascript">
   loadArrays();
</script>

</form>
</body>
</html>
```

3. Save the file again, and open it in a browser to make sure the form is displayed correctly. If it's not, check your code against hiTechMailingListForm.html in your student data files. Next, save the file as **hiTechMailingList.html**, and enter the code

for the <head> section, starting on the line under the opening <html> tag. Notice the following points:

- Arrays are loaded as parallel arrays.

- The loadArrays() function calls the loadForm() function with an argument of 0 so that the first record is displayed.

- Record numbers have been left identical with the subscript numbers, starting with 0.

- Notice the data validation to check for empty and nonnumeric data: The Previous button doesn't accept a subscript less than 0.

```
<head>
<script type="text/javascript">

// Program name: hiTechMailingList.html
// Purpose: Creates an updateable mailing list form
// Author: Paul Addison
// Date last modified: 01-Sep-2011

// Declare variables and constants
var SIZE = 24;          // size of arrays
var index;              // index for loops
var currentPos = 0;     // current record subscript
var lastName;           // last name array
var firstName;          // first name array
var city;               // city array
var state;              // state array
```

4. Enter the code for the function that loads the arrays:

```
function loadArrays() {
   lastName = new Array
      ("Adams", "Baker", "Chalmers", "Dawber,
 "Englebert", "Fraser", "Grover", "Heimlich",
 "Iverson", "Jackson", "Kellogg", "Landry",
 "Matheson", "Norman", "Osterling", "Paulson",
 "Robbins", "Sterling", "Tarkington", "Urbanik",
 "Valencia", "Wilson", "Yardley", "Zerza");

   firstName = new Array
      ("Paul", "Merri", "Elizabeth", "Michael",
 "Carla", "Kris", "Yvonne", "Debbie", "Paula",
 "Peggy", "Lynn", "Randy", "Eddie", "David",
 "Carolyn", "James", "Darla", "Darrell", "Ricky",
 "Beth", "Mitchell", "Denise", "Scott", "Daniel");

   city = new Array
      ("Annapolis", "Boston", "Charleston",
 "Dallas", "Englewood", "Frankfort", "Griffith",
```

```
      "Houston", "Iowa City", "Jacksonville",
      "Kalamazoo", "LaCrosse", "Memphis", "Norman",
      "Oberlin", "Portland", "Quincy", "Raleigh",
      "San Jose", "Tempe", "Virginia City",
      "West Lafayette", "Yorba City", "Zephyrhills");
```

```
   state = new Array
        ("MD", "MA", "SC", "TX", "CO", "IN", "IN",
   "TX", "IA", "FL", "MI", "WI", "TN", "OK", "OH",
   "OR", "MA", "NC", "CA", "AZ", "VA", "IN", "FL",
   "FL");
```

5.   Next, call the function to load the form with record 0:

```
   loadForm(0);
}
```

6.   Add the function that loads the form. The argument is the record number 0 to 23 or codes for the Previous, Next, First, Last, or GoTo buttons.

```
function loadForm(sub) {
   // sub is an argument representing a button
   // that was clicked

   // Check for nonentry of record number
   if (sub == "" || sub == null || isNaN(sub) ) {
      sub = 0;
   }

   // Set position if Previous button is clicked
   // Disallow moving to a subscript < 0
   if (sub == -2) {
      sub = currentPos - 1;
      if (sub < 0) sub = 0;
   }

   // Set position if Next button is clicked
   // Disallow moving to a subscript > SIZE
   if (sub == -1) {
      sub = currentPos + 1;
      if (sub >= SIZE) sub = SIZE - 1;
   }

   // Set position if Last button is clicked
   if (sub == -3) {
      sub = SIZE - 1;
   }

   // Note current position
   currentPos = sub;
   document.Mail.message.value=currentPos;
```

```
      document.Mail.lastName.value = lastName[sub];
      document.Mail.firstName.value = firstName[sub];
      document.Mail.city.value = city[sub];
      document.Mail.state.value = state[sub];

      // Replace value in Go To text box
      document.Mail.subscript.value = sub;
    }
```

7. Change the data in the arrays. (Again, note that the change is temporary because JavaScript doesn't write to text files.) Then add the closing tags for the <head> section.

```
function changeField(field, fieldValue) {

    // see which text box was changed
    // and change array value
    if (field == "lastName")↵
  lastName[currentPos] = fieldValue;
    if (field == "firstName")↵
  firstName[currentPos] = fieldValue;
    if (field == "city")↵
  city[currentPos] = fieldValue;
    if (field == "state")↵
  state[currentPos] = fieldValue;
  }

</script>
</head>
```

8. Save the file again, and open it in a browser. Try using all the navigation buttons, entering a record number, and changing data in existing records. Your browser page should look similar to Figure 11-5. If it doesn't, check your file against hiTechMailingList.html in your student data files.

448

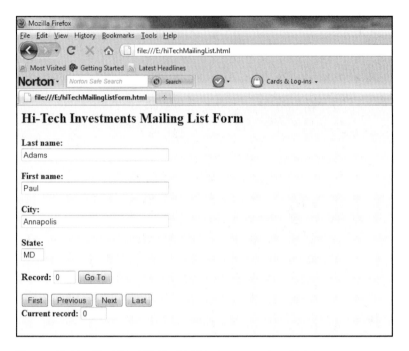

Figure 11-5   The hiTechMailingList.html program in a Web browser

Detective Work

Try changing the hiTechMailingList.html code so that the record numbers vary from 1 to 24 instead of 0 to 23. When you're finished, turn the revised code in to your instructor.

Chapter Summary

- Programming requires understanding the problems to be solved and knowing what tools are available and when to apply them.

- A typical data-processing program consists of a preparation section, a processing loop for data records, and a finish-up section.

- Applying programming tools to new situations makes you more creative and flexible in problem solving.

- Top-down design, a proven methodology for developing programs, is especially useful for getting a program's overall design in place and allowing refinement of details to occur over time.

- Thorough module and program testing ensures that a program can handle invalid data or no data and its parts interact with each other correctly.

- Data sets are data values created for the purpose of testing program logic.

- Field testing is an important component of software engineering that involves preparing software for use by business, industry, and the public.

Key Terms

data sets—Groups of data values created for the purpose of testing program logic, which include values before, at, and after the values specified in conditions.

field testing—The process of testing software in an environment that simulates actual operating conditions; used to measure accuracy and performance, analyze user behavior, and gather users' suggestions.

finish-up module—The closing section of a data-processing program; includes reporting results and totals.

housekeeping—The preparation tasks performed before processing data records.

processing module—Typically, a loop that processes each data record that's input by a user or contained in a data file.

software engineering—The process of designing software by using prescribed methods and best practices and preparing software for commercial and public release.

Review Questions

True/False

1. Many data processing applications have a common pattern of performing housekeeping tasks, processing records until the end of input, and finishing up. True or False?

2. Top-down design focuses on the details of modules. True or False?

3. Programmers should be able to understand what a program is meant to accomplish by reading the comments. True or False?

4. Arrays are always preferable to a series of variables. True or False?

5. Well-designed data sets can be used to test a program's logic. True or False?

6. The JavaScript function isNaN() can be used to test for nonnumeric data. True or False?

7. If nothing is entered in a text box, pressing Enter, clicking OK, and clicking Cancel produce the same results. True or False?

8. Field testing should be done only when a software product is going to be sold commercially. True or False?

Multiple Choice

1. You can simulate shuffling a deck of cards by using arrays and which of the following?

    a. Case statement

    b. random number generator

    c. null value

    d. text box

2. Top-down design encourages using modules that can be developed later, called _____.

    a. functions

    b. flowcharts

    c. decision tables

    d. stubs

3. When you have several conditions and multiple outcomes, which of the following tools is useful? (Choose all that apply.)

    a. IPO chart

    b. decision table

    c. binary tree

    d. hierarchy chart

4. When the user is to be given a choice of activities, you typically use which of the following?

    a. array

    b. menu system

    c. sentinel

    d. binary tree

5. When you need to keep track of several similar variables, you should consider using a(n) _____.

    a. array

    b. menu system

    c. sentinel

    d. binary tree

6. When testing a module for accuracy, which of the following techniques is suitable? (Choose all that apply.)

    a. creating comprehensive data sets

    b. changing variable names

    c. testing data at the borders

    d. developing stubs

7. Software testing includes checking a module's interaction with _____.

    a. random number generators

    b. high-speed processors

    c. other modules

    d. For loops

8. Beginning programmers can field-test their programs by doing which of the following? (Choose all that apply.)

    a. having other people attempt to "break" them

    b. asking programmers to read the comments

    c. converting them to another language

    d. having other people run the program and asking for their feedback

Discussion Questions

1. How are top-down design and thorough testing of software used in program development?

2. Why is developing an algorithm in pseudocode encouraged as a first step instead of writing code in a programming language?

3. What are the advantages of field-testing your programs?

Hands-On Activities

Hands-On Activity 11-1

Write a pseudocode program that prompts the user for a keyboard character and the number of rows and columns, and then displays a solid rectangle consisting of rows and columns of the specified character. Save the file as characterBoxFilled.txt.

Hands-On Activity 11-2

Use JavaScript to implement the algorithm in Hands-On Activity 11-1. Convert your pseudocode to JavaScript, and then test your program. Save the file as characterBoxFilled.html.

Hands-On Activity 11-3

Modify the pseudocode program in Hands-On Activity 11-1 so that the user-specified character is used to create the outline of a rectangle, with the inside left blank. Save the file as characterBoxOutlined.txt.

Hands-On Activity 11-4

Use JavaScript to implement the algorithm in Hands-On Activity 11-3. *Hint*: You need to set a fixed-width font for this rectangle to be rendered correctly in HTML, and you need a "nonbreaking" space because HTML condenses adjacent multiple spaces into one space. Add this line between the <body> and <script> tags:
```
<font face="Courier New">
```

Use this line to set a nonbreaking space:
```
var BL = " ";  // HTML literal blank (nonbreaking space)
```

Finally, add the closing </font> tag between the </script> and </body> tags. Convert your pseudocode to JavaScript, and then test your program. Save the file as characterBoxOutlined.html.

CASE STUDY: Automating It's War!

You made the card game War fully functional in Chapter 9. In this chapter, you have learned some guidelines for designing programs from scratch, so in this case study, you develop a new version of the game that's automated to simulate the way it's normally played. Here's how the game works:

- The card deck is shuffled and dealt to two players.

- The players play the top card in their hands on each play.

- The winner of the hand takes two cards and adds them to the pile of cards won.

- In case of a tie, the next card from each player's hand is added to the hold pile, in addition to the two cards played for the hand. (Adding the next card to the hold pile represents the card that's laid face down when a tie occurs in the real card game.)

- Points aren't counted. The winner is the one who wins all the cards when the other player loses all the cards.

- When a player's hand runs out, it's replenished by the pile of cards the player has won. The cards are shuffled before the player uses them.

Discussion:

- In "Applying Tools to New Situations" earlier in this chapter, you learned how to shuffle a deck of cards and distribute them evenly to two players, and you use similar techniques for this program.

- To analyze your automated game, keep track of the number of hands played.

- You need an array for each player's winnings and one for the hold pile. Each array should keep track of the highest subscript used so that cards can be added.

- When a player's hand needs to be replenished, the array of cards won is copied into the array for the player's hand. The number of cards in the player's hand is reset to the number that was in the array of cards won, and the array of cards won is set back to 0.

- Before play starts, your program should ask for the names of the two players.

- Each hand's results should be displayed onscreen, indicating which card each player played and who won the hand.

- In case of a tie, the two cards (representing face-down cards) added to the hold pile should be displayed.

- Because completing the game might take several hundred hands (as you know if you've played the game before) and require scrolling down the browser page, add an alert box to report the game's results when it ends. This alert box should include the winner's name and the number of hands played.

- Some notational shortcuts are used, such as incrementing a subscript in the same statement in which it's used instead of incrementing it separately, as in the statement `cardName1 = playerDeck1[playerIndex1++]`.

Start by developing the pseudocode for the game. When you finish, you convert it to JavaScript. Open a new document in Notepad, and save it as autoWarGame.txt. Enter the documentation lines and declare the variables:

```
Start

// Program name: Automated War Game (Chapter 11)
// Purpose: A simulation of the card game War played with
//    deck shuffling and card counting, until one player wins
//    all the cards.
//    Cards are shuffled and assigned to the two players.
//    For each hand, the next card in the deck is played.
//    If card values are equal, the cards are added to a
//       hold array.
//    If card values are unequal, both cards played are added
//       to the player's winnings array, as are any cards in
//       the hold area.
//    If a player runs out of cards, cards in the winnings
//       array are transferred to the player's hand.
//    No score is kept. The game is played until one player
//       has all the cards.
// Author: Paul Addison
// Date last modified: 01-Sep-2011

    // Declare variables and constants
    Declare Numeric numPlays = 0      // # of plays in game
    Declare Numeric DECK_SIZE = 52    // # of cards in deck
    Declare String player1, player2   // names of players
    Declare String winner             // name of winner

    Declare Numeric index                    // array index
    Declare Numeric deckSubscript            // subscript for deck
    Declare Numeric numPlayerCards1 = 0  // # cards player 1
    Declare Numeric numPlayerCards2 = 0  // # cards player 2

    Declare String cardName1        // card played player 1
    Declare String cardName2        // card played player 2
    Declare Numeric cardPoints1     // card points player 1
    Declare Numeric cardPoints2     // card points player 2
```

Create arrays for the card deck, the assigned cards, each player's winnings, and the hold pile:

```
// Create card deck array, array of card deck points,
// and array of assigned cards
Declare String cardDeck[] =
    "2C", "3C", "4C", "5C", "6C", "7C", "8C", "9C",
    "10C", "JC", "QC", "KC", "AC",
    "2D", "3D", "4D", "5D", "6D", "7D", "8D", "9D",
    "10D", "JD", "QD", "KD", "AD",
    "2H", "3H", "4H", "5H", "6H", "7H", "8H", "9H",
    "10H", "JH", "QH", "KH", "AH",
    "2S", "3S", "4S", "5S", "6S", "7S", "8S", "9S",
    "10S", "JS", "QS", "KS", "AS"

// Create a parallel array to track assigned cards
// Initialize values to false
Declare Boolean cardAssigned[DECK_SIZE]
For index = 0 to DECK_SIZE - 1
    cardAssigned[index] = False
End For

// Create array of cards for each player's hand
// Declare indexes for current card being played
// and highest index
Declare String playerDeck1[DECK_SIZE]
Declare String playerDeck2[DECK_SIZE]
Declare Numeric playerIndex1 = 0
Declare Numeric playerIndex2 = 0

// Create array of cards for each player's winnings
// Declare indexes for highest index
Declare String playerWinnings1[DECK_SIZE]
Declare String playerWinnings2[DECK_SIZE]
Declare Numeric winningsIndex1 = 0
Declare Numeric winningsIndex2 = 0

// Create array for hold pile
Declare String holdPile[DECK_SIZE]
Declare Numeric holdIndex
Declare Numeric numHoldCards = 0
```

Next, add the function for dealing cards to the players. Notice that the Random() function generates a number from 0 to 51 that corresponds to the subscripts:

```
// Initialize player decks
For index = 0 to (DECK_SIZE / 2) - 1
    // Choose random card until an unassigned one is found
    Do
        deckSubscript = Random(0, DECK_SIZE - 1)
    While cardAssigned[deckSubscript]
```

```
// Deal card to player 1, mark as assigned
playerDeck1[index] = cardDeck[deckSubscript]
numPlayerCards1++
cardAssigned[deckSubscript] = True

// Choose random card until an unassigned one is found
Do
    deckSubscript = Random(0, DECK_SIZE - 1)
While cardAssigned[deckSubscript]

// Deal card to player 2, mark as assigned
playerDeck2[index] = cardDeck[deckSubscript]
numPlayerCards2++
cardAssigned[deckSubscript] = True
End For
```

Welcome the user and get the players' names:

```
// Welcome the user
Display "Welcome to the game of War!"

// Ask for names of the two players
Display "Enter name of the first player: "
Input player1
Display "Enter name of the second player: "
Input player2
```

Start the main loop, and draw the card off the top of each player's deck:

```
// Play as long as each player has cards
While numPlayerCards1 > 0 And numPlayerCards2 > 0

    // Draw next card from player decks
    //  and display card names
    cardName1 = playerDeck1[playerIndex1++]
    cardName2 = playerDeck2[playerIndex2++]
```

Decrement each player's card count, and replenish the player's hand if the count is down to 0. You write the modules—replenish(1) and replenish(2)—to perform this task later. The argument to these modules is the player number.

```
    // Decrement card counts
    // If card count is down to 0, fill from winnings deck
    numPlayerCards1--
    If numPlayerCards1 <= 0 Then
       Call replenish(1)
    End If

    numPlayerCards2--
    If numPlayerCards2 <= 0 Then
       Call replenish(2)
    End If
```

Display the players and names of the card played. Also, call the function to get point counts for the cards. You write this function later. The argument to the function is the card name.

```
// Display card names
Display player1 + "'s card: " + cardName1 + ", " +↵
player2 + "'s card: " + cardName2

// Get point counts for cards from function
cardPoints1 = getPoints(cardName1)
cardPoints2 = getPoints(cardName2)
```

Compare the cards, and handle the case of one player having a higher card. Include comments explaining that the winner gets the cards played and the hold cards.

```
// Compare cards
// Cards played and hold cards go to winnings pile
// In case of tie, cards go to hold pile
If cardPoints1 > cardPoints2 Then
// player 1 wins hand
   Display player1 + " wins hand."

   // Add player cards to winnings deck
   playerWinnings1[winningsIndex1++] = cardName1
   playerWinnings1[winningsIndex1++] = cardName2

   // Add cards to winnings deck, if any,
   //   from hold pile and clear hold pile
   For holdIndex = 0 to numHoldCards - 1
      playerWinnings1[winningsIndex1++] =↵
   holdPile[holdIndex]
   End For
   numHoldCards = 0
   If numPlayerCards1 <= 0 Then
      Call replenish(1)
   End If

Else If cardPoints2 > cardPoints1 Then
// player 2 wins hand

   Display player2 + " wins hand."
   // Add player cards to winnings deck
   playerWinnings2[winningsIndex2++] = cardName1
   playerWinnings2[winningsIndex2++] = cardName2

   // Add cards to winnings deck, if any,
   //   from hold pile and clear hold pile
   For holdIndex = 0 to numHoldCards - 1
      playerWinnings2[winningsIndex2++] =↵
   holdPile[holdIndex]
   End For
   numHoldCards = 0
   If numPlayerCards2 <= 0 Then
      Call replenish(2)
   End If
```

Now enter the code for handling a tie. The cards played go to a hold pile, and each player draws another card that goes to the hold pile. Both players' card counts need to be checked again, and their hands should be replenished if the count is down to 0. The cards given up in case of a tie should be displayed. This is the end of the main loop!

```
    Else
    // tie hand

        Display "Tie hand."
        // Add player cards to hold pile
        holdPile[numHoldCards++] = cardName1
        holdPile[numHoldCards++] = cardName2

        // Each player puts one card in hold pile
        If numPlayerCards1 >= 1 Then
            Display player1 + " gave up " +↵
playerDeck1[playerIndex1]
            holdPile[numHoldCards++] =↵
playerDeck1[playerIndex1++]
            numPlayerCards1--
            // player might be out of cards
            If numPlayerCards1 <= 0 Then
                Call replenish(1)
            End If
        End If

        If numPlayerCards2 >= 1 Then
            Display player2 + " gave up " +↵
playerDeck2[playerIndex2]
            holdPile[numHoldCards++] =↵
playerDeck2[playerIndex2++]
            numPlayerCards2--
            // player might be out of cards
            If (numPlayerCards2 <= 0) Then
                Call replenish(2)
            End If
        End If

    End If

// End While loop
End While
```

To end the main module, determine and display the winner, and then thank the user. For debugging purposes, include the case of the game ending but both players having cards left. This outcome shouldn't happen, but including this case tells you whether it does.

```
// Determine and display name of winner
Display "Game over."

If numPlayerCards2 <= 0 Then
```

```
      winner = player1
   Else If numPlayerCards1 <= 0 Then
      winner = player2
   Else
      winner = "NOBODY"
      Display "ERROR...Game ended,"
      Display "but both players have cards!"
   End If

   Display "Game over. " + winner + " is the winner in "↵
+ numPlays + " plays."

   // Thank the user
   Display "Thank you for playing the game of War!"

Stop
```

Now write the module that shuffles the player's winning pile and replenishes the player's hand from the array of cards won. You know how many cards are in this array (from the index for the winning hands array), so use a loop to copy each card into the player's hand. (You know the player's hand is empty, or the module wouldn't have been called). Remember that the argument is the player number, so you know which array to replenish. Display a message that the player's hand is being replenished and include the number of cards. Use the same shuffling technique to assign the cards you used when first dealing the deck.

```
// Module to replenish player's hand from winning pile
Module replenish(Numeric playerNum)

   // Declare variables
   Declare Numeric index          // loop index
   Declare Numeric deckSubscript  // deck subscript

   If playerNum == 1 Then
      Display player1 + "'s hand replenished with " +↵
winningsIndex1 + " cards."
      For deckSubscript = 0 to winningsIndex1 - 1
         cardAssigned[deckSubscript] = False
      End For
      For index = 0 to winningsIndex1 - 1
         Do
            deckSubscript = Random(0, winningsIndex1 - 1)
         While cardAssigned[deckSubscript]

         playerDeck1[index] = playerWinnings1[deckSubscript]
         cardAssigned[deckSubscript] = True
      End For

      numPlayerCards1 = winningsIndex1
      playerIndex1 = 0
      winningsIndex1 = 0

   Else If playerNum == 2 Then
```

```
      Display player2 + "'s hand replenished with " +⏎
winningsIndex2 + " cards."
      For deckSubscript = 0 to winningsIndex2 - 1
         cardAssigned[deckSubscript] = False
      End For
      For index = 0 to winningsIndex2 - 1
         Do
            deckSubscript = Random(0, winningsIndex2 - 1)
         While cardAssigned[deckSubscript]

         playerDeck2[index] = playerWinnings2[deckSubscript]
         cardAssigned[deckSubscript] = True
      End For

      numPlayerCards2 = winningsIndex2
      playerIndex2 = 0
      winningsIndex2 = 0
   End If

End Module
```

Finally, write the function to get the point count for each card. The first character of the card name is enough to determine the point value (only the 10 card starts with the digit 1). A Case structure takes slightly less code than an If/Else If structure, although both would do the same job.

```
// Function to get number of points for a card
Function Numeric getPoints(String cardName)

   // Declare constants and variables
   // First character of card name is extracted
   Declare String firstChar = substring(cardName,0,1)
   // Point value assigned based on first character
   Declare Numeric points

   Select firstChar
      Case "2": points = 2
      Case "3": points = 3
      Case "4": points = 4
      Case "5": points = 5
      Case "6": points = 6
      Case "7": points = 7
      Case "8": points = 8
      Case "9": points = 9
      Case "1": points = 10
      Case "J": points = 11
      Case "Q": points = 12
      Case "K": points = 13
      Case "A": points = 14
      Default: Display "ERROR: Bad card value: " + cardName
   End Select
   Return points

End Function
```

By now, you have had a lot of practice in converting pseudocode to JavaScript. As you've learned, developing pseudocode first makes converting your algorithm to any programming language easier. As long as you know the language's syntax, you can convert your pseudocode because the logic is the same.

Remember that both modules and functions are considered functions in JavaScript, and they're entered in the <head> section. Because you have already developed them in your pseudocode, you can create the <head> section first and convert your module and function to JavaScript functions. Then you can create the <body> section and convert your main module.

Open a new document in Notepad, and save it as autoWarGame.html. Convert your pseudocode to JavaScript, save the file again, and open it in a browser. It might take several hundred plays before one player wins the automated game. Figure 11-6 shows the first page of what output from this game might look like, including the alert box displaying the game's results. If you don't get any output or it's incorrect, compare it with autoWarGame-solution.html in your student data files.

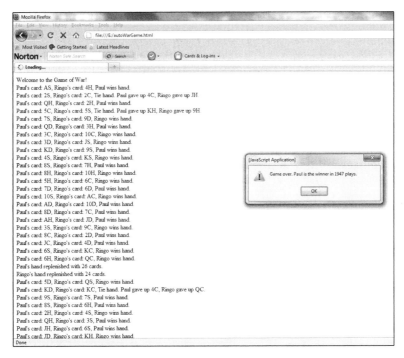

Figure 11-6   The autoWarGame.html program in a Web browser

You've modified your War game program to create an automated card game that simulates shuffling and dealing cards, playing hands, assigning cards, resolving ties, determining a winner, and counting plays. That's quite a lot for a beginning programmer!

CHAPTER 12

Sorting Data

In this chapter, you learn to:

◎ Explain the advantages of sorting

◎ Describe the concept of common sorting algorithms

◎ Explain the logic of the bubble sort, selection sort, and insertion sort

◎ Use the JavaScript sorting method on numeric and nonnumeric data

◎ Sort arrays in ascending or descending order

◎ Program and use common sorting algorithms in JavaScript

"Good order is the foundation of all things."
—EDMUND BURKE, IRISH ORATOR, PHILOSOPHER, AND
POLITICIAN (1729–1797)

People like order. Putting things in order helps people find what they want more quickly and see patterns and trends, such as how many items have low or high values. It also makes grouping items and counting items in categories easier, and as you saw in Chapter 10, it makes binary searches possible. Putting data items in order is called **sorting**, and this process is categorized as an **ascending sort** (low to high values) or a **descending sort** (high to low values). Sorting is often done on arrays because sorted array elements can be referenced in memory and moved around more easily. Data in other kinds of data structures, such as linked lists and binary trees, can be sorted, too.

Programmers write efficient routines for sorting, but because sorting is such a common process, many programming languages have built-in sorting routines. It's similar to writing a function for calculating square roots based on your knowledge of the "longhand" method. You can write your own, but square root functions have been written for almost every language and are far more convenient. So why is a chapter on sorting included in this book? Learning about sorting algorithms helps you understand essential concepts of programming: variables, temporary variables, values, data types, data structures, comparisons, loops, and more. Sorting is a valuable exercise in learning to think like a programmer.

Introduction to Sorting Algorithms

Suppose you have a numeric array of six elements, declared like this:

```
Declare Numeric someNums[] = 8, 3, 9, 6, 10, 2
```

This array can be represented graphically as shown in Figure 12-1.

Subscript	[0]	[1]	[2]	[3]	[4]	[5]
Value	8	3	9	6	10	2

Figure 12-1   The someNums array in unsorted order

If you sort the array into ascending order, it ends up looking like Figure 12-2.

Subscript	[0]	[1]	[2]	[3]	[4]	[5]
Value	2	3	6	8	9	10

Figure 12-2   The someNums array sorted into ascending order

There are several algorithms for sorting data, including the following ones discussed in this chapter:

- A **bubble sort** is the most straightforward sorting algorithm but often the least efficient. It involves comparing adjacent elements and swapping them, if needed, until all elements are in their correct positions. Several swaps might be done on each pass through the elements, and the process might take almost as many passes through the array as there are elements.

- A **selection sort** finds which element belongs in a particular position on each pass through the array and moves it there. It's more efficient than a bubble sort because only one swap is made in each pass.

- An **insertion sort** builds a sorted array by determining where each element should be in the sorted part of the array and inserting it in that position while moving all other sorted elements over one position.

Sorting an array of data elements involves moving them around. In addition, a sorting algorithm can involve switching the places of two elements being compared, a process called **swapping**. Beware, however: This process often isn't as simple as it seems. Suppose you want to swap the values of someNums[0] and someNums[1], which currently contain the values 8 and 3. You might be tempted to try the following method:

```
someNums[0] = someNums[1]
someNums[1] = someNums[0]
```

Here's the problem with this method: The first step puts the value 3 in someNums[0], but it replaces the value 8 that was there because a variable can hold only one value at a time. When you get to the second step, someNums[0] contains a 3, and the assignment statement replaces 3 with 3. Therefore, the value 8 is lost.

When you swap the values of two variables or array elements, you need a third variable, a temporary one, to hold one of the values until the swap is completed. If you declare a numeric variable called temp, for example, the following code accomplishes the swap:

```
temp = someNums[0]
someNums[0] = someNums[1]
someNums[1] = temp
```

The Bubble Sort Algorithm

The bubble sort's logic is uncomplicated. Like all sorting algorithms, it sorts an array's items into ascending or descending order by making several passes through the array, comparing adjacent elements, and swapping them if necessary.

You can also make an ascending bubble sort move the smallest value to the leftmost location first, and then work toward the right of the array.

To see how a bubble sort works, start with an algorithm to sort an array into ascending order. On the first pass, when two adjacent elements are compared, if the one on the left has a greater value than the one on the right, they're swapped. This way, each comparison ensures that the greater value is always placed on the right, and at the end of the first pass, the greatest value is in the rightmost position.

If you picture the array vertically instead of horizontally, with the highest subscript at the top, the largest value rises, or "bubbles up," to the top during the first pass as follows:

• The first comparison is between elements [0] and [1]: 8 and 3. The greater element is on the left, so the 8 and 3 are swapped.

• The second comparison looks at elements [1] and [2]: 8 and 9. They don't need to be swapped because the greater element is on the right.

• The third comparison looks at elements [2] and [3], 9 and 6, and swaps them.

• The fourth comparison looks at elements [3] and [4]: 9 and 10. They don't need to be swapped because the greater element is on the right.

• The fifth comparison looks at elements [4] and [5], 10 and 2, and swaps them.

The first pass transforms the array as shown in Figure 12-3. Bold numbers have been swapped after a comparison.

Subscript	[0]	[1]	[2]	[3]	[4]	[5]
Original order	8	3	9	6	10	2
Comparison #1	**3**	**8**	9	6	10	2
Comparison #2	3	8	9	6	10	2
Comparison #3	3	8	**6**	**9**	10	2
Comparison #4	3	8	6	9	10	2
Comparison #5	3	8	6	9	**2**	**10**

Figure 12-3   Bubble sort, first pass

On the second pass, the comparison just needs to go to the next to last position because the greatest value, 10, has already been placed in the last position, subscript [5]. The second highest value is placed in the next to last position on this pass (see Figure 12-4). The numbers in the last column are blue to indicate that they're already in their final positions and aren't included in this pass.

Subscript	[0]	[1]	[2]	[3]	[4]	[5]
Original order	3	8	6	9	2	10
Comparison #1	3	8	6	9	2	10
Comparison #2	3	6	8	9	2	10
Comparison #3	3	6	8	9	2	10
Comparison #4	3	6	8	2	9	10

Figure 12-4   Bubble sort, second pass

Each successive pass includes one less element. Figures 12-5, 12-6, and 12-7 show the third, fourth, and fifth passes.

Subscript	[0]	[1]	[2]	[3]	[4]	[5]
Original order	3	6	8	2	9	10
Comparison #1	3	6	8	2	9	10
Comparison #2	3	6	8	2	9	10
Comparison #3	3	6	2	8	9	10

Figure 12-5   Bubble sort, third pass

Subscript	[0]	[1]	[2]	[3]	[4]	[5]
Original order	3	6	2	8	9	10
Comparison #1	3	6	2	8	9	10
Comparison #2	3	2	6	8	9	10

Figure 12-6   Bubble sort, fourth pass

Subscript	[0]	[1]	[2]	[3]	[4]	[5]
Original order	3	2	6	8	9	10
Comparison #1	2	3	6	8	9	10

Figure 12-7   Bubble sort, fifth and final pass

The total number of passes is one less than the number of elements because the element remaining in the leftmost position doesn't need to be compared with anything. The number of comparisons made in each pass is one less than the number of elements remaining to be sorted because an element must be compared with the element next to it.

When you're sorting in ascending order, use the greater than operator (>) in the comparison to swap adjacent elements if the first element is greater than the second. To sort in descending order, use the less than operator (<) to swap elements if the first element is less than the second.

In this example, you're sorting an array in ascending order (low to high), so you need to swap adjacent elements if the first element is greater than the second. If you want to sort elements in descending order, you swap them if the first element is less than the second.

The programming logic for a bubble sort requires two loops: an outer loop for each pass through the array and an inner loop to compare elements during a pass. In the following example, assume that the array and all variables have been declared, and the array has been initialized:

```
// Bubble sort logic
// Outer loop works from last array element
//    down to the first
// Inner loop steps through array, comparing
//    and swapping elements if necessary
For maxElement = ARRAYSIZE - 1 To 1 Step - 1
   For index = 0 To maxElement - 1
      If someNums[index] > someNums[index + 1] Then
         temp = someNums[index]
         someNums[index] = someNums[index + 1]
         someNums[index + 1] = temp
      End If
   End For
End For
```

If you add steps for declaring and initializing the array, you can convert this pseudocode to JavaScript, as shown in the following steps.

PROGRAM 12-1 JavaScript Program bubbleSort.html

Remember to add a blank line after the code section in each step.

1. Open a new document in Notepad, and save it as **bubbleSort.html.** Enter the starting HTML tags and the program documentation lines:

```
<html>
<body>
<script type="text/javascript">

// Program name: bubbleSort.html
// Purpose: Use a bubble sort on an array
// Author: Paul Addison
// Date last modified: 01-Sep-2011
```

2. Declare your constants and variables, and then declare and initialize the array:

```
// Declare constants and variables
var BR = "<br />";    // line break
```

(continues)

(continued)

```
var ARRAYSIZE = 6;     // array size
var maxElement;        // last element in pass
var index;             // array index
var temp;              // swap variable

// Declare and initialize the array
var someNums = new Array(8, 3, 9, 6, 10, 2);
```

3. Display a header identifying the sorting method, and display the array in its original order:

```
// Identify the sorting method
// Display the array before sorting
document.write("BUBBLE SORT" + BR);
document.write("Before sorting:" + BR);
for (index = 0; index < ARRAYSIZE; index++) {
   document.write(someNums[index] + BR);
}
```

4. Enter the code to perform the bubble sort:

```
// Outer loop works from last array element
//    down to the first
// Inner loop steps through array, comparing
//    and swapping elements if necessary
for (maxElement = ARRAYSIZE - 1; maxElement > 0; ↵
  maxElement--) {
   for (index = 0; index < maxElement; index++) {
      if (someNums[index] > someNums[index + 1]) {
         temp = someNums[index];
         someNums[index] = someNums[index + 1];
         someNums[index + 1] = temp;
      }
   }
}
```

5. Display the array in its new sorted order, and then add the closing HTML tags:

```
// Display the array after sorting
document.write("After sorting:" + BR);
for (index = 0; index < ARRAYSIZE; index++) {
   document.write(someNums[index] + BR);
}

</script>
</body>
</html>
```

6. Save the file again, and open it in a browser (see Figure 12-8). The numbers should be sorted in ascending order.

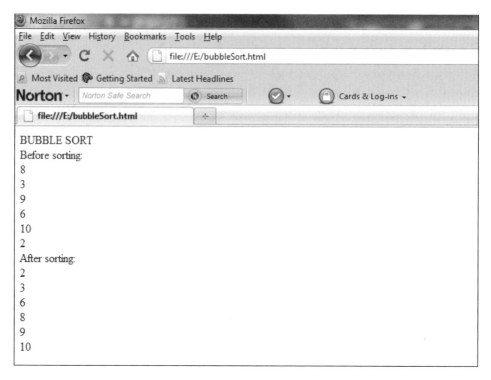

Figure 12-8   The bubbleSort.html program in a Web browser

There's a way to improve the bubble sort algorithm's efficiency. What if the array elements are already sorted, or the array is sorted after one or two passes? As with the sequential search algorithm in Chapter 10, when you used the found variable to indicate when a match was found, you can use a variable (swapsMade) to indicate whether a pass has been completed with no swaps made.

Using this variable involves changing the outer For loop to a Do While loop to add the new condition. (This means separating the initializing and decrementing of the maxElement variable from the condition in the outer For loop.) The swapsMade variable is initialized to false at the start of each pass and set to true whenever a swap is made. The Do While loop repeats only if the swapsMade variable's value is changed to true during the pass. The adjusted pseudocode looks like this, with changes to the code bolded:

```
// Bubble sort logic
// Outer loop works from last array element
//    down to the first
// Inner loop steps through the array, comparing
//    and swapping elements if necessary
```

```
Declare Boolean swapsMade
maxElement = ARRAYSIZE - 1
Do
   swapsMade = False
   For index = 0 To maxElement - 1
      If someNums[index] > someNums[index + 1] Then
         swapsMade = True
         temp = someNums[index]
         someNums[index] = someNums[index + 1]
         someNums[index + 1] = temp
      End If
   End For
   maxElement -= 1
While maxElement > 0 And swapsMade
```

The Selection Sort Algorithm

A selection sort also requires passes through an array, but it makes one fewer pass than the number of array elements. For an ascending sort, the array is scanned for the smallest value on the first pass, and when its position is determined, it's swapped with the element at subscript [0]. On the second pass, the next smallest value (of the remaining elements) is found, and it's swapped with the element at subscript [1]. This algorithm is more efficient than a bubble sort because only one swap is made during a pass.

Figure 12-9 shows a selection sort. The numbers moved in each pass are bold. If a number is already in its correct position, it's left in place. After a number is in place, it's shown in blue.

Subscript	[0]	[1]	[2]	[3]	[4]	[5]
Original order	8	3	9	6	10	2
Pass #1 (0)	2	3	9	6	10	8
Pass #2 (1)	2	3	9	6	10	8
Pass #3 (2)	2	3	6	9	10	8
Pass #4 (3)	2	3	6	8	10	9
Pass #5 (4)	2	3	6	8	9	10

Figure 12-9   Selection sort, all passes

The following example shows the selection sort's logic expressed in pseudocode. Notice that because you're doing an ascending sort, you find the smallest value first by setting the first element as the minimum value, and then resetting the minimum to any element that's less than the current minimum. If the minimum value isn't already in the current position, it's swapped with the element in the current position. The variable for the current element is this example is currEl.

```
// Selection sort algorithm
// Outer loop designates a position
//   from first to last element
For currEl = 0 To ARRAYSIZE - 1
   minValue = someNums[currEl]
   minPosition = currEl

   // Inner loop steps through array,
   //   finding smallest value
   For index = currEl + 1 To ARRAYSIZE - 1
      If someNums[index] < minValue Then
         minValue = someNums[index]
         minPosition = index
      End If
   End For

   // Swap minimum value with element at
   //   designated position if different
   If minPosition != currEl Then
      temp = someNums[currEl]
      someNums[currEl] = someNums[minPosition]
      someNums[minPosition] = temp
   End If
End For
```

If you add steps for declaring and initializing the array, you can convert this pseudocode to JavaScript, as shown in the following steps.

 PROGRAM 12-2 JavaScript Program selectionSort.html

Remember to add a blank line after the code section in each step.

1. Open a new document in Notepad, and save it as **selectionSort.html.** Enter the starting HTML tags and the program documentation lines:

```
<html>
<body>
<script type="text/javascript">

// Program name: selectionSort.html
// Purpose: Use a selection sort on an array
// Author: Paul Addison
// Date last modified: 01-Sep-2011
```

(continues)

(continued)

2. Declare your constants and variables, and then declare and initialize the array:

```
// Declare constants and variables
var BR = "<br />";    // line break
var ARRAYSIZE = 6;    // array size
var currEl;           // array position to fill
var index;            // array index
var minValue;         // current lowest value
var minPosition;      // position of minimum
var temp;             // swap variable

// Declare and initialize the array
var someNums = new Array(8, 3, 9, 6, 10, 2);
```

3. Display a header identifying the sorting method, and display the array in its original order:

```
// Identify the sorting method
// Display the array before sorting
document.write("SELECTION SORT" + BR);
document.write("Before sorting:" + BR);
for (index = 0; index < ARRAYSIZE; index++) {
   document.write(someNums[index] + BR);
}
```

4. Enter the code to perform the selection sort:

```
// Outer loop designates a position
//    from first to last element
for (currEl = 0; currEl < ARRAYSIZE; currEl++) {
   minValue = someNums[currEl];
   minPosition = currEl;

   // Inner loop steps through array,
   //   finding smallest value
   for
 (index = currEl + 1; index < ARRAYSIZE; index++) {
      if (someNums[index] < minValue) {
         minValue = someNums[index];
         minPosition = index;
      }
   }
   // Swap minimum value with element at
   //    designated position if different
   if (minPosition != currEl) {
      temp = someNums[currEl];
      someNums[currEl] = someNums[minPosition];
      someNums[minPosition] = temp;
   }
}
```

(continues)

(continued)

5. Display the array in its new sorted order, and then add the closing HTML tags:

```
// Display the array after sorting
document.write("After sorting:" + BR);
for (index = 0; index < ARRAYSIZE; index++) {
    document.write(someNums[index] + BR);
}

</script>
</body>
</html>
```

6. Save the file again, and open it in a browser. Your output should look like Figure 12-10.

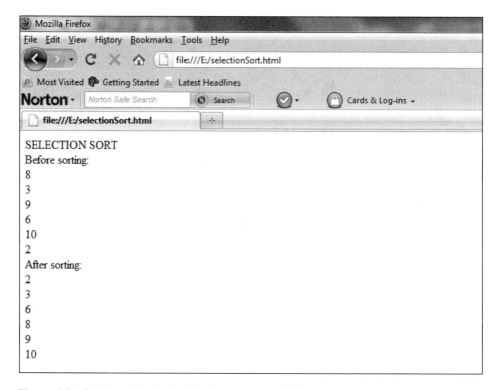

Figure 12-10   The selectionSort.html program in a Web browser

The Insertion Sort Algorithm

The insertion sort algorithm builds a sorted array one element at a time. Suppose you want to sort an array in ascending order. An insertion sort looks at the value of the second element and "pulls" it temporarily—that is, the element is held in a separate variable until its place in the array can be determined. If the value of the first element is greater than the pulled value, the first element is shifted to the second position, and the pulled element is inserted in the first position.

Next, an insertion sort looks at the third position and pulls it temporarily. If the value of the second element is greater than the pulled value, it's shifted to the third position. If the value of the first element is greater, it's shifted to the second position; if it's not, the pulled value is placed in the second position.

Each array element is pulled and compared with the sorted array built so far, which consists of elements with lower subscript values (to the left when represented graphically). If the value to the left is greater than the pulled value, it's shifted to the right, and the pulled value moves to the left. If it's not, the pulled value is inserted in this position.

The loop for pulled values starts with subscript [1] because each pulled value is compared with the value at its left, continuing to the highest subscript (ARRAYSIZE - 1). A nested While loop compares the pulled value with the value in the "insert position," shifting this element to the right if it's greater than the pulled position or inserting the pulled value at this position if it's not. If the pulled value gets all the way back to position 0, it's placed there. The insertion sort's logic is expressed in pseudocode as follows:

```
// Insertion sort algorithm
// Loop pulls each element from 1 to the end of the array
For pulledIndex = 1 to ARRAYSIZE - 1
   pulledValue = someNums[pulledIndex]
   insertIndex = pulledIndex

   // If element to the left is greater,
   //    shift it to the right
   //    and look at the next element to the left
   While insertIndex > 0 ↵
 And someNums[insertIndex - 1] > pulledValue
       someNums[insertIndex] = someNums[insertIndex - 1]
       insertIndex = insertIndex - 1
   End While

   // Insert the pulled value when the shifting ends
   someNums[insertIndex] = pulledValue
End For
```

All sorting algorithms use an outer For loop to go through an array. The bubble and insertion sorts also use a nested For loop to compare and swap elements, but the insertion sort uses a nested While loop because an element isn't placed until its correct position is determined.

Figures 12-11 through 12-15 show an insertion sort pulling and placing one element at a time. Elements in gray aren't affected by the step, and bold elements are being pulled, shifted, or placed by the sorting process.

	[0]	[1]	[2]	[3]	[4]	[5]
3 is pulled	8	3	9	6	10	2
8 is greater, so it's shifted to [1]		8	9	6	10	2
3 placed at [0]	3	8	9	6	10	2

Figure 12-11   Insertion sort, placing element [1]

	[0]	[1]	[2]	[3]	[4]	[5]
9 is pulled	3	8	9	6	10	2
8 isn't greater, so 9 is left in place	3	8	9	6	10	2

Figure 12-12   Insertion sort, placing element [2]

	[0]	[1]	[2]	[3]	[4]	[5]
6 is pulled	3	8	9	6	10	2
9 is greater, so it's shifted to [3]	3	8		9	10	2
8 is greater, so it's shifted to [2]	3		8	9	10	2
3 isn't greater, so 6 is placed at [1]	3	6	8	9	10	2

Figure 12-13   Insertion sort, placing element [3]

	[0]	[1]	[2]	[3]	[4]	[5]
10 is pulled	3	6	8	9	10	2
9 isn't greater, so 10 is left in place	3	6	8	9	10	2

Figure 12-14   Insertion sort, placing element [4]

	[0]	[1]	[2]	[3]	[4]	[5]
2 is pulled	3	6	8	9	10	2
10 is greater, so it's shifted to [5]	3	6	8	9		10
9 is greater, so it's shifted to [4]	3	6	8		9	10
8 is greater, so it's shifted to [3]	3	6		8	9	10
6 is greater, so it's shifted to [2]	3		6	8	9	10
3 is greater, so it's shifted to [1]		3	6	8	9	10
2 is placed at [0]	2	3	6	8	9	10

Figure 12-15   Insertion sort, placing element [5]

If you add steps for declaring and initializing the array, you can convert the previous pseudocode to JavaScript, as shown in the following steps.

 PROGRAM 12-3 JavaScript Program insertionSort.html

Remember to add a blank line after the code section in each step.

1. Open a new document in Notepad, and save it as **insertionSort.html**. Enter the starting HTML tags and the program documentation lines:

```
<html>
<body>
<script type="text/javascript">

// Program name: insertionSort.html
// Purpose: Use an insertion sort on an array
// Author: Paul Addison
// Date last modified: 01-Sep-2011
```

2. Declare the constants and variables for the program, and then declare and initialize the array:

```
// Declare constants and variables
var BR = "<br />";     // line break
var ARRAYSIZE = 6;     // array size
var pulledIndex;       // index of element to place
var pulledValue;       // value of element to place
var insertIndex;       // index of element shifted
var insertValue;       // value of element shifted
var index;             // general array index

// Declare and initialize the array
var someNums = new Array(8, 3, 9, 6, 10, 2);
```

3. Display a header identifying the sorting method, and display the array in its original order:

```
// Identify the sorting method
// Display the array before sorting
document.write("INSERTION SORT" + BR);
document.write("Before sorting:" + BR);
for (index = 0; index < ARRAYSIZE; index++) {
   document.write(someNums[index] + BR);
}
```

4. Enter the code to perform the insertion sort:

```
// Loop pulls each element
//    from 1 to the end of the array
```

(continues)

478

(continued)

```
for (pulledIndex = 1; pulledIndex < ARRAYSIZE; ↵
pulledIndex++) {
    pulledValue = someNums[pulledIndex];
    insertIndex = pulledIndex;

    // If element to the left is greater,
    //    shift it to the right
    //    and look at next element to the left
    while (insertIndex > 0 && ↵
someNums[insertIndex - 1] > pulledValue) {
        someNums[insertIndex] = ↵
someNums[insertIndex - 1];
        insertIndex = insertIndex - 1;
    }
    // Insert the pulled value when shifting ends
    someNums[insertIndex] = pulledValue;
}
```

5. Display the array in its new sorted order, and then add the closing HTML tags:

```
// Display the array after sorting
document.write("After sorting:" + BR);
for (index = 0; index < ARRAYSIZE; index++) {
    document.write(someNums[index] + BR);
}

</script>
</body>
</html>
```

6. Save the file again, and open it in a browser. Your output should look like Figure 12-16.

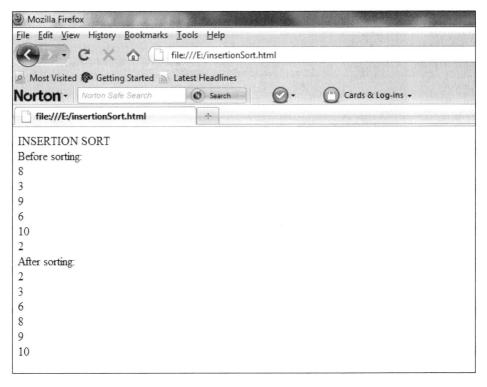

Figure 12-16   The insertionSort.html program in a Web browser

The JavaScript `sort()` Method

As mentioned, many programming languages have built-in sorting methods. JavaScript has the `sort()` method that works on arrays, but it sorts in **lexigraphical order**, which is based on character values, not numeric values. For example, the number 300 is sorted before 5 because the digit "3" comes before "5" in lexigraphical order. When you're sorting string data, it's sorted alphabetically as you'd expect.

In the following example, you set up an array of string data and then call the `sort()` method, using the following syntax to sort the array:

```
arrayName.sort();
```

Other sorting algorithms include the shell, heap, merge, and quick sorts. You can see animations of these sorts and the ones described in this chapter at *www.sorting-algorithms.com*.

480

PROGRAM 12-4 JavaScript Program
stringJavaScriptSort.html

Remember to add a blank line after the code section in each step.

1. Open a new document in Notepad, and save it as **stringJavaScriptSort.html**. Enter the starting HTML tags and the program documentation lines:

```
<html>
<body>
<script type="text/javascript">

// Program name: stringJavaScriptSort.html
// Purpose: Use JavaScript's built-in
//    sort() method on string data
// Author: Paul Addison
// Date last modified: 01-Sep-2011
```

2. Declare your constants and variables, and then declare and initialize the array:

```
// Declare constants and variables
var BR = "<br />";    // line break
var ARRAYSIZE = 6;    // array size

// Declare and initialize the array
var someNums = new Array("Greece", "Argentina", ↵
"New Zealand", "Japan", "Iceland", "Poland");
```

3. Display a header identifying the sorting method, and display the array in its original order:

```
// Identify the sorting method
// Display the array before sorting
document.write("JAVASCRIPT SORT" + BR);
document.write("Before sorting:" + BR);
for (index = 0; index < ARRAYSIZE; index++) {
   document.write(someNums[index] + BR);
}
```

4. Call the built-in JavaScript sorting method:

```
// Call JavaScript sort() method
someNums.sort();
```

5. Display the array in its new sorted order, and then add the closing HTML tags:

```
// Display the array after sorting
document.write("After sorting:" + BR);
for (index = 0; index < ARRAYSIZE; index++) {
   document.write(someNums[index] + BR);
}
```

(continues)

(continued)

```
    </script>
    </body>
    </html>
```

6. Save the file again, and open it in a browser. Your output should look like Figure 12-17.

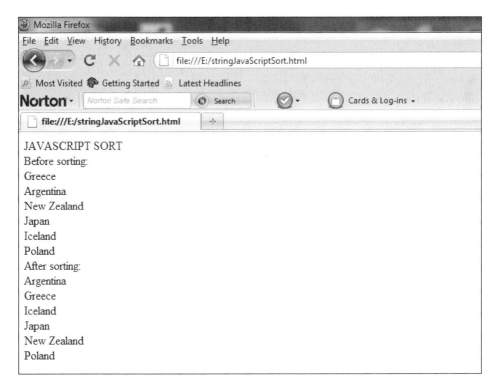

Figure 12-17 The stringJavaScriptSort.html program in a Web browser

The sort() method arranges array elements in ascending order. To reverse the order of array elements, you use the JavaScript method reverse(), which has the following syntax:

arrayName.reverse();

So if you want to sort a string array in descending order, you can use the following pair of statements:

arrayName.sort();
arrayName.reverse();

Detective Work

Next, try modifying the stringJavaScriptSort.html program to sort numeric data. Open the file in Notepad again, and save it as numericJavaScriptSort.html. Change the first display line to say, `"JAVASCRIPT SORT WITH NUMERIC ARRAY:"`. Next, change the statement that declares and initializes the array to use numeric values, as shown:

```
var someNums = new Array(8, 3, 9, 6, 10, 2);
```

Save the file again, and open it in a browser. Your output should look like Figure 12-18. If it doesn't, compare your file with numericJavaScriptSort-solution.html in your student data files.

```
Mozilla Firefox
File  Edit  View  History  Bookmarks  Tools  Help

    C  X  ⌂    file:///E:/numericJavaScriptSort.html

Most Visited   Getting Started   Latest Headlines

Norton ·   Norton Safe Search      Search         Cards & Log-ins ▾

  file:///E:/numericJavaScriptSort.html

JAVASCRIPT SORT WITH NUMERIC ARRAY:
Before sorting:
8
3
9
6
10
2
After sorting:
10
2
3
6
8
9
```

Figure 12-18   The numericJavaScriptSort.html program in a Web browser

Do you see that the number 10 is sorted before the number 2? That's because of the lexigraphical sorting that JavaScript does, which treats numbers as characters. The solution in JavaScript is to create a function that essentially forces a numeric comparison of the numbers and places the one with the lower numeric value before the other. The function looks like this:

```
function numericSort(a, b) {
    return a - b;
}
```

 When you used the JavaScript sort() method with string data, you called it
with no arguments. An optional argument called a function reference can be
used with the sort() method; it bases the sorting order of any two array elements on the value the function returns. In this case, the numericSort function reference returns the value of the first argument minus the second (a - b).
The result can be a negative number, 0, or a positive number. If it returns a positive
number, it means the first number is greater than the second, and the sort() method
sorts the second argument before the first so that the array is sorted in numeric ascending order. Also, if you call the function reference with the statement return b - a;,
the elements are sorted in numeric ascending order.

Now modify your program with the changes shown in bold in the
following lines. First, open numericJavaScriptSort.html in Notepad, if
necessary, and save it as numericJavaScriptSortModified.html. Note
that because you're creating a <head> section, you should move your
documentation lines into it.

```
<html>
<head>
<script type="text/javascript">

// Program name: numericJavaScriptSortModified.html
// Purpose: Use JavaScript's built-in
//    sort() method on numeric data and add
//    a function reference
// Author: Paul Addison
// Date last modified: 01-Sep-2011

// Function to force numeric sort
function numericSort(a, b) {
    return a - b;
}

</script>
</head>

<body>
<script type="text/javascript">

// Declare constants and variables
var BR = "<br />";      // line break
var ARRAYSIZE = 6;      // array size
var index;              // general array index

// Declare and initialize the array
var someNums = new Array(8, 3, 9, 6, 10, 2);

// Identify the sorting method
// Display the array before sorting
document.write("JAVASCRIPT SORT WITH NUMERIC ARRAY ");
```

```
document.write("AND SORTING FUNCTION REFERENCE" + BR);
document.write("Before sorting:" + BR);
for (index = 0; index < ARRAYSIZE; index++) {
    document.write(someNums[index] + BR);
}

// Call JavaScript sort() method
//   using numericSort function reference
someNums.sort(numericSort);

// Display the array after sorting
document.write("After sorting:" + BR);
for (index = 0; index < ARRAYSIZE; index++) {
    document.write(someNums[index] + BR);
}

</script>
</body>
</html>
```

Save the file again, and open it in a browser. It should sort the numbers correctly this time (see Figure 12-19).

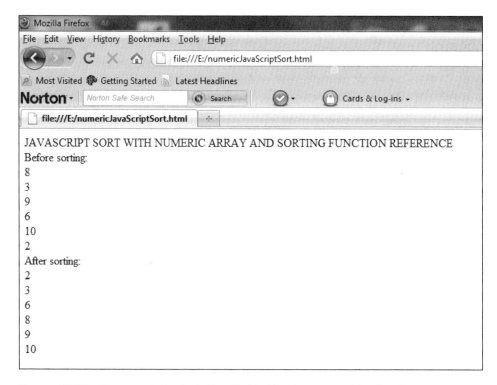

Figure 12-19 The numericJavaScriptSortModified.html program with a function reference included

Programmer's Workshop

In this chapter, you have learned four ways to sort an array: bubble sort, selection sort, insertion sort, and JavaScript's sort() method. Some ways are more efficient than others, but often the array size affects the sorting algorithm's efficiency. Many sorting algorithms are more efficient with smaller arrays, and other algorithms become more efficient as the arrays get larger.

In this Programmer's Workshop, you count the number of comparisons in the bubble sort algorithm when used with varying array sizes. Then you compute the ratio of comparisons to the number of elements. By modifying the bubble sort program to allow different array sizes, you can determine whether the bubble sort becomes more or less efficient as the array gets larger.

Discussion:

- You prompt the user for the array size.

- To populate the array with values, you can fill it with random numbers within the range of the array size.

- An accumulator variable called numComps counts the number of comparisons, and a calculated variable called compElemRatio contains the ratio of comparisons to the number of elements.

- To save space, you can separate array elements with a space instead of a line break, as you did in this chapter's examples.

  1. Start Notepad, open the **bubbleSort.html** file you created for Program 12-1, and save it as **bubbleSortTester.html**. Modify the comment lines in bold:

     ```
     <html>
     <body>
     <script type="text/javascript">

     // Program name: bubbleSortTester.html
     // Purpose: Test bubble sort efficiency with
     //    different array sizes
     // Author: Paul Addison
     // Date last modified: 01-Sep-2011
     ```

  2. Modify the variables and constants shown in bold so that the array size isn't preset, and declare variables for the timer:

     ```
     // Declare constants and variables
     var BR = "<br />";   // line break
     var ES = "";         // empty string for prompt
     var ARRAYSIZE;       // array size
     ```

```
var maxElement;        // last element in pass
var index;             // array index
var temp;              // swap variable
var numComps = 0;      // number of comparisons
var compElemRatio;     // comparison/element ratio
```

3. Modify the code to add a prompt for the array size, declare the array with that size, and populate it by using the random number generator function:

```
// Prompt user for the array size
ARRAYSIZE = prompt("How many elements?",ES);

// Declare and initialize the array
var someNums = new Array(ARRAYSIZE);
for (index = 0; index < ARRAYSIZE; index++) {
    someNums[index] = ↵
  Math.floor(Math.random() * ARRAYSIZE);
}
```

4. Modify the heading identifying the sorting method, and modify the presort display to use a space instead of a line break between array elements:

```
// Identify the sorting method
// Display the array before sorting
document.write("BUBBLE SORT/RANDOM NUMBERS" + BR);
document.write("Before sorting:" + BR);
for (index = 0; index < ARRAYSIZE; index++) {
    document.write(someNums[index] + " ");
}
```

5. The logic of the bubble sort remains unchanged, except you insert a statement to increment the number of comparisons inside the nested loop:

```
// Outer loop works from last array element
//    down to the first
// Inner loop steps through array, comparing
//    and swapping elements if necessary
for (maxElement = ARRAYSIZE - 1; maxElement > 0;
↵
  maxElement--) {
    for (index = 0; index < maxElement; index++) {
        numComps++;
        if (someNums[index] > someNums[index + 1]) {
            temp = someNums[index];
            someNums[index] = someNums[index + 1];
            someNums[index + 1] = temp;
        }
    }
}
```

6. Modify the postsort display to use a space instead of a line break after each array element:

```
// Display the array after sorting
document.write(BR + "After sorting:" + BR);
for (index = 0; index < ARRAYSIZE; index++) {
    document.write(someNums[index] + " ");
}
```

7. Before the closing HTML tags, insert the code to display the number of comparisons, and compute and display the ratio of comparisons to the number of elements:

```
// Compute and display ratio of comparisons
//    to number of elements
compElemRatio = numComps / ARRAYSIZE;
document.write(BR);
document.write("# of comparisons: " + numComps);
document.write(BR);
document.write("Comparisons to elements ratio: ");
document.write(compElemRatio.toFixed(2) + BR);

</script>
</body>
</html>
```

8. Save the file again, and open it in a browser. If your program doesn't work correctly, compare your file with bubbleSortTester.html in your student data files. Figure 12-20 shows what the output might look like with 25 random numbers.

9. Now test your program again by entering these values for the number of elements: **25**, **50**, **100**, **200**, **400**, **800**, **1600**, **3200**, and **6400**. As the number of elements doubles, what happens to the ratio of comparisons per element? Does the bubble sort become more or less efficient as the array gets larger?

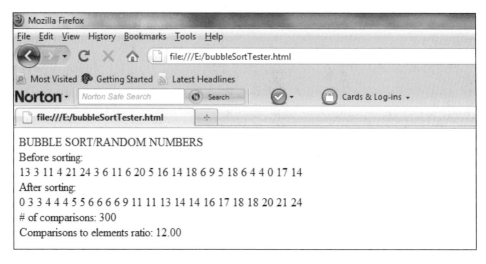

BUBBLE SORT/RANDOM NUMBERS
Before sorting:
13 3 11 4 21 24 3 6 11 6 20 5 16 14 18 6 9 5 18 6 4 4 0 17 14
After sorting:
0 3 3 4 4 4 5 5 6 6 6 6 9 11 11 13 14 14 16 17 18 18 20 21 24
# of comparisons: 300
Comparisons to elements ratio: 12.00

Figure 12-20   The bubbleSortTester.html program in a Web browser

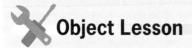

Object Lesson

You have learned how to create objects and arrays. Would it surprise you to learn that you can create an array of objects? In this Object Lesson, you create an Account class for River Bank and Trust, similar to the one you created in Chapter 3, but this time, you store Account objects in an array.

To display accounts in order, alphabetically by last name, you sort the array by using the lastName property. To get the last name from an Account record, you need to write a getLastName() function, which returns the value of the lastName field from the current object.

Discussion:

- The user should be asked how many new accounts to create, and this number is used as the array size.

- The user should be prompted for data values for each account, and then the program should call the constructor function to create an Account object with these values and assign each object to an array element.

- After all new accounts have been entered, the program should do the following:

  - Sort the account array by using the lastName property of objects.

- Display account information by calling the display() function for each object.

- Adjust subscripts to add 1 to them when they're displayed so that they're easier for nonprogrammers to understand.

This program is similar to AccountClass-2.html from Chapter 3, so you might want to review that program first.

1. Open a new document in Notepad, and save it as **AccountArrayClass.html**. Enter the starting HTML tags and program documentation lines:

```
<html>
<head>
<script type="text/javascript">

// Program name: AccountArrayClass.html
// Purpose: Create an array of Account objects
//     and sort the display by using an index array
// Author: Paul Addison
// Date last modified: 01-Sep-2011
```

2. Enter the constructor function:

```
// Constructor function for the Account class
function Account(type, num, lName, fName, bal) {
    this.acctType = type;
    this.acctNumber = num;
    this.lastName = lName;
    this.firstName = fName;
    this.acctBal = bal;
    this.getLastName = getLastName;
    this.display = display;
}
```

3. Enter the function for returning the last name of the current object, used when sorting the array:

```
// Function to return last name
function getLastName() {
    return this.lastName;
}
```

4. Enter the display() function and the tags to end the <head> section:

```
// Function to display object info
function display() {
    document.write("Account type: " +↵
  this.acctType + BR);
    document.write("Account number: " +↵
  this.acctNumber + BR);
    document.write("Last name: " +↵
  this.lastName + BR);
    document.write("First name: " +↵
```

```
        this.firstName + BR);
           document.write("Account balance: " +
        this.acctBal + BR);
           document.write(BR);
    }
```

```
</script>
</head>
```

5. Start the \<body\> section and declare variables and constants, including variables for the data fields of the Account class:

```
<body>
<script type="text/javascript">

// Variables and constants
var BR = "<br />";    // line break
var ES = "";          // empty string for prompt
var index;            // array index
var userIndex;        // index adjusted for user
var ARRAYSIZE;        // array size
var aType;            // account type
var aNumber;          // account number
var aLastName;        // last name
var aFirstName;       // first name
var aBal;             // starting balance
var maxElement;       // last element in pass
var temp;             // swap variable
```

6. Prompt the user for the number of accounts, and create the account array with this size:

```
// Prompt user for number of accounts
ARRAYSIZE = prompt("How many accounts?",ES);

// Create an array for accounts
var acctArray = new Array(ARRAYSIZE);
```

7. Use a For loop to prompt for each data field for an Account record, and then call the constructor to create an Account object and assign it to the current array element:

```
// Create a series of Account objects
for (index = 0; index < ARRAYSIZE; index++) {
   userIndex = index + 1;
   aType = prompt("#" + userIndex +
 ": Enter account type (C or S):",ES);
   aNumber = prompt("#" + userIndex +
 ": Enter account number (7 digits):",ES);
   aLastName = prompt("#" + userIndex +
 ": Enter last name:",ES);
   aFirstName = prompt("#" + userIndex +
 ": Enter first name:",ES);
   aBal = prompt("#" + userIndex +
 ": Enter starting balance:",ES);
```

```
    acctArray[index] = new Account ↵
     (aType, aNumber, aLastName, aFirstName, aBal);
    }
```

8. Enter the code to sort the account array based on the lastName property:

```
// Sort the account array based on last name
// Bubble sort algorithm is used
for (maxElement = ARRAYSIZE - 1; maxElement > 0; ↵
 maxElement--) {
    for (index = 0; index < maxElement; index++) {
        if (acctArray[index].getLastName() > ↵
 acctArray[index + 1].getLastName()) {
            temp = acctArray[index];
            acctArray[index] = acctArray[index + 1];
            acctArray[index + 1] = temp;
        }
    }
}
```

9. Use a For loop to call the display() function for each array element, using the reordered numbers in the index array as the subscripts for the account array:

```
// Display heading
// Display array elements in sorted order
document.write("RIVER BANK AND TRUST" + BR);
for (index = 0; index < ARRAYSIZE; index++) {
    userIndex = index + 1;
    acctArray[index].display();
}
```

10. Thank the user, and end the program:

```
// Thank the user
document.write("Thank you!" + BR);

</script>
</body>
</html>
```

11. Save the file again, and open it in a browser. Test it by entering the following records. The output should look like Figure 12-21; if it doesn't, compare your work with AccountArrayClass.html in your student data files.

- C, 7676767, Piperson, Jon, 1200.00
- S, 1212121, Adams, Abigail, 650.00
- C, 9898989, Spaid, Bill, 800.00

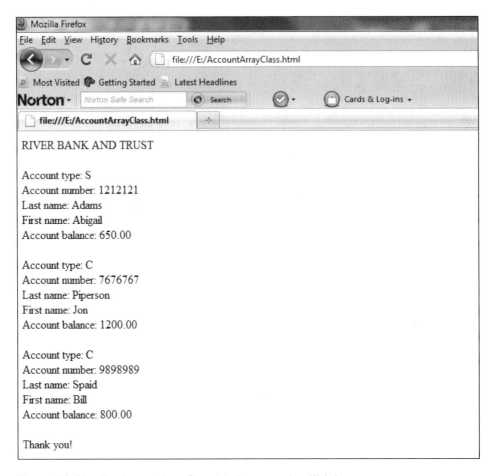

Figure 12-21   The AccountArrayClass.html program in a Web browser

Detective Work

Next, try modifying the AccountArrayClass.html program so that it sorts the records by account number instead of last name. Open your AccountArrayClass.html file, if needed, and save it as AccountArrayClassByAcct.html. *Hint:* You need to change the getLastName() function to return the account number instead. Also, because all account numbers should be seven digits, a lexigraphical sort should produce the same results as a numeric sort. Save the file, and open it in a browser. If the program doesn't work correctly, check it against AccountArrayClassByAcct-solution.html in your student data files.

Chapter Summary

- Data is sorted to help locate information more quickly.

- Arrays work well with sorting algorithms because all elements are in memory and easily referenced.

- Data can be sorted in ascending order (low to high numbers or alphabetically) or in descending order (high to low numbers or reverse alphabetical order).

- To sort in ascending order, an element is swapped or moved if its value is greater than the next element, so the greater than operator (>) is used. To sort in descending order, the less than operator (<) is used.

- Many sorting algorithms swap the values of two variables, which requires using a third (temporary) variable.

- A bubble sort compares adjacent values and swaps them if necessary.

- A selection sort finds which element belongs in a particular position on each pass through the array and moves it there.

- An insertion sort builds a sorted array by determining where each element should be in the sorted part of the array and inserting it in that position while moving all other sorted elements over one position.

- JavaScript has its own sorting method, sort(), but it sorts lexigraphically, so another function is needed to force a numeric comparison of elements' values when the array data is numeric.

- JavaScript also has the reverse() method for reversing the order of elements in an array.

Key Terms

ascending sort—A sorting category that places items in low to high order; with numeric data, the items are in order from low to high numeric values, and with string data, they're in alphabetical order.

bubble sort—A sorting algorithm that involves comparing adjacent elements and swapping them, if needed, until all elements are in their correct positions.

descending sort—A sorting category that places items in high to low order; with numeric data, the items are in order from high to low numeric values, and with string data, they're in reverse alphabetical order.

insertion sort—A sorting algorithm that builds a sorted array by determining where each element should be in the sorted part of the array and inserting it in that position while moving all other sorted elements over one position.

lexigraphical order—A sort that looks at character values for sorting (including digits in numbers), instead of sorting by numeric values.

selection sort—A sorting algorithm that finds which element belongs in a particular position on each pass through the array and moves it there.

sorting—The process of arranging data items in order.

swapping—Switching the order of two elements in an array for the purpose of sorting them in a specified order.

Review Questions

True/False

1. An ascending sort for numbers means arranging them from high to low values. True or False?

2. Numeric data can be sorted in ascending or descending order, but string data can be sorted only in ascending order. True or False?

3. A bubble sort scans the array on each pass and makes one swap in each pass. True or False?

4. When arranging items in ascending order, a bubble sort places the largest value in the first array position at the end of the first pass. True or False?

5. A selection sort compares adjacent values in each pass and swaps array elements as needed. True or False?

6. A selection sort can sort only in ascending order. True or False?

7. An insertion sort builds a sorted array one element at a time. True or False?

8. An insertion sort needs a parallel array to hold array elements while they're being shifted. True or False?

9. The JavaScript sort() method sorts data numerically. True or False?

10. All sorting algorithms work more efficiently on smaller arrays than on larger arrays. True or False?

Multiple Choice

1. The data values 899, 566, 299, 45, and 3 are in which order?

    a. ascending

    b. descending

    c. lexigraphical

    d. binary

2. The data values "Harrison", "Matheson", "Quincy", and "Young" are in which order? (Choose all that apply.)

    a. ascending

    b. descending

    c. lexigraphical

    d. alphabetical

3. To swap two array elements, a _____ variable is needed.

    a. string

    b. numeric

    c. temporary

    d. null

4. On its first pass through an array of 10 elements, a bubble sort makes _____ comparisons.

    a. 8

    b. 9

    c. 10

    d. 11

5. A bubble sort's efficiency can be improved by a variable that indicates _____.

    a. whether a value being searched for was found

    b. whether any comparisons were made during a pass through the array

    c. whether any swaps were made during a pass through the array

    d. whether the array has any duplicate values

6. A selection sort, on its first pass through an array of 10 elements, makes no more than _____ swap(s).

    a. 0

    b. 1

    c. 9

    d. 10

7. An insertion sort pulls an element from the array and _____ other array elements until the correct location for the pulled element is determined.

    a. deletes

    b. increments

    c. shifts

    d. initializes

8. Which JavaScript method reverses the order of elements in an array?

    a. `sort()`

    b. `reverse()`

    c. `backward()`

    d. `sortDescending()`

---

9. The JavaScript sort() method called by a string array with no arguments sorts elements in what order? (Choose all that apply.)

   a. alphabetic

   b. lexigraphical

   c. numeric

   d. ascending

10. How do you sort a numeric array with the JavaScript sort() method?

   a. Sort the array, and then use the reverse() method.

   b. Use a function reference as the argument to the sort() method.

   c. Use the parseInt() function on the array elements.

   d. JavaScript sorts in numeric order automatically.

Discussion Questions

1. What are some reasons for sorting collections of data?

2. How does the swapsMade variable described for the bubble sort increase the sort's efficiency?

3. How can you list array elements in sorted order yet preserve their original order in the array?

Hands-On Activities

Hands-On Activity 12-1

Open the bubbleSort.html file you created for Program 12-1, and save it as bubbleSortString.html. Populate the array with string data instead of numeric data, and then test it with these states as data: "Georgia", "Colorado", "Iowa", "Florida", "Kentucky", and "Arizona".

Hands-On Activity 12-2

Open the bubbleSort.html file, and save it as bubbleSortDescending.html. Modify the program with numeric data to sort an array in descending order by using a different comparison operator, and then test the program. *Hint:* Only one change is required in addition to modifying the program documentation lines.

Hands-On Activity 12-3

Open the selectionSort.html file, and save it as selectionSortDescending.html. Modify the program to sort an array in descending order, and then test it. *Hint:* When you sorted in descending order, you were looking for the minimum value to place first; now look for the maximum value.

Hands-On Activity 12-4

Open the insertionSort.html file, and save it as insertionSortDescending.html. Modify the program to sort an array in descending order by using a different comparison operator, and then test the program. *Hint:* Only one change is required in addition to modifying the program documentation lines.

CASE STUDY: The War Is Over!

The Case Study concluded in Chapter 11 when you automated the War card game.

CHAPTER 13

Recursion

In this chapter, you learn to:

◎ Explain the process of recursion

◎ Describe the biggest danger of recursion and how to prevent it

◎ Explain how modules are pushed and popped to and from memory

◎ Describe the logic of classic recursion problems, including factorials, the Fibonacci sequence, and the Towers of Hanoi

◎ Code and test some examples of recursion

"In order to understand recursion, you must first understand recursion."

—UNKNOWN PUNDIT

Have you ever stood between two mirrors and looked into one to see a reflection of a reflection of a reflection, until it was so small you couldn't see it at all? This image might help you visualize a programming technique called **recursion**, which is a process in which a module calls itself. Does this definition mean it could result in a never-ending process, such as an infinite loop? Yes, it can, if it's not set up correctly. To prevent a neverending recursion process, you must make sure to build a **base case** into the procedure, which is an event that doesn't call itself and must be reached eventually.

Any recursive procedure can be accomplished by nonrecursive means, so what's the point of recursion? Just as learning about sorting routines helps you understand code and algorithms, understanding recursion can help you understand concepts about programming and computer operation. It's a useful programming exercise.

Recursive Procedures

First, take a look at an example of a problem that can have a recursive solution. For any positive integer n, the value of the sumUpTo() function is defined as the sum of all numbers from 1 up to n. You can set up this problem easily as the following loop:

```
// Function to add numbers from 1 up to the argument
Function Numeric sumUpTo(Numeric num)
   Declare Numeric result = 0    // answer
   Declare Numeric index         // For loop index

   // For loop adds numbers to total
   For index = 0 to num
      num = num + index
   End For
End Function
```

However, there's another way to approach this problem (assuming the argument is 5):

- The sum up to 5 can be defined as 5 plus the sum up to 4.

- The sum up to 4 can be defined as 4 plus the sum up to 3.

- The sum up to 3 can be defined as 3 plus the sum up to 2.

- The sum up to 2 can be defined as 2 plus the sum up to 1.

- Finally, the sum up to 1 can simply be defined as 1. This is the base case.

The function can be written in pseudocode as follows:

```
// Function to add numbers from 1 up to the argument
Function Numeric sumUpTo(Numeric num)
```

```
    If num == 1 Then
        Return 1
    Else
        Return num + sumUpTo(num - 1)
    End If
End Function
```

So if the function is called from the main module with the statement
runningTotal = sumUpTo(5), the steps take place in the following
order, as shown in Figure 13-1:

1.   sumUpTo(5) returns 5 + sumUpTo(4).

2.   sumUpTo(4) returns 4 + sumUpTo(3).

3.   sumUpTo(3) returns 3 + sumUpTo(2).

4.   sumUpTo(2) returns 2 + sumUpTo(1).

5.   sumUpTo(1) returns 1 to sumUpTo(2).

6.   sumUpTo(2) returns 2 + 1 (3) to sumUpTo(3).

7.   sumUpTo(3) returns 3 + 3 (6) to sumUpTo(4).

8.   sumUpTo(4) returns 4 + 6 (10) to sumUpTo(5).

9.   sumUpTo(5) returns 5 + 10 (15) to the main module, where it's
     stored in the variable runningTotal.

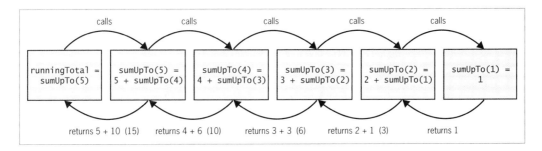

Figure 13-1   Steps in the recursive procedure sumUpTo()

Memory Stacks

One reason modular programming is encouraged is that it's an efficient way to manage computer memory. Because variables declared
in a module are local, and arguments passed by value are copied
into local variables, a module can run like an independent program.
A program's main module occupies a designated place in memory
called the **stack**, and when a call to another module is made, the main
module's execution is suspended, and the program code for the other
module is placed in an unused area of memory, which can be thought
of as being above the main module area.

In other words, a memory stack contains the main program, and when another module is running, it's said to be placed, or **pushed**, onto the memory stack until it's finished executing. At this point, it's removed, or **popped**, from the stack, along with all local variables. That's why variables declared in a module aren't available to other modules: They no longer exist when the module ends.

In Figure 13-2, the main module executes until the double() module is called, and then the code for the double() module is pushed onto the memory stack. The value of the variable num (which is 3) is passed to the module, where it's copied into the variable n. When the double() module finishes executing, its code is popped from the stack, and the main module resumes execution. In the figure, the grayed-out sections of code aren't currently running.

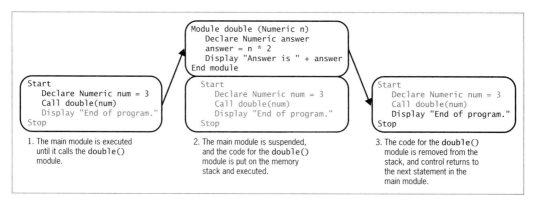

Figure 13-2   A module stacked on the main module when it's called

Modules can also call other modules, and each new call results in the new module's code being pushed onto the stack and being popped off the stack when it's finished. You can imagine the problem if a module were to call itself repeatedly, with nothing to terminate the process. New copies of the module would continue to be pushed onto the stack until no memory is left, a condition called a **stack overflow**. It's what occurs if a recursive procedure contains no base case.

Now that you have seen an example of recursion, it's time to examine other examples in the following sections and see how a base case can be used to prevent a stack overflow.

Examples of Recursion

Some examples of problems that can be solved recursively are so well known that they're considered classic. They include factorials, the Fibonacci sequence, the sum of squares, and the Towers of Hanoi.

Factorials

The factorial of a number is the product of all positive integers from that number down to 1. For example, the factorial of 5 is 5 * 4 * 3 * 2 * 1, or 120. As mentioned, any recursive procedure can be described nonrecursively, so you can define a nonrecursive factorial function like this:

```
Function Numeric factorial(Numeric num)
   // Declare variables
   Declare Numeric fact = 1    // factorial result
   Declare Numeric index       // loop index

   // Loop
   For index = num to 1 Step -1
      fact = fact * index
   End For
   Return fact
End Function
```

Here's another way of looking at this problem:

- The factorial of 5 is the same as 5 times the factorial of 4.

- The factorial of 4 is the same as 4 times the factorial of 3.

- The factorial of 3 is the same as 3 times the factorial of 2.

- The factorial of 2 is the same as 2 times the factorial of 1.

- The factorial of 1 is 1.

In other words, a factorial can be defined as factorial(n) = n * factorial(n - 1), with factorial(1) defined as 1. You can express a recursive algorithm for calculating a factorial like this:

```
Function Numeric factorial(Numeric num)
   // Call function recursively until reaching 1
   If num == 1 Then
      Return 1
   Else
      Return num * factorial(num - 1)
   End If
End Function
```

Suppose you want to find the factorial of the number 4 and store it in a variable called fact. The main module includes the statement fact = factorial(4), and the program proceeds as follows:

- The first time the main module calls the factorial() function with the value 4 as an argument, the function calls itself with the value 3.

- A new instance of the function starts with the value 3 and calls factorial() with the value 2.

- This instance of the function calls factorial() with the value 1.

- The last instance of the function returns the value 1 and ends.

- Now the instance that had the value 2 can return its value (2 * 1, or 2) and end.

- The instance called with the value 3 returns 3 * 2, or 6, and ends.

- The original instance called with the value 4 returns 4 * 6, or 24, to the main module and ends.

- Program execution then returns to the main module, where the value 24 is assigned to the variable `fact`.

Figure 13-3 shows how the `factorial()` module continues to call itself until it returns 1 and begins supplying actual values to the remaining open functions.

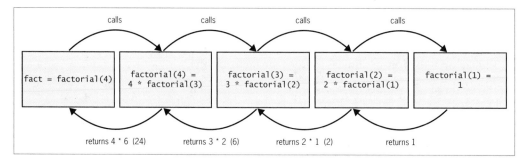

Figure 13-3 Steps in the recursive procedure `factorial()`

PROGRAM 13-1 JavaScript Program factorial.html

This program includes a statement in the `factorial()` function to indicate the order in which functions are being called. Remember to add a blank line after the code section in each step.

1. Open a new document in Notepad, and save it as **factorial.html**. Enter the starting HTML tags and program documentation lines:

```
<html>
<head>
<script type="text/javascript">

// Program name: factorial.html
// Purpose: Use recursion to calculate a factorial
// Author: Paul Addison
// Date last modified: 01-Sep-2011
```

(continues)

(continued)

2. Enter the code for the `factorial()` function and the tags
   to end the `<head>` section:

```
// This function defines a factorial
// If the number is 1, the function returns a 1
// Otherwise, it calls itself with an argument
//    of the number - 1
function factorial(num) {
  document.write("Processing the factorial of: "↵
 + num + BR);
  if (num == 1) return 1;
  else return (num * factorial(num - 1));
}

</script>
</head>
```

3. Start the `<body>` section and declare constants and
   variables:

```
<body>
<script type="text/javascript">

// Declare constants and variables
var BR = "<br />";   // line break
var ES = "";         // empty string
var num;             // number user enters
var numFactorial;    // factorial calculated
```

4. Prompt for the number, call the `factorial()` function, and
   display the result:

```
// Prompt user for a number
// Call factorial function and display the result
num = prompt("Enter a number:",ES);
numFactorial = factorial(num);
document.write("The factorial of " + num + " is "↵
 + numFactorial + BR);

</script>
</body>
</html>
```

5. Save the file again, and open it in a browser. If you enter
   the number 7, your output should look like Figure 13-4.

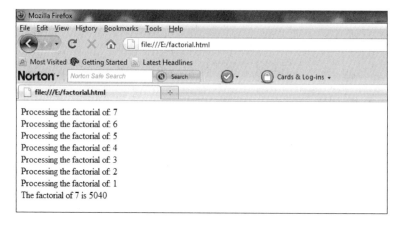

Figure 13-4 The factorial.html program in a Web browser

The Fibonacci sequence was mentioned in the 2006 movie *The DaVinci Code*. The 10-digit bank account number of murder victim Jacques Saunière was made up of the first eight non-zero numbers in the Fibonacci sequence (1123581321). Some definitions of the Fibonacci sequence don't include zero.

The Fibonacci Sequence

In mathematics, the Fibonacci sequence is defined as follows: The first number is 0, the second number is 1, and any number following is the sum of the two previous numbers. The sequence looks like this:

0, 1, 1, 2, 3, 5, 8, 13, 21, 34, 55, 89, 144 ...

Interestingly, this mathematical sequence appears in nature. For example, the numbers of clockwise and counterclockwise spirals in a sunflower (and many other flowers) are two consecutive numbers in the Fibonacci series, such as 34 and 55. In addition, starting with the number 55 in the sequence, the ratio of any number to its previous number in the sequence rounds to 1.618, known as the "golden ratio." The Fibonacci sequence offers another opportunity to study recursion.

The Fibonacci number at any position (after the first two numbers in the sequence) is the sum of the Fibonacci number at two positions before the current one and the Fibonacci number at one position before the current one. Therefore, for any integer *n* greater than or equal to 2, you can represent its position in the Fibonacci sequence, starting the position numbering at 0, as follows:

fibonacci(*n*) = fibonacci(*n* – 2) + fibonacci(*n* – 1)

In this expression, the values of fibonacci(0) and fibonacci(1) are predefined as 0 and 1.

A recursive algorithm for the Fibonacci sequence can be expressed in pseudocode like this:

```
Function Numeric fibonacci(Numeric num)
   // Call function recursively until reaching 0 or 1
   If num == 0 Or num == 1 Then
      Return num
   Else
      Return fibonacci(num - 2) + fibonacci(num - 1)
   End If
End Function
```

PROGRAM 13-2 JavaScript Program fibonacci.html

This program determines the Fibonacci number at a given position in the sequence, and then runs a loop to construct the entire sequence up to that position. Note that for better readability, the constant cs is declared for a comma followed by a space, used to separate numbers in the sequence.

1. Open a new document in Notepad, and save it as **fibonacci.html**. Enter the starting HTML tags and program documentation lines:

```
<html>
<head>
<script type="text/javascript">

// Program name: fibonacci.html
// Purpose: Use recursion to calculate a Fibonacci
//    sequence up to a given position in the
//    sequence, starting with position 0
// Author: Paul Addison
// Date last modified: 01-Sep-2011
```

2. Define the Fibonacci function and end the `<head>` section:

```
// This function defines a Fibonacci sequence
// If number is 0, the function returns a 0
// If number is 1, the function returns a 1
// If number is higher than 1, it returns the
//    Fibonacci value of the number - 2, plus the
//    Fibonacci value of the number - 1

function fibonacci(num) {
   if (num == 0 || num == 1) return num;
   else return (fibonacci(num - 2) + ↵
 fibonacci(num - 1));
}
</script>
</head>
```

(continues)

(continued)

3. Start the `<body>` section and declare constants and variables:

```
<body>
<script type="text/javascript">

// Declare constants and variables
var BR = "<br />";    // line break
var ES = "";          // empty string
var CS = ", ";        // comma/space combination
var num;              // # of sequence position
var index;            // loop index
```

4. Prompt the user, call the function, and display the result:

```
// Prompt user for a number
// Call fibonacci function and display the result
num = prompt("Enter a number:",ES);
document.write("The Fibonacci number at position "↵
   + num + " is " + fibonacci(num) + BR);
```

5. Call the `fibonacci()` function to display the complete sequence up to the position, and then display the Fibonacci number at that position:

```
// Construct Fibonacci sequence to given position
document.write("The sequence to that position: ");
for (index = 0; index < num; index++) {
// include comma and space after each number
   document.write(fibonacci(index) + CS);
}
// no comma and space after last number
document.write(fibonacci(num) + BR);

</script>
</body>
</html>
```

6. Save the file again, and open it in a browser. If you enter the number 12, your browser output should look like Figure 13-5.

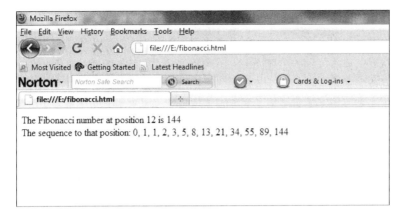

Figure 13-5   The fibonacci.html program in a Web browser

Sum of Squares

Now that you're learning to think recursively, you can see many patterns that use recursion, as when the same operation can be performed on smaller and smaller numbers until a base case is reached, often when the numbers get down to 1 or 0.

A problem similar to calculating a factorial is computing the sum of squares up to a certain number. For any positive number n, the sum of squares equals $1^2 + 2^2 + 3^2$, and so on up to n^2. Viewing the problem recursively, the sum of squares for n is $n^2 + (n - 1)^2 + (n - 2)^2$, and so on down to 1. As a result, for any positive integer, the sum of squares can be defined as (num * num) + sumOfSquares(num - 1), shown in the following example:

```
Function Numeric sumOfSquares(Numeric num)
   // Base case returns 1
   // Anything else returns square of current number
   //    plus the sum of squares of smaller numbers
   If (num == 1) Then
      Return 1
   Else
      Return (num * num) + sumOfSquares(num - 1)
   End If
End Function
```

Next, you see how to write a JavaScript program that uses this function.

PROGRAM 13-3 JavaScript Program
sumOfSquares.html

1. Open a new document in Notepad, and save it as **sumOfSquares.html**. Enter the starting HTML tags and program documentation lines:

```
<html>
<head>
<script type="text/javascript">

// Program name: sumOfSquares.html
// Purpose: Use recursion to sum all squares
//    up to a given number
// Author: Paul Addison
// Date last modified: 01-Sep-2011
```

2. Enter the code for the function, and then end the <head> section:

```
// This function calculates the sum of squares
//    up to a given number
// If the number is 1, the function returns 1
// Otherwise, it returns its square
//    plus the sum of squares to the number - 1
function sumOfSquares(num) {
  if (num == 1) return 1;
  else return (num * num) + sumOfSquares(num - 1);
}
</script>
</head>
```

3. Start the <body> section and declare constants and variables:

```
<body>
<script type="text/javascript">

// Declare constants and variables
var BR = "<br />";  // line break
var ES = "";        // empty string
var userNum;        // number user enters
var sumSq;          // sum of squares calculated
```

4. Prompt the user, call the function, display the result, and end the program:

```
// Prompt user for a number
// Call sumOfSquares function and display result
userNum = prompt("Enter a number:",ES);
sumSq = sumOfSquares(userNum);
```

(continues)

(continued)

```
document.write("The sum of squares up to "↵
 + userNum + " is " + sumSq + BR);

</script>
</body>
</html>
```

5. Save the file again, and open it in a browser. If you enter the number 30, your output should look like Figure 13-6.

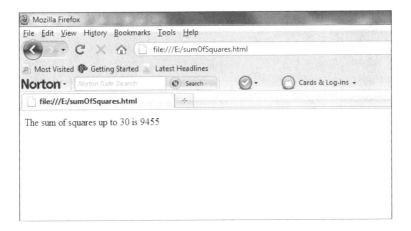

Figure 13-6 The sumOfSquares.html program in a Web browser

The Towers of Hanoi

Another classic example of recursion is the puzzle called the Towers of Hanoi. It's attributed to the French mathematician Edouard Lucas and is based on a legend about a temple in Vietnam, with 64 golden discs stacked on three posts. The priests in the temple have been moving these discs in accordance with the puzzle's rules since the 1800s. The legend says that when the puzzle is completed, the world will come to an end.

 It has been calculated that completing this puzzle with 64 discs and one move per second would take about 585 billion years. Fortunately, it takes far fewer moves when starting with fewer discs.

The game based on this puzzle is played with three pegs and a stack of discs. Initially, the discs are in order on the first peg, with the smallest on top and the largest on the bottom. The goal is to move them from the first peg to a different peg while following these rules:

- You can move only one disc at a time, from one peg to another.

- You can't place a larger disc on a smaller disc.

This puzzle can be solved by using recursion. The code controlling what seems to be a complicated process is actually quite simple. To play the game, you use one peg as the source, one peg as the target, and the third peg as a spare during the moves. Call the pegs A, B, and C from left to right, and number the discs starting with 1 as the smallest to *n* as the largest.

If you have only one disc, you can move it directly from Peg A (the source) to Peg C (the target), as shown in Figure 13-7. In this example, *n* is 1.

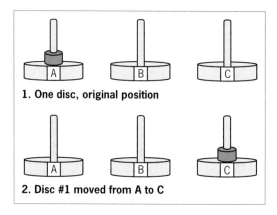

1. One disc, original position

2. Disc #1 moved from A to C

Figure 13-7   The Towers of Hanoi played with one disc

If you have two discs, the algorithm requires using the spare peg and divides the moves into three parts (see Figure 13-8): moving the smaller disc to the spare peg, moving the larger disc to the target peg, and then moving the smaller disc from the spare peg to the target peg, as follows:

- Move Disc #1 from Peg A to Peg B.

- Move Disc #2 from Peg A to Peg C.

- Move Disc #1 from Peg B to Peg C.

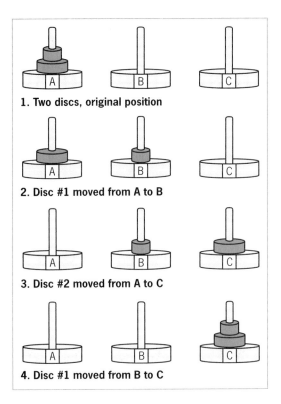

1. Two discs, original position

2. Disc #1 moved from A to B

3. Disc #2 moved from A to C

4. Disc #1 moved from B to C

Figure 13-8   The Towers of Hanoi played with two discs

If you have three discs, you move the smallest two discs to the spare peg, move the largest disc to the target peg, and then move the smallest two discs from the spare peg to the target peg, like this (see Figure 13-9):

• Move Disc #1 from Peg A to Peg C.

• Move Disc #2 from Peg A to Peg B.

• Move Disc #1 from Peg C to Peg B.

• Move Disc #3 from Peg A to Peg C.

• Move Disc #1 from Peg B to Peg A.

• Move Disc #2 from Peg B to Peg C.

• Move Disc #1 from Peg A to Peg C.

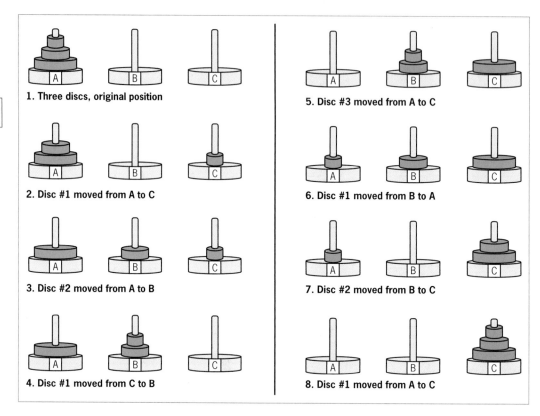

1. Three discs, original position

2. Disc #1 moved from A to C

3. Disc #2 moved from A to B

4. Disc #1 moved from C to B

5. Disc #3 moved from A to C

6. Disc #1 moved from B to A

7. Disc #2 moved from B to C

8. Disc #1 moved from A to C

Figure 13-9   The Towers of Hanoi played with three discs

As a programmer, the pattern you should see is that for *n* discs, you move *n* - 1 discs to the spare peg, disc *n* to the target peg, and then *n* - 1 discs from the spare peg to the target peg. A module to move the discs can be called recursively with *n* - 1 discs, and the base case of *n* = 0 stops the recursive calls. You might also have noticed that when the number of discs is odd, the first move is from Peg A to Peg C, and when the number of discs is even, the first move is from Peg A to Peg B so that the final stack is on Peg C. The order of target and spare pegs in the parameters is different from their order in the recursive call, so they alternate with each new recursive call, as follows:

```
Module moveDiscs(Integer n, sourcePeg, targetPeg, sparePeg)
    If (n > 0) Then
        moveDiscs(n - 1, sourcePeg, sparePeg, targetPeg)
        // Move disc from sourcePeg to targetPeg
        moveDiscs(n - 1, sparePeg, targetPeg, sourcePeg)
    End If
End Module
```

To use this module as a function in a JavaScript program, you can ask the user how many discs are on the first peg and match the peg names with the parameters (A = source, C = target, and B = spare).

PROGRAM 13-4: JavaScript Program
towersOfHanoi.html

1. Open a new document in Notepad, and save it as
   towersOfHanoi.html. Enter the starting HTML tags and
   program documentation lines:

```
<html>
<head>
<script type="text/javascript">

// Program name: towersOfHanoi.html
// Purpose: Use recursion to solve the
//    Towers of Hanoi puzzle
// Author: Paul Addison
// Date last modified: 01-Sep-2011
```

2. Enter the code for the recursive function to move the
   discs and add the tags to end the <head> section.

```
// This function simulates the Towers of Hanoi game
function moveDiscs ↵
(n, sourcePeg, targetPeg, sparePeg) {
   // Move all but largest disc from source to
   //    spare by calling moveDiscs() recursively
   //    with (n - 1) discs
   // Move largest disc from source to target
   // Move all but largest disc from spare to
   //    target by calling moveDiscs() recursively
   //    with (n - 1) discs
   // n = 0 is base case that stops recursive calls
   if (n > 0) {
      moveDiscs(n - 1, sourcePeg, sparePeg, ↵
 targetPeg);
      document.write("Moving Disc " + n + " from " ↵
 + sourcePeg + " to " + targetPeg + BR);
      moveDiscs(n - 1, sparePeg, targetPeg, ↵
 sourcePeg);
   }
}

</script>
</head>
```

(continues)

(continued)

3. Enter the tags to start the `<body>` section, declare constants and variables, and display a program heading:

```
<body>
<script type="text/javascript">

// Declare constants and variables
var BR = "<br />";   // HTML line break
var ES = "";         // empty string
var numDiscs;        // number of discs

// Display a program heading
document.write("Towers of Hanoi" + BR + BR);
```

4. Prompt the user for the number of discs, and then call the `moveDiscs()` function:

```
// Prompt user for number of discs
// Call moveDiscs() function, starting with:
//    Peg A = source, Peg C = target, Peg B = spare
numDiscs = prompt("How many discs on the peg?",ES);
moveDiscs(numDiscs, "Peg A", "Peg C", "Peg B");
```

5. Thank the user and end the program:

```
// Thank the user and end the program
document.write(BR + "Discs are now in order.");
document.write(BR + "Thank you." + BR);

</script>
</body>
</html>
```

6. Save the file again, and open it in a browser. If you enter 4 for the number of discs, your output should look like Figure 13-10.

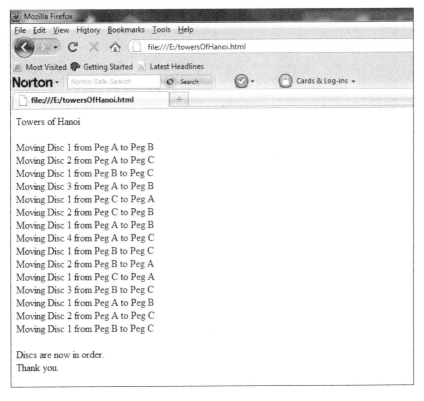

Figure 13-10   The towersOfHanoi.html program in a Web browser

In this chapter, you have learned what recursion is, with a variety of programming examples to see it in action. In the Programmer's Workshop, you apply recursion to an ancient mathematics problem.

Programmer's Workshop

The greatest common denominator (GCD) of two numbers is the largest integer that can be divided by both numbers evenly (with no remainder). The mathematician Euclid discovered a method for computing the GCD. If the two numbers are called x and y, and $x >= y$ and $y >= 0$, the following test can be made:

- If $y = 0$, the GCD is x.

- If not, set x to y, set y equal to the remainder after dividing x by y, and try this process again.

Used in a function, if y (which is smaller than or equal to x) isn't 0, call the function again with y as the new x, and the remainder (modulus) as the new y. Euclid determined that if you keep repeating this process, eventually the remainder will be 0 (the base case).

In this workshop, you write a recursive function in pseudocode, and then write a JavaScript program that asks for two numbers, calls the function, and returns the GCD.

Start with the IPO process:

- What outputs are requested? The greatest common denominator (GCD) for any two integers

- What inputs do you have available? Two nonnegative integers entered by the user (numeric, x and y)

- What processing is required?

  - Make certain the first number is greater than or equal to the second by comparing them and swapping their order, if necessary.

  - Call a function that divides x by y and checks to see whether the remainder is 0. If it isn't, call the function again, with y as the first number and the remainder as the second.

Discussion:

- The name of the function can be simply GCD.

- The function needs only two parameters: x and y. Before these arguments are passed, check that the first is greater than or equal to the second, and both are greater than or equal to 0.

- To translate the two parts of the test into pseudocode, you use a straightforward selection statement, with the first part returning the result and the second part issuing a recursive call with new arguments.

In pseudocode, the GCD() function looks like this:

```
Function Numeric GCD(Numeric x, Numeric y)
    If y = 0 Then
        Return x
    Else
        Return GCD(y, x % y)
    End If
End Function
```

To create a JavaScript program, you need to put the GCD() function in the <head> section, and write a <body> section that asks the user for two numbers and makes sure both are greater than or equal to 0.

Next, the GCD() function is called to make sure the first argument is greater than or equal to the second.

1. Open a new document in Notepad, and save it as **greatestCommonDenominator.html**. Enter the starting HTML tags and program documentation lines:

```
<html>
<head>
<script type="text/javascript">

// Program name: greatestCommonDenominator.html
// Purpose: Use recursion to find the GCD
//    Assumptions: x >= y and y >= 0
// Author: Paul Addison
// Date last modified: 01-Sep-2011
```

2. Enter the code for the recursive GCD() function and the tags to end the <head> section:

```
function GCD(x, y) {
    if (y == 0) return x;
    else return GCD(y, x % y);
}

</script>
</head>
```

3. Enter the tags to start the <body> section, declare constants and variables, and display a program heading:

```
<body>
<script type="text/javascript">

// Declare constants and variables
var BR = "<br />";     // HTML line break
var ES = "";           // empty string
var num1, num2;        // two numbers for GCD
var theGCD;            // returned GCD

// Display program heading
document.write("Greatest Common Denominator" + BR)
```

4. Prompt the user for two nonnegative numbers and validate them:

```
// Prompt user for two numbers
// Validate that they're >= 0
do {
    num1 = prompt("Enter first number (>= 0):",ES);
} while (num1 < 0);

do {
    num2 = prompt("Enter second number (>= 0):",ES);
} while (num2 < 0);
```

5. Call the GCD() function, display the results, thank the user, and end the program:

```
// Call GCD function
if (num1 >= num2) theGCD = GCD(num1, num2);
else theGCD = GCD(num2, num1);

// Display the results
document.write("The GCD is: " + theGCD + BR);

// Thank the user and end the program
document.write("Thank you." + BR);

</script>
</body>
</html>
```

6. Save the file again, and open it in a browser. If you enter the numbers 72 and 48, your output should look like Figure 13-11.

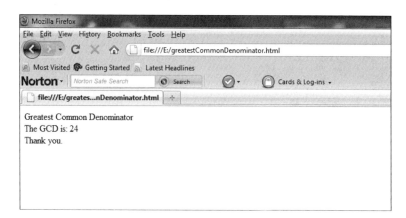

Figure 13-11 The greatestCommonDenominator.html program in a Web browser

You have just calculated the greatest common denominator of two numbers by using recursion. In the Object Lesson, you use a constructor function that calls itself recursively.

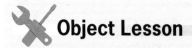 **Object Lesson**

Constructor functions can also be called recursively. As with the functions you have worked with in this chapter, you must have a base case.

Imagine you have heard a news broadcast stating that the Age of the Zantillians is coming, and only descendants of the great Tofu Zantilli in the past five generations will be permitted to survive. You're commanded to write a program requiring each person to enter his or her father's name, grandfather's name, and so on, until it's determined whether the person is a true Zantillian.

Now that you know about recursion, you write a prompt asking the user for his or her father's first and last name and use this information to instantiate a `Father` object. When the object is created, the constructor function checks to see whether the father's name is Tofu Zantilli; if so, it displays a congratulatory message. If not, the function sees whether five generations have been counted; if so, it displays a message of condolence. If neither outcome happens, the function calls itself recursively, prompting for the grandfather's name while adding 1 to the number of generations.

There are two base cases: when an ancestor is discovered to be Tofu Zantilli and when five generations have been counted. Whether a person is determined to be a Zantillian or not, his or her ancestry should be displayed going back five generations or back to Tofu Zantilli.

Discussion:

- The constructor should accept the father's first and last name and the number of generations counted.

- The two base cases should be checked for whether the name equals `"Tofu Zantilli"` and the number of generations has reached the limit. Only then should the program prompt the user to enter a new father.

- An array should be used to store the object for each father.

- A function should be called that asks for the name of the first father and calls the constructor function, but if more names are needed, the constructor function should prompt for them and then call itself to instantiate them.

- To display the user's ancestry, call a function that uses a loop to pass each element of the `fatherArray` array to a `displayName()` function that displays the name.

1. Open a new document in Notepad, and save it as **zantillian.html**. Enter the starting HTML tags and program documentation lines:

```
<html>
<head>
<script type="text/javascript">

// Program name: zantillian.html
// Purpose: Create Father objects and see whether
```

```
//   you're a Zantillian; you are if you had an
//   ancestor named Tofu Zantilli in the past five
//   generations
// Author: Paul Addison
// Date last modified: 01-Sep-2011
```

2. Declare variables needed in the constructor function and the array of Father objects:

```
// Declare variables
var BR = "<br />";      // HTML line break
var ES = "";            // empty string
var hisName;            // father's name
var NUM_GENS = 5;       // max # generations
var numFathers = 0;     // # fathers listed - 1
var i;                  // loop index

// Declare fatherArray as array of Father objects
var fatherArray = new Array(NUM_GENS);
```

3. Write the function that gets the father's name and calls the constructor function:

```
// Function that gets name and calls constructor
function checkZantillian() {
    hisName = prompt("Your father's name?",ES);
    fatherArray[numFathers] = new Father(hisName);
}
```

4. Write the constructor function for the Father class. If one of the two base cases is reached, a message is displayed. Otherwise, the constructor calls itself recursively.

```
// Constructor function for the Father class
function Father(nameArg) {
    this.fName = nameArg;
    this.displayName = displayName;

    if (nameArg.toLowerCase() == "tofu zantilli") {
        document.write↵
("All hail the true Zantillian!" + BR);
    }
    else if (numFathers >= NUM_GENS - 1) {
        document.write↵
("Sorry, you are not a true Zantillian." + BR);
    }
    else {
        numFathers++;
        hisName = prompt("His father's name?",ES);
        fatherArray[numFathers] = new Father(hisName);
    }
}
```

5. Write the function that loops to call the `displayName()` function for each of the user's ancestors, up to five. Then enter the code for the `displayName()` function and end the <head> section.

```
// Function to display ancestry
function displayAncestry() {
   document.write(BR);
   for (i = 0; i <= numFathers; i++) {
      if (i == 0) document.write("Your father: ");
      else document.write("His father: ");
      fatherArray[i].displayName();
   }
}

// Function to display name
function displayName() {
   document.write(this.fName + BR);
}

</script>
</head>
```

6. Start the <body> section, declare the line break constant, and display a program heading:

```
<body>
<script type="text/javascript">

// Declare constant
var BR = "<br />";    // HTML line break

// Display program heading
document.write("Zantillian Ancestry" + BR);
```

7. Call the functions to see whether the user is a Zantillian and display the user's ancestry:

```
// Call function to see whether user is Zantillian
// Call function to display ancestry
checkZantillian();
displayAncestry();
```

8. Thank the user and call it quits:

```
// Thank the user and end the program
document.write("Thank you!" + BR);

</script>
</body>
</html>
```

9. Save the file again, and open it in a browser. If you enter five names that don't include Tofu Zantilli, your output should look like Figure 13-12.

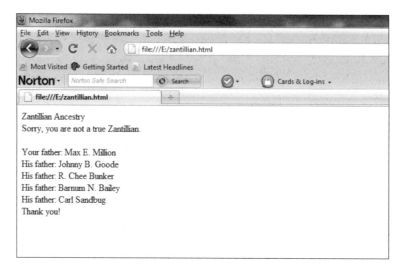

Figure 13-12   The zantillian.html program in a Web browser

Chapter Summary

- A recursive module is one that calls itself.

- Any recursive algorithm can be written as a nonrecursive algorithm.

- When a module is called, its code is stacked on top of the calling module's code.

- When a module is finished, its code is popped off the memory stack.

- A recursive module needs a base case so that calls to itself stop eventually.

- Factorials, the Fibonacci sequence, and the Towers of Hanoi are classic examples of recursion.

Key Terms

base case—A condition in a recursive module that returns a definite value; it causes the module to stop calling itself.

popped—The process of taking a section of code for a module off the memory stack when the module has finished running.

pushed—The process of adding a section of code for a module to a memory stack when the module is called.

recursion—A process in which a module calls itself.

stack—The part of memory that holds modules while they're running. The main module is thought of as occupying a low area of memory, and the code for each module is placed above the main module while it's running.

stack overflow—A condition in which available memory has been used up. One cause of a stack overflow is a recursive module that never gets to a base case.

Review Questions

True/False

1. Recursive functions can always be written in a nonrecursive way. True or False?

2. Recursive function calls can be terminated only at the operating system level. True or False?

3. The base case causes a program with a recursive function to crash. True or False?

4. A factorial can be computed recursively by returning the number times the factorial of 1 minus the number. True or False?

5. A recursive function must return a value. True or False?

6. A Fibonacci sequence can be computed recursively by using a single For loop. True or False?

Multiple Choice

1. A recursive function must have a _____ to keep calls from repeating infinitely.

   a. best case

   b. worst case

   c. base case

   d. zero case

2. What happens when a module is called? (Choose all that apply.)

    a. The calling module is suspended temporarily.

    b. The code for the called module is removed from memory.

    c. The user is prompted as to whether to continue.

    d. The code for the called module is added to memory.

3. Memory added to a stack is said to be _____ onto the stack.

    a. pushed

    b. popped

    c. dropped

    d. squeezed

4. Memory taken off a stack is said to be _____ from the stack.

    a. pushed

    b. popped

    c. dropped

    d. squeezed

5. The series 0, 1, 1, 2, 3, 5, 8, 13, and so on is called which of the following?

    a. sum of squares

    b. factorial series

    c. Fibonacci sequence

    d. Towers of Hanoi

6. A recursive module can do which of the following? (Choose all that apply).

    a. Call itself until a base case is reached.

    b. Return a definite value when a base case is reached.

    c. Use up all available memory if a base case isn't reached.

    d. Call another module.

7. When more memory is added to a stack than it can hold, which of the following occurs?

   a. infinite loop

   b. stack overflow

   c. recursive call

   d. garbage collection

Discussion Questions

1. Are there any practical advantages of recursion?

2. What happens when a recursive function doesn't have a base case?

3. With increased memory in today's computers, is a stack overflow still a concern?

Hands-On Activities

Hands-On Activity 13-1

Write a nonrecursive function in pseudocode to create and display a Fibonacci sequence for a given number of elements. (*Hint*: Use a For loop.) You don't have to write a complete program, just the function. Save the file as nonRecursiveFibonacci.txt.

Hands-On Activity 13-2

Create and test a JavaScript program based on the pseudocode function in Hands-On Activity 13-1. Save the file as nonRecursiveFibonacci.html.

Hands-On Activity 13-3

Create and test a JavaScript program with a recursive function named power() that calculates the value of a base number raised to an exponent. The base and exponent are the two arguments to the function. The base can be any number, but the exponent must be greater than or equal to 0. The algorithm is as follows: If the exponent is 0, return 1; if the exponent is 1, return the base; and if the exponent is greater than 1, return the base times the power() function of the base and the exponent minus 1. The function should be defined in the <head> section, and in the <body> section, the program should ask for two numbers, make sure the exponent is greater than or equal to 0, call the power() function, and display the result. Save the file as powerFunction.html.

HTML Tutorial

HTML Basics

As explained in Chapter 2, Hypertext Markup Language (HTML) describes the layout and appearance of text in a browser page. Although it's used mainly to develop Web pages, it's used in this book as a container for programs written in JavaScript. For this reason, the HTML code included in chapters has consisted mostly of tags for rendering JavaScript along with a few HTML tags introduced in Object Lessons to enhance the look of form-based programs.

You can do the tutorial in this appendix before, during, or after the chapters in this book. It's not necessary for developing and testing the book's JavaScript programs, but it can be used to make your browser pages more attractive. If you go on to do any Web site development, knowledge of basic HTML tags will help you.

This appendix is by no means a complete reference on HTML. To learn about its hundreds of features, you're encouraged to try free online tutorials, especially the ones available at *www.w3schools.com*. This appendix doesn't cover XHTML, document type definitions, or Cascading Style Sheets because they apply to designing Web pages and Web sites. HTML is used in this book simply as a framework for local (non-Internet) browser pages. However, all code complies with HTML 4.0 standards, including the use of opening and closing tags as well as empty tags. In addition, the `<strong>` and `<em>` tags (for bold and italic text), which can be modified with style sheets, are used instead of presentational tags, such as `<b>` and `<i>` for bold and italics.

HTML files are stored as text files, so you can use a simple text editor, such as Notepad (Windows) or TextEdit (Macintosh), to create, save, and modify them. To do the tutorial, you need only a text editor and a browser to view the HTML pages you create. You don't need to be connected to the Internet.

Tags and Empty Tags

Sections of HTML files are called elements and are delineated with tags, which consist of the element name enclosed by angle brackets (< and >). If sections of HTML files contain content, such as text, opening and closing tags are used to enclose the content. The closing tag simply adds a forward slash (/) before the element name. For example, the <html> and </html> tags are the first and last tags in an HTML file, used to enclose the file's entire contents.

HTML files are usually divided into two main sections:

- The <head> section contains documentation and other information about the file, including the browser page's title between the <title> and </title> tags. As you learned in Chapter 8, code for JavaScript functions is also placed in the <head> section.

- The <body> section contains the part of the file to be displayed on the browser page. Text in the <body> section that isn't inside a <script> section or isn't part of a tag appears on the browser page.

Sections delineated by HTML tags can be placed inside other sections and can contain other sections, but sections can't overlap. For example, the following code is valid:

```
<strong><em><font face = "Arial">
Pie in the sky!
</font></em></strong>
```

However, the following code isn't valid because the <em> and <strong> sections overlap:

```
<em><font face = "Arial"><strong>
Pie in the sky!
</font></em></strong>
```

Most browsers have tabs you can use to keep several pages open in a single browser window. When you create a title in HTML, it appears in the browser's title bar and in the page tab. To start this tutorial, try creating a title by following these steps:

1. Open a new document in Notepad, and save it as **titleBar.html**. Enter the following code:

    ```
    <html>
    <head>
    <title>
    My First Browser Page
    </title>
    </head>

    <body>
    Look at the title bar!
    </body>
    </html>
    ```

2. Leave Notepad open. Save the file again, and open it in a browser (see Figure A-1). Notice that the title "My First Browser Page" is displayed in both the title bar and the page tab.

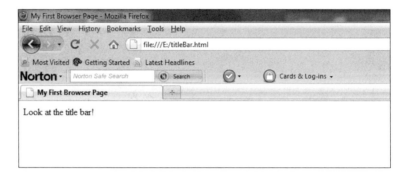

Figure A-1   The titleBar.html file in a Web browser

3. The text in the body of a browser page appears in the default font and color set in your browser. To see or change your browser's default font and color, use one of these methods, depending on which browser you use:

- In Mozilla Firefox, click **Tools**, **Options** from the menu. In the Options dialog box, click the **Content** icon at the top, and check the settings in the Fonts & Colors section. When you're finished, click **Cancel**.

- In Internet Explorer, click **Tools**, **Internet Options** from the menu. In the General tab, click the **Fonts** button. After viewing your font settings, click **OK** or **Cancel**. To see text colors, click the **Colors** button in the General tab of the Internet Options dialog box. When you're finished, click **Cancel** in the Colors dialog box and the Internet Options dialog box. To change the text size, click the **Page** drop-down list at the upper right, click **Text Size**, and select one of the five options.

- In Safari, click the **Tools** toolbar icon (looks like a cogwheel), click **Preferences**, and then click **Appearance**. You can then view fonts and sizes for variable-width fonts (such as Times New Roman) and fixed-width fonts (such as Courier). When you're finished, close the Appearance window.

- In Google Chrome, you can change fonts and font size by clicking the **Tools** toolbar icon (looks like a wrench), and then clicking **Options**, **Under the Hood**. Scroll down to the Web Content section, and click **Change font and language settings**. View the settings, and then click **Cancel** when you're done. To change default colors in Chrome, you have to change themes by clicking the **Tools** toolbar icon, and then clicking **Options**, **Personal Stuff**, and **Get themes**.

If a tag is simply an instruction with no page content, it's called an empty tag. Instead of a closing tag, the slash appears just before the right angle bracket, as in <br /> for the line break tag. Line breaks, blank lines, spaces, and other nonvisible characters are known as "white space," and browsers usually condense consecutive white space characters into a single space. Therefore, a browser doesn't display a line break on a page just because your HTML file has a line break in it. You must insert the line break tag in your HTML file to force the line break on the browser page, as shown in these steps:

1. Return to Notepad, click **File**, **Save As** from the menu, and save the file you're working on as **lineBreaks.html**. Then insert the two lines shown in bold in the following code:

```
<html>
<head>
<title>
My First Browser Page
</title>
</head>

<body>
Look at the title bar!
This is the second line of the body section.
This is the third line.
</body>
</html>
```

2. Save the file again, and open it in your browser (see Figure A-2). As you can see, the two lines you added in the HTML file aren't displayed on their own lines in the browser page; they're just separated with a single space.

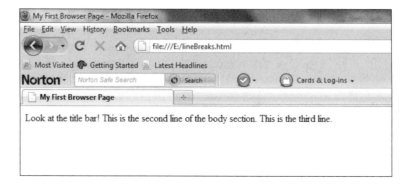

Figure A-2   The lineBreaks.html file in a Web browser

3.   Return to Notepad, click **File**, **Save As** from the menu, and save the file you're working on as **lineBreaks2.html**. Then insert the two line break tags shown in bold:

```
<html>
<head>
<title>
My First Browser Page
</title>
</head>

<body>
Look at the title bar!<br />
This is the second line of the body section.<br />
This is the third line.
</body>
</html>
```

4.   Save the file again, and open it in your browser (see Figure A-3). The two new lines are now separated with line breaks.

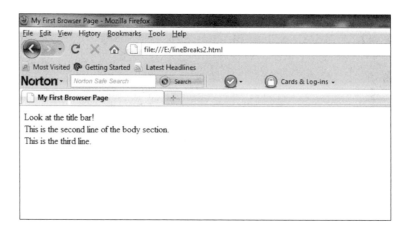

Figure A-3   The lineBreaks2.html file with line breaks

Another empty tag is <hr /> for a horizontal rule, which is a line that extends horizontally across the browser page.

1. Return to Notepad, click **File**, **Save As** from the menu, and save the file you're working on as **ruler.html**. Then insert the code shown in bold. One is the tag for a horizontal rule, and one is a new line of text.

```
<html>
<head>
<title>
My First Browser Page
</title>
</head>

<body>
Look at the title bar! <br />
This is the second line of the body section. <br />
This is the third line.
<hr />
This line of text appears below the horizontal rule.
</body>
</html>
```

2. Save the file again, and open it in your browser (see Figure A-4). The browser page now includes a horizontal rule and a line of text below it.

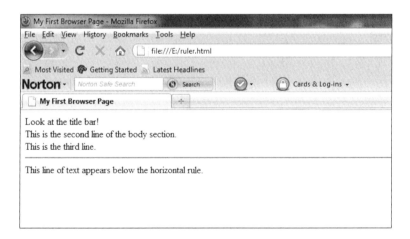

Figure A-4   The ruler.html file in a Web browser

Attributes and Values

Some tags include other information to clarify how the element is to be displayed on the browser page. This information is often specified in an attribute-value pair. An attribute is a property of an element, such as size or color, and a value is a number or text describing the property. To assign a value to a property, use an equals sign in this format:

```
<elementName attribute = "value">
```

You can find a list of color names supported by all major browsers at www.w3schools.com/html/ html_colornames.asp.

For example, you can specify your browser page's background color with the bgcolor attribute in the <body> tag. You can use any recognized color name enclosed in quotation marks for the bgcolor attribute's value. If you want the background color to be cyan (a light blue), you add this information to the <body> tag, as shown in this example:

```
<body bgcolor="cyan">
```

1. Return to Notepad, click **File**, **Save As** from the menu, and save the file you're working on as **colorPages.html**. Then modify the <body> tag as shown in the following bold line:

```
<html>
<head>
<title>
My First Browser Page
</title>
</head>

<body bgcolor="Lavender">
Look at the title bar! <br />
This is the second line of the body section. <br />
This is the third line.
<hr />
This line of text appears below the horizontal rule.
</body>
</html>
```

2. Save the file again, and open it in your browser (see Figure A-5). The page background is now lavender.

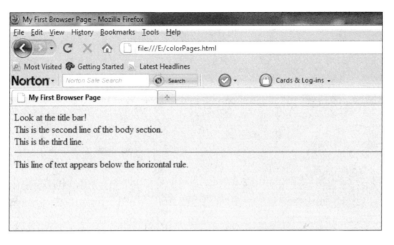

Figure A-5   The colorPages.html file in a Web browser

Block-Level Elements

HTML treats certain elements as blocks so that they can be displayed differently than other sections of the HTML file. Block-level elements include headings and paragraphs. Headings are identified by a tag consisting of h and a number from 1 to 6, representing text sizes from largest to smallest: <h1></h1>, <h2></h2>, and so on. Unless heading tags are defined in a style tag or a style sheet, text in a heading section is displayed as bold with the size determined by the number. The following tag, for example, renders Frank's Fruit Market in bold text in the largest available size on a browser page:

 You can define specifications for how to display content between heading tags with a style tag or in a Cascading Style Sheet. These topics are beyond the scope of this tutorial, but you can find more information in online HTML tutorials.

```
<h1>Frank's Fruit Market</h1>
```

A paragraph is also considered a block-level element. Paragraphs start with a <p> tag, end with a </p> tag, and are separated on a browser page with a blank line.

1. Return to Notepad, open a new document, and save it as **fruitMarket.html**. Enter the following code:

```
<html>
<head>
<title>
Welcome to Frank's Fruit Market!
</title>
</head>

<body bgcolor="AliceBlue">
<h1>Frank's Fruit Market</h1>
<h2>300 Myrtle Street<br />
Dover, DE 19901</h2>
```

```
<p>We invite you to visit Frank's Fruit Market
Monday through Friday between the hours of
8:00 am and 4:30 pm.</p>

<p>Only the freshest fruits are sold at Frank's.
All produce is locally grown and checked daily.
Free samples of seasonal fruit are available
at our customer counter.</p>

</body>
</html>
```

2. Save the file again, and open it in your browser (see Figure A-6). Notice that the two headings are different sizes.

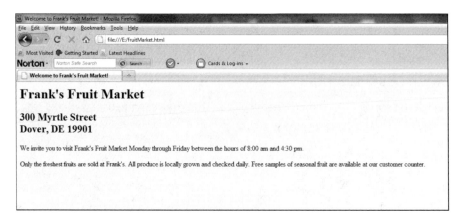

Figure A-6   The fruitMarket.html file in a Web browser

Text Enhancements

As you've seen, content in heading tags is rendered as bold text. What if you want to make regular text bold or italic to emphasize it? Specific tags for bold and italic text are available, but many designers prefer using `<strong>` for bold and `<em>` (emphasize) for italics so that style tags and style sheets can be used to define "strong" and "emphasized" text in a variety of ways. If no style sheets or tags are used, the default is rendering text in `<strong>` tags as bold and text in `<em>` tags as italic.

1. Return to Notepad, click **File**, **Save As** from the menu, and save the file you're working on as **fruitMarket2.html**. Then insert the two tag pairs shown in bold:

```
<html>
<head>
<title>
Welcome to Frank's Fruit Market!
</title>
</head>
```

```
<body bgcolor="AliceBlue">
<h1>Frank's Fruit Market</h1>
<h2>300 Myrtle Street<br />
Dover, DE 19901</h2>

<p>We invite you to visit <strong>Frank's Fruit
Market</strong> Monday through Friday between the hours of
8:00 am and 4:30 pm.</p>

<p>Only the freshest fruits are sold at Frank's.
All produce is locally grown and checked daily.
Free samples of seasonal fruit are available
at our <em>customer counter</em>.</p>

</body>
</html>
```

2. Save the file again, and open it in your browser (see Figure A-7). The name of the business is now displayed in bold text, and the words "customer counter" are in italics.

Figure A-7   The fruitMarket2.html file in a Web browser

Ordered and Unordered Lists

Creating lists in HTML is easy. You have a choice of numbered (ordered) lists or bulleted (unordered) lists. The tag pair for an ordered list is <ol> </ol>, and for an unordered list, it's <ul> </ul>. List items are specified with the <li> </li> tag pair and are usually indented in the code simply to improve readability. The browser indents them on the page automatically. Here's an example of the format for an ordered list:

```
<ol>
    <li>First list item</li>
    <li>Second list item</li>
</ol>
```

Good programming style includes making sure your code is easy to read.

1. Return to Notepad, click **File**, **Save As** from the menu, and save the file you're working on as **fruitMarket3.html**. Then insert the code shown in bold. Notice that the text in the last paragraph is now used for items in the ordered list.

```
<html>
<head>
<title>
Welcome to Frank's Fruit Market!
</title>
</head>

<body bgcolor="AliceBlue">
<h1>Frank's Fruit Market</h1>
<h2>300 Myrtle Street<br />
Dover, DE 19901</h2>

<p>We invite you to visit
<strong>Frank's Fruit Market</strong>
Monday through Friday between the hours of
8:00 am and 4:30 pm.</p>

<p>This week, we have lots of fresh:
<ul>
    <li>Strawberries</li>
    <li>Raspberries</li>
    <li>Blueberries</li>
    <li>Blackberries</li>
</ul>
</p>

<p>Here are three good reasons
to shop at Frank's Fruit Market:
<ol>
    <li>Only the freshest fruits are sold at Frank's. ↵
    </li>
    <li>All produce is locally grown and checked daily.</li>
    <li>Free samples are available at our
<em>customer counter</em>.</li>
</ol>
</p>

</body>
</html>
```

2. Save the file again, and open it in your browser (see Figure A-8). Your browser page now has an unordered list and an ordered list.

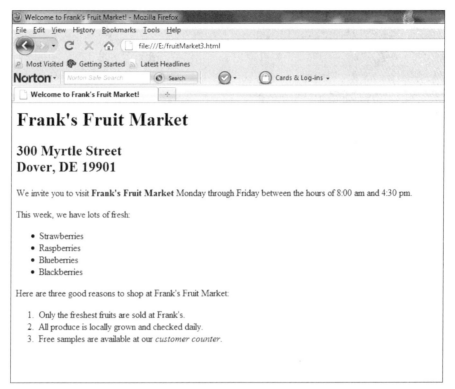

Tables

HTML makes it possible to organize an area of the browser page into a table, which consists of rows and columns intersecting in cells, similar to a spreadsheet. Cells are represented by table data elements. They normally take up the space of one row and column but can be made to span more than one row or column.

A table is defined with the <table> </table> tag pair. A row consists of the content between the <tr> and </tr> tags, and each data element in a row is contained between the <td> (table data) and </td> tags. A special data element called a header, designated with the <th> (for "table header") and </th> tags, displays text in bold and centers it in the cell.

You can investigate Web references and online tutorials, such as *www.w3schools.com*, to see how to make table cells span multiple rows and columns.

Common attributes of the `<table>` tag, although they aren't required, include the following:

- `width`—Specified in pixels or in a percentage of the page width

- `border`—Set as 0 (for no border) or a line thickness in pixels

- `cellspacing`—Specifies the number of blank pixels between table cells

- `cellpadding`—Specifies the margin around content inside a cell

1. Return to Notepad, open a new document, and save it as **rainfall.html**. Enter the following code:

```
<html>
<head>
<title>
Rainfall Amounts
</title>
</head>

<body bgcolor="GhostWhite">
<h2>
Rainfall Amounts for the Week beginning June 5, 2011
</h2>

<table width="50%" border="1" cellpadding="3">
<tr>
    <th>Sunday</th><th>Monday</th><th>Tuesday</th>
    <th>Wednesday</th><th>Thursday</th><th>Friday</th>
    <th>Saturday</th>
<tr>
    <td>.00"</td><td>.16"</td><td>1.55"</td><td>.34"</td>
    <td>.00"</td><td>.00"</td><td>.88"</td>
</tr>
</table>

</body>
</html>
```

2. Save the file again, and open it in your browser (see Figure A-9). Because the `width` attribute was specified as 50%, the table takes up half the width of the browser page when viewed full screen. (Note that this screenshot has been cropped because of page width limitations.)

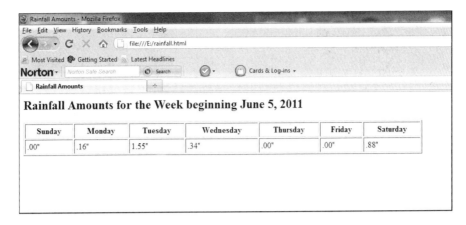

Figure A-9   The rainfall.html file in a Web browser

Images

Including images is a good way to enhance a browser page visually. You use the `<img>` tag to place an image at a specified location. The most important attribute-value pair is the `src` attribute, which specifies the image's filename. This attribute can also be used to specify the image's location, but if it's stored in the same folder as the HTML file, you don't need to include a folder name or pathname.

The file designation `"flowers/carnation.jpg"` means the folder containing the HTML file also contains a folder named flowers, and the carnation.jpg file is stored in the flowers folder. If you're specifying an image that requires a drive letter on your system, you must use the file protocol in the image file designation. The format consists of the word `file`, a colon, three forward slashes, and then the pathname (including the drive letter, a slash, each folder name followed by a slash, and the filename), as in this example: `"file:///e:/flowers/carnation.jpg"`. You can also use a complete URL if the file is available on the Web, as in `"http://www.flowerswelove.com/flowers/carnation.jpg"`.

Other attributes include `height` and `width` in pixels, but they aren't required if the image is going to be displayed at its actual size. However, including them can speed up loading the image because they tell the browser how much space to reserve for the image, instead of requiring the operating system to determine the size first. These attributes are also useful if you want to display the image at a different size. If you specify only the height or width, the other dimension is calculated for you, keeping the same height-to-width ratio as the original. (If the specified height or width isn't the same as the actual image, loading might actually be slowed down while the computer resizes the display.)

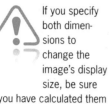

If you specify both dimensions to change the image's display size, be sure you have calculated them to match the original's height-to-width ratio, or the image will look distorted.

You can also use the border attribute to display a border around the image; you use the same values as with a table's border attribute.

In this next example, you load the image isleOfSkye.jpg from your student data files; it's 480 × 360 pixels. Specify a border of 1 pixel, and have the image loaded at its original size.

1. Return to Notepad, open a new document, and save it as
    scotland.html. Enter the following code:

```
<html>
<head>
<title>
Isle of Skye, Scotland
</title>
</head>

<body bgcolor="LightYellow">
<h2>Welcome to the Isle of Skye in Scotland!</h2>

<img src="isleOfSkye.jpg" border="1" width="480"
height="360" /><br />
<strong>A rushing mountain stream on the Isle of Skye.
</strong><br />
<em>(Photo by Paul Addison)</em>

</body>
</html>
```

2. Save the file again, and open it in your browser (see Figure A-10).
    The image is displayed with a heading above it and a caption
    below it.

Figure A-10   The scotland.html file in a Web browser

Comments in HTML

Whether you're going through this tutorial before, during, or after writing JavaScript programs in the chapters, remember that JavaScript code is placed between the HTML file's `<script>` and `</script>` tags and in the `<head>` section, the `<body>` section, or both.

HTML comments are used in the non-JavaScript sections of the file. As with JavaScript, comments in an HTML file aren't displayed on the browser page. However, HTML comments are written differently than JavaScript comments are. In HTML, comments begin with a left angle bracket, an exclamation point, and two dashes (or hyphens).

The comment text comes next, and the comment ends with two dashes followed by a right angle bracket. Here's an example of some comments in the non-JavaScript section of an HTML file:

```
<html>
<head>

<!-- A one-line comment in HTML -->

<!--
Here's an example of using a multiple-line comment
in HTML. All text between the opening and closing
comment tags is considered a comment. This format is
different from JavaScript comments.
-->

</head>
</html>
```

Don't get your comment styles mixed up. If you put comments in the wrong place or in the wrong format, they might show up as text on the browser page.

To see the HTML code for a Web page, including its comments, use one of these methods:

- Mozilla Firefox: Click **View**, **Page Source** from the menu.

- Internet Explorer: Click **View**, **Source** from the menu.

- Safari: Click **View**, **View Source** from the menu.

The HTML code for creating forms is covered in Chapter 3, so form tags aren't included in this appendix.

- Google Chrome: Click the **Tools** toolbar icon, and then click **Tools**, **View source**.

Because this book is about learning programming concepts with JavaScript, a minimal amount of HTML code is used. Therefore, comments are placed in the `<script>` section in the JavaScript format, which starts each comment with two slashes.

Now that you know how to use common HTML tags, you might want to apply them to the JavaScript programs in this book to make them more attractive. One reminder, however: If you want JavaScript output to be formatted with tags, you can't simply put tags in the JavaScript section. You have to use a `document.write()` statement and include the tag as a string to send the tag to the browser for interpretation. The examples in the book do this regularly. For example, in several programs, you declared a string constant named BR, assigned the line break tag as its value, and included BR as output in `document.write()` statements, as shown:

```
var BR = "<br />";    // HTML line break
document.write("This is one short line." + BR);
```

Arguments to `document.write()` statements are enclosed in quotation marks, so if the HTML tag values you use also need quotation marks, use single quotation marks for the HTML tag values inside the double quotation marks for the document.write() arguments, like this:

```
document.write("<font color='Orange' size='20'>");
```

1. Return to Notepad, open a new document, and save it as **javaScriptUsingHTMLTags.html**. Enter the following code:

```
<html>
<head>
<title>
JavaScript Using HTML Tags
</title>

<!-- HTML comments start like this
Program name: javaScriptUsingHTMLTags.html
Purpose: Use JavaScript to output HTML tags
Author: Paul Addison
Date last modified: 01-Sep-2011
-->

</head>

<body>
<script type="text/javascript">

// Declare constant
var BR = "<br />";    // HTML line break

// JavaScript comments start with two slashes
// Set the browser background color to beige
document.write("<body bgcolor='Beige'>");

// Set the text color to orange
// and the font size to 20 points
document.write("<font color='Orange' size='20'>");

// Display a hello message
document.write("Hello, World!" + BR);

// Change font back to the default
document.write("</font>");

// Display a goodbye message
document.write("Goodbye!" + BR);

</script>
</body>
</html>
```

2. Save the file again, and open it in your browser (see Figure A-11).

Figure A-11 The javaScriptUsingHTMLTags.html file in a Web browser

Table A-1 summarizes the HTML tags used in this appendix.

HTML tag	Description	Examples of attributes
`<html>`	Declares file as an HTML file	
`<head>`	Delineates the section where information about the Web page, such as the title, is stored	
`<title>`	Specifies the title of the Web page displayed in the browser's title bar	
`<body>`	Delineates the section containing instructions to render the Web page	`bgcolor`
`<script>`	Delineates the section containing code in a scripting language, such as JavaScript	`type`
`<b>`	Renders text as bold	
`<i>`	Renders text as italic	
`<strong>`	Makes text stand out (default is bold)	
`<em>`	Emphasizes text (default is italics)	
`<p>`	Indicates a paragraph	
` `	Line break (empty tag)	
`<hr />`	Horizontal rule (empty tag)	
`<h1>` to `<h6>`	Formats headings; six sizes available	
`<font>`	Sets font attributes	`face, color, size`
`<ol>`	Creates an ordered (numbered) list	
`<ul>`	Creates an unordered (bulleted) list	
`<li>`	Specifies a list item	

Table A-1 HTML tags used in this appendix *(continues)*

(continued)

HTML tag	Description	Examples of attributes
`<table>`	Sets up a table	`width, border, cellspacing, cellpadding`
`<tr>`	Specifies a row in a table	
`<td>`	Specifies a cell in a table	
`<th>`	Specifies a header cell in a table (bold and centered)	
`<img>`	Displays an image	`src, width, height, border`
`<!--`	Opening comment tag	
`-->`	Closing comment tag	

Table A-1   HTML tags used in this appendix

Index

571